Expert Political Judgment

Expert
Political Judgment

HOW GOOD IS IT?
HOW CAN WE KNOW?

Philip E. Tetlock

PRINCETON UNIVERSITY PRESS

PRINCETON AND OXFORD

Published by Princeton University Press, 41 William Street, Princeton, New Jersey 08540

In the United Kingdom: Princeton University Press, 3 Market Place, Woodstock, Oxfordshire OX20 1SY

Sixth printing, and first paperback printing, 2006
Paperback ISBN-13: 978-0-691-12871-9
Paperback ISBN-10: 0-691-12871-5

THE LIBRARY OF CONGRESS HAS CATALOGED THE CLOTH EDITION OF THIS BOOK AS FOLLOWS

Tetlock, Philip.
  Expert political judgment : how good is it? how can we know? / Philip E. Tetlock.
    p.   cm.
  Includes bibliographical references and index.
  ISBN-13: 978-0-691-12302-8 (alk. paper)
  ISBN-10: 0-691-12302-0 (alk. paper)
   1. Political psychology.   2. Ideology.   I. Title.
  JA74.5.T38 2005
  320'.01'9—dc22   2004061694

British Library Cataloging-in-Publication Data is available

This book has been composed in Sabon

Printed on acid-free paper. ∞

pup.princeton.edu

Printed in the United States of America

10

To Jenny, Paul, and Barb

Contents

Acknowledgments

THE JURY is out on just how much bad judgment I showed by undertaking the good-judgment project. The project dates back to the year I gained tenure and lost my generic excuse for postponing projects that I knew were worth doing, worthier than anything I was doing back then, but also knew would take a long time to come to fruition. As I write twenty years later, the data are still trickling in and the project now threatens to outlast not just my career but me. Some long-term forecasts that experts offered will not come due until 2026. But most of the data are tabulated, some surprising patterns have emerged, and I see no reason for delaying the write-up into my retirement.

Of course, a project of this duration requires the cooperation of many people over many years. My greatest collective debt is to the thoughtful professionals who patiently worked through the often tedious batteries of questions on what could have been, what is, and what might yet be. I told them at the outset that I did not intend to write a book that named names, or that, by exploiting hindsight bias, incited readers to glorify those who got it right or ridicule those who got it wrong. I promised strict confidentiality. The book that would emerge from this effort would be variable-centered, not person-centered. The focus would be on the links between *how* people think and *what* they get right or wrong, at various junctures, in a kaleidoscopically shifting world. I realize that the resulting cognitive portrait of expert political judgment is not altogether flattering, but I hope that research participants, even the "hedgehogs" among them, do not feel shabbily treated. I level no charges of judgmental flaws that do not also apply to me.

Another great debt is to the many colleagues who offered methodological and theoretical advice that saved me from making an even bigger fool of myself than I may have already done. Barbara Mellers, Paul Tetlock, and Phillip Rescober offered invaluable guidance on how to design measures of forecasting skill that were sensitive to the variety of ingenious objections that forecasters raised when either high probability events failed to materialize or low probability events did materialize. And colleagues from several disciplines—including psychology, political science, economics, history, and the hybrid field of intelligence analysis—made suggestions at various junctures in this long journey that, in my opinion at least, improved the final product. I cannot remember the source of every insightful observation at every stage of this project, but this list should include in roughly chronological order from 1984 to 2004: Peter Suedfeld, Aaron Wildavsky, Alexander George, George Breslauer, Danny Kahneman, Robyn Dawes, Terry Busch, Yuen Foong Khong, John Mercer, Lynn Eden, Amos Tversky, Ward Edwards, Ron Howard, Arie Kruglanski, James March, Joel Mokyr, Richard Herrmann, Geoffrey Parker, Gary Klein, Steve Rieber, Yaacov Vertzberger, Jim Goldgeier, Erika Henik, Rose McDermott, Cass Sunnstein, and Hal Arkes. In the final phases of this project, Paul Sniderman and Bob Jervis played a particularly critical role in helping to sharpen the central arguments of the book. Needless to say, though, none of the aforementioned bears responsibility for those errors of fact or interpretation that have persisted despite their perceptive advice.

I also owe many thanks to the many former and current students who have worked, in one capacity or another, on various components of this project. They include Charles McGuire, Kristen Hannum, Karl Dake, Jane Bernzweig, Richard Boettger, Dan Newman, Randall Peterson, Penny Visser, Orie Kristel, Beth Elson, Aaron Belkin, Megan Berkowitz, Sara Hohenbrink, Jeannette Porubin, Meaghan Quinn, Patrick Quinn, Brooke Curtiss, Rachel Szteiter, Elaine Willey, and Jason Mills. I also greatly appreciate the staff support of Deborah Houy and Carol Chapman.

Turning to institutional sponsors, this project would have been impossible but for generous financial and administrative support from the following: the John D. and Catherine T. MacArthur Foundation Program in International Security, the Institute of Personality and Social Research of the University of California, Berkeley, the Institute on Global Conflict and Cooperation at the University of California, the Center for Advanced Study in the Behavioral Sciences in Palo Alto, the Mershon Center of the Ohio State University, the Social Science Research Council, the National Science Foundation, the United States Institute of Peace, the Burtt Endowed Chair in the Psychology Department at the Ohio State University, and the Mitchell Endowed Chair at the Haas School of Business at the University of California, Berkeley.

Finally, I thank my family—especially, Barb, Jenny, and Paul—for their infinite forbearance with my workaholic ways.

Preface

AUTOBIOGRAPHICAL exercises that explore why the researcher opted to go forward with one project rather than another have often struck me as self-dramatizing. What matters is the evidence, not why one collected it. Up to now, therefore, I have hewed to the just-the-facts conventions of my profession: state your puzzle, your methods, and your answers, and exit the stage.

I could follow that formula again. I have long been puzzled by why so many political disagreements—be they on national security or trade or welfare policy—are so intractable. I have long been annoyed by how rarely partisans admit error even in the face of massive evidence that things did not work out as they once confidently declared. And I have long wondered what we might learn if we approached these disputes in a more aggressively scientific spirit—if, instead of passively watching warring partisans score their own performance and duly pronounce themselves victorious, we presumed to take on the role of epistemological referees: soliciting testable predictions, scoring accuracy ourselves, and checking whether partisans change their minds when they get it wrong.

I initially implemented my research plan tentatively, in a trial-and-error fashion in small-scale forecasting exercises on the Soviet Union in the mid-1980s, and then gradually more boldly, in larger-scale exercises around the world over the next decade. My instinct was to adopt and, when necessary, adapt methods of keeping score from my home discipline of psychology: correspondence measures of how close political observers come to making accurate predictions and logical-process measures of the degree to which observers play fair with evidence and live up to reputational bets that require them to update their beliefs.

Without giving too much away, I can say that surprises are in store. We shall discover that the best forecasters and timeliest belief updaters shared a self-deprecating style of thinking that spared them some of the big mistakes to which their more ideologically exuberant colleagues were prone. There is often a curiously inverse relationship between how well forecasters thought they were doing and how well they did.

I could now exit the stage. But the project makes more sense when traced to its origins: my first close-up contact with the ingenuity and determination that political elites display in rendering their positions impregnable to evidence. The natural starting point is a 1984 meeting at the National Research Council, the administrative branch of the National Academy of Sciences. I was a freshly tenured professor from Berkeley and the most junior (nonmember of the academy) member of the committee. The committee had been convened—as academic committees often are—to midwife the birth of another committee. This new committee would have an ambitious—critics said pretentious—mandate: to explore the contributions of the social sciences, not to the humdrum, usual-suspect problems of early childhood education or affirmative action, but to rescuing civilization itself from nuclear incineration.

Just because we want an answer, even desperately want one, does not mean we have an answerable question. Science is, by one famous definition, the art of the solvable,[1] and I was not alone in fearing that our humanitarian reach exceeded our scientific grasp. Although the clock on the cover of the *Bulletin of the Atomic Scientists* had edged closer to midnight than at any other time aside from the Cuban missile crisis of October 1962, it was obvious to most around the table that we had no metric for gauging our proximity to nuclear war, something that had not yet happened and might never happen. The clock-setters were guessing. Indeed, it was not clear how the classic methods of clarifying causality, experimental and statistical control, could even be applied to explain the nonoccurrence of an event (nuclear war) that qualified as sui generis if ever one did, or to the challenge of extrapolating its continued nonoccurrence.[2]

Thoughtful activists replied that too much thought can be paralyzing. One speaker dismissed "worrywarts" who find themselves hurtling down a mountain highway in a bus with a demented driver at the wheel, but who would rather debate the sines and cosines on the next curve than wrestle control from the maniac (an allusion to Ronald Reagan) who was about to send them plunging to their doom.[3] Another speaker posed two possible futures: in one you must explain to your irradiated and slowly dying children why you did nothing as the world edged toward nuclear apocalypse, and in the other you must explain to your bemused colleagues why you thought the end was imminent when everything worked out well. Easy choice, he thought.

Academic administrators defuse debates of this sort by artful obfuscation. The activists got a committee but not the putschist committee they

---

[1] P. B. Medawar, *The Art of the Soluble* (London: Methuen, 1967).

[2] My closing chapter in the first volume sponsored by the committee makes this point— about the limits of our knowledge—more delicately than I make it here. See P. E. Tetlock, R. Jervis, J. Husband, P. Stern, and C. Tilly, eds., *Behavior, Society, Nuclear War*, vol. 1 (New York: Oxford University Press, (1989). See also the discussion of nuclear theology in J. Nye, "Nuclear Learning and U.S.-Soviet Security Regimes," *International Organization* 4 (1987): 371–402.

[3] J. Schell, *The Fate of the Earth* (New York: Avon, 1982).

wanted—one that would issue thundering, Linus Pauling–style indictments of warmongers. The worrywarts, who doubted the wisdom of any committee, got the kind of committee they would have wanted had they wanted one: a politically innocuous but academically respectable forum for assessing the sines and cosines on the curvy political road ahead.

I took it upon myself to canvas professional opinion on the American-Soviet relationship. What did the experts know, or think they know, about Soviet intentions? How did they judge whether American policy had struck the right balance between deterrence and reassurance in dealing with the Soviets? Looking back over the previous forty years, did they see any, or perhaps many, "missed opportunities" to promote peaceful cooperation? In probing these "foundational" beliefs, I was struck by how frequently influential observers offered confident, but flatly contradictory, assessments that were impervious to the arguments advanced by the other side. Hawks saw the Soviet Union as an evil empire that had to be contained through deterrence; doves saw a series of misunderstandings rooted in rigid mind-sets and exploited by self-serving interest groups; and self-styled owls flit between these polar oppositions, crafting proposals that blended hawks' determination to deter and doves' desire to reassure.[4]

Two decades later, it is hard to re-create the mood of apprehension among doves. They felt that the Reagan administration was dragging us precariously close to the precipice.[5] In hindsight, it is tempting to be condescending. We now know that in March 1985, Mikhail Gorbachev became General Secretary of the Communist Party and introduced sweeping reforms. The fear of all-out nuclear war dissipated as thoughtful observers turned their attention to nuclear terrorism and about what would happen to the massive Soviet stock of weapons of mass destruction when the Russian government could no longer pay the military custodians of those weapons their pittance salaries. The epicenter of controversy shifted.[6] Animated debates between hawks and doves gave way to spirited exchanges over managing transitions from socialism to capitalism, coping with resurgent nationalism and fundamentalism, and saving humanity from ecocatastrophes. Cold war thinking was passé.

---

[4] G. Allison, A. Carnesale, and J. Nye, *Hawks, Doves, and Owls: An Agenda for Avoiding Nuclear War* (New York: W.W. Norton, 1985); P. E. Tetlock, "Policy-makers' Images of International Conflict," *Journal of Social Issues* 39 (1983): 67–86.

[5] For examples of how worried some were, see M. Deutsch, "The Prevention of World War III: A Psychological Perspective," *Political Psychology* 4 (1983): 3–31; R. White, *Fearful Warriors: A Psychological Profile of U.S.-Soviet Relations* (New York: Free Press, 1984).

[6] On the sharp transition between cold war and post–cold war thinking, see T. Friedman, *The Lexus and the Olive Tree* (New York: Farrar, Straus & Giroux, 1999).

Was it foolish to have gotten so worked up? Many conservatives believe so: the National Research Council erred in creating a committee that lent even limited legitimacy to a gaggle of academic Chicken Littles. One respected colleague chided me: "So the sky was not falling." The much ridiculed Reagan administration was right to have kept on upping the ante in the geopolitical poker game until the Kremlin folded out.[7]

Liberals saw things differently.[8] They worried that bellicose rhetoric and a massive defense buildup were setting in motion a cycle of hostility in which each side exaggerates the aggressive intent of the other and, by preparing for the worst, guarantees the worst. Many, moreover, have not changed their minds: they still insist that the cold war would have ended just as swiftly in a world with a two-term Carter presidency and Mondale follow-ups. Conservative "triumphalism" reminded one prominent scientist of a man who wins a round of Russian roulette and proclaims himself a genius. We were lucky that Gorbachev, rather than a vodka-guzzling neo-Stalinist, was waiting in the wings to take over. This scholar conjured up scenarios in which the Politburo, angered by American provocations, elevated an "apparatchik thug" to general secretary in 1985 and began to play major-league forms of the game of nuclear brinkmanship that North Korea, in minor-league form, is playing today. Civilization would soon be tottering on the brink.

Here we see the first, but not the last, example of a popular belief system defense among inaccurate forecasters, the close-call counterfactual: "Well, I predicted x and x did not happen, but it almost did. You who laugh reveal the poverty of your historical imaginations."[9] Declining empires do not usually accept relegation to the dustbin of history as peacefully as the Soviet Union. Talk about the inevitability of collapse, about how internal weakness and external pressure forced the hands of the Soviet leadership, tells us less about the probability distribution of possible worlds than it does about the self-deceptive tricks that hindsight plays

[7] Indeed, doctrinaire deterrence theorists stressed the dangers of appearing weak in many arenas. On the domestic front, they didn't like mollycoddling criminals and, after the demise of the Soviet Union, they warned against appeasing international scofflaws such as North Korea and Iraq. For the view that foreign policy priorities are extensions of primitive interpersonal priorities, see L. S. Etheredge, A World of Men (Cambridge: MIT Press, 1980). For qualifications, see R. Herrmann, P. E. Tetlock, and P. Visser, "Mass Public Decisions on Going to War: A Cognitive-Interactionist Framework," American Political Science Review 93 (1999): 553–74. Liberals are not always more doveish than conservatives. When the attitude object excites enough antipathy—apartheid in South Africa or ethnic cleansing in Yugoslavia—many are eager to "get tough."

[8] Tetlock, "Policy-makers' Images of International Conflict," 67–86.

[9] For documentation of how pervasive this belief-system defense is, see P. E. Tetlock, "Close-call Counterfactuals and Belief System Defenses: I Was Not Almost Wrong but I Was Almost Right," Journal of Personality and Social Psychology 75 (1998): 230–42.

on the mind. We too easily convince ourselves that we knew all along what was going to happen when, in fact, we were clueless.

Political partisans will sometimes suspect me of playing favorites. In some quarters, I am already under a cloud of suspicion. Why dwell on a forecasting fiasco for the left? Do I have a neoconservative agenda of showing that, not only were the Cassandras of the left wrong, they try to cover up this massive mistake with gibberish about counterfactual worlds in which events dovetail suspiciously smoothly with the apocalyptic movie-script scenarios that their Hollywood friends penned twenty years ago?[10]

But, alas for the political right, the turning point in Soviet political history in March 1985, provides a less than ideal opportunity for gloating. The data reveal ample grounds for embarrassment across the spectrum of once-fashionable opinion. Conservatives were no better forecasters than liberals. In fact, many were slower than liberals to acknowledge Gorbachev's commitment to reform, some dismissing him as an apparatchik in "Gucci garb" right up to the coup attempt of August 1991. They were blindsided by the emergence of a mutant reformer like Gorbachev from deep within the bowels of a totalitarian system that they had postulated to be drearily uniform and infallibly self-reproducing. Contrary to Richard Pipes and Jeanne Kirkpatrick, the Soviets had not mastered the technology of ideological cloning.[11] The pudgy grey gerontocrats of the Politburo, dutifully lined up in their furry hats on the Kremlin wall every November 7, looked alike but did not think alike. To justify their tardiness on the "Gorbachev call," conservatives often resorted to another popular belief system defense: "OK, I made a mistake, but it was the right mistake." The error of underestimating the Soviet threat was more serious than that of overestimating it.[12]

[10] I cannot refute every suspicion that the hypersensitive might form of my motives. Various views wind up looking silly at various points. But this book is not dedicated to testing rival political theories; its mission is to shed light on the workings of the minds of political observers. When advocates of a point of view are far off the mark, readers have an array of options, including concluding that (a) forecasters misinterpreted the theory; (b) forecasters had the right theory but no real-world savvy, so they fed the wrong antecedent conditions into the deductive machinery of their theory which, in the tradition of garbage in, garbage out, duly spat out idiotic predictions; (c) the theory is flawed in minor ways that tinkering can fix; (d) the theory is flawed in fundamental ways that require revising core assumptions. True believers in a theory will reach option (d) only after they have been dragged kicking and screaming through options (a), (b), and (c), whereas debunkers should leap straight to option (d) at the first hint of a glitch.

[11] R. Pipes, "Gorbachev's Party Congress: How Significant for the United States?" (Miami, FL: Soviet and East European Studies Program Working Paper Series, 1986).

[12] Conservatives also risk having the tables turned on them if they mock the "Reagan was just lucky" defense. Across the many forecasting exercises in this book, conservatives are as likely as liberals to resort to the close-call defense in trying to rescue floundering forecasts.

There is, of course, nothing exceptional about experts being blindsided by events. Nor is there anything unusual about partisans duking it out over ambiguous data. In politics, there is always someone eager to claim credit and deny blame and someone else ready to undercut the claims and denials. When we all insist on keeping our own scorecards, we should not be astonished by self-righteous eruptions of disagreements over "who won." Absent strong reminders of what we once thought, we all too easily slip into believing our own self-promotional puffery.

This account sets the stage for unveiling the impetus behind this book. Inspiration was born from my exasperation at self-serving scorekeeping and the difficulty of inducing advocates of rival perspectives to answer the question "What would make you change your mind?" I set out on a mission that perhaps only a psychologist (and I am one) would be naïve enough to undertake: to "objectify" good political judgment by identifying standards for judging judgment that would command assent across the spectrum of reasonable opinion. This book, for better or for worse, is the result.

Expert Political Judgment

CHAPTER 1

Quantifying the Unquantifiable

> I do not pretend to start with precise questions. I do not think
> you can start with anything precise. You have to achieve such
> precision as you can, as you go along.
> —BERTRAND RUSSELL

EVERY DAY, countless experts offer innumerable opinions in a dizzying array of forums. Cynics groan that expert communities seem ready at hand for virtually any issue in the political spotlight—communities from which governments or their critics can mobilize platoons of pundits to make prepackaged cases on a moment's notice.

Although there is nothing odd about experts playing prominent roles in debates, it is odd to keep score, to track expert performance against explicit benchmarks of accuracy and rigor. And that is what I have struggled to do in twenty years of research of soliciting and scoring experts' judgments on a wide range of issues. The key term is "struggled." For, if it were easy to set standards for judging judgment that would be honored across the opinion spectrum and not glibly dismissed as another sneaky effort to seize the high ground for a favorite cause, someone would have patented the process long ago.

The current squabble over "intelligence failures" preceding the American invasion of Iraq is the latest illustration of why some esteemed colleagues doubted the feasibility of this project all along and why I felt it essential to push forward anyway. As I write, supporters of the invasion are on the defensive: their boldest predictions of weapons of mass destruction and of minimal resistance have not been borne out.

But are hawks under an obligation—the debating equivalent of Marquis of Queensbury rules—to concede they were wrong? The majority are defiant. Some say they will yet be proved right: weapons will be found—so, be patient—or that Baathists snuck the weapons into Syria—so, broaden the search. Others concede that yes, we overestimated Saddam's arsenal, but we made the right mistake. Given what we knew back then—the fragmentary but ominous indicators of Saddam's intentions— it was prudent to over- rather than underestimate him. Yet others argue that ends justify means: removing Saddam will yield enormous long-term benefits if we just stay the course. The know-it-all doves display a double failure of moral imagination. Looking back, they do not see how terribly things would have turned out in the counterfactual world in which Saddam remained ensconced in power (and France wielded de facto veto power over American security policy). Looking forward, they do not see how wonderfully things will turn out: freedom, peace, and prosperity flourishing in lieu of tyranny, war, and misery.[1]

The belief system defenses deployed in the Iraq debate bear suspicious similarities to those deployed in other controversies sprinkled throughout this book. But documenting defenses, and the fierce conviction behind them, serves a deeper purpose. It highlights why, if we want to stop running into ideological impasses rooted in each side's insistence on scoring its own performance, we need to start thinking more deeply about how we think. We need methods of calibrating expert performance that transcend partisan bickering and check our species' deep-rooted penchant for self-justification.[2]

The next two sections of this chapter wrestle with the complexities of the process of setting standards for judging judgment. The final section previews what we discover when we apply these standards to experts in the field, asking them to predict outcomes around the world and to comment on their own and rivals' successes and failures. These regional forecasting exercises generate winners and losers, but they are not clustered along the lines that partisans of the left or right, or of fashionable academic schools of thought, expected. *What* experts think matters far less than *how* they think. If we want realistic odds on what will happen next, coupled to a willingness to admit mistakes, we are better off turning to experts who embody the intellectual traits of Isaiah Berlin's prototypical fox—those who "know many little things," draw from an eclectic array of traditions, and accept ambiguity and contradiction as inevitable features of life—than we are turning to Berlin's hedgehogs—those who "know one big thing," toil devotedly within one tradition, and reach for formulaic solutions to ill-defined problems.[3] The net result is a double irony: a perversely inverse relationship between my prime exhibit indicators of good judgment and the qualities the media prizes in pundits—the tenacity required to prevail in ideological combat—and the qualities

---

[1] For a passionate affirmation of these defenses, see W. Safire, "The New Groupthink," *New York Times*, July 14, 2004, A27.

[2] The characterization of human beings as rationalizing rather than rational animals is as old as Aristotle and as new as experimental social psychology. See Z. Kunda, *Social Cognition: Making Sense of People* (Boston: MIT Press, 1999).

[3] I. Berlin, "The Hedgehog and the Fox," in *The Proper Study of Mankind* (New York: Farrar, Straus & Giroux, 1997), 436–98. Berlin traces the distinction—via Erasmus—2,600 years to a shadowy source on the edge of recorded Greek history: the soldier-poet Archilocus. The metaphorical meaning oscillates over time, but it never strays far from eclectic cunning (foxes) and dogged persistence (hedgehogs).

science prizes in scientists—the tenacity required to reduce superficial complexity to underlying simplicity.

HERE LURK (THE SOCIAL SCIENCE EQUIVALENT OF) DRAGONS

It is a curious thing. Almost all of us think we possess *it* in healthy measure. Many of us think we are so blessed that we have an obligation to share *it*. But even the savvy professionals recruited from academia, government, and think tanks to participate in the studies collected here have a struggle defining *it*. When pressed for a precise answer, a disconcerting number fell back on Potter Stewart's famous definition of pornography: "I know it when I see *it*." And, of those participants who ventured beyond the transparently tautological, a goodly number offered definitions that were in deep, even irreconcilable, conflict. However we set up the spectrum of opinion—liberals versus conservatives, realists versus idealists, doomsters versus boomsters—we found little agreement on either who had *it* or what *it* was.

The elusive *it* is good political judgment. And some reviewers warned that, of all the domains I could have chosen—many, like medicine or finance, endowed with incontrovertible criteria for assessing accuracy—I showed suspect scientific judgment in choosing good political judgment. In their view, I could scarcely have chosen a topic more hopelessly subjective and less suitable for scientific analysis. Future professional gatekeepers should do a better job stopping scientific interlopers, such as the author, from wasting everyone's time—perhaps by posting the admonitory sign that medieval mapmakers used to stop explorers from sailing off the earth: *hic sunt dragones*.

This "relativist" challenge strikes at the conceptual heart of this project. For, if the challenge in its strongest form is right, all that follows is for naught. Strong relativism stipulates an obligation to judge each worldview within the framework of its own assumptions about the world—an obligation that theorists ground in arguments that stress the inappropriateness of imposing one group's standards of rationality on other groups.[4] Regardless of precise rationale, this doctrine imposes a blanket ban on all

---

[4] Extreme relativism may be a mix of anthropological and epistemological posturing. But prominent scholars have advanced strong "incommensurability arguments" that claim clashing worldviews entail such different standards of evidence as to make mutual comprehension impossible. In philosophy of science: P. Feyerabend, *Against Method: Outline of an Anarchistic Theory of Knowledge* (London: Humanities Press, 1975). In moral theory, A. MacIntyre, *Whose Justice? Which Rationality?* (London: Duckworth, 1988). Such arguments carry strong implications for how to do research. We should adopt a nonjudgmental approach to judgment, one limited to compiling colorful ethnographic catalogs of the odd ideas that have prevailed at different times and places.

efforts to hold advocates of different worldviews accountable to common norms for judging judgment. We are barred from even the most obvious observations: from pointing out that forecasters are better advised to use econometric models than astrological charts or from noting the paucity of evidence for Herr Hitler's "theory" of Aryan supremacy or Comrade Kim Il Sung's juche "theory" of economic development.

Exasperation is an understandable response to extreme relativism. Indeed, it was exasperation that, two and a half centuries ago, drove Samuel Johnson to dismiss the metaphysical doctrines of Bishop Berkeley by kicking a stone and declaring, "I refute him thus." In this spirit, we might crankily ask what makes political judgment so special. Why should political observers be insulated from the standards of accuracy and rigor that we demand of professionals in other lines of work?

But we err if we shut out more nuanced forms of relativism. For, in key respects, political judgment is especially problematic. The root of the problem is not just the variety of viewpoints. It is the difficulty that advocates have pinning each other down in debate. When partisans disagree over free trade or arms control or foreign aid, the disagreements hinge on more than easily ascertained claims about trade deficits or missile counts or leaky transfer buckets. The disputes also hinge on hard-to-refute counterfactual claims about what would have happened if we had taken different policy paths and on impossible-to-refute moral claims about the types of people we should aspire to be—all claims that partisans can use to fortify their positions against falsification. Without retreating into full-blown relativism, we need to recognize that political belief systems are at continual risk of evolving into self-perpetuating worldviews, with their own self-serving criteria for judging judgment and keeping score, their own stocks of favorite historical analogies, and their own pantheons of heroes and villains.

We get a clear picture of how murky things can get when we explore the difficulties that even thoughtful observers run into when they try (as they have since Thucydides) to appraise the quality of judgment displayed by leaders at critical junctures in history. This vast case study literature underscores—in scores of ways—how wrong Johnsonian stone-kickers are if they insist that demonstrating defective judgment is a straightforward "I refute him thus" exercise.[5] To make compelling indictments of political judgment—ones that will move more than one's ideological soul

[5] For excellent compilations, and analyses, of such arguments, see R. Jervis, *Perception and Misperception in International Politics* (Princeton, NJ: Princeton University Press, 1976); R. E. Neustadt and E. R. May, *Thinking in Time* (New York: Free Press, 1986); Y. Vertzberger, *The World in Their Minds* (Stanford, CA: Stanford University Press, 1990); Y. F. Khong, *Analogies at War* (Princeton, NJ: Princeton University Press, 1993); B. W. Jentleson, ed., *Opportunities Missed, Opportunities Seized: Preventive Diplomacy in the*

mates—case study investigators must show not only that decision makers sized up the situation incorrectly but also that, as a result, they put us on a manifestly suboptimal path relative to what was once possible, and they could have avoided these mistakes if they had performed due diligence in analyzing the available information.

These value-laden "counterfactual" and "decision-process" judgment calls create opportunities for subjectivity to seep into historical assessments of even exhaustively scrutinized cases. Consider four examples of the potential for partisan mischief:

a. How confident can we now be—sixty years later and after all records have been declassified—that Harry Truman was right to drop atomic bombs on Japan in August 1945? This question still polarizes observers, in part, because their answers hinge on guesses about how quickly Japan would have surrendered if its officials had been invited to witness a demonstration blast; in part, because their answers hinge on values—the moral weight we place on American versus Japanese lives and on whether we deem death by nuclear incineration or radiation to be worse than death by other means; and, in part, because their answers hinge on murky "process" judgments—whether Truman shrewdly surmised that he had passed the point of diminishing returns for further deliberation or whether he acted impulsively and should have heard out more points of view.[6]

b. How confident can we now be—forty years later—that the Kennedy administration handled the Cuban missile crisis with consummate skill, striking the perfect blend of firmness to force the withdrawal of Soviet missiles and of reassurance to forestall escalation into war? Our answers hinge not only on our risk tolerance but also on our hunches about whether Kennedy was just lucky to have avoided dramatic escalation (critics on the left argue that he played a perilous game of brinkmanship) or about whether Kennedy bollixed an opportunity to eliminate the Castro regime and destabilize the Soviet empire (critics on the right argue that he gave up more than he should have).[7]

Post–Cold War World (Lanham, MD: Rowman & Littlefield, 1999); F. I. Greenstein, The Presidential Difference: Leadership Styles from FDR to Clinton (New York: Free Press, 2000); D. W. Larson and S. A. Renshon, Good Judgment in Foreign Policy (Lanham, MD: Rowman & Littlefield, 2003).

[6] D. McCullough, Truman (New York: Simon & Schuster, 1992); B. J. Bernstein, "The Atomic Bombing Reconsidered," Foreign Affairs 74 (1995): 147.

[7] D. Welch and J. Blight, "The Eleventh Hour of the Cuban Missile Crisis: An Introduction to the ExComm Tapes," International Security 12 (1987/88): 5–92; S. Stern, "Source Material: The 1997 Published Transcripts of the JFK Cuban Missile Crisis Tapes: Too Good to be True?" Presidential Studies Quarterly 3 (1997): 586–93.

    c. How confident can we now be—twenty years later—that Reagan's admirers have gotten it right and the Star Wars initiative was a stroke of genius, an end run around the bureaucracy that destabilized the Soviet empire and hastened the resolution of the cold war? Or that Reagan's detractors have gotten it right and the initiative was the foolish whim of a man already descending into senility, a whim that wasted billions of dollars and that could have triggered a ferocious escalation of the cold war? Our answers hinge on inevitably speculative judgments of how history would have unfolded in the no-Reagan, rerun conditions of history.[8]

    d. How confident can we be—in the spring of 2004—that the Bush administration was myopic to the threat posed by Al Qaeda in the summer of 2001, failing to heed classified memos that baldly announced "bin Laden plans to attack the United States"? Or is all this 20/20 hindsight motivated by desire to topple a president? Have we forgotten how vague the warnings were, how vocal the outcry would have been against FBI-CIA coordination, and how stunned Democrats and Republicans alike were by the attack?[9]

Where then does this leave us? Up to a disconcertingly difficult to identify point, the relativists are right: judgments of political judgment can never be rendered politically uncontroversial. Many decades of case study experience should by now have drummed in the lesson that one observer's simpleton will often be another's man of principle; one observer's groupthink, another's well-run meeting.

But the relativist critique should not paralyze us. It would be a massive mistake to "give up," to approach good judgment solely from first-person pronoun perspectives that treat our own intuitions about what constitutes good judgment, and about how well we stack up against those intuitions, as the beginning and end points of inquiry.

This book is predicated on the assumption that, even if we cannot capture all of the subtle counterfactual and moral facets of good judgment, we can advance the cause of holding political observers accountable to independent standards of empirical accuracy and logical rigor. Whatever their allegiances, good judges should pass two types of tests:

---

[8] J. Matlock, *Autopsy on an Empire: the American Ambassador's Account of the Collapse of the Soviet Union* (New York: Random House, 1995); B. Farnham, "Perceiving the End of Threat: Ronald Reagan and the Gorbachev Revolution," in *Good Judgment in Foreign Policy*, 153–90. R. L. Garthoff, *The Great Transition: American-Soviet Relations and the End of the Cold War* (Washington, DC: Brookings Institution, 1994).

[9] The debate on this case has only begun. But the 9/11 Presidential Commission has laid out a thoughtful framework for conducting it (The 9/11 Commission Report. New York: Norton, 2004).

1. Correspondence tests rooted in empiricism. How well do their private beliefs map onto the publicly observable world?
2. Coherence and process tests rooted in logic. Are their beliefs internally consistent? And do they update those beliefs in response to evidence?

In plain language, good judges should both "get it right" and "think the right way."[10]

This book is also predicated on the assumption that, to succeed in this ambitious undertaking, we cannot afford to be parochial. Our salvation lies in multimethod triangulation—the strategy of pinning down elusive constructs by capitalizing on the complementary strengths of the full range of methods in the social science tool kit. Our confidence in specific claims should rise with the quality of converging evidence we can marshal from diverse sources. And, insofar as we advance many interdependent claims, our confidence in the overall architecture of our argument should be linked to the sturdiness of the interlocking patterns of converging evidence.[11]

Of course, researchers are more proficient with some tools than others. As a research psychologist, my comparative advantage does not lie in doing case studies that presuppose deep knowledge into the challenges confronting key players at particular times and places.[12] It lies in applying the distinctive skills that psychologists collectively bring to this challenging topic: skills honed by a century of experience in translating vague speculation about human judgment into testable propositions. Each chapter of

---

[10] On the fundamental status of correspondence and coherence standards in judging judgment, see K. Hammond, *Human Judgment and Social Policy: Irreducible Uncertainty, Inevitable Error, Unavoidable Injustice* (New York: Oxford University Press, 1996).

[11] This project offers many examples of interlocking convergence: our hedgehog-fox measure of cognitive style predicts indicators of good judgment similar to those predicted by kindred measures elsewhere; our qualitative analysis of forecasters' explanations for their predictions dovetails with our quantitative analyses of why foxes outperformed hedgehogs; our findings of poky belief updating among forecasters, especially hedgehogs, mesh well with laboratory research on "cognitive conservatism." Psychologists will see here the cumulative logic of construct validation. See D. T. Campbell and D. W. Fiske, "Convergent and Discriminant Validation by the Multitrait-Multimethod Matrix," *Psychological Bulletin* 56 (1959): 81–105.

[12] I avoid ambitious conceptions of good judgment that require, for instance, my judging how skillfully policy makers juggle trade-offs among decision quality (is this policy the best policy given our conception of national interest?), acceptability (can we sell this policy?), and timeliness (how should we factor in the costs of delay?). (A. L. George, *Presidential Decision-Making in Foreign Policy* [Boulder, CO: Westview, 1980]) I also steer clear of conceptions that require my judging whether decision makers grasped "the essential elements of a problem and their significance" or "considered the full range of viable options." (S. Renshon, "Psychological Sources of Good Judgment in Political Leaders, in *Good Judgment in Foreign Policy*, 25–57).

this book exploits concepts from experimental psychology to infuse the abstract goal of assessing good judgment with operational substance, so we can move beyond anecdotes and calibrate the accuracy of observers' predictions, the soundness of the inferences they draw when those predictions are or are not borne out, the evenhandedness with which they evaluate evidence, and the consistency of their answers to queries about what could have been or might yet be.[13]

The goal was to discover how far back we could push the "doubting Thomases" of relativism by asking large numbers of experts large numbers of questions about large numbers of cases and by applying no-favoritism scoring rules to their answers. We knew we could never fully escape the interpretive controversies that flourish at the case study level. But we counted on the law of large numbers to cancel out the idiosyncratic case-specific causes for forecasting glitches and to reveal the invariant properties of good judgment.[14] The miracle of aggregation would give us license to tune out the kvetching of sore losers who, we expected, would try to justify their answers by arguing that our standardized questions failed to capture the subtleties of particular situations or that our standardized scoring rules failed to give due credit to forecasts that appear wrong to the uninitiated but that are in some deeper sense right.

The results must speak for themselves, but we made progress down this straight and narrow positivist path. We can construct multimethod composite portraits of good judgment in chapters 3, 4, and 5 that give zero weight to complaints about the one-size-fits-all ground rules of the project and that pass demanding statistical tests. If I had stuck to this path, my life would have been simpler, and this book shorter. But, as I listened to the counterarguments advanced by the thoughtful professionals who participated in this project, it felt increasingly high-handed to dismiss every complaint as a squirmy effort to escape disconfirmation.

---

[13] My approach represents a sharp shift away from case-specific "idiographic" knowledge (who gets what right at specific times and places?) toward more generalizable or "nomothetic" knowledge (who tends to be right across times and places?). Readers hoping for the scoop on who was right about "shock therapy" or the "Mexican bailout" will be disappointed. Readers should stay tuned, though, if they are curious why some observers manage to assign consistently more realistic probabilities across topics.

[14] The law of large numbers is a foundational principle of statistics, and Stigler traces it to the eighteenth century. He quotes Bernoulli: "For even the most stupid of men, by some instinct of nature . . . is convinced that the more observations have been made, the less danger there is of wandering from one's goal." And Poisson: "All manner of things are subject to a universal law that we may call the law of large numbers . . . : if we observe a large number of events of the same nature, dependent upon constant causes and upon causes that vary irregularly . . . we will find the ratios between the numbers of these events are approximately constant." (S. Stigler, 1986, *The History of Statistics: The Measurement of Uncertainty Before 1900* [Cambridge: Harvard University Press, 1986], 65, 185)

My participants knew my measures—however quantitative the veneer— were fallible. They did not need my permission to argue that the flaws lay in my procedures, not in their answers.

We confronted more and more judgment calls on how far to go in accommodating these protests. And we explored more and more adjustments to procedures for scoring the accuracy of experts' forecasts, including *value adjustments* that responded to forecasters' protests that their mistakes were the "right mistakes" given the costs of erring in the other direction; *controversy adjustments* that responded to forecasters' protests that they were really right and our reality checks wrong; *difficulty adjustments* that responded to protests that some forecasters had been dealt tougher tasks than others; and even *fuzzy-set adjustments* that gave forecasters partial credit whenever they claimed that things that did not happen either almost happened or might yet happen.

We could view these scoring adjustments as the revenge of the relativists. The list certainly stretches our tolerance for uncertainty: it requires conceding that the line between rationality and rationalization will *often* be blurry. But, again, we should not concede too much. Failing to learn everything is not tantamount to learning nothing. It is far more reasonable to view the list as an object lesson in how science works: tell us your concerns and we will translate them into scoring procedures and estimate how sensitive our conclusions about good judgment are to various adjustments. Indeed, these sensitivity analyses will reveal the composite statistical portraits of good judgment to be robust across an impressive range of scoring adjustments, with the conditional likelihood of such patterns emerging by chance well under five in one hundred (likelihood conditional on null hypothesis being true).

No number of statistical tests will, however, compel principled relativists to change their minds about the propriety of holding advocates of clashing worldviews accountable to common standards—a point we drive home in the stock-taking closing chapter. But, in the end, most readers will not be philosophers—and fewer still relativists.

This book addresses a host of more pragmatic audiences who have learned to live with the messy imperfections of social science (and be grateful when the epistemological glass is one-third full rather than annoyed about its being two-thirds empty). Our findings will speak to psychologists who wonder how well laboratory findings on cognitive styles, biases, and correctives travel in the real world, decision theorists who care about the criteria we use for judging judgment, political scientists who wonder who has what it takes to "bridge the gap" between academic abstractions and the real world, and journalists, risk consultants, and intelligence analysts who make their livings thinking in "real time" and might be curious who can "beat" the dart-throwing chimp.

I can promise these audiences tangible "deliverables." We shall learn how to design correspondence and coherence tests that hold pundits more accountable for their predictions, even if we cannot whittle their wiggle room down to zero. We shall learn why "what experts think" is so sporadic a predictor of forecasting accuracy, why "how experts think" is so consistent a predictor, and why self-styled foxes outperformed hedgehogs on so wide a range of tasks, with one key exception where hedgehogs seized the advantage. Finally, we shall learn how this patterning of individual differences sheds light on a fundamental trade-off in all historical reasoning: the tension between defending our worldviews and adapting those views to dissonant evidence.

Tracking Down an Elusive Construct

Announcing bold intentions is easy. But delivering is hard: it requires moving beyond vague abstractions and spelling out how one will measure the intricate correspondence and coherence facets of the multifaceted concept of good judgment.

Getting It Right

Correspondence theories of truth identify good judgment with the goodness of fit between our internal mental representations and corresponding properties of the external world. Just as our belief that grass is green owes its truth to an objective feature of the physical world—grass reflects a portion of the electromagnetic spectrum visible to our eyes—the same can be said for beliefs with less precise but no less real political referents: wars break out, economies collapse. We should therefore credit good judgment to those who see the world as it is—or soon will be.[15] Two oft-derived corollaries are: (1) we should bestow bonus credit on those farsighted souls who saw things well before the rest of us—the threat posed by Hitler in the early 1930s or the vulnerability of the Soviet Union in the early 1980s or the terrorist capabilities of radical Islamic organizations in the 1990s or the puncturing of the Internet bubble in 2000; (2) we should penalize those misguided souls who failed to see

---

[15] Our correspondence measures focused on the future, not the present or past, because we doubted that the sophisticated specialists in our sample would make the crude partisan errors of fact ordinary citizens make (see D. Green, B. Palmquist, and E. Schickler, *Partisan Hearts and Minds* [New Haven, CT: Yale University Press, 2002]). Pilot testing confirmed these doubts. Even the most dogmatic Democrats in our sample knew that inflation fell in the Reagan years, and even the most dogmatic Republicans knew that budget deficits shrank in the Clinton years. To capture susceptibility to biases among our respondents, we needed a more sophisticated mousetrap.

things long after they became obvious to the rest of us—who continued to believe in a monolithic Communist bloc long after the Sino-Soviet rupture or in Soviet expansionism through the final Gorbachev days.

Assessing this superficially straightforward conception of good judgment proved, however, a nontrivial task. We had to pass through a gauntlet of five challenges.[16]

1. *Challenging whether the playing fields are level.* We risk making false attributions of good judgment if some forecasters have been dealt easier tasks than others. Any fool can achieve close to 100 percent accuracy when predicting either rare outcomes, such as nuclear proliferation or financial collapse, or common ones, such as regular elections in well-established democracies. All one need do is constantly predict the higher base rate outcome and—like the proverbial broken clock—one will look good, at least until skeptics start benchmarking one's performance against simple statistical algorithms.

2. *Challenging whether forecasters' "hits" have been purchased at a steep price in "false alarms."* We risk making false attributions of good judgment if we fixate solely on success stories—crediting forecasters for spectacular hits (say, predicting the collapse of the Soviet Union) but not debiting them for false alarms (predicting the disintegration of nation-states—e.g., Nigeria, Canada—still with us). Any fool can also achieve high hit rates for any outcome—no matter how rare or common—by indiscriminately attaching high likelihoods to its occurrence. We need measures that take into account all logically possible prediction-outcome matchups: saying x when x happens (hit); saying x when x fails to happen (false alarm or overprediction); saying $\sim x$ when $\sim x$ happens (correct rejection); and saying $\sim x$ when x happens (miss or underprediction).

3. *Challenging the equal weighting of hits and false alarms.* We risk making false attributions of good judgment if we treat political reasoning as a passionless exercise of maximizing aggregate accuracy. It is profoundly misleading to talk about forecasting accuracy without spelling out the trade-offs that forecasters routinely make between the conflicting risks of overprediction (false alarms: assigning high probabilities to events that do not occur) and underprediction (misses: assigning low probabilities to events that do occur).[17] Consider but two illustrations:

---

[16] For thoughtful discussions of correspondence measures, see A. Kruglanski, *Lay Epistemics and Human Knowledge* (New York: Plenum Press, 1989; D. A. Kenny, *Interpersonal Perception* (New York: Guilford Press, 1994).

[17] John Swets, *Signal Detection Theory and ROC Analysis in Psychology and Diagnostics* (Mahwah, NJ: Lawrence Erlbaum, 1996).

a. Conservatives in the 1980s justified their suspicions of Gorbachev by insisting that underestimating Soviet strength was the more serious error, tempting us to relax our guard and tempting them to test our resolve. By contrast, liberals worried that overestimating the Soviets would lead to our wasting vast sums on superfluous defense programs and to our reinforcing the Soviets' worst-case suspicions about us.

b. Critics of the Western failure to stop mass killings of the 1990s in Eastern Europe or central Africa have argued that, if politicians abhorred genocide as much as they profess in their brave "never again" rhetoric, they would have been more sensitive to the warning signs of genocide than they were. Defenders of Western policy have countered that the cost of false-alarm intrusions into the internal affairs of sovereign states would be prohibitive, sucking us into a succession of Vietnam-style quagmires.

Correspondence indicators are, of course, supposed to be value neutral, to play no favorites and treat all mistakes equally. But we would be remiss to ignore the possibility we are misclassifying as "wrong" forecasters who have made value-driven decisions to exaggerate certain possibilities. Building on past efforts to design correspondence indicators that are sensitive to trade-offs that forecasters strike between over- and underprediction, the Technical Appendix lays out an array of value adjustments that give forecasters varying benefits of the doubt that their mistakes were the "right mistakes."[18]

4. *Challenges of scoring subjective probability forecasts.* We cannot assess the accuracy of experts' predictions if we cannot figure out what they predicted. And experts were reluctant to call outcomes either impossible or inevitable. They hedged with expressions such as "remote chance," "maybe," and "odds-on favorite." Checking the correctness of vague verbiage is problematic. Words can take on many meanings: "likely" could imply anything from barely better than 50/50 to 99 percent.[19] Moreover, checking the correctness

---

[18] J. Swets, R. Dawes, and J. Monahan, "Psychological Science Can Improve Diagnostic Decisions, *Psychological Science in the Public Interest*, 1 (2000): 1–26. These mental exercises compel us to be uncomfortably explicit about our priorities. Should we give into the utilitarian temptation to save lives by ending a long war quickly via a tactical nuclear strike to "take out" the enemy leadership? Or should we define good judgment as the refusal to countenance taboo trade-offs, as the wise recognition that some things are best left unthinkable? See P. E. Tetlock, O. Kristel, B. Elson, M. Green, and J. Lerner, (2000). "The Psychology of the Unthinkable: Taboo Trade-Offs, Forbidden Base Rates, and Heretical Counterfactuals, *Journal of Personality and Social Psychology*, 78 (2000): 853–70.

[19] Many studies have examined the varied meanings that people attach to verbal expressions of uncertainty: W. Bruine de Bruin, B. Fischhoff, S. G. Millstein, and B. L. Felscher,

of numerical probability estimates is problematic. Only judgments of zero (impossible) and 1.0 (inevitable) are technically falsifiable. For all other values, wayward forecasters can argue that we stumbled into improbable worlds: low-probability events sometimes happen and high-probability events sometimes do not.

To break this impasse, we turned to behavioral decision theorists who have had success in persuading other reluctant professionals to translate verbal waffling into numerical probabilities as well as in scoring these judgments.[20] The key insight is that, although we can never know whether there was a .1 chance in 1988 that the Soviet Union would disintegrate by 1993 or a .9 chance of Canada disintegrating by 1998, we can measure the accuracy of such judgments across many events (saved again by the law of large numbers). These aggregate measures tell us how discriminating forecasters were: do they assign larger probabilities to things that subsequently happen than to things that do not? These measures also tell us how well calibrated forecasters were: do events they assign .10 or .50 or .90 probabilities materialize roughly 10 percent or 50 percent or 90 percent of the time? And the Technical Appendix shows us how to tweak these measures to tap into a variety of other finer-grained conceptions of accuracy.

5. *Challenging reality.* We risk making false attributions of good judgment if we fail to recognize the existence of legitimate ambiguity about either what happened or the implications of what happened for the truth or falsity of particular points of view.

Perfect consensus over what happened is often beyond reach. Partisan Democrats and Republicans will remain forever convinced that the pithiest characterization of the 2000 presidential election is that the other side connived with judicial hacks to steal it. Rough agreement is, however, possible as long as we specify outcomes precisely enough to pass the litmus tests in the Methodological Appendix. The most important of these was the clairvoyance test: our measures had to define possible futures so clearly that, if we handed experts' predictions to a true clairvoyant, she could tell us, with no need for clarifications ("What did you

---

"Verbal and Numerical Expressions of Probability: 'It's a Fifty-Fifty Chance.'" *Organizational Behavior and Human Decision Processes* 81 (2000): 115–23.

[20] The pioneering work focused on weather forecasters. See A. H. Murphy, "Scalar and Vector Partitions of the Probability Score, Part I, Two-Stage Situation," *Journal of Applied Meteorology* 11 (1972): 273–82; A. H. Murphy, "Scalar and Vector Partitions of the Probability Score, Part II, N-State Situation," *Journal of Applied Meteorology* 12 (1972): 595–600. For extensions, see R. L. Winkler, "Evaluating Probabilities: Asymmetric Scoring Rules," *Management Science* 40 (1994): 1395–1405.

mean by a Polish Peron or . . . ?"), who got what right. This test rules out oracular pronouncements of the Huntington or Fukuyama sort: expect clashes of civilizations or end of history. Our measures were supposed to focus, to the degree possible,[21] on the unadorned facts, the facts before the spinmeisters dress them up: before "defense spending as percentage of GDP" is rhetorically transformed into "reckless warmongering" or "prudent precaution."

The deeper problem—for which there is no ready measurement fix—is resolving disagreements over the implications of what happened for the correctness of competing points of view. Well before forecasters had a chance to get anything wrong, many warned that forecasting was an unfair standard—unfair because of the danger of lavishing credit on winners who were just lucky and heaping blame on losers who were just unlucky.

These protests are not just another self-serving effort of ivory tower types to weasel out of accountability to real-world evidence. Prediction and explanation are not as tightly coupled as once supposed.[22] Explanation is possible without prediction. A conceptually trivial but practically consequential source of forecasting failure occurs whenever we possess a sound theory but do not know whether the antecedent conditions for applying the theory have been satisfied: high school physics tells me why the radiator will freeze if the temperature falls below 32°F but not how cold it will be tonight. Or, consider cases in which we possess both sound knowledge and good knowledge of antecedents but are stymied because outcomes may be subject to chaotic oscillations. Geophysicists understand how principles of plate tectonics produce earthquakes and can monitor seismological antecedents but still cannot predict earthquakes.

Conversely, prediction is possible without explanation. Ancient astronomers had bizarre ideas about what stars were, but that did not stop them from identifying celestial regularities that navigators used to guide ships for centuries. And contemporary astronomers can predict the rhythms of solar storms but have only a crude understanding of what causes these potentially earth-sizzling eruptions. For most scientists, prediction is not enough. Few scientists would have changed their minds about astrology if Nancy Reagan's astrologer had chalked up a string of spectacular forecasting successes. The result so undercuts core beliefs that the scientific community would have, rightly, insisted on looking long and hard for other mechanisms underlying these successes.

---

[21] The caveat is critical. The more experts knew, the harder it often became to find indicators that passed the clairvoyance test. For instance, GDP can be estimated in many ways (we rely on purchasing power parity), and so can defense spending.

[22] F. Suppe, *The Structure of Scientific Theories* (Chicago: University of Chicago Press, 1973); S. Toulmin, *Foresight and Understanding: An Inquiry into the Aims of Science* (New York: Harper & Row, 1963).

These arguments highlight valid objections to simple correspondence theories of truth. And the resulting complications create far-from-hypothetical opportunities for mischief. It is no coincidence that the explanation-is-possible-without-prediction argument surges in popularity when our heroes have egg on their faces. Pacifists do not abandon Mahatma Gandhi's worldview just because of the sublime naïveté of his remark in 1940 that he did not consider Adolf Hitler to be as bad as "frequently depicted" and that "he seems to be gaining his victories without much bloodshed";[23] many environmentalists defend Paul Ehrlich despite his notoriously bad track record in the 1970s and 1980s (he predicted massive food shortages just as new technologies were producing substantial surpluses);[24] Republicans do not change their views about the economic competence of Democratic administrations just because Martin Feldstein predicted that the legacy of the Clinton 1993 budget would be stagnation for the rest of the decade;[25] social democrats do not overhaul their outlook just because Lester Thurow predicted that the 1990s would witness the ascendancy of the more compassionate capitalism of Europe and Japan over the "devil take the hindmost" American model.[26]

Conversely, it is no coincidence that the prediction-is-possible-without-explanation argument catches on when our adversaries are crowing over their forecasting triumphs. Our adversaries must have been as lucky in victory as we were unlucky in defeat. After each side has taken its pummeling in the forecasting arena, it is small wonder there are so few fans of forecasting accuracy as a benchmark of good judgment.

Such logical contortions should not, however, let experts off the hook. Scientists ridicule explanations that redescribe past regularities as empty tautologies—and they have little patience with excuses for consistently poor predictive track records. A balanced assessment would recognize that forecasting is a fallible but far from useless indicator of our understanding of causal mechanisms. In the long run (and we solicit enough forecasts on enough topics that the law of large numbers applies), our confidence in a point of view should wax or wane with its predictive successes and failures, the exact amounts hinging on the aggressiveness of forecasters' ex ante theoretical wagers and on our willingness to give weight to forecasters' ex post explanations for unexpected results.

[23] C. Cerf, and V. S. Navasky, eds., *The Experts Speak: The Definitive Compendium of Authoritative Misinformation* (New York: Pantheon Books, 1984).

[24] A. Sen, *Poverty and Famines* (New York: Oxford University Printing House, 1981).

[25] M. Feldstein, "Clinton's Revenue Mirage," *Wall Street Journal*, April 6, 1993, A14.

[26] See Lester Thurow, *Head to Head: The Coming Economic Battle among Japan, Europe, and America* (New York: Murrow, 1992).

Thinking the Right Way

One might suppose there must be close ties between correspondence and coherence/process indicators of good judgment, between getting it right and thinking the right way. There are connections but they are far from reliably deterministic. One could be a poor forecaster who works within a perfectly consistent belief system that is utterly detached from reality (e.g., paranoia). And one could be an excellent forecaster who relies on highly intuitive but logically indefensible guesswork.

One might also suppose that, even if our best efforts to assess correspondence indicators bog down in disputes over what really or nearly happened, we are on firmer ground with coherence/process indicators. One would again be wrong. Although purely logical indicators command deference, we encounter resistance even here. It is useful to array coherence/process indicators along a rough controversy continuum anchored at one end by widely accepted tests and at the other by bitterly contested ones.

At the close-to-slam-dunk end, we find violations of logical consistency so flagrant that few rise to their defense. The prototypic tests involve breaches of axiomatic identities within probability theory.[27] For instance, it is hard to defend forecasters who claim that the likelihood of a set of outcomes, judged as a whole, is less than the sum of the separately judged likelihoods of the set's exclusive and exhaustive membership list.[28] Insofar as there are disputes, they center on how harshly to judge these mistakes: whether people merely misunderstood instructions or whether the mistakes are by-products of otherwise adaptive modes of thinking or whether people are genuinely befuddled.

At the controversial end of the continuum, competing schools of thought offer unapologetically opposing views on the standards for judging judgment. These tests are too subjective for my taste, but they foreshadow later controversies over cognitive styles. For instance, the more committed observers are to parsimony, the more critical they are of those who fail to organize their belief systems in tidy syllogisms that deduce historical outcomes from covering laws and who flirt with close-call counterfactuals that undercut basic "laws of history"; conversely, the less committed observers are to parsimony, the more critical they are of the "rigidity" of those who try to reduce the quirkiness of history to theoretical formulas. One side's rigor is the other's dogmatism.

[27] L. Savage, *The Foundations of Statistics* (New York: Wiley, 1954); W. Edwards, "The Theory of Decision Making," *Psychological Bulletin* 51 (1954): 380–417.

[28] It requires little ingenuity to design bets that turn violators of this minimalist standard of rationality into money pumps. People do, however, often stumble. See A. Tversky, and D. Koehler, "Support Theory: A Nonextensional Representation of Subjective Probability," *Psychological Review* 101 (1994): 547–67.

In the middle of the continuum, we encounter consensus on what it means to fail coherence/process tests but divisions on where to locate the pass-fail cutoffs. The prototypic tests involve breaches of rules of fair play in the honoring of *reputational bets* and in the evenhanded treatment of evidence in *turnabout thought experiments.*

To qualify as a good judge within a Bayesian framework—and many students of human decision making as well as high-IQ public figures such as Bill Gates and Robert Rubin think of themselves as Bayesians—one must own up to one's reputational bets. The Technical Appendix lays out the computational details, but the core idea is a refinement of common sense. Good judges are good belief updaters who follow through on the logical implications of reputational bets that pit their favorite explanations against alternatives: if I declare that x is .2 likely if my "theory" is right and .8 likely if yours is right, and x occurs, I "owe" some belief change.[29]

In principle, no one disputes we should change our minds when we make mistakes. In practice, however, outcomes do not come stamped with labels indicating whose forecasts have been disconfirmed. Chapter 4 shows how much wiggle room experts can create for themselves by invoking various belief system defenses. Forecasters who expected the demise of Canada before 2000 can argue that Quebec almost seceded and still might. And Paul Ehrlich, a "doomster" known for his predictions of ecocatastrophes, saw no need whatsoever to change his mind after losing a bet with "boomster" Julian Simon over whether real prices of five commodities would increase in the 1980s. After writing a hefty check to Simon to cover the cost spread on the futures contracts, Ehrlich defiantly compared Simon to a man who jumps from the Empire State Building and, as he passes onlookers on the fiftieth floor, announces, "All's well so far."[30]

How should we react to such defenses? Philosophers of science who believe in playing strictly by ex ante rules maintain that forecasters who rewrite their reputational bets, ex post, are sore losers. Sloppy relativism will be the natural consequence of letting us change our minds—whenever convenient—on what counts as evidence. But epistemological liberals will demur. Where is it written, they ask, that we cannot revise reputational bets, especially in fuzzy domains where the truth is rarely either-or? A

[29] P. E. Tetlock, "Theory-Driven Reasoning about Possible Pasts and Possible Futures," *American Journal of Political Science* 43 (1999): 335–36. Sherman Kent, the paragon of intelligence analysts, was an early advocate of translating vague hunches into precise probabilistic odds (S. Kent, *Collected Essays* (U.S. Government: Center for the Study of Intelligence, 1970), http://www.cia.gov/csi/books/shermankent/toc.html.

[30] For an account of the Ehrlich-Simon bet, see John Tierney, "Betting on the Planet," *New York Times Magazine,* December 2, 1990, 52–53, 74–81.

balanced assessment here would concede that Bayesians can no more purge subjectivity from coherence assessments of good judgment than correspondence theorists can ignore complaints about the scoring rules for forecasting accuracy. But that does not mean we cannot distinguish desperate patch-up rewrites that delay the day of reckoning for bankrupt ideas from creative rewrites that stop us from abandoning good ideas.[31] Early warning signs that we are slipping into solipsism include the frequency and self-serving selectivity with which we rewrite bets and the revisionist scale of the rewrites.

Shifting from forward-in-time reasoning to backward-in-time reasoning, we relied on turnabout thought experiments to assess the willingness of analysts to change their opinions on historical counterfactuals. The core idea is, again, simple. Good judges should resist the temptation to engage in self-serving reasoning when policy stakes are high and reality constraints are weak. And temptation is ubiquitous. Underlying all judgments of whether a policy was shrewd or foolish are hidden layers of speculative judgments about how history would have unfolded had we pursued different policies.[32] We have warrant to praise a policy as great when we can think only of ways things could have worked out far worse, and warrant to call a policy disastrous when we can think only of ways things could have worked out far better. Whenever someone judges something a failure or success, a reasonable rejoinder is: "Within what distribution of possible worlds?"[33]

Turnabout thought experiments gauge the consistency of the standards that we apply to counterfactual claims. We fail turnabout tests when we apply laxer standards to evidence that reinforces as opposed to undercuts our favorite what-if scenarios. But, just as some forward-in-time reasoners balked at changing their minds when they lost reputational bets, some backward-in-time reasoners balked at basing their assessments of the probative value of archival evidence solely on information available before they knew how the evidence would break. They argued that far-fetched claims require stronger evidence than claims they felt had strong support from other sources. A balanced assessment here requires confronting a dilemma: if we only accept evidence that confirms

[31] Suppe, *The Structure of Scientific Theories*; P. Laudan, *Progress and Its Problems* (Berkeley: University of California Press, 1986).

[32] We discover how reliant we are on hidden counterfactuals when we probe the underpinnings of attributions of good or bad judgment to leaders. The simplest rule—"If it happens on your watch . . ."—has the advantage of reducing reliance on counterfactuals but the disadvantage of holding policy makers accountable for outcomes outside their control. Most of us want leeway for the possibilities that (a) some leaders do all the right things but—by bad luck—get clobbered; (b) other leaders violate all the rules of rationality and—by sheer dumb luck—prosper.

[33] David K. Lewis, *Counterfactuals* (Cambridge: Harvard University Press, 1973).

our worldview, we will become prisoners of our preconceptions, but if we subject all evidence, agreeable or disagreeable, to the same scrutiny, we will be overwhelmed. As with reputational bets, the question becomes how much special treatment of favorite hypotheses is too much. And, as with reputational bets, the bigger the double standard, the greater are the grounds for concern.

PREVIEW OF CHAPTERS TO FOLLOW

The bulk of this book is devoted to determining how well experts perform against this assortment of correspondence and coherence benchmarks of good judgment.

Chapters 2 and 3 explore correspondence indicators. Drawing on the literature on judgmental accuracy, I divide the guiding hypotheses into two categories: those rooted in *radical skepticism*, which equates good political judgment with good luck, and those rooted in *meliorism*, which maintains that the quest for predictors of good judgment, and ways to improve ourselves, is not quixotic and there are better and worse ways of thinking that translate into better and worse judgments.

Chapter 2 introduces us to the radical skeptics and their varied reasons for embracing their counterintuitive creed. Their guiding precept is that, although we often talk ourselves into believing we live in a predictable world, we delude ourselves: history is ultimately one damned thing after another, a random walk with upward and downward blips but devoid of thematic continuity. Politics is no more predictable than other games of chance. On any given spin of the roulette wheel of history, crackpots will claim vindication for superstitious schemes that posit patterns in randomness. But these schemes will fail in cross-validation. What works today will disappoint tomorrow.[34]

Here is a doctrine that runs against the grain of human nature, our shared need to believe that we live in a comprehensible world that we can master if we apply ourselves.[35] Undiluted radical skepticism requires us to believe, *really believe*, that when the time comes to choose among

[34] The exact time of arrival of disappointment may, though, vary. The probability of black or red on a roulette spin should be independent of earlier spins. But political-economic outcomes are often interdependent. If one erroneously predicted the rise of a "Polish Peron," one would have also been wrong about surging central government debt-to-GDP ratios, inflation, corruption ratings, and so on. Skeptics should predict as much consistency in who gets what right as there is interdependence among outcomes.

[35] Radical skepticism as defined here should not be confused with radical relativism as defined earlier. Radical skeptics do not doubt the desirability or feasibility of holding different points of view accountable to common correspondence and coherence tests; they doubt only that, when put to these tests, experts can justify their claims to expertise.

controversial policy options—to support Chinese entry into the World Trade Organization or to bomb Baghdad or Belgrade or to build a ballistic missile defense—we could do as well by tossing coins as by consulting experts.[36]

Chapter 2 presents evidence from regional forecasting exercises consistent with this debunking perspective. It tracks the accuracy of hundreds of experts for dozens of countries on topics as disparate as transitions to democracy and capitalism, economic growth, interstate violence, and nuclear proliferation. When we pit experts against minimalist performance benchmarks—dilettantes, dart-throwing chimps, and assorted extrapolation algorithms—we find few signs that expertise translates into greater ability to make either "well-calibrated" or "discriminating" forecasts.

Radical skeptics welcomed these results, but they start squirming when we start finding patterns of consistency in who got what right. Radical skepticism tells us to expect nothing (with the caveat that if we toss enough coins, expect some streakiness). But the data revealed more consistency in forecasters' track records than could be ascribed to chance. Meliorists seize on these findings to argue that crude human-versus-chimp comparisons mask systematic individual differences in good judgment.

Although meliorists agree that skeptics go too far in portraying good judgment as illusory, they agree on little else. Cognitive-content meliorists identify good judgment with a particular outlook but squabble over which points of view represent movement toward or away from the truth. Cognitive-style meliorists identify good judgment not with *what* one thinks, but with *how* one thinks. But they squabble over which styles of reasoning—quick and decisive versus balanced and thoughtful—enhance or degrade judgment.

Chapter 3 tests a multitude of meliorist hypotheses—most of which bite the dust. *Who* experts were—professional background, status, and so on—made scarcely an iota of difference to accuracy. Nor did *what* experts thought—whether they were liberals or conservatives, realists or institutionalists, optimists or pessimists. But the search bore fruit. *How* experts thought—their style of reasoning—did matter. Chapter 3 demonstrates the usefulness of classifying experts along a rough cognitive-style continuum anchored at one end by Isaiah Berlin's prototypical hedgehog and at the other by his prototypical fox.[37] The intellectually aggressive hedgehogs knew one big thing and sought, under the banner of parsimony,

---

[36] The unpalatability of a proposition is weak grounds for rejecting it. But it often influences where we set our thresholds of proof. (P. E. Tetlock, "Political or Politicized Psychology: Is the Road to Scientific Hell Paved with Good Moral Intentions?" *Political Psychology* 15 [1994]: 509–30)

[37] Berlin, "The Hedgehog and the Fox."

to expand the explanatory power of that big thing to "cover" new cases; the more eclectic foxes knew many little things and were content to improvise ad hoc solutions to keep pace with a rapidly changing world.

Treating the regional forecasting studies as a decathlon between rival strategies of making sense of the world, the foxes consistently edge out the hedgehogs but enjoy their most decisive victories in long-term exercises inside their domains of expertise. Analysis of explanations for their predictions sheds light on how foxes pulled off this cognitive-stylistic coup. The foxes' self-critical, point-counterpoint style of thinking prevented them from building up the sorts of excessive enthusiasm for their predictions that hedgehogs, especially well-informed ones, displayed for theirs. Foxes were more sensitive to how contradictory forces can yield stable equilibria and, as a result, "overpredicted" fewer departures, good or bad, from the status quo. But foxes did not mindlessly predict the past. They recognized the precariousness of many equilibria and hedged their bets by rarely ruling out anything as "impossible."

These results favor meliorism over skepticism—and they favor the pro-complexity branch of meliorism, which proclaims the adaptive superiority of the tentative, balanced modes of thinking favored by foxes,[38] over the pro-simplicity branch, which proclaims the superiority of the confident, decisive modes of thinking favored by hedgehogs.[39] These results also domesticate radical skepticism, with its wild-eyed implication that experts have nothing useful to tell us about the future beyond what we could have learned from tossing coins or inspecting goat entrails. This tamer brand of skepticism—skeptical meliorism—still warns of the dangers of hubris, but it allows for how a self-critical, dialectical style of reasoning can spare experts the big mistakes that hammer down the accuracy of their more intellectually exuberant colleagues.

Chapter 4 shifts the spotlight from whether forecasters get it right to whether forecasters change their minds as much as they should when they get it wrong. Using experts' own reputational bets as our benchmark, we discover that experts, especially the hedgehogs, were slower than they should have been in revising the guiding ideas behind inaccurate forecasts.[40] Chapter 4 also documents the belief system defenses that experts use to justify rewriting their reputational bets after the fact: arguing that, although the predicted event did not occur, it eventually will

[38] For a review of work on cognitive styles, see P. Suedfeld, and P. E. Tetlock, "Cognitive styles," in *Blackwell International Handbook of Social Psychology: Intra-Individual Processes*, vol. 1, ed. A. Tesser and N. Schwartz (London: Blackwell, 2000).

[39] G. Gigerenzer and P. M. Todd, *Simple Heuristics That Make Us Smart* (New York: Oxford University Press, 2000).

[40] H. J. Einhorn and R. M. Hogarth, "Prediction, Diagnosis and Causal Thinking in Forecasting," *Journal of Forecasting* 1 (1982): 23–36.

(off on timing) or it nearly did (the close call) and would have but for . . . (the exogenous shock). Bad luck proved a vastly more popular explanation for forecasting failure than good luck proved for forecasting success.

Chapter 5 lengthens the indictment: hedgehogs are more likely than foxes to uphold double standards for judging historical counterfactuals. And this double standard indictment is itself double-edged. First, there is the selective openness toward close-call claims. Whereas chapter 4 shows that hedgehogs only opened to close-call arguments that insulated their forecasts from disconfirmation (the "I was almost right" defense), chapter 5 shows that hedgehogs spurn similar indeterminacy arguments that undercut their favorite lessons from history (the "I was not almost wrong" defense). Second, chapter 5 shows that hedgehogs are less likely than foxes to apologize for failing turnabout tests, for applying tougher standards to agreeable than to disagreeable evidence. Their defiant attitude was "I win if the evidence breaks in my direction" but "if the evidence breaks the other way, the methodology must be suspect."

Chapters 4 and 5 reinforce a morality-tale reading of the evidence, with sharply etched good guys (the spry foxes) and bad guys (the self-assured hedgehogs). Chapter 6 calls on us to hear out the defense before reaching a final verdict. The defense raises logical objections to the factual, moral, and metaphysical assumptions underlying claims that "one group makes more accurate judgments than another" and demands difficulty, value, controversy and fuzzy-set scoring-rule adjustments as compensation. The defense also raises the psychological objection that there is no single, best cognitive style across situations.[41] Overconfidence may be essential for achieving the forecasting coups that posterity hails as visionary. The bold but often wrong forecasts of hedgehogs may be as forgivable as high strikeout rates among home-run hitters, the product of a reasonable trade-off, not grounds for getting kicked off the team. Both sets of defenses create pockets of reasonable doubt but, in the end, neither can exonerate hedgehogs of all their transgressions. Hedgehogs just made too many mistakes spread across too many topics.

Whereas chapter 6 highlighted some benefits of the "closed-minded" hedgehog approach to the world, chapter 7 dwells on some surprising

---

[41] For expansions of this argument, see P. E. Tetlock, R. S. Peterson, and J. M. Berry, Flattering and Unflattering Personality Portraits of Integratively Simple and Complex Managers," *Journal of Personality and Social Psychology* 64 (1993): 500–511; P. E. Tetlock and A. Tyler, "Winston Churchill's Cognitive and Rhetorical Style," *Political Psychology* 17 (1996): 149–70. P. E. Tetlock, D. Armor, and R. Peterson, "The Slavery Debate in Antebellum America: Cognitive Style, Value Conflict, and the Limits of Compromise," *Journal of Personality and Social Psychology* 66 (1994): 115–26.

costs of the "open-minded" fox approach. Consultants in the business and political worlds often use scenario exercises to encourage decision makers to let down their guards and imagine a broader array of possibilities than they normally would.[42] On the plus side, these exercises can check some forms of overconfidence, no mean achievement. On the minus side, these exercises can stimulate experts—once they start unpacking possible worlds—to assign too much likelihood to too many scenarios.[43] There is nothing admirably open-minded about agreeing that the probability of event A is less than the compound probability of A and B, or that x is inevitable but alternatives to x remain possible. Trendy open-mindedness looks like old-fashioned confusion. And the open-minded foxes are more vulnerable to this confusion than the closed-minded hedgehogs.

We are left, then, with a murkier tale. The dominant danger remains hubris, the mostly hedgehog vice of closed-mindedness, of dismissing dissonant possibilities too quickly. But there is also the danger of cognitive chaos, the mostly fox vice of excessive open-mindedness, of seeing too much merit in too many stories. Good judgment now becomes a metacognitive skill—akin to "the art of self-overhearing."[44] Good judges need to eavesdrop on the mental conversations they have with themselves as they decide how to decide, and determine whether they approve of the trade-offs they are striking in the classic exploitation-exploration balancing act, that between exploiting existing knowledge and exploring new possibilities.

Chapter 8 reflects on the broader implications of this project. From a philosophy of science perspective, there is value in assessing how far an exercise of this sort can be taken. We failed to purge all subjectivity from judgments of good judgment, but we advanced the cause of "objectification" by developing valid correspondence and coherence measures of good judgment, by discovering links between how observers think and how they fare on these measures, and by determining the robustness of these links across scoring adjustments. From a policy perspective, there is value in using publicly verifiable correspondence and coherence benchmarks to gauge the quality of public debates. The more people know about pundits' track records, the stronger the pundits' incentives to compete by improving the epistemic (truth) value of their products, not just by pandering to communities of co-believers.

---

[42] Peter Schwarz, *The Art of the Long View* (New York: Doubleday, 1991).

[43] For a mathematical model for understanding the effects of "unpacking" on probability judgments, A. Tversky and D. Koehler, "Support Theory: A Nonextensional Representation of Subjective Probability," *Psychological Review* 101 (1994): 547–67.

[44] H. Bloom, *Shakespeare: The Invention of the Human* (New York: Riverhead, 1998).

These are my principal arguments. Like any author, I hope they stand the test of time. I would not, however, view this project as a failure if hedgehogs swept every forecasting competition in the early twenty-first century. Indeed, this book gives reasons for expecting occasional reversals of this sort. This book will count as a failure, as a dead end, only if it fails to inspire follow-ups by those convinced they can do better.

CHAPTER 2

The Ego-deflating Challenge of Radical Skepticism

> Among all forms of mistake, prophecy is the most gratuitous.
> —GEORGE ELIOT, *Middlemarch*

> What I've said that turned out to be right will be considered
> obvious, and what was wrong will be humorous.
> —BILL GATES, *The Road Ahead*

IT IS COMMONPLACE to lament the sad state of political forecasting.
Moreover, suspicions that the entire enterprise is intellectually bankrupt
have only been fortified by the most recent forecasting fiasco: the unan-
imous declaration by quantitative modelers of presidential elections at
the American Political Science Association in August 2000 that we
could ignore the frantic rhetorical posturing of the next few months.
Election campaigns are tales full of sound and fury but of no significance because of the offsetting effects of each side's propaganda broad-
sides. The die had been cast: Gore would defeat Bush by decisive, even
landslide, margins.[1]

We revisit this incident in chapter 5, so here it must suffice to caution
against drawing sweeping conclusions from a single data point. The
current chapter has three missions: (1) to explore why radical skeptics
believe the social science quest for predictive laws to be ill-conceived;
(2) to weave their arguments into a composite set of six hypotheses,
the core tenets of skepticism, that tell us what to expect when a diverse
array of experts tries to predict an even more diverse array of real-
world events; (3) to present evidence that suggests that, although skepticism about the predictive powers of experts is warranted, the skeptics
do sometimes overreach: "who gets what right" is not just a matter of
blind luck.

---

[1] For thoughtful postmortems, see L. M. Bartels and J. Zaller, "Presidential Vote Models: A Recount," *Political Science and Politics* 34 (2001): 9–20; M. S. Lewis-Beck, and C.
Tien, "Modeling the Future: Lessons from the Gore Forecast," *Political Science and Politics*
34 (2001): 21–24; C. Wlezien, "On Forecasting the Presidential Vote," *Political Science
and Politics* 34 (2001): 25–32; J. E. Campbell, "The Referendum That Didn't Happen: The
Forecasts of the 2000 Presidential Election," *Political Science and Politics* 34 (2001):
33–38.

RADICAL SKEPTICISM

Radical skeptics naturally gravitate toward a punctuated equilibrium view of politics.[2] On the one hand, they must concede the obvious. Politics is sometimes drearily predictable. No expertise was required to know that war would not erupt in Scandinavia in the 1990s. In stable systems, we can often do well by relying on simple, predict-the-past algorithms. On the other hand, radical skeptics are keenly aware that all hell sometimes breaks loose. These bouts of severe unpredictability are, moreover, unpredictable, as unpredictable as the meteors that intermittently smash into our planet and radically alter the course of evolution, making—among other things—our branch of intelligent life possible.

Several of our more reluctant research participants suspected that unpredictability was more the rule than the exception in politics. Invoking Machiavelli, one cautioned that good (forecasting) judgment is more a matter of *fortuna* than of *virtu*.[3] A second opined that Tolstoy had the "right take on great men": those with reputations for farsightedness were lucky and how lucky becomes clear when we survey their mistakes as well as their triumphs. For example, Churchill gets credit for seeing the Nazi menace before almost everyone else, perhaps saving European Jews from total extermination, but he was not endowed with any preternatural gift. He may have merely had a lower threshold than others for seeing threats to British interests. After all, he did claim, in his campaign against self-government for India,[4] to see ominous similarities between Gandhi and Hitler. A third puzzled over the paradoxes that arise in sizing up the judgment of that master practitioner of Realpolitik, Joseph Stalin. On the plus side of the amoral impact ledger, Stalin achieved total command of the Soviet Union and expanded Russian influence deeper into central Europe than any czar. On the minus side, he ignored warnings of an imminent Nazi invasion in 1941, attributing them to a British plot. We are thus left with a riddle: How could someone so pathologically paranoid on the home front have been so oblivious to the threat posed by a regime dedicated to annihilating "Judaeo-Bolshevism"?[5] A fourth observed that even renowned speculators, such as George Soros, who brought the Bank of England to its knees in 1992, spotted the Thai baht's weakness in 1997, and anticipated the Russian default of 1998, are eventually humbled. As Soros ruefully remarked on his "shorting"

[2] S. J. Gould, *Bully for Brontosaurus: Reflections in Natural History* (New York: W. W. Norton, 1991).

[3] H. F. Pitkin, *Fortune Is a Woman: Gender and Politics in the Thought of Niccolo Machiavelli* (Berkeley: University of California Press, 1984).

[4] Martin Gilbert, *Churchill: A Life* (New York: Holt, 1991).

[5] G. Gorodetsky, *Grand Delusion* (New Haven, CT: Yale University Press, 1999).

Internet stocks too soon, "We had our head handed to us."[6] Of course, Soros was "just off on timing." The NASDAQ fell by 60 percent by 2001. Looking ahead, it remains to be seen whether the rampaging bulls of the late twentieth century have been set up to be mowed down in the early twenty-first century or the new-economy visionaries are right that things are different this time, and that Dow 36,000 is around the corner.

Skeptics also stress the fine line between success and failure. Churchill's career was almost ruined in 1916 by his sponsorship of the disastrous Gallipoli campaign designed to knock the Ottoman Empire out of World War I. But Churchill insisted, and some historians agree, that the plan "almost worked" and would have if it had been more res-olutely implemented.[7] Conversely, Stalin arguably escaped his share of blame for his blunders because, in the end, he was victorious. Stalin nearly lost everything but was saved by Hitler's even bigger blunders.

On close scrutiny, reputations for political genius rest on thin evidential foundations: genius is a matter of being in the right place at the right time. Hero worshippers reveal their own lack of historical imagination: their in-capacity to see how easily things could have worked out far worse as a re-sult of contingencies that no mortal could have foreseen. Political geniuses are just a close-call counterfactual away from being permanently pilloried as fools.

Varieties of Radical Skepticism

Figure 2.1 splits radical skeptics into two lines of intellectual descent: ontological skeptics who point to fundamental properties of the world that make it impossible to achieve forecasting accuracy beyond crude ex-trapolation algorithms and psychological skeptics who point to funda-mental properties of the human mind that make it inevitable that experts will miss whatever predictability has not been precluded "in principle."

ONTOLOGICAL SKEPTICS

This camp is populated by an odd assortment of path-dependency the-orists, complexity theorists, game theorists, and probability theorists.

Path dependency. Polya's urn is a simple game that makes a profound point: life can alternate—quite unpredictably—between periods of boring predictability and wild unpredictability.[8] Players confront an urn with

---

[6] G. Soros, *Open Society: Reforming Global Capitalism* (New York: Public Affairs, 2000).

[7] Gilbert, *Churchill.*

[8] B. Arthur, *Increasing Returns and Path-Dependence in the Economy* (Ann Arbor: University of Michigan Press, 1994); P. Pierson, "Increasing Returns, Path Dependence, and the Study of Politics," *American Political Science Review* 94 (2000): 251–67.

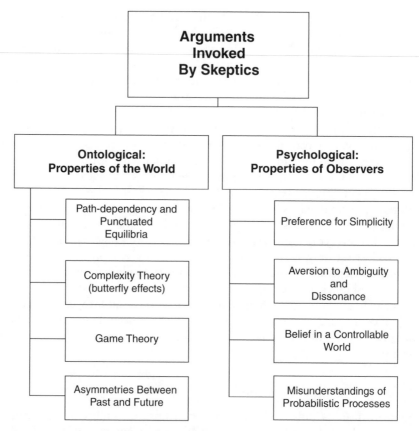

Figure 2.1. The varied grounds that skeptics have for suspecting that observers will never be able to predict better than either chance or extrapolation algorithms. The more arguments one endorses, the more entrenched one's skepticism toward the possibility of forecasting in complex social systems.

two balls, one red and one green. Players remove a ball, at random, and return it, plus an additional ball of the same color. And they repeat this procedure until they fill the urn. Polya urn processes have three defining characteristics:[9] they are initially unpredictable (in the beginning, the final outcome could range anywhere from 99.9 percent red to .01 percent red), they become increasingly inflexible (later draws contribute only minutely to the final distribution), and they show how small initial advantages can quickly accumulate, making it hard to change direction.

Path-dependency theorists argue that many historical processes should be modeled as quirky path-dependent games with the potential to yield

[9] Arthur, *Increasing Returns*, 112–14.

increasing returns. They maintain that history has repeatedly demonstrated that a technology can achieve a decisive advantage over competitors even if it is not the best long-run alternative.[10] These theorists have also not limited themselves to explaining the triumph of QWERTY typewriters, VHS recorders, and Microsoft Windows. They have locked bigger game into their explanatory sights.

The most ambitious application of increasing returns has been to the long-simmering controversy over "the rise of the West" (and the concomitant failure of the "Rest"). How did a comparative handful of Europeans, inhabiting a cultural backwater a thousand years ago, become the dominant force on the planet, reducing peoples on every other continent to tributary status?[11] It was not obvious that Europe and its colonial offshoots would achieve global hegemony. China and Islam seemed like formidable contenders as late as A.D. 1300 or 1400. From an increasing-returns perspective, the key lies in the tiny advantages that Europe had in preconditions for growth: a fragile web of coevolving institutions that encouraged property rights and rule of law (giving entrepreneurs some protection from confiscation), a measured tolerance of free inquiry (facilitating a common pool of knowledge from which innovators could draw), market competition (rewarding ingenuity), and a competitive state system in which states that lagged economically soon faltered militarily. This synergistic combination underlies the exponential expansion of European influence that began around A.D. 1500 and, in a few centuries, propelled a laggard civilization ahead of its more sophisticated rivals.[12]

Not everyone, however, is sold on the wide applicability of increasing-returns, path-dependency views of history. Traditionalists subscribe to decreasing-returns approaches that portray both past and future as deducible from assumptions about how farsighted economic actors, working within material and political constraints, converge on unique equilibria. For example, Daniel Yergin notes how some oil industry observers in the early 1980s used a decreasing-returns framework to predict, thus far correctly, that OPEC's greatest triumphs were behind it.[13] They expected the sharp rises in oil prices in the late 1970s to stimulate conservation,

[10] Douglas C. North, *Institutions, Institutional Change and Economic Performance* (Cambridge: Cambridge University Press, 1990); D. C. North and R. P. Thomas, *The Rise of the Western World: A New Economic History* (New York: Cambridge University Press, 1973).

[11] Jack Goldstone, "Europe's Peculiar Path: The Unlikely Transition to Modernity," in *Unmaking the West: What-If Scenarios That Rewrite World History*, ed. P. E. Tetlock, R. N. Lebow, and G. Parker (Ann Arbor: University of Michigan Press, 2006).

[12] J. Mokyr, "King Kong and Cold Fusion: Entities That Never Were but Could Have Been," in Tetlock, Lebow, and Parker, *Unmaking the West*.

[13] D. Yergin, *The Prize: The Epic Quest for Oil, Money, and Power* (New York: Simon & Schuster, 1991).

exploration, and exploitation of other sources of energy, which would put downward pressure on oil prices. Each step from the equilibrium is harder than the last. Negative feedback stabilizes social systems because major changes in one direction are offset by counterreactions. Good judges appreciate that forecasts of prolonged radical shifts from the status quo are generally a bad bet.

Can forecasters tell us, ex ante, when to apply an increasing- or decreasing-returns framework? Skeptics doubt we can even make such determinations ex post: too much hinges on metaphysical guesswork. Who, this side of God, knows whether history has a diverging branching structure that leads to a variety of possible worlds, or a converging structure that, notwithstanding detours, channels us into destinations predetermined long ago?

Complexity Theorists. One could grant the ubiquity of path dependency but still embrace a moderate brand of skepticism that links good judgment to the ability to identify leverage points.[14] A persistent mediator, such as Jimmy Carter at Camp David, might broker a peace that would otherwise have been lost, or a shrewd philanthropist, such as George Soros, might have a pretty good track record of picking projects that have impact disproportionate to the expenditure, such as photocopy machines for Soviet bloc countries or funds to pay unemployed Soviet scientists who might otherwise have sold their services to rogue states eager to obtain weapons of mass destruction.

Radical skeptics deny even this role for good judgment. Embracing complexity theory, they argue that history is a succession of chaotic shocks reverberating through *incomprehensibly intricate* networks. To back up this claim, they point to computer simulations of physical systems that show that, when investigators link well-established nonlinear relationships into positive feedback loops, tiny variations in inputs begin to have astonishingly large effects.[15]

McCloskey illustrates the point with a textbook problem of ecology: predicting how the population of a species next year will vary as a function of this year's population.[16] The model is $x_{t+1} = f(x_t)$, a one-period-back nonlinear differential equation. The simplest equation is the hump: $x_{t+1} = \beta x_t [1 - x_t]$, where the tuning parameter, β, determines the hump's shape by specifying how the population of deer at $t + 1$ depends on the population in the preceding period. More deer mean more reproductive

[14] J. Gleick, *Chaos: Making a New Science* (New York: Viking, 1987).

[15] P. Bak and K. Chen, "Self-Organized Criticality," *Scientific American* 264 (January 1991): 46–53.

[16] D. McCloskey, "History, Differential Equations, and the Problem of Narration," *History and Theory* 30 (1991): 21–36.

opportunities, but more deer also exhaust the food supply and attract wolves. The higher β is, the steeper the hump and the more precipitous the shift from growth to decline. McCloskey shows how a tiny shift in beta from 3.94 to 3.935 can alter history. The plots of populations remain almost identical for several years but, for mysterious tipping-point reasons, the hypothetical populations decisively part ways twenty-five years into the simulation.

These tipping-point models are so compelling because they resonate so deeply with human experience. Who among us cannot imagine our lives unfolding differently but for tiny accidents of fate that shaped the jobs we hold, the people we marry, and so on? Counterfactual historians aggressively extend such "bifurcation point" arguments when they try to show it is "easy" to unravel not just the fates of individuals but also those of nations.[17] One eminent practitioner of this genre, Robert Fogel, argues that, even as late as the 1850s, "the overarching role of contingent circumstances in the victory of the antislavery movement needs to be emphasized. There never was a moment between 1854 and 1860 in which the triumph of the anti-slavery coalition was assured."[18] And just as the Civil War was not foreordained, many historians insist that there was nothing inevitable about the war's outcome. Accounts of military campaigns in the Civil War (and other wars) abound with tales of how—in the spirit of the nursery rhyme—horseshoe-nail-sized causes determined the outcomes of battles.[19]

We could endlessly multiply these examples of great oaks sprouting from little acorns. For radical skeptics, though, there is a deeper lesson: the impossibility of picking the influential acorns before the fact. Joel Mokyr compares searching for the seeds of the Industrial Revolution to "studying the history of Jewish dissenters between 50 A.D. and 50 B.C. We are looking for something that at its inception was insignificant, even bizarre, but destined to change the life of every man and woman in the West."[20]

Academics often disdain such arguments. Butterfly effect arguments undercut their pet theories: wars break out not due to grand causes—primordial hatreds or power imbalances—but to petty ones—royal

[17] See R. Cowley, *What If? The World's Foremost Military Historians Imagine What Might Have Been: Essays* (New York: Putnam, 1999); Tetlock, Lebow, and Parker, *Unmaking the West.*

[18] Robert Fogel, *Without Consent or Contract: The Rise and Fall of American Slavery* (Boston: Houghton Mifflin, 1989).

[19] J. M. McPherson, *The Battle Cry of Freedom: The Civil War Era* (New York: Oxford University Press, 1988).

[20] Joel Mokyr, *The Economics of the Industrial Revolution* (Totowa, NJ: Rowman & Allanheld, 1985).

carriage drivers making wrong turns, giving astonished assassins, who had just botched their jobs earlier that day, second chances to do it right. There is not much scholarly panache in documenting cause-effect linkages of this sort, one triviality after another, no better than "journalism."[21] McCloskey, however, gets the last word: "The disdain for assigning large events small causes is not rational in a world that is partly non-linear." If our fates are the products of extraordinary strings of coincidences, "it is ostrich-like foolishness to bury our heads in the sand and pretend that we live in a neatly deterministic and predictable world."[22]

Game Theorists. The rivalry between Sherlock Holmes and the evil genius Professor Moriarty illustrates how indeterminacy can arise as a natural by-product of rational agents second-guessing each other. When the two first met, Moriarty was eager, too eager, to display his capacity for interactive thinking by announcing: "All I have to say has already crossed your mind." Holmes replied: "Then possibly my answer has crossed yours." As the plot unfolds, Holmes uses his superior "interactive knowledge" to outmaneuver Moriarty by unexpectedly getting off the train at Canterbury, thwarting Moriarty who had calculated that Paris was Holmes's rational destination. Convoluted though it is, Moriarty failed to recognize that Holmes had already recognized that Moriarty would deduce what a rational Holmes would do under the circumstances, and the odds now favored Holmes getting off the train earlier than once planned.[23]

Indeterminacy problems of this sort are the bread and butter of behavioral game theory. In the "guess the number" game, for example, contestants pick a number between 0 and 100, with the goal of making their guess come as close as possible to two-thirds of the average guess of all the contestants.[24] In a world of only rational players—who base their guesses on the maximum number of levels of deduction—the equilibrium is 0. However, in a contest run at Richard Thaler's prompting by the *Financial Times*,[25] the most popular guesses were 33 (the right guess if everyone else chooses a number at random, producing an average guess of 50) and 22 (the right guess if everyone thinks through the preceding argument and picks 33). Dwindling numbers of respondents carried the

[21] McCloskey, "History, Differential Equations," 36.

[22] Ibid.

[23] Arthur Conan Doyle, *The Complete Sherlock Holmes* (New York: Garden City, 1938).

[24] Rosmarie Nagel, "Unraveling in Guessing Games: An Experimental Study," *American Economic Review* 85 (1995): 1313–26.

[25] Richard Thaler, "From Homo Economics to Homo Sapiens," *Journal of Economic Perspectives* 14 (2000): 133–41.

deductive logic to the third stage (picking two-thirds of 22) or higher, with a tiny hypereducated group recognizing the logically correct answer to be 0. The average guess was 18.91 and the winning guess, 13, which suggests that, for this newspaper's readership, a third order of sophistication was roughly optimal.

But defenders of forecasting accuracy benchmarks of good judgment can argue that all is not lost, that we can model how people play such games by distinguishing two types of sophistication. Logically sophisticated but psychologically naïve players guess zero: they see the right answer but exaggerate how many others do. Logically and psychologically sophisticated players see the right answer and appreciate how many, or few, others also "get it." Good judgment requires their mix of logical and psychological savvy.

Radical skeptics can counter, however, that many games have inherently indeterminate multiple or mixed strategy equilibria. They can also note that one does not need to buy into a hyperrational model of human nature to recognize that, when the stakes are high, players will try to second-guess each other to the point where political outcomes, like financial markets, resemble random walks.[26] Indeed, radical skeptics delight in pointing to the warehouse of evidence that now attests to the unpredictability of the stock market. Burton Malkiel documents that most mutual funds did not outperform market averages over the past thirty years. He also finds little consistency in performance. Big winners in the 1970s often flopped in the 1980s and 1990s. Good judgment requires hanging in for the long haul (the random walk meanders around an upward trend) and resisting the siren calls of technical analysts who promise to divine the future from the entrails of past trends and of hot-tip market-timers who are oddly eager to share breathtaking opportunities with strangers.[27]

At this point, some readers will give skeptics a dose of their own medicine. Have the naysayers not heard of superstar investors such as Peter Lynch, Warren Buffett, and George Soros, who beat their competitors (and market averages) with eerie consistency? But die-hard skeptics are unfazed: they endorse the blasphemous thought that these objects of adulation just got lucky. The skeptics offer a striking analogy. Imagine

---

[26] This is no recent insight. Carl von Clausewitz noted how "war most closely resembles a card game." It helps to be dealt good cards, but seasoned poker players know there is no quicker route to losing one's shirt than by playing too predictably. (Carl von Clausewitz, *On War*, ed. and trans. Michael Howard and Peter Paret [Princeton, NJ: Princeton University Press, 1976]); see also Erik Gartzke, "War Is in the Error Term," *International Organization* 53 [1999]: 567–87; R. Jervis, "The Future of World Politics," *International Security* 16 [1991/1992]: 39–73.)

[27] William A. Sherden, *The Fortune Sellers* (New York: Wiley, 1998).

tossing each of one hundred coins one hundred times. By chance, a small set will yield improbable streaks of heads or tails. Financial geniuses are statistical flukes—no more mysterious than a few coins landing heads five or ten consecutive times.

Probability Theorists. Even readers swayed by the foregoing arguments may remain reluctant to "go all the way" with radical skepticism. One source of this reluctance is the repeated success that almost all of us feel we have had in explaining the past. Whether we anchor our explanations of the past in qualitative case studies or in multivariate regression models, hope springs eternal that our accounts of what just happened will confer predictive leverage on what will happen next.

Robyn Dawes pours cold water on this comforting thought. The outcomes we most want to forecast—usually disasters—tend to be rare. And Dawes argues that, even for rare events we can explain reasonably well, such as airplane crashes, there is no guarantee we will do as well at predicting the future. If anything, we can almost guarantee the opposite: disappointment.[28]

Dawes illustrates his thesis with the grisliest job of the National Transportation Safety Board (NTSB): piecing together postmortems of plane crashes. The crash of Western flight 903 in Mexico City on October 31, 1979, captures the challenges NTSB investigators confront. The plane landed at night on the left runway—which was closed to traffic because it was under construction—and crashed into a truck. Looking backward into time, investigators identified at least five plausible causes of the crash.

> *Fatigue.* Fifteen minutes before the crash the pilot said, "Morning, Dan," and Dan responded with a muffled "Morning." Dan, the navigator, had had only four hours' sleep in the last twenty-four hours. The pilot had had five hours. Later Dan said, "I think I'm going to sleep all night" (all said about ten minutes prior to his death).
>
> *Poor Visibility.* Air traffic control then instructed the pilots to approach by tracking the radar beam on the left runway but shifting to the right for landing. Only the right runway was illuminated by approach lights. However visibility was poor, so the construction on the left runway and the lack of landing lights was not apparent.
>
> *Radio Failure.* Two minutes before the crash, the pilot asked, "What happened to that fucking radio?" The copilot replied, "I just don't have any idea. . . . It just died." The pilots thus had no radio contact two minutes before landing on the wrong runway.

---

[28] R. Dawes, "The Prediction of the Future Versus an Understanding of the Past: A Basic Asymmetry," *American Journal of Psychology* 106 (1993): 1–24.

Vague Communication. After radio contact was restored, sixty-five seconds before the crash, the air traffic controller told the pilots, "26 of 5, you are left of the track." By bad luck, the plane had been slightly left of the left runway. The pilot replied, "Yeah, we know." If the tower had been explicit, the crash might have been averted.

Stress. Forty-three seconds prior to the crash, an ever-burdened air traffic controller confused the two runways. "OK, sir. Approach lights on runway 23 left by the runway closed to traffic." In fact, the radar beam was on the left runway and the approach lights on the right runway, which was not closed to traffic. Thirteen seconds later, the pilot realized that the plane was heading to the wrong runway, but it was too late.

This sad tale is laced with quirky details, but it contains lessons of broad applicability. We often want to know why a particular consequence—be it a genocidal bloodbath or financial implosion—happened when and how it did. Examination of the record identifies a host of contributory causes. In the plane crash, five factors loom. It is tempting to view each factor by itself as a necessary cause. But the temptation should be resisted. Do we really believe that the crash could *not* have occurred in the wake of other antecedents? It is also tempting to view the five causes as jointly sufficient. But believing this requires endorsing the equally far-fetched counterfactual that, had something else happened, such as a slightly different location for the truck, the crash would still have occurred.

Exploring these what-if possibilities might seem a gratuitous reminder to families of victims of how unnecessary the deaths were. But the exercise is essential for appreciating why the contributory causes of one accident do not permit the NTSB to predict plane crashes in general. Pilots are often tired; bad weather and cryptic communication are common; radio communication sometimes breaks down; and people facing death frequently panic. The NTSB can pick out, post hoc, the ad hoc combination of causes of any disaster. They can, in this sense, explain the past. But they cannot predict the future. The only generalization that we can extract from airplane accidents may be that, absent sabotage, crashes are the result of a confluence of improbable events compressed into a few terrifying moments.

If a statistician were to conduct a prospective study of how well retrospectively identified causes, either singly or in combination, predict plane crashes, our measure of predictability—say, a squared multiple correlation coefficient—would reveal gross unpredictability. Radical skeptics tell us to expect the same fate for our quantitative models of wars, revolutions, elections, and currency crises. Retrodiction is enormously easier than prediction.

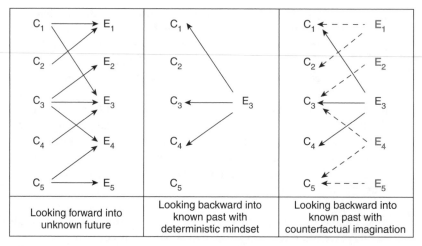

Looking forward into unknown future	Looking backward into known past with deterministic mindset	Looking backward into known past with counterfactual imagination

Figure 2.2. The first panel displays the bewildering array of possible relationships between causal antecedents and possible futures when the observer does not yet know which future will need to be explained. The second panel displays a simpler task. The observer now knows which future materialized and identifies those antecedents "necessary" to render the outcome inevitable. The third panel "recomplexifies" the observer's task by imagining ways in which once-possible outcomes could have occurred, thereby recapturing past states of uncertainty that hindsight bias makes it difficult to reconstruct. The dotted arrows to faded E's represent possible pathways between counterfactual worlds and their conjectured antecedents.

How can this be? Looking forward in time, we confront the first panel of figure 2.2. We don't yet know what we have to explain. We need to be alert to the multiplicity of ways in which potential causes could produce a multiplicity of potential effects. Let's call this complex pattern the "many-many relationship between antecedents and conse-quences." Looking backward in time, we confront the second panel of figure 2.2. We now do know what we need to explain. We can concentrate our explanatory efforts on why one of the many once-possible conse-quences occurred. Let's call this simple pattern the "many-one relation-ship between antecedents and consequences." The pattern is, however, deceptively simple. It plays on the cognitive illusion that the reasons we can identify why a known outcome had to occur give us a basis for pre-dicting when similar outcomes will occur.

Retrospective explanations do not travel well into the future. The best protection against disappointment is that recommended in the third panel of figure 2.2: work through counterfactual thought exercises that punc-ture the deceptive simplicity of the many-one relationship by imagining ways in which outcomes we once deemed possible could have come about. Chapter 7 will show that, although these exercises do not boost our predictive accuracy, they do check our susceptibility to hindsight bias: our tendency to exaggerate the degree to which we saw it coming all along. Humility is attainable, even if forecasting accuracy is not.

Psychological Skeptics

Ontological skeptics need no psychology. They trace indeterminacy to properties of the external world—a world that would be just as unpredictable if we were smarter. Psychological skeptics are not so sure. They suspect there are opportunities to peer into the future that we miss for reasons linked to the internal workings of the human mind. Psychological skeptics are thus more open to meliorist arguments that observers with the "right mental stuff" will prove better forecasters. Indeed, every obstacle that psychological skeptics identify to good judgment is an invitation to "we could fix it" interventions. Here we identify four key obstacles: (1) our collective preference for simplicity; (2) our aversion to ambiguity and dissonance; (3) our deep-rooted need to believe we live in an orderly world; and (4) our seemingly incorrigible ignorance of the laws of chance.

PREFERENCE FOR SIMPLICITY

However cognitively well equipped human beings were to survive on the savannah plains of Africa, we have met our match in the modern world. Picking up useful cues from noisy data requires identifying fragile associations between subtle combinations of antecedents and consequences. This is exactly the sort of task that work on probabilistic-cue learning indicates people do poorly.[29] Even with lots of practice, plenty of motivation, and minimal distractions, intelligent people have enormous difficulty tracking complex patterns of covariation such as "effect $y1$ rises in likelihood when $x1$ is falling, $x2$ is rising, and $x3$ takes on an intermediate set of values."

Psychological skeptics argue that such results bode ill for our ability to distill predictive patterns from the hurly-burly of current events.[30] Insofar

[29] B. Brehmer, "In One Word: Not from Experience," *Acta Psychologica* 45 (1980): 223–41; P. D. Werner, T. L. Rose, and J. A. Yesavage, "Reliability, Accuracy, and Decision-Making Strategy in Clinical Predictions of Imminent Dangerousness," *Journal of Consulting and Clinical Psychology* 51 (1983): 815–25; H. Einhorn and R. Hogarth, "Confidence in Judgment: Persistence of the Illusion of Validity," *Psychological Review* 85 (1978): 395–416.

[30] R. Dawes, "Behavioral Decision Making and Judgment," in *The Handbook of Social Psychology*, 4th ed., vol. 1., ed. D. T. Gilbert, S. T. Fiske, and G. Lindzey, 497–548. (New York: McGraw-Hill, 1998); S. Fiske and S. Taylor, *Social Cognition* (New York: McGraw-Hill, 1991). Widespread reliance on simple heuristics is widely blamed for the poor showing—although there is vigorous debate over how often these simple heuristics lead us astray.

as history repeats itself, it does not do so in a ploddingly mechanistic fashion.[31] Much analogical reasoning from history is, however, plodding. Consider the impact of the Vietnam War on the political consciousness of late twentieth-century pundits who saw a variety of conflicts, almost surely too great a variety, as Vietnam-style quagmires. The list includes Nicaragua, Haiti, Bosnia, Colombia, Afghanistan, and Iraq (all new American Vietnams), Afghanistan (the Soviet Union's Vietnam), Chechnya (Russia's Vietnam), Kashmir (India's Vietnam), Lebanon (Israel's Vietnam), Angola (Cuba's Vietnam), the Basque territory (Spain's Vietnam), Eritrea (Ethiopia's Vietnam), Northern Ireland (Britain's Vietnam), and Kampuchea (Vietnam's Vietnam).[32] We know—from many case studies—that overfitting the most superficially applicable analogy to current problems is a common source of error.[33] We rarely hear policy makers, in private or public, invoking mixtures of probabilistic analogies: "Saddam resembles Hitler in his risk taking, but he also has some of the shrewd street smarts of Stalin, the vaingloriousness of Mussolini, and the demagoguery of Nasser, and the usefulness of each analogy depends on the context."

AVERSION TO AMBIGUITY AND DISSONANCE

People for the most part dislike ambiguity—and we shall discover in chapter 3 that this is especially true of the hedgehogs among us. History, however, heaps ambiguity on us. It not only requires us to keep track of many things; it also offers few clues as to which things made critical differences. If we want to make causal inferences, we have to guess what would have happened in counterfactual worlds that exist—if "exist" is the right word—only in our imaginative reenactments of what-if scenarios. We know from experimental work that people find it hard to resist filling in the missing data points with ideologically scripted event sequences.[34] Indeed, as chapter 5 will show, observers of world politics are often enormously confident in their counterfactual beliefs,[35] declaring with eerie certainty that they know pretty much exactly what would have happened in counterfactual worlds that no one can visit or check out.

[31] Robert Jervis, *Perception and Misperception in International Politics* (Princeton, NJ: Princeton University Press, 1976).

[32] P. E. Tetlock, "Social Psychology and World Politics," in Fiske, Gilbert, and Lindzey, *Handbook of Social Psychology*.

[33] R. E. Neustadt and E. R. May, *Thinking in Time: The Uses of History for Decision-Makers* (New York: Free Press, 1986).

[34] H. Einhorn and R. Hogarth, "Behavioral Decision Theory," *Annual Review of Psychology* 31 (1981): 53–88.

[35] P. E. Tetlock and P. Visser, "Thinking about Russia: Possible Pasts and Probable Futures," *British Journal of Social Psychology* 39 (2000): 173–96; G. W. Breslauer and P. E. Tetlock, *Learning in U.S. and Soviet Foreign Policy* (Boulder, CO: Westview Press, 1991).

People for the most part also dislike dissonance—a generalization that again particularly applies to the hedgehogs we shall meet in chapter 3. They prefer to organize the world into neat evaluative gestalts that couple good causes to good effects and bad to bad.[36] Unfortunately, the world can be a morally messy place in which policies that one is predisposed to detest sometimes have positive effects and policies that one embraces sometimes have noxious ones. Valued allies may have frightful human rights records; free trade policies that improve living standards in the Third World may reward companies that exploit child labor; despised terrorists may display qualities that, in other contexts, we might laud as resourceful and even courageous; regimes in rogue states may have more popular support than we care to admit. Dominant options— that beat the alternatives on all possible dimensions—are rare.

NEED FOR CONTROL

Most of us find it irksome to contemplate making life-and-death decisions on no sounder basis than a coin toss.[37] Nihilistic fatalism of this sort runs against the mostly can-do grain of human nature. Moreover, it should be especially irksome to the specialists in our sample, people who make their living thinking and writing about varied facets of international affairs, to adopt this despairing stance, undercutting as it does not just their worldviews but also their livelihoods. This argument suggests that people will generally welcome evidence that fate is not capricious, that there is an underlying order to what happens. The core function of political belief systems is not prediction; it is to promote the comforting illusion of predictability.

THE UNBEARABLE LIGHTNESS OF OUR UNDERSTANDING OF RANDOMNESS

No amount of methodological hocus-pocus will improve the accuracy of our forecasts in games of pure chance. If a casino with a financial death wish installed a roulette wheel with 60 percent black and 40 percent red slots and kept payoffs unchanged, the best strategy would always be to bet on the most likely outcome: black. The worst strategy would be to look for patterns until one convinces oneself that one has found a formula that justifies big bets on the less likely outcome. The reward for thought, at least thought of the gambler's-fallacy caliber, will be to hemorrhage money.[38]

---

[36] R. P. Abelson, E. Aronson, W. McGuire, T. Newcomb, M. Rosenberg, and P. Tannenbaum, eds. *Theories of Cognitive Consistency: A Sourcebook* (Chicago: Rand McNally, 1968).

[37] E. J. Langer, "The Illusion of Control," *Journal of Personality and Social Psychology* 32 (1975): 311–28.

[38] On the dangers of being "too clever" in pursuit of patterns in random data, see Ward Edwards, "Probability Learning in 1000 Trials," *Journal of Experimental Psychology*, 62 (1961): 385–94.

Our reluctance to acknowledge unpredictability keeps us looking for predictive cues well beyond the point of diminishing returns.[39] I witnessed a demonstration thirty years ago that pitted the predictive abilities of a classroom of Yale undergraduates against those of a single Norwegian rat. The task was predicting on which side of a T-maze food would appear, with appearances determined—unbeknownst to both the humans and the rat—by a random binomial process (60 percent left and 40 percent right). The demonstration replicated the classic studies by Edwards and by Estes: the rat went for the more frequently rewarded side (getting it right roughly 60 percent of the time), whereas the humans looked hard for patterns and wound up choosing the left or the right side in roughly the proportion they were rewarded (getting it right roughly 52 percent of the time). Human performance suffers because we are, deep down, deterministic thinkers with an aversion to probabilistic strategies that accept the inevitability of error. We insist on looking for order in random sequences. Confronted by the T-maze, we look for subtle patterns like "food appears in alternating two left/one right sequences, except after the third cycle when food pops up on the right." This determination to ferret out order from chaos has served our species well. We are all beneficiaries of our great collective successes in the pursuit of deterministic regularities in messy phenomena: agriculture, antibiotics, and countless other inventions that make our comfortable lives possible. But there are occasions when the refusal to accept the inevitability of error—to acknowledge that some phenomena are irreducibly probabilistic—can be harmful.

Political observers run the same risk when they look for patterns in random concatenations of events. They would do better by thinking less. When we know the base rates of possible outcomes—say, the incumbent wins 80 percent of the time—and not much else, we should simply predict the more common outcome. But work on base rate neglect suggests that people often insist on attaching high probabilities to low-frequency events.[40] These probabilities are rooted *not* in observations of relative frequency in relevant reference populations of cases, but rather in case-specific hunches about causality that make some scenarios more "imaginable" than others. A plausible story of how a government might suddenly collapse counts for far more than how often similar outcomes have occurred in the past. Forecasting accuracy suffers when intuitive causal reasoning trumps extensional probabilistic reasoning.[41]

[39] Dawes, "Behavioral Decision Making."

[40] J. Koehler, "The Base-Rate Fallacy Reconsidered: Descriptive, Normative, and Methodological Challenges," *Behavioral and Brain Sciences* 19 (1996): 1–53.

[41] A. Tversky and D. Kahneman, "Extensional Versus Intuitive Reasoning: The Conjunction Fallacy in Probability Judgment," *Psychological Review* 90 (1983): 293–315; on

Psychological skeptics are also not surprised when people draw strong lessons from brief runs of forecasting failures or successes. Winning forecasters are often skilled at concocting elaborate stories about why fortune favored their point of view. Academics can quickly spot the speciousness of these stories when the forecaster attributes her success to a divinity heeding a prayer or to planets being in the correct alignment. But even these observers can be gulled if the forecaster invokes an explanation in intellectual vogue.

At this point, skeptics throw up their hands. They remind us of the perils of drawing confident inductive inferences from small samples of unknown origin and, if in a patient mood, append a lecture on the logical fallacy of affirming the consequent: "Beware of people who argue, "If A, then B," observe B, and then declare, "A is true." If you go down that path, you will wind up awarding "forecaster of the year" awards to an unseemly procession of cranks. Who wants to congratulate apartheid supporters in South Africa for their prescient predictions of the dismal state of sub-Saharan Africa? Much mischief can be wrought by transplanting this hypothesis-testing logic, which flourishes in controlled lab settings, into the hurly-burly of real-world settings where ceteris paribus never is, and never can be, satisfied.

Advancing Testable Hypotheses

Combining these varied grounds for radical skepticism, we can appreciate how reasonable people could find themselves taking the seemingly unreasonable position that experts add precious little, perhaps nothing, to our ability to see into the future. Moreover, skeptics make testable predictions about the unpredictability of the world. The six core tenets of radical skepticism are as follows:

1. *Debunking hypotheses: humans versus chimps and extrapolation algorithms of varying sophistication.* Like the weather, the political world has pockets of turbulence: political and financial crises during which we, the consumers of expertise, feel the greatest need for guidance but such guidance will be least useful. Even the most astute observers will fail to outperform random prediction generators— the functional equivalent of dart-throwing chimps—in affixing realistic likelihoods to possible futures.

---

the difficulty of knowing what the relevant reference classes are, see R. Jervis, "Representativeness in Foreign Policy Judgments," *Political Psychology* 7 (1986): 483–505.

Of course, it is not always obvious when one has entered or exited turbulence. Turbulence is the exception. It is far easier ex post than ex ante to pinpoint the qualitative breakpoints that mark where old patterns of predictability break down and new ones emerge.[42] The right performance baseline ceases to be blind chance in the often long periods of stability between episodes of turbulence. We should therefore raise the bar and ask whether experts can outperform not the chimp but extrapolation algorithms of varying sophistication. The Technical Appendix describes several such algorithms: (a) crude base rate algorithms that attach probabilities to outcomes that correspond to the frequency with which those outcomes pop up in narrowly or widely defined comparison populations of cases; (b) cautious or aggressive case-specific extrapolation algorithms that, for each state in our sample, predict the continuation of its recent past into its near-term future; (c) formal statistical equations (such as generalized autoregressive distributed lag models) that piece together optimal linear combinations of predictors in the dataset.

If past work on clinical versus statistical prediction is a guide, we should expect human forecasters to achieve levels of performance far closer to the chimp and simple extrapolation algorithms than to the formal statistical ones. There is an additional twist, though. Psychological skeptics add that many humans will fall below even extrapolation algorithms. When good case-based stories are circulating for expecting unusual outcomes, people will base their confidence largely on these stories and ignore the cautionary base rates. Coups, economic collapse, and so on are rare events in most places. Predicting them vastly inflates the likelihood of getting it wrong.[43]

2. *The diminishing marginal returns from expertise hypothesis.* Radical skeptics have a fallback if experts manage to outpredict the chimp and extrapolation algorithms. They can argue that, whatever modest advantage expertise may confer, we quickly reach the point of diminishing returns. The attentive reader of the *New York Times* is likely to be as adept at picking up predictive cues as renowned area study specialists. It follows that, on average, specialists on Canada—who casually tracked events in the USSR in the elite

---

[42] P. G. Allen, "Econometric Forecasting," in *Principles of Forecasting*, ed., J. S. Armstrong, 303–62 (Boston: Kluwer, 2001); M. Singer and A. B. Wildavsky, *The Real World Order: Zones of Peace, Zones of Turmoil* (Chatham, NJ: Chatham House, 1996).

[43] This is not to imply that it is easy to figure out which base rates to use. Should we limit ourselves to the recent past or to the region narrowly defined or to the specific nation in question? Our mindless algorithms use a range of base rates that vary in time span (five, ten, and twenty-five years), regime-type specificity (stable democracies, unstable ones, dictatorships, and so on) and regional specificity (Nigeria, West Africa, Africa, the world).

press—should assign as realistic probabilities to possible Soviet futures as did certified Sovietologists. Dilettante trespassers will "win" as often as "lose" against experts on their home turf.

3. *The fifteen minutes of fame hypothesis.* We have laid the basis for another counterintuitive corollary of radical skepticism: expect little consistency in who surpasses or falls short of these minimalist performance benchmarks. Occasionally, to be sure, some will do better and others worse by virtue of the interconnections among outcomes being forecast. Those "lucky enough" to anticipate the demise of the Soviet Union should also enjoy the benefits of a string of successful predictions of political and economic liberalization in Eastern Europe. But there should be no presumption that (a) experts who are good forecasters inside their domains of expertise will be good outside those domains; (b) experts with certain points of view or styles of thinking who do well at one historical juncture will do well at other junctures.

4. *The loquacious overconfidence (or hot air) hypothesis.* Although knowledge beyond a bare minimum should not enhance forecasting accuracy, it should bestow on experts the cognitive resources to generate more elaborate and convincing rationales for their forecasts. Thus, as expertise rises, confidence in forecasts should rise faster than the accuracy of forecasts, producing substantial overconfidence by the time we reach the highest rungs of the expertise ladder. The most distinctive cognitive marker of expertise should be relatively extreme and elaborately justified probability judgments that fare poorly against the evidence.

5. *The seduced by fame, fortune, and power hypothesis.* The more frequently experts are asked to offer their opinions on current events to the media, business, or government, the greater the temptation to offer quotable quotes and good sound bites. Ego-enhancing contact with outsiders counts as a factor that, like expertise itself, should increase confidence without increasing accuracy, thus further fueling overconfidence. Of course, causality can also work in the other direction. The media can be seduced by the charismatically overconfident.

6. *The indefinitely sustainable illusion hypothesis.* Radical skeptics expect minimal consistency in who gets what right across time and topics. But psychologists are not surprised that people persist in believing there is a great deal of consistency, the forecasting equivalent of hot hands in basketball.[44] The illusion of consistency is rooted in both cognitive biases (pervasive misunderstandings about

---

[44] T. Gilovich, R. Vallone, and A. Tversky, "The Hot Hand in Basketball: On the Misperception of Random Sequences," *Cognitive Psychology* 17 (1985): 295–314.

the workings of chance) and motivational biases (the need to believe that we do not make life-and-death decisions whimsically). We should thus expect (a) the frequent emergence of shortfalls between what the public hopes experts can deliver and what experts can deliver; (b) the frequent widening of these shortfalls whenever historical forces increase how desperate people are for guidance but not how skilled experts are at providing it.

METHODOLOGICAL BACKGROUND

Readers more interested in results than in methods can skip ahead to the section entitled "The Evidence." It is, however, a mistake for serious scholars to do so. The fact is there is no single best approach to testing the six hypotheses. No study will be without "fatal flaws" for those inclined to find them. Critics can always second-guess the qualifications of the forecasters or the ground rules or content of the forecasting exercises. This chapter therefore makes no claim on the final word.

The Methodological Appendix does, however, give us four good reasons for supposing the current dataset is unusually well suited for testing the core tenets of radical skepticism. Those reasons are as follows:

1. *The sophistication of the research participants who agreed— admittedly with varying enthusiasm—to play the role of forecasters.* This makes it hard to argue that if we had recruited "real heavyweights," we would now be telling a more flattering tale about expertise. And, although defenders of expertise can always argue that an intellectually heftier or a more politically connected sample would have done better, we can say—without breaking our confidentiality promises spelled out in the appendix—that our sample of 284 participants was impressive on several dimensions. Participants were highly educated (the majority had doctorates and almost all had postgraduate training in fields such as political science (in particular, international relations and various branches of area studies), economics, international law and diplomacy, business administration, public policy, and journalism); they had, on average, twelve years of relevant work experience; they came from many walks of professional life, including academia, think tanks, government service, and international institutions; and they showed themselves in conversation to be remarkably thoughtful and articulate observers of the world scene.
2. *The broad, historically rolling cross section of political, economic, and national security outcomes that we asked forecasters to try to*

anticipate between 1988 and 2003. This makes it hard to argue that the portrait of good judgment that emerges here holds only for a few isolated episodes in recent history: objections of the canonical form "Sure, they got the collapse of the USSR or the 1992 U.S. election right, but did they get . . . " A typical forecasting exercise elicited opinions on such diverse topics as GDP growth in Argentina, the risk of nuclear war in the Indian subcontinent, and the pace of "democratization" and "privatization" in former Communist bloc countries. Many participants made more than one hundred predictions, roughly half of which pertained to topics that fell within their self-reported domains of expertise and the other half of which fell outside their domains of expertise.

3. *The delicate balancing acts that had to be performed in designing the forecasting exercises.* On the one hand, we wanted to avoid ridiculously easy questions that everyone could get right: "Yes, I am 100 percent confident that stable democracies will continue to hold competitive elections." On the other hand, we wanted to avoid ridiculously hard questions that everyone knew they could not get right (or even do better than chance): "No, I can only give you just-guessing levels of confidence on which party will win the American presidential election of 2012." In groping for the right balance, therefore, we wanted to give experts the flexibility to express their degrees of uncertainty about the future. To this end, we used standardized format, subjective probability scales. For instance, the scale for judging each possibility in the three-possible-future exercises looked like this (with the added option that forecasters could assign .33 to all possibilities (by checking the "maximum uncertainty box") when they felt they had no basis for rating one possibility likelier than any other):

In groping for the right balance, we also formulated response options so that experts did not feel they were being asked to make ridiculously precise point predictions. To this end, we carved the universe of possible futures into exclusive and exhaustive categories that captured broad ranges of past variation in outcome variables.

The Methodological Appendix inventories the major categories of questions by regions, topics, and time frames. These questions tapped perceptions of who was likely to be in charge of the legislative or executive branches of government after the next election (e.g., How likely is it that after the next election, the party that currently has the most representatives in the legislative branch(es) of government will *retain this status (within plus or minus a plausible delta), will lose this status,* or *will strengthen its position?*), perceptions of how far the government will fall into debt (e.g., How likely is it—in either a three or six-year frame—that the annual central government operating deficit as percentage of GDP will *fall below, within, or above* a specified comparison range of values (based on the variance in values over the last six years)?), and perceptions of national security threats (e.g., How likely is it—within either a three- or six-year frame—that defense spending as a percentage of central government expenditure will *fall below, within, or above* a specified comparison range of values [again, set by the immediately preceding patterns]?).

4. *The transparency and rigor of the rules for assessing the accuracy of the forecasts.* Transparency makes it hard to argue that the game was rigged against particular schools of thought. Rigor makes it hard for losing forecasters to insist that, although they might appear to have been wrong, they were—in some more profound sense—right. We rely exclusively in this chapter—and largely in later chapters—on aggregate indices of accuracy logically derived from thousands of predictions.

Some readers may, however, still wonder exactly how we can assess the accuracy of probability judgments of unique events. The answer is via the miracle of aggregation. Granted, the true probabilities of each outcome that did occur remain shrouded in mystery (we know only the value is not zero), and so too are the true probabilities of each outcome that failed to occur (we know only the value is not 1.0). However, if we collect enough predictions, we can still gauge the relative frequency with which outcomes assigned various probabilities do and do not occur. To take an extreme example, few would dispute that someone whose probability assignments to possible outcomes closely tracked the relative frequency of those outcomes (events assigned x percent likelihood occurred about x percent of the time) should be considered a better forecaster than someone whose probability assignments bore no relationship to the relative frequency of outcomes.

The Technical Appendix details the procedures for computing the key measure of forecasting accuracy, the probability score, which is defined as the average deviation between the ex ante probabilities that experts assign possible futures and the ex post certainty values that the researchers assign those futures once we learn what did (1.0) or did not (0.0) happen.[45] To get the best possible score, zero, one must be clairvoyant: assigning a probability of 1.0 to all things that subsequently happen and a probability of zero to all things that do not. To get the worst possible score, 1.0, one must be the opposite of clairvoyant, and infallibly declare impossible everything that later happens and declare inevitable everything that does not.

Probability scores, however, provide only crude indicators of how large the gaps are between subjective probabilities and objective reality. Answering more fine-grained questions requires decomposing probability scores into more precise indicators. Readers should be alerted to three curve ball complications:

a. *Are some forecasters achieving better (smaller) probability scores by playing it safe and assigning close-to-guessing probabilities?* To explore this possibility, we need to break probability scores into two component indicators—calibration and discrimination—that are often posited to be in a trade-off relationship. The calibration index taps the degree to which subjective probabilities are aligned with objective probabilities. Observers are perfectly calibrated when there is precise correspondence between subjective and objective probabilities (and thus the squared deviations sum to zero). Outcomes assigned 80 percent likelihoods happen about 80 percent of the time, those assigned a 70 percent likelihood happen about 70 percent of the time, and so on. The discrimination index taps forecasters' ability to do better than a simple predict-the-base-rate strategy. Observers get perfect discrimination scores when they infallibly assign probabilities of 1.0 to things that happen and probabilities of zero to things that do not.

To maximize calibration, it often pays to be cautious and assign probabilities close to the base rates; to maximize discrimination, it often pays to be bold and assign extreme probabilities. The first panel of figure 2.3 shows how a playing-it-safe strategy—assigning probabilities that never stray from the midpoint values of .4, .5, and .6—can produce excellent (small) calibration scores but poor (small) discrimination scores. The second and third panels show how it is possible to achieve both excellent calibration and discrimination scores. Doing so, though, does require skill: mapping probability values onto variation in real-world outcomes.

---

[45] A. H. Murphy and R. L. Winkler, "Probability Forecasts: A Survey of National Weather Service Forecasters," *Bulletin of the American Meteorological Society* 55 (1974): 1449–53. Murphy, "Scalar and Vector Partitions, Parts I and II."

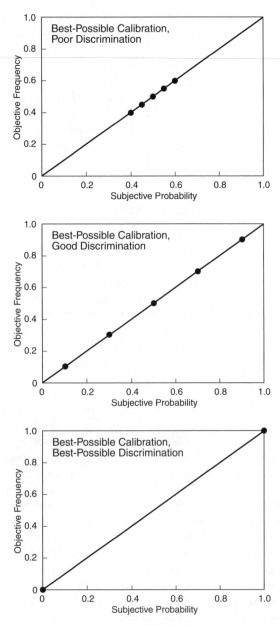

Figure 2.3. It is possible to be perfectly calibrated but achieve a wide range of discrimination scores: poor (the fence-sitting strategy), good (using a broad range of values correctly), and perfect (using only the most extreme values correctly).

b. *Did some forecasters do better merely because they were dealt easier tasks?* Probability scores can be inflated either because experts were error prone or because the task was hard. Distinguishing these alternatives requires statistical procedures for estimating: (1) task difficulty (tasks are easy to the degree either there is little variance in outcomes—say, predicting rain in Phoenix—or there is variance that can be captured in simple statistical models—say, predicting seasonal variation in temperature in Toronto); (2) the observed variation in performance can be attributed to variation in skill rather than task difficulty.

c. *Are some forecasters getting worse probability scores because they are willing to make many errors of one type to avoid even a few of another?* Forecasters can obtain bad scores because they either overpredict (assign high probabilities to things that never happen) or underpredict (assign low probabilities to things that do happen). What looks initially like a mistake might, however, be a reflection of policy priorities. Experts sometimes insisted, for example, that it is prudent to exaggerate the likelihood of change for the worse, even at a steep cost in false alarms. Assessing such claims requires value-adjusting probability scores in ways that give experts varying benefits of the doubt when they under- or overestimate particular outcomes.

THE EVIDENCE

The methodological stage has been set for testing the core tenets of radical skepticism. Figure 2.4 presents the average calibration and discrimination scores for 27,451 forecasts which have been broken down into experts' versus dilettantes' predictions of shorter or longer-term futures of the domestic-political, economic, and national-security policies of countries in either the zones of turbulence or stability. A calibration score of .01 indicates that forecasters' subjective probabilities diverged from objective frequencies, on average, by about 10 percent; a score of .04, an average gap of 20 percent. A discrimination score of .01 indicates that forecasters, on average, predicted about 6 percent of the total variation in outcomes; a score of .04, that they captured 24 percent.

The Debunking Hypotheses: Humanity versus Algorithms of Varying Sophistication

Figure 2.5 plots the average calibration and discrimination of human forecasters, of four forms of mindless competition—including: (a) the

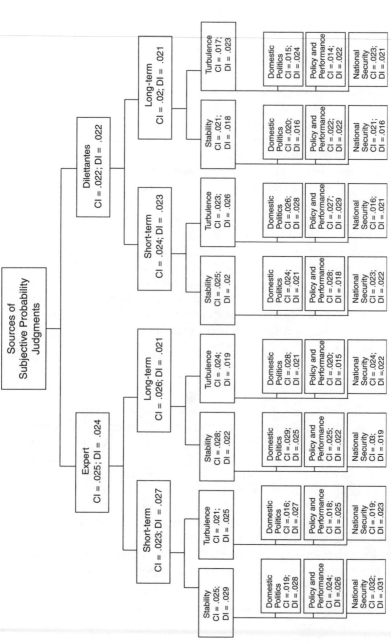

Figure 2.4. The calibration (CI) and discrimination (DI) scores of all subjective probability judgments entered into later data analyses. The first-tier breakdown is into judgments made by experts versus dilettantes; the second-tier breakdown is into shorter-versus longer-term predictions; the third-tier breakdown is into predictions for states in the zone of stability versus the zone of turbulence; and the final breakdown (into three boxes nested under each third-tier label) is into predictions for domestic politics (e.g., who is in charge?), government policy and performance (e.g., what are spending priorities and how well is the economy doing?), and national security (e.g., has there been violent conflict inside or outside state borders?).

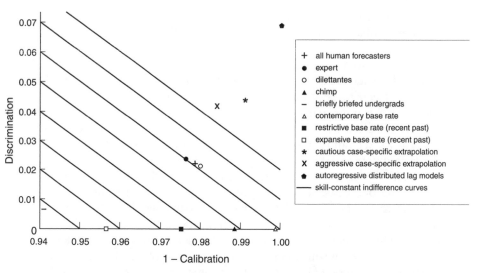

Figure 2.5. The calibration and discrimination scores achieved by human forecasters (experts and dilettantes), by their mindless competition (chimp random guessing, restrictive and expansive base-rate extrapolation, and cautious and aggressive case-specific extrapolation algorithms), and by the sophisticated statistical competition. Each curve represents a set of equal-weighting calibration-discrimination trade-offs that hold overall forecasting skill (probability score) constant. Higher curves represent improving overall performance.

chimp strategy of assigning equal probabilities; (b) the expansive and re-strictive base-rate strategies of assigning probabilities corresponding to the frequency of outcomes in the five year periods preceding forecasting periods in which we assess human performance (inserting values derived either from the entire dataset or from restricted subsets of cases such as the former Soviet bloc); (c) the contemporary-base-rate strategy of as-signing probabilities corresponding to the frequency of outcomes in the actual forecasting periods; (d) the cautious and aggressive case-specific strategies of assigning either high or very high probabilities to the hypoth-esis that the most recent trend for a specific country will persist—and of the sophisticated competition that drew on autoregressive distributed lag models.

Radical skeptics should mostly welcome the initial results. Humanity barely bests the chimp, losing on one key variable and winning on the other. We lose on calibration. There are larger average gaps between human probability judgments and reality than there are for those of the hypothetical chimp. But we win on discrimination. We do better at as-signing higher probabilities to occurrences than to nonoccurrences than does the chimp. And the win on discrimination is big enough to offset the loss on calibration and give humanity a superior overall probability score (reflected in the clustering of the human data points on the constant-probability-score diagonal just above that for the chimp).

Defenders of our collective cognitive dignity also get faint solace when we compare human forecasting accuracy to that of algorithms that mechanically assign probabilities to events that correspond to estimates of the base rate frequencies of those events. Humanity does manage to edge out the restrictive and expansive base-rate algorithms which assumed that the near to medium-term future would—in aggregate—look exactly like the near to medium-term past. But humanity can only eke out a tie against the contemporary-base-rate strategy which, by exploiting aggregated outcome knowledge up to the present, achieves virtually perfect calibration. Of course, one could argue that little stigma attaches to this loss. The shortcut to good calibration is to assign probabilities that correspond to the best available data on the base-rate frequencies of the usual trichotomy of possibilities—perpetuation of status quo (50.5 percent), change in the direction of more of something (28.5 percent), and change in the direction of less of something (21 percent). The contemporary base rate algorithm accomplishes no great feat by predicting that events with a base-rate frequency of 51 percent in the current forecasting period have a 51 percent likelihood of occurring in that same period. The algorithm "cheats:" it peeks at outcome data to which no other competitor has advance access.

Overall, we can put negative or positive spins on these results. The negative spin tells a tale of hubris: people bet on case-specific hunches that low-frequency events would occur and they pay the price for this bias—base-rate neglect—in the form of inferior calibration scores. The critical driver of human probability judgments was not how commonly do events of this sort occur; rather, it was "how easily do compelling causal scenarios come to mind?"

The positive spin is a tale of courageous observers venturing out on limbs to tell us things we did not already know about a volatile world. Humans overpredicted lower-frequency events: departures from the status quo—either in the direction of less of something (which, in turn, could have been either bad [e.g., lower GDP growth] or good [e.g., declining corruption ratings]) or in the direction of more of something (which, in turn, could have been either bad [e.g., greater central government debt] or good [e.g., greater political freedom]).

This positive spin analysis implies that we should "forgive" human forecasters for losing on calibration but winning on discrimination. The chimp and base-rate algorithms did not make even token efforts to discriminate. As a matter of policy, they always assigned the same probabilities across the board and received the lowest possible score, zero. By contrast, humans tried to discriminate and were somewhat successful (a value of .03 on the y axis translates into "explaining" roughly 18 percent of the total variation in forecasting outcomes.) The probability score curves in figure 2.5 (curves that plot logically possible trade-offs between calibration and discrimination, holding overall accuracy constant) suggest that people may indeed have paid a reasonable calibration price to achieve this level of discrimination: the human probability score function is higher than the chimp's and roughly equal to the contemporary base-rate algorithm. One could also argue that these probability score functions underestimate the net human advantage because they treat calibration and discrimination equally, whereas discrimination should be valued over calibration.[46] In many real-world settings, it is more vital to assign sharply higher probabilities to events that occur—even if at the cost of embarrassing false alarms or misses—than it is to attach probabilities to events that tightly covary with the objective likelihood of occurrence across the full zero-to-one scale.

But we lose these "excuses" when we turn to the case-specific extrapolation algorithms, which assign different probabilities to outcomes as a function of the distinctive outcome histories of each case. Humanity now loses on both calibration and discrimination.

This latter result demolishes two of humanity's principal defenses. It neutralizes the argument that forecasters' modest showing on calibration was a price worth paying for the bold, roughly accurate predictions that only human beings could deliver (and that were thus responsible for their earlier victories on discrimination). And it pours cold water on the comforting notion that human forecasters failed to outperform minimalist benchmarks because they had been assigned an impossible mission—in effect, predicting the unpredictable. Translating the predictions of the crude case-specific extrapolation algorithms, as well as the sophisticated time series forecasting equations, into subjective probability equivalents, we discover that, whereas the best human forecasters were hard-pressed to predict more than 20 percent of the total variability in outcomes (using the DI/VI "omniscience" index in the Technical Appendix), the crude case-specific algorithms could predict 25 percent to 30 percent of the variance and the generalized autoregressive distributed lag models explained on average 47 percent of the variance.[47]

[46] Yates, Judgment and Decision Making.

[47] Readers might find it surprising that simple case-specific extrapolation algorithms sometimes performed almost as well as formal time series models (of the generalized autoregressive distributed lag sort). We should expect this type of result whenever the true stochastic process governing the variable being forecasted (call it y_t) is approximated by an autoregressive process of order one and no other variables are useful predictors of y_t. In this situation, rational forecasters will adopt simple rules such as always predict the next period's value will be $y_{t-1} + (1 - \text{rho}) * m$, where y_{t-1} is the last period's value, rho is some constant less than or equal to 1 which indicates the variable's "persistence," and m is the unconditional mean to which the variable reverts over time (e.g., when rho = 1, the variable follows a random walk). Only the variable's past value has predictive usefulness for the future.

These results plunk human forecasters into an unflattering spot along the performance continuum, distressingly closer to the chimp than to the formal statistical models. Moreover, the results cannot be dismissed as aberrations: figure 2.4 shows that human calibration and discrimination scores do not vary much across a broad swath of short- and long-term forecasts in policy domains and states in both the zones of stability (North America, Western Europe, and Japan) and turbulence (Eastern Europe, the Middle East, Africa, South Asia, and Latin America). Surveying these scores across regions, time periods, and outcome variables, we find support for one of the strongest debunking predictions: *it is impossible to find any domain* in which humans clearly outperformed crude extrapolation algorithms, less still sophisticated statistical ones.[48]

The Diminishing Marginal Predictive Returns Hypothesis

Figures 2.5 and 2.6 bolster another counterintuitive prediction of radical skepticism. Figure 2.5 shows that, collapsing across all judgments, experts on their home turf made neither better calibrated nor more discriminating forecasts than did dilettante trespassers. And Figure 2.6 shows that, at each level along the subjective probability scale from zero to 1.0, expert and dilettante calibration curves were strikingly similar. People who devoted years of arduous study to a topic were as hard-pressed as colleagues casually dropping in from other fields to affix realistic probabilities to possible futures.

The case for performance parity between experts and dilettantes is strong. But experts have several possible lines of defense. One is to argue that we have failed to identify the "real experts" among the experts—and that if we define expertise more selectively, we will find that it confers a real forecasting advantage. This argument does not hold up well when we make the standard distinctions among degrees and types of expertise. More refined statistical comparisons failed to yield any effects on either calibration or discrimination that could be traced to amount of experience (seniority) or types of expertise (academic, government or private sector background, access to classified information, doctoral degree or not, or status of university affiliation). There was also little sign that expertise by itself, or indicators of degrees of expertise, improved performance when we broke forecasting questions into subtypes: short-term versus long-term, zone of stability versus turbulence, and domestic political, economic policy/performance, and national security issues.

[48] W. M. Grove and P. Meehl, "Comparative Efficiency of Informal (Subjective, Impressionistic) and Formal (Mechanical, Algorithmic) Prediction Procedures: The Clinical-Statistical Controversy," *Psychology, Public Policy, and Law* 2 (1996): 293–323.

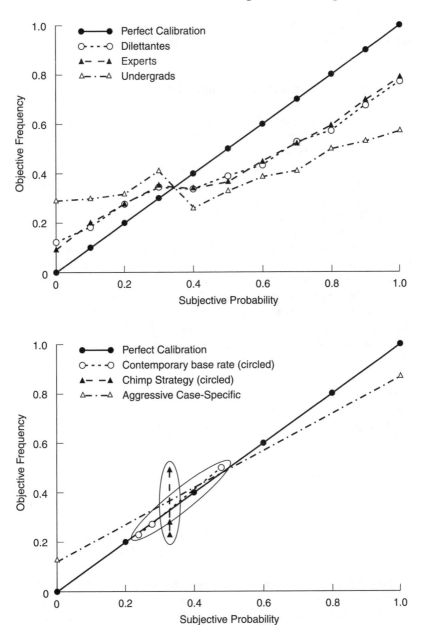

Figure 2.6. The first panel compares the calibration functions of several types of human forecasters (collapsing over thousands of predictions across fifty-eight countries across fourteen years). The second panel compares the calibration functions of several types of statistical algorithms on the same outcome variables.

A second, more promising, line of defense shifts from identifying superexperts to raising the status of the so-called dilettantes. After all, the dilettantes are themselves experts—sophisticated professionals who are well versed in whatever general purpose political or economic theories might confer predictive leverage. Their only disadvantage is that they know a lot less about certain regions of the world. And even that disadvantage is mitigated by the fact most dilettantes tracked a wide range of current events in elite news outlets.

To shed further light on where the point of diminishing marginal predictive returns for expertise lies, on how far down the ladder of cognitive sophistication we can go without undercutting forecasting skill, we compared experts against a humbler, but still human, benchmark: briefly briefed Berkeley undergraduates. In 1992, we gave psychology majors "facts on file" summaries, each three paragraphs long, that presented basic information on the polities and economies of Russia, India, Canada, South Africa, and Nigeria. We then asked students to make their best guesses on a standard array of outcome variables. The results spared experts further embarrassment. Figure 2.5 shows that the undergraduates were both less calibrated and less discriminating than professionals working either inside or outside their specialties. And figure 2.6 shows that the calibration curve for undergraduates strays far further from the diagonal of perfect calibration than do the expert or dilettante curves (hence far worse calibration scores).

These results suggest that, although subject matter expertise does not give a big boost to performance, it is not irrelevant. If one insists on thinking like a human being rather than a statistical algorithm, on trying to figure out on a case-by-case basis the idiosyncratic balance of forces favoring one or another outcome, it is especially dangerous doing so equipped only with the thin knowledge base of the undergraduates. The professionals—experts and dilettantes—possessed an extra measure of sophistication that allowed them to beat the undergraduates soundly and to avoid losing by ignominiously large margins to the chimp and crude extrapolation algorithms. That extra sophistication would appear to be pegged in the vicinity of savvy readers of high-quality news sources such as the *Economist*, the *Wall Street Journal*, and the *New York Times*, the publications that dilettantes most frequently reported as useful sources of information on topics outside their specialties.

At this juncture, defenders of expertise have exhausted their defense within a probability scoring framework that treats all errors—overpredicting or underpredicting change for the better or worse—as equal. To continue the scientific fight, they must show that, although experts made as many and as large "mistakes" as dilettantes—where the bigger mistakes mean bigger gaps between subjective probabilities and objective frequencies—experts made mostly the "right mistakes," mistakes with good policy rationales such as "better safe than sorry" and "don't cry wolf too often," whereas dilettantes underpredicted and overpredicted willy-nilly.

Unfortunately for this defense, experts and dilettantes have similar mistake profiles. Both exaggerate the likelihood of change for the worse.[49] Such outcomes occur 23 percent of the time, but experts assign average probabilities of .35, dilettantes, .29. Both also exaggerate the likelihood of change for the better. Such outcomes occur 28 percent of the time and experts assign average subjective probabilities of .34, dilettantes, .31. It follows that experts and dilettantes must underestimate the likelihood of the status quo by complementary margins.

But the mistake profiles of experts versus dilettantes, and of humans versus chimps, were not identical. Experts overpredict change significantly more than both dilettantes and the chimp strategy. So, there is potential for catch-up by value-adjusting probability scores that give experts varying benefits of the doubt. The Technical Appendix shows how to value-adjust probability scores by (a) identifying the mistakes that forecasters are, on balance, most prone to make; (b) solving for values of k that narrow the gaps between subjective probabilities and objective reality in proportion to the average size of the dominant mistake (generously assuming that forecasters' dominant mistake was, on balance, the right mistake given their error avoidance priorities).

Figure 2.7 shows the impact of value-adjusting probability scores. The unadjusted probability scores are at the base of each arrow. These scores are the sum of overpredictions (assigning high probabilities to things that do not happen) and underpredictions (assigning low probabilities to things that do happen). The better scores thus migrate upward and rightward. Once again, the unadjusted score for the case-specific algorithm (A) falls on a superior probability score function than that for human beings (either experts or dilettantes) which, in turn, falls on a superior probability score function than that for the chimp.

---

[49] Readers might notice here a shift in classifications of outcomes—from the value-neutral "change in the direction of more or less of something" to the value-laden "change for the better or worse." The conversion was generally unproblematic because, in carrying out these value adjustments, we simply adopted the consensus expert perspective on what was good or bad and dropped those variables on which there was sharp disagreement. Experts overwhelmingly agreed, for instance, that the change for the better involved greater GDP, lower unemployment, lower central government debt as percentage of GDP, less armed conflict within or between states, lower corruption, greater transparency, greater political and economic freedom, and fewer nuclear-armed states. The results are not materially different, however, when we allow for individual differences in value perspectives (such as conservatives favoring more aggressive privatization transitions from socialism than did liberals or euro skeptics preferring abandoning the currency convergence project and euro enthusiasts hoping for the opposite, and the quite frequent emergence of disagreements about whether leadership change would be desirable in particular countries).

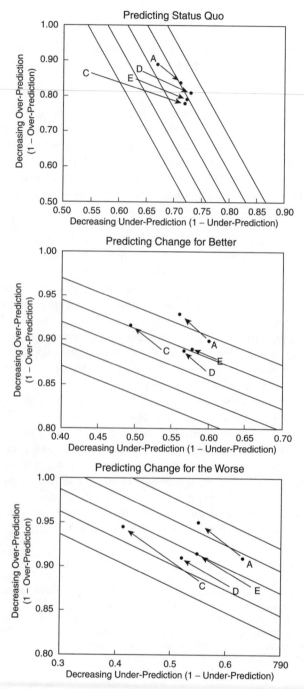

Figure 2.7. The impact of the k-value adjustment (procedure) on performance of experts (E), dilettantes (D), chimps (C), and an aggressive case-specific extrapolation algorithm (A) in three different forecasting tasks: distinguishing status quo from change for either better or worse, distinguishing change for better from either status quo or change for worse, or distinguishing change for worse from either status quo or change for better.

Longer arrows mean bigger value-adjustment effects, and the tip of each arrow is the value-adjusted probability score. Panel 1 shows that, when we focus on predicting continuation of the status quo (as opposed to change for either the better or worse), the optimal value adjustment decreases the "penalties" for underprediction, at some price in overprediction. Panel 2 shows that, when we focus on predicting change for the better, the optimal adjustment decreases the penalties for overprediction, at some price in underprediction. Panel 3 shows that, when we focus on predicting change for the worse, the optimal value adjustment decreases the penalties for overprediction, at some price in underprediction.

Catch-up is so elusive, and the chimp is the biggest beneficiary of adjustments, because the long-term expected value of the chimp strategy errs most consistently (always underestimating probabilities of events that happen more than 33 percent of the time or overestimating probabilities of events that happen less than 33 percent of the time). Adjustments thus bring the chimp to approximate parity with humans. Experts, dilettantes, and case-specific extrapolation algorithms benefit less because they make more complicated mixtures of errors, alternately under- or overpredicting change for the better or worse.

The net result is that, value adjustments do not give much of a boost to either experts in particular or humanity in general. Of course, there are still grounds for appeal. The current round of value adjustments corrects only for the dominant error a forecaster makes and do not allow that it might be prudent to alternate between under- and overpredicting change for the better or worse across contexts. One could thus argue for more radical (arguably desperate) value adjustments that give forecasters even more benefit of the doubt that their errors represent the right mistakes. This encounter with value adjustments will not therefore be our last. But, for reasons laid out in the Technical Appendix and chapter 6, we should beware that the more generous we make value adjustments, the greater the risk of our becoming apologists for poor forecasting. The reductio ad absurdum is value adjustments tailored so exquisitely that, whatever mistakes we make, we insist on correcting them.

Qualifications noted, the consistent performance parity between experts and dilettantes—even after value adjustments—suggests that radical skeptics are right that we reach the point of diminishing marginal predictive returns for knowledge disconcertingly quickly.

The Fifteen Minutes of Fame Hypothesis

Radical skeptics see experts' failure to outperform dilettantes as further evidence there is little consistency in "who gets what right" across regions, topics, or time—at least any more consistency than we should expect from the intercorrelations among outcomes in the forecasting environment. According to the Andy Warhol hypothesis, everybody, no matter how silly, is ultimately entitled to his or her fifteen minutes of fame, plus or minus a random disturbance value. Forecasting skill should be roughly as illusory as hot hands in basketball.

Radical skeptics need not be too perturbed by the strong consistency in who got what right across time. Forecasters who received superior calibration and discrimination scores in their short-term predictions of political and economic trends also received superior scores in their longer-term predictions (correlations of .53 and .44). These correlations are of approximately the magnitude one would expect from the predictive power of time series and regression models that captured the autoregressive continuity of, and the intercorrelations among, outcome variables. Radical skeptics should, however, be perturbed by the consistency coefficients across domains: knowledge of who did well within their specialties allowed us to identify far beyond chance accuracy those with good calibration and discrimination scores outside their specialties (correlations of .39 and .31). These latter strands of continuity in good judgment cut across topics with virtually zero statistical and conceptual overlap—from predicting GDP growth in Argentina to interethnic wars in the Balkans to nuclear proliferation in South Asia to election outcomes in Western Europe and North America. To be consistent, radical skeptics must dismiss such results, significant at the .01 level, as statistical flukes.

From a meliorist perspective, the more reasonable response is to start searching for attributes that distinguish forecasters with better and worse track records. Chapter 3 picks up this challenge in earnest. Here it must suffice to say that it is possible to build on the initial findings of consistency in forecasting performance—to show that these individual differences are not a stand-alone phenomenon but rather correlate with a psychologically meaningful network of other variables, including cognitive style. For current purposes, though, these effects have the status of anomalies—irritating blotches on the skeptics' otherwise impressive empirical record (something they will try to trivialize by attributing it to confounds or artifacts), but a source of potential comfort to meliorists who insist that, even within the restricted range of plausible worldviews and cognitive styles represented in this elite sample of forecasters, some ways of thinking about politics translate into superior performance.

The Hot Air Hypothesis

Radical skeptics have been dealt a setback, but that should not prevent us from testing their remaining hypotheses. We have seen that forecasters pay a steep calibration price for attaching high likelihoods to low-frequency events. The hot air hypothesis asserts that experts are more susceptible to this form of overconfidence than dilettantes because experts "know too much": they have so much case-specific knowledge at their fingertips, and are so skilled at marshalling that knowledge to construct compelling cause-effect scenarios, that they talk themselves into assigning extreme probabilities that stray further from the objective base-rate probabilities. As expertise rises, we should therefore expect confidence in forecasts to rise faster, far faster, than forecast accuracy.

We should, though, be careful. Regression-toward-the-mean effects can mimic overconfidence. If we make the safe assumption there is measurement error in our indicators of subjective probability and objective frequency, we should expect purely by chance that when experts assign extremely confident probabilities to outcomes—say zero (impossible) or 1.0 (sure thing)—those outcomes will materialize more than 0 percent and less than 100 percent of the time (exactly how much more or less is a function of the correlation between subjective and objective probabilities and the size of the standard deviations—see Technical Appendix). The key question is whether the magnitude of the observed overconfidence—either that things will (1.0) or will not happen (zero)—exceeds what we would expect based on chance.

To answer this question, we need to determine whether the average probability judgment is significantly different from the average objective frequency for each of the three superordinate classes of events: no change versus change for either the better or worse. Consistent with the systematic error hypothesis, a series of t-tests reveal significant probability-reality gaps for both experts and dilettantes. Both groups assign too high probabilities to change, especially change for the worse, and too low probabilities to the status quo. And consistent with the hot air hypothesis, we find bigger probability-reality gaps for experts than for dilettantes. Experts pay a penalty for using the extreme end points of the probability scale more often: pronouncing outcomes either impossible (zero) or almost impossible (.1) and either inevitable (1.0) or almost inevitable (.9). Of all the predictions experts made, 30.3 percent declared outcomes either impossible or highly unlikely and 6.9 percent declared outcomes either certain or highly likely. By contrast, dilettantes were more diffident, assigning only 25.8 percent of their predictions to the lowest probabilities and 4.7 percent to the highest. Given we already know that experts and dilettantes are roughly equally adept at assigning probabilities (the impossible or nearly impossible happen about 15 percent of the time for both groups and sure things or almost sure things fail to happen about 27 percent of the time for both groups), the arithmetic dictates that experts have more big mistakes to explain away than do dilettantes.

Assessing the core claim of the hot air hypothesis—that one-sided justifications are pumping up overconfidence among experts—requires moving beyond ticks on probability scales and coding forecasters' rationales for their predictions. As described in the Methodological Appendix, we asked all participants to provide explanations for their forecasts on one topic within their field of expertise and on one topic outside their field. These thought protocols were then subjected to content analyses that assessed, among other things, verbosity, number of arguments favoring each possible future, and the balance of arguments favoring or opposing the most likely future. The results confirmed that: (a) the more relevant expertise forecasters possessed, the more elaborate their justifications for their forecasts. The average number of causal arguments advanced for "most likely futures" in experts' thought protocols was 5.4, whereas the average number for dilettantes was 2.9, a highly significant difference; (b) the more lopsidedly these arguments favored the most likely future (the ratio of pro to con arguments), the higher the perceived likelihood of the future ($r = .45$).

Clinching the argument requires, however, demonstrating the mediating role of thoughts in producing differential confidence among experts and dilettantes. Here, regression analysis revealed that the tendency for experts to make more extreme predictions than dilettantes vanishes when we control statistically for the links between expertise and loquacity (number of arguments) and extremity and loquacity. The expertise-extremity relationship also disappears when we control for the lopsidedness of the argument count in favor of the most likely future. In both cases, the relevant partial correlations fell below .10.

The Seduction Hypothesis

The final tenets of radical skepticism, the fifth and sixth, deal not with the accuracy of expert advice but rather with the forces that drive supply and demand for such advice. The fifth tenet declares that the expert community has too great a vested interest in self-promotion to cease and desist from supplying snake oil forecasting products. If this sounds a tad harsh, it is meant to be. Hard-core skeptics do not mince words when it comes to appraising the gullibility of their fellow citizens, the forecasting skills of their colleagues, and the psychological obstacles that make it difficult both for citizens to recognize that the imperial expert has no clothes and for experts to acknowledge the naked truth.

Inspection of correlation coefficients culled from the forecasting exercises illustrates how supply-side processes may prime the pump of overconfident advice that flows from well-placed epistemic communities into the policy world. We asked a large group of participants how often they advised policy makers, consulted with government or business, and were solicited by the media for interviews. Consistent with the seduction-by-fame-fortune-and-power hypothesis, experts in demand were more overconfident than their colleagues who eked out existences far from the limelight, $r(136) = .33$, $p < .05$. A similar correlation links overconfidence and the number of media mentions that participants received, according to a Google search count ($r = .26$). Both relationships fell to nonsignificance after controlling for a cognitive-style measure derived from the thought protocols. More "balanced" thinkers (who were prone to frame arguments in "on the one hand" and "on the other" terms) were less overconfident ($r = .37$) and less in the limelight ($r = .28$). Of course, causality surely flows in both directions. On one hand, overconfident experts may be more quotable and attract more media attention. On the other, overconfident experts may also be more likely to seek out the attention. The three principals—authoritative-sounding experts, the ratings-conscious media, and the attentive public—may thus be locked in a symbiotic triangle. It is tempting to say they need each other too much to terminate a relationship merely because it is based on an illusion. We return to these issues in chapter 8, where we take up Richard Posner's thesis that there are systematic distortions in the media markets for intellectual commentary.

The Indefinitely Sustainable Illusion Hypothesis

This final hypothesis declares that, no matter how unequivocal the evidence that experts cannot outpredict chimps or extrapolation algorithms, we should expect business to unfold as usual: pundits will continue to warn us on talk shows and op-ed pages of what will happen unless we dutifully follow their policy prescriptions. We—the consumers of expert pronouncements—are in thrall to experts for the same reasons that our ancestors submitted to shamans and oracles: our uncontrollable need to believe in a controllable world and our flawed understanding of the laws of chance. We lack the willpower and good sense to resist the snake oil products on offer. Who wants to believe that, on the big questions, we could do as well tossing a coin as by consulting accredited experts?

A simple experiment on Berkeley undergraduates illustrates the demand side of the equation. We presented one of two fictitious scenarios in sub-Saharan Africa: either a low-stakes decision in which the worst-case outcome was a minor escalation of tensions between two ethnic groups inhabiting the same country or a high-stakes decision in which the worst-case outcome was a bloodbath with many thousands of deaths. Students then judged how much confidence they would have in policy advice from one of two sources: a panel of prestigious social scientists drawn from major universities but lacking specialized knowledge of the region and an otherwise identical panel that did possess specialized knowledge of the region. The will to believe in the predictive and prescriptive powers of expertise should be strongest when observers believe that lives hang in the balance. Consistent with this notion, increasing the stakes boosted the perceived likelihood of only the relevant experts being right (from 65 percent to 79 percent), not that of the irrelevant ones (54 percent to 52 percent). Responsible people reach for the best possible advice; to do anything else would be, well, irresponsible. The mystique of expertise is so rooted in our culture that failing to consult the right experts is as unconscionable a lapse of due diligence as failing to consult witch doctors or Delphic oracles in other times.

The experiment also sheds light on how political accountability can foster reliance on expertise. We asked participants to imagine that government officials made a decision that worked out either badly or well after they had consulted either relevant or less clearly relevant experts. When people imagined a policy failure, they attached greater responsibility to officials who failed to consult the right experts. To be sure, going through the right process motions does not immunize one from criticism: consulting the right people and failing is still not as good as succeeding, regardless of whom one consults. But it takes some sting out of the criticism.

Here, then, is a reason for skeptics to despair. Even if they win all the scientific battles, they may still lose the political war. Defeat is likely, in part, because it will be hard to convince those with their hands on the levers of power to accept the unsettling implications of the skeptics' warnings. Defeat is also likely, in part, because, even if skeptics overcome this formidable psychological barrier, they face an even more formidable societal one. Given prevailing accountability norms and practices, even decision makers who believe the skeptics are right should continue soliciting advice from the usual suspects. They know that the anticipated blame from a policy fiasco in which they bypassed the relevant experts substantially exceeds that from a fiasco in which they ritualistically consulted the relevant experts.

GROPING TOWARD COMPROMISE: SKEPTICAL MELIORISM

The radical skeptics' assault on the ivory-tower citadels of expertise inflicted significant, if not irreparable, reputational damage. Most experts found it ego deflating to be revealed as having no more forecasting skill than dilettantes and less skill than simple extrapolation algorithms. These are not results one wants disseminated if one's goal is media acclaim or lucrative consulting contracts, or even just a bit of deference from colleagues to one's cocktail-party kibitzing on current events. Too many people will have the same reaction as one take-no-prisoners skeptic: "Insisting on anonymity was the only farsighted thing those characters did."[50]

There is, then, a case for closing the scientific case and admonishing pundits to bring their inflated self-concepts into alignment with their modest achievements. But the case for cloture also has weaknesses. Several pockets of evidence suggest the meliorist search for correlates of good judgment is not as quixotic as radical skeptics portray it. There are numerous hints that crude human-versus-mindless-algorithm or expert-versus-dilettante comparisons are masking systematic individual differences in forecasting skill. The meliorists may be right that good judgment is not reducible to good luck.

The die-hard skeptics will resist. They see no point in taking what meliorists consider the natural next step: moving beyond generalizations about forecasters as a whole and exploring variation in forecasting skill that permits us to answer more subtle questions of the form "Who was right about what, when, and why?" There is no point because we now know that variation in forecasting skill is roughly normally distributed, with means hovering not much above chance and slightly below case-specific extrapolation algorithms. Would we not expect exactly these patterns if experts on average had almost no forecasting skill, but some lucky souls got higher scores and others lower ones? To be sure, if one looks long enough, one will find something that correlates with something else. But one will have frittered away resources in pursuit of will-o'-the-wisp relationships that will fail to hold up in new periods just as surely as will Aunt Mildred's astrological guide that served her so well at roulette last week. Truth in advertising requires presenting any search

---

[50] Readers who themselves meet the definition of political expert used here (see Methodological Appendix) might feel unfairly singled out. They should not. Although this project was not designed to compare how well experts from various fields perform prediction tasks, we can safely assert that political experts are far from alone in thinking they are better forecasters than they are. The co-existence of highly knowledgeable experts and anemic forecasting performance is a common phenomenon. See C. Camerer and E. Johnson, "The Process-Performance Paradox in Expert Judgment: How Can Experts Know So Much and Predict So Badly?" in *Toward a General Theory of Expertise*, ed. K. A. Ericsson and J. Smith, 195–217 (New York: Cambridge University Press, 1991); H. Arkes, "Overconfidence in Judgmental Forecasting," in *Principles of Forecasting*, ed. S. Armstrong, 495–516 (Boston: Kluwer, 2001). It is also fair to say that political experts are not alone in their susceptibility to biases documented in later chapters, including belief perseverance, base-rate neglect, and hindsight bias. See N. V. Dawson, H. R. Arkes, C. Siciliano, R. Blinkhorn, M. Lakshmanan, and M. Petrelli, "Hindsight Bias: An Impediment to Accurate Probability Estimation in Clinicopathologic Conferences," *Medical Decision Making* 8 (1988): 259–64; W. D. Gouvier, M. Uddo-Crane, and L. M. Brown, "Base Rates of Postconcussional Symptoms," *Archives of Clinical Neuropsychology* 3 (1988): 273–78; G. B. Chapman and A. S. Elstein, "Cognitive Processes and Biases in Medical Decision Making," in *Decision Making in Health Care,* ed. G. B. Chapman and F. A. Sonnenberg, 183–210 (Cambridge: Cambridge University Press, 2000).

beyond chapter 2 not as one for correlates of ability to make stunningly accurate forecasts but rather as one for correlates of ability to avoid the massive mistakes that drive the forecasting skill of certain groups deep into negative territory, below what one could achieve by relying on base rates or predict-the-past algorithms.

It would be rash to ignore the skeptics' warnings. But it would also be rash to ignore the strong hints that certain brands of meliorism have validity. Uninspiring though absolute levels of forecasting skill have been—relative differences in skill are consequential. Experts who speak truth to power are not about to be replaced by extrapolation algorithms. And, among these experts, there is no shortage of competing views on the conceptual recipe for good judgment. Proponents of these views regularly dispense their conflicting advice in magazines, in conferences, and on television talk shows—advice that has rhetorical force only insofar as the audience grants that the source knows something about the future that the source's sparring partners do not. Tax cuts will either promote or impede or have no effect on GDP growth; pursuing ballistic missile defense projects will have either good, bad, or mixed effects. The current approach holds out the promise of determining which perspectives are linked to more accurate predictions. Keeping a rough tally of who gets what right could serve the same public-service functions as the tallying exercises of the *Wall Street Journal* or the *Economist* serve in the domains of equity markets and macroeconomics: provide reality checks on self-promotional puffery and aid to consumers in judging the quality of competing vendors in the marketplace of ideas.

Finally, regardless of whether it is rash to abandon the meliorist search for the Holy Grail of good judgment, most of us feel it is. When we weigh the perils of Type I errors (seeking correlates of good judgment that will prove ephemeral) against those of Type II errors (failing to discover durable correlates with lasting value), it does not feel like a close call. We would rather risk anointing lucky fools over ignoring wise counsel. Radical skepticism is too bitter a doctrinal pill for most of us to swallow.

The comparisons are not, however, always so soothing. There are domains in which experts are remarkably well calibrated and their performance towers over that of dilettantes. See A. H. Murphy and R. L. Winkler, "Probability Forecasting in Meterology," *Journal of the American Statistical Association* 79 (1984): 489–500; G. Keren, "Facing Uncertainty in the Game of Bridge: A Calibration Study," *Organizational Behavior and Human Decision Processes* 39 (1987): 98–114.

The differences across domains are probably due to a combination of factors. Quick, unequivocal feedback on the accuracy of predictions promotes superior performance. So too do norms within the profession that encourage confronting, rather than rationalizing away, mistakes (an especially severe shortcoming in the political domain that we document in chapter 4 and for which we propose possible solutions in chapter 8).

CHAPTER 3

Knowing the Limits of One's Knowledge

FOXES HAVE BETTER CALIBRATION AND DISCRIMINATION SCORES THAN HEDGEHOGS

> The fox knows many things but the hedgehog knows one big thing.
>
> —Isaiah Berlin

> The test of a first-rate intelligence is the ability to hold two opposing ideas in the mind at the same time, and still retain the ability to function.
>
> —F. Scott Fitzgerald

Behavioral scientists often disagree over not only the facts but also over what is worth studying in the first place. What one school of thought dismisses as a minor anomaly of no conceivable interest to any gainfully employed grown-up, another school elevates to center stage. So it is here. The competing perspectives on good judgment in chapter 1— skepticism and meliorism—offer starkly different assessments of the wisdom of searching for correlates of forecasting skill. Skeptics argue that chapter 2 settled the debate: good judgment and good luck are roughly one and the same. Meliorists sigh that chapter 3 finally gets us to the core issue: Why are some people quite consistently better forecasters than others?

Chapter 3 gives meliorism as fair a methodological shake as chapter 2 gave skepticism. The chapter is organized around a two-track approach to the search for good judgment: the rigor of a quantitative, variable-centered approach that follows a clear hypothesis-testing logic, and the richness of a looser qualitative approach that explores the patterns running through the arguments that our forecasters advanced for expecting some outcomes and rejecting others.

The first track is sensitive to skeptics' concerns about capitalizing on chance. It caps the potentially limitless list of meliorist hunches by targeting only the most influential hypotheses that could be culled from either formal arguments in the research literature or informal comments of research participants. Its strength is the clarity with which it defines previously vague concepts and lays out explicit standards of proof. The second track throws skeptics' caution to the wind. It pursues the search for the cognitive underpinnings of good judgment in an impressionistic, even opportunistic, fashion. It calls on us to be good listeners, to pick up those patterns of reasoning that distinguish the most from the least accurate forecasters. Its strength is its power to yield evocative accounts of why particular groups outperformed others when they did.

Of course, there is a rigor-richness trade-off. We purchase rigor by shaving off subtleties that are hard to count; we purchase richness by capitalizing on coincidental connections between what experts say and what subsequently happens. Fortunately, the knowledge game is not zero-sum here. In the end, the two search strategies yield reassuringly similar results. We discover that an intellectual trait widely considered a great asset in science—the commitment to parsimony—can be a substantial liability in real-world forecasting exercises.

The Quantitative Search for Good Judgment

Skeptics see chapter 3 as a fool's errand because they see enormous risks of capitalizing on chance when investigators get free license to fish in large empirical ponds until they finally catch something that correlates with forecasting accuracy. It was essential, therefore, to impose priorities in searching the vast universe of ways in which we human beings differ from one another. We could not test all possible meliorist hypotheses, but we could test three sizable subsets: those bearing on individual differences among experts in their backgrounds and accomplishments, in the *content* of their belief systems, and in their *styles* of reasoning.

Demographic and Life History Correlates

One can always second-guess the bona fides of the sample, but a lot of meliorist folk wisdom about good judgment bit the dust in this round of analyses. As table 3.1 shows, the list of close-to-zero, zero-order correlates is long. It made virtually no difference whether participants had doctorates, whether they were economists, political scientists, journalists, or historians, whether they had policy experience or access to classified information, or whether they had logged many or few years of experience in their chosen line of work. As noted in Chapter 2, the only consistent predictor was, ironically, fame, as indexed by a Google count: better-known forecasters—those more likely to be fêted by the media—were less well calibrated than their lower-profile colleagues.

TABLE 3.1
Individual Difference Predictors of Calibration of Subjective Probability
Forecasts

Individual Difference Predictors	Forecasting Accuracy	
	Correlations	Standardized Betas (with standard errors)
I. Professional Background		
(a) Education (Ph.D. or not)	+.02	+.001 (.03)
(b) Years of professional experience (1 to 36)	+.00	+.02 (.03)
(c) Academic or nonacademic work	−.03	+.05 (.04)
(d) Access to classified information	+.02	+.01 (.05)
(e) Contact with media (1–7 scale: never to every week)	−.12	−.09 (.08)
Gender (female = 1)	.05	.08 (.08)
(f) Self-rate relevance of expertise	.09	.03 (.07)
II. Ideological-Theoretical Orientation		
(a) Left-Right	+.07	+.01 (.05)
(b) Idealist-Realist	+.06	−.03 (.06)
(c) Doomster-Boomster	+.20*	−.12 (.04)*
III. Cognitive Style		
(a) Hedgehog-Fox	.35**	+.29 (.04)**
(b) Integratively complex thought protocols	.31	+.25 (.05)**
(c) Extremism	.30	+.09 (.06)

* .05 significance
** .01 significance
Adjusted R^2 = .29 (N = 177)

Content Correlates

Political belief systems vary on many dimensions, and the lengthier the
laundry list of predictors, the greater the risk of capitalizing on chance.
To preempt such objections, I used maximum likelihood factor analysis
to reduce an unwieldy number of questionnaire items (thirteen) to a
manageable number of thematic composites (a three-factor solution).[1]
Table 3.2 presents the loadings of each variable on each factor. The
higher a variable's loading on a factor, and the lower its loadings on
other factors, the more important the variable is in uniquely defining the
factor. The resulting factors were as follows.

[1] Factor analysis selects factors by initially maximizing the likelihood that the variance-
covariance matrix is generated by a single factor plus normally distributed disturbances.

TABLE 3.2
Variable Loadings in Rotated Factor Matrix from Maximum Likelihood Factor
Analysis (Quartimin Rotation) of Belief Systems Items

Variable	Left-Right	Institutionalist-Realist	Doomster-Boomster
1. Strong trend toward global economic interdependence	−0.09	−0.18	+0.52*
2. Faith in power of markets to stimulate prosperity	+0.39*	+0.05	+0.70*
3. Downplay negative environmental externalities of free markets	+0.44*	−0.18	+0.68*
4. Downplay negative effects of markets on social equality	+0.58*	−0.21	+0.29
5. Balance-of-power politics remains the dominant regulating principle in world politics	+0.25	+0.61*	−0.14
6. Mistake to dismiss international institutions as totally subordinate to whims of great powers	−0.14	−0.43*	+0.09
7. Optimistic about long-term growth potential of world economy	+0.17	−0.03	+0.66*
8. Concerned about pushing limits of sustainable development	−0.19	−0.14	−0.53*
9. Reassurance is more important than deterrence in international relations	−0.29*	−0.53*	+0.02
10. Financial contagion a greater threat than moral hazard in deciding to aid insolvent governments	−0.18	−0.33*	−0.03
11. Powerful subnational identifications will soon transform boundaries of dozens of existing states	+0.21	+0.29*	−0.04
12. Pervasive tendency to under-estimate fragility of ecosystems	−0.11	−0.08	−0.40*
13. Self-identification with left-right	+0.59*	+0.12	+0.28

Note: Asterisks highlight five highest loadings for each factor and bold labels atop each column highlight meaning of high loadings.

LEFT VERSUS RIGHT

The left wanted to redress inequalities within and across borders, expressed reservations about rapid transitions from socialist to market economies and about the impact of trade liberalization and unrestricted capital flows on countries with weak regulatory institutions, and worried about nasty side effects on the poor and the natural environment. The right were enthusiastic about market solutions but had grave reservations about "governmental meddling" that shifted attention from wealth creation to wealth distribution. To quote one: "Government failure is far more common than market failure."

INSTITUTIONALISTS VERSUS REALISTS

Realists agreed that, new world order rhetoric to the side, world politics remains a "jungle." They were wary of subordinating national policy to international institutions and of trusting words and promises when money and power are at stake. They also worried about the power of "matrioshka nationalisms" in which secessionists break up existing states but then splinter into factions seeking to secede from the secession.[2] Institutionalists saw more potential for moving beyond the "cutthroat" logic of realism, nationalism, and deterrence. They stressed the necessity of coordinating national policy with international bodies, the capacity of new ideas to transform old definitions of national interests, and the dangers of failing to take into account the concerns of other parties.

DOOMSTERS VERSUS BOOMSTERS

Boomsters emphasized the resilience of ecosystems (their capacity to "snap back") and the ingenuity of human beings in coping with scarcity (when the going gets tough, the tough get going and come with cost-effective substitutes for nonrenewable resources). They put priority on developing economic growth and high-technology solutions, and the

---

(*Note 1 con'd from p. 69*) Extracting the single factor from the data yields a residual variance-covariance matrix from which the additional factors are selected by repeating the likelihood maximization process. After applying several factoring methods and rotation procedures, we settled on a maximum likelihood solution with quartimin rotation (that did not force factors into orthogonal alignments). The retention of three factors was justified by the pattern of decline in eigenvalues and by the improving fit to the data from more formal goodness-of-fit tests. For details, see L. R. Fabrigar, D. T. Wegener, R. C. MacCallum, and E. J. Strahan, "Evaluating the Use of Exploratory Factor Analysis in Psychological Research," *Psychological Methods* 4(3) (1999): 272–99. F. J. Floyd and K. F. Widaman, "Factor Analysis in the Development and Refinement of Clinical Assessment Instructions," *Psychological Assessment* 7(3) (1995): 286–99.

[2] D. P. Moynihan, *Pandemonium* (New York: Oxford University Press, 1997).

most radical believed that humanity was on the verge, with advances in artificial intelligence and molecular biology, of entering a posthuman phase of history populated by beings smarter, healthier, and happier than the dim, diseased, and depressed hominids roaming the planet in the late twentieth century. Doomsters stressed the fragility of ecosystems and the urgency of promoting sustainable development and living within the "carrying capacity constraints" of the planet. Radical doomsters believed that humanity is on the wrong track, one leading to "grotesque" income gaps between haves and have-nots, to "criminal plundering" of nature, and to growing violence in the underdeveloped world as scarcity aggravates ethnic and religious grievances.

Taken together, the three factors reveal a lot about the worldviews of participants.[3] But these content factors offer little help in our search for broad bandwidth predictors of forecasting skill. Figure 3.1—which divides respondents into low, moderate, or high scorers on each factor—shows that neither low nor high scorers enjoy any notable advantage on either calibration or discrimination. This null result holds up across the zones of turbulence and stability, and across forecasting topics. Figure 3.1 does, however, offer a glimmering of hope that the meliorist quest for correlates of good judgment is not quixotic. Moderates consistently bested extremists on calibration—an advantage that they did not purchase by sacrificing discrimination.[4]

Although the content factors proved anemic predictors of overall performance, it was easy to identify times and places at which one or another faction could crow over its successes. We shall soon see that, consistent with the fifteen minutes of fame hypothesis, who is up versus down can shift rapidly from case to case, and even from moment to moment within cases.

Cognitive Style Correlates

The search for correlates of good judgment across time and topics became more successful when the spotlight shifted from *what* experts thought to *how* they thought. Table 3.3 presents the thirteen items used to measure cognitive style, as well as the results of a maximum likelihood factor analysis. The low and high variable loadings on the first factor bear a striking resemblance to Isaiah Berlin's famous distinction

---

[3] The first and third factors were correlated ($r = .43$). Boomsters tilted to the right, doomsters to the left. The second factor was moderately correlated ($r = 0.27$) with the first but negligibly with the third (.09). Realists and materialists favored the right; institutionalists and idealists, the left.

[4] Regression analyses, technically more appropriate, tell the same story. The tertile (and later quartile) splits do, though, simplify presentation.

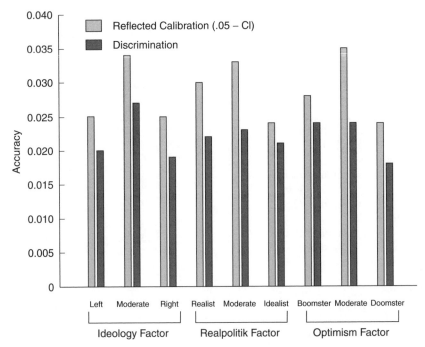

Figure 3.1. Calibration and discrimination scores as a function of forecasters' attitudes on the left-right, realism-idealism, and boomster-doomster "content" scales derived from factor analysis. The data are collapsed across all forecasting domains, including the zone of turbulence and the zone of stability, and forecasting topics, including political, economic, and national security. Higher (reflected) calibration scores indicate greater ability to assign subjective probabilities that correspond to objective relative frequency of outcomes. Higher discrimination scores indicate greater ability to assign higher probabilities to events that occur than to those that do not.

between hedgehogs and foxes in the history of ideas.[5] Low scorers look like hedgehogs: thinkers who "know one big thing," aggressively extend the explanatory reach of that one big thing into new domains, display bristly impatience with those who "do not get it," and express considerable confidence that they are already pretty proficient forecasters, at least in the long term. High scorers look like foxes: thinkers who know many small things (tricks of their trade), are skeptical of grand schemes, see explanation and prediction not as deductive exercises but rather as exercises in flexible "ad hocery" that require stitching together diverse sources of information, and are rather diffident about their own forecasting

[5] Berlin, "The Hedgehog and the Fox."

TABLE 3.3
Variable Loadings in Rotated Factor Matrix from the Maximum Likelihood
Analysis of the Style-of-Reasoning Items (higher loadings indicate more foxlike
cognitive style [column 1] or more decisive style [column 2]

	Loading	
Items	Hedgehog-Fox Factor	Decisiveness Factor
1. Self-identification as fox or hedgehog (Berlin's definition)	+0.42	−0.04
2. More common error in judging situations is to exaggerate complexity of world	−0.20	+0.14
3. Closer than many think to achieving parsimonious explanations of political processes	−0.29	+0.05
4. Politics is more cloudlike than clocklike	+0.26	−0.02
5. More common error in decision making is to abandon good ideas too quickly	−0.31	+0.22
6. Having clear rules and order at work is essential for success	−0.09	+0.31
7. Even after making up my mind, I am always eager to consider a different opinion	+0.28	−0.07
8. I dislike questions that can be answered in many ways	−0.35	+0.05
9. I usually make important decisions quickly and confidently	−0.23	+0.26
10. When considering most conflicts, I can usually see how both sides could be right	+0.31	+0.01
11. It is annoying to listen to people who cannot make up their minds	−0.18	+0.14
12. I prefer interacting with people whose opinions are very different from my own	+0.23	−0.10
13. When trying to solve a problem, I often see so many options it is confusing	+0.08	−0.27

prowess, and—like the skeptics in chapter 2—rather dubious that the cloudlike subject of politics can be the object of a clocklike science.[6]

The measure of cognitive style correlates only feebly with the three content factors (all r's < .10). Hedgehogs and foxes can be found in all factions. But they are not randomly distributed across the three dimensions of political thought. Foxes were more likely to be centrists. When we assess sample-specific extremism—by computing the squared deviation of each expert's score on each dimension from the mean on that dimension—the resulting measures correlate at .31 with preference for a hedgehog style of reasoning. These relationships will help later to pinpoint where hedgehogs—of various persuasions—made their biggest mistakes.[7]

Most notable, though, is the power of the hedgehog-fox dimension of cognitive style as a broad bandwidth predictor of forecasting skill. The hedgehog-fox dimension did what none of the "content" measures of political orientation, and none of the measures of professional background, could do: distinguish observers of the contemporary scene with superior forecasting records, across regions, topics, and time.

[6] Of course, impressive though the correspondence is between our empirical dimension and Berlin's conceptual distinction, the mapping is imperfect. Factor analysis transforms Sir Isaiah's dichotomy into a measurement continuum that treats "hedgehogness" and "foxiness" as matters of degree, not all or none. Psychologists are familiar with this dimension of human personality. It bears a family resemblance to the generic openness factor in multivariate studies of personality structure as well as to several measures of cognitive style in the psychological literature, especially those of need for closure and integrative complexity (see, for example, O. P. John, "The 'Big Five' Factor Taxonomy: Dimensions of Personality in the Natural Language and in Questionnaires," in *Handbook of Personality*, ed. L. A. Pervin (New York: Guilford Press, 1990); A. W. Kruglanski and D. M. Webster, "Motivated Closing of the Mind: 'Seizing' and 'freezing,'" *Psychological Review* 103 (1996): 263–68; also P. Suedfeld and P. E. Tetlock, "Cognitive Styles," in *Blackwell International Handbook of Social Psychology*, vol. 1, ed. A. Tesser and N. Schwartz (London: Blackwell, 2001). High need-for-closure, integratively simple individuals are like Berlin's hedgehogs: they dislike ambiguity and dissonance in their personal and professional lives, place a premium on parsimony, and prefer speedy resolutions of uncertainty that keep prior opinions intact. Low need-for-closure, integratively complex individuals are like Berlin's foxes: they are tolerant of ambiguity and dissonance, curious about other points of view, and open to the possibility they are wrong.

[7] Political psychologists have a long-standing interest in the linkages between cognitive style and political ideology. The current results run against the dominant grain in this literature. Most studies have found that those on the political right tend to score higher on psychological measures of preferences for simplicity and closure than those on the left and the center of the ideological spectrum. (See J. T. Jost, J. Glaser, A Kruglanski, and F. Sulloway, "Political Conservatism as Motivated Social Cognition," *Psychological Bulletin* 129 [2003]: 339–75.) By contrast, we have found that those on the left and right ends of the spectrum in our sample obtain roughly comparable scores on such measures and both groups score higher than those toward the center of the spectrum. It would be a mistake though to make too much of this inconsistency—a mistake for at least three reasons. First,

Figure 3.2 plots the calibration and discrimination scores of thirty-two subgroups of forecasters (resulting from a $4 \times 2 \times 2 \times 2$ division and identified by the legend in the figure caption).

The results affirm the modest meliorist contention that the crude human-versus-chimp, and expert-versus-dilettante comparisons in chapter 2 mask systematic, not just random, variation in forecasting skill. Some cognitive-stylistic subspecies of humans consistently outperformed others. On the two most basic measures of accuracy—calibration and discrimination—foxes dominate hedgehogs. The calibration scores of foxes and fox-hogs (first and second quartile scorers on the cognitive-style scale) hover in the vicinity of .015, which means they assign subjective probabilities (1.0, .9, .8, . . .) that deviate from objective frequency (.88, .79, .67, . . .) by, on average, 12 percent; by contrast, the hedgehogs and hedge-foxes (third and fourth quartile scorers on the cognitive-style scale) have calibration scores hovering around .035, which means a subjective probability–objective reality gap, on average, of 18 percent. The discrimination scores of foxes and fox-hogs average .03 (which means they capture about 18 percent of the variance in their predictions), whereas those for hedgehogs and hedge-foxes average .023 (which means they capture about 14 percent of the variance).

But the results do not support the bolder meliorist contention that certain styles of thinking reliably yield forecasting accuracy comparable or superior to those of formal statistical models. Only the best-performing foxes come close to the forecasting accuracy of crude case-specific extrapolation algorithms (numbers 35 and 36 in upper right of fig. 3.2) and none even approach the autoregressive distributed lag models (number 37 in far upper right).

Figure 3.2 thus brackets human performance. It reveals how short of omniscience the best forecasters fall: they are lucky to approach 20 percent of that epistemic ideal across all exercises, whereas extrapolation

---

the research literature is not monolithic. In my own past work, I have found support for both the rigidity-of-the-right and the ideologue hypotheses. Much hinges on the proportions of true believers from the left and the right in one's sample. (See P. E. Tetlock, "Cognitive Structural Analysis of Political Rhetoric: Methodological and Theoretical Issues, in *Political Psychology: A Reader*, ed. S. Iyengar and W. J. McGuire, 380–407 (Durham, NC: Duke University Press, 1992.) Second, the research literature offers no precise guidance on how far to the left or right one must go to observe hypothesized shifts in cognitive style. Third, causality is murky. On the one hand, cognitive style may shape the content of one's political views. Hedgehogs may be drawn to all-encompassing abstractions and foxes may be drawn to blurrier compromise positions. On the other hand, the content of one's political views may shape one's style of reasoning. Cognitive style may simply be a by-product of the moral-political values that we hold dear and the frequency with which the world forces us to make tough choices. Reciprocal determinism is probably at work.

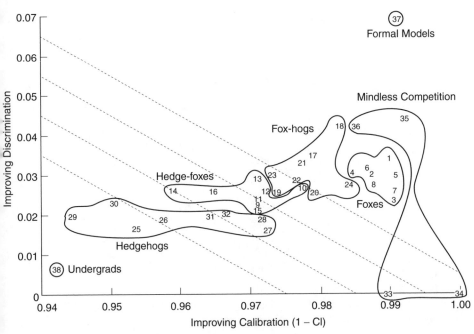

Figure 3.2. How thoroughly foxes and fox-hog hybrids (first and second quartiles on cognitive-style scale) making short-term or long-term predictions dominated hedgehogs and hedge-fox hybrids (fourth and third quartiles) making short- and long-term predictions on two indicators of forecasting accuracy: calibration and discrimination. Key to translating numbers into identifiable subgroups and tasks: pure foxes (1–8), pure hedgehogs (25–32), fox-hog hybrid (17–24) and hedge-fox hybrid (9–16); moderates (1–4, 9–12, 17–20, 25–28) and extremists (5–8, 13–16, 21–24, 29–32); experts (1–2, 5–6, 9–10, 13–14, 17–18, 21–22, 25–26, 29–30) and dilettantes (3–4, 7–8, 11–12, 15–16, 19–20, 23–24, 27–28, 31–32), short-term (2, 4, 6, 8, 10, 12, 14, 16, 18, 20, 22, 24, 26, 28, 30, 32) and long-term (1, 2, 5, 7, 9, 11, 13, 15, 17, 19, 21, 23, 25, 27, 29, and 31); mindless algorithms (chimp—33), base-rate extrapolation (34), and moderate and extreme case-specific extrapolation (35, 36); the average performance of formal statistical models (generalized autoregressive distributed lag—37), and Berkeley undergraduates (38).

algorithms approach 30 percent and formal models 50 percent.[8] And it reveals how far human performance can fall—to the point where highly educated specialists are explaining less than 7 percent of the variance

[8] As described in the Technical Appendix, one way to estimate proportion of variance predicted (an omniscience ratio) is to divide DI scores by the total variability in outcomes (VI) and multiplying by 100.

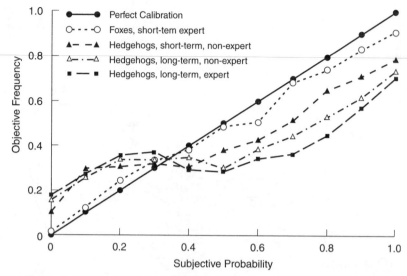

Figure 3.3. The calibration functions of four groups of forecasters compared to the ideal of perfect calibration (diagonal). The further functions stray from the diagonal, the larger and worse the resulting calibration scores.

and fall on lower aggregate skill curves than the chimpanzee's equal-guessing strategy.[9]

Figures 3.3 and 3.4 supplement figure 3.2. Figure 3.3 plots a series of calibration functions that show how well the fox-hedgehog difference holds up across the entire subjective probability scale, how close foxes come to the diagonal of perfect calibration when they make short-term predictions within their domain of expertise, and how far hedgehogs stray from this ideal when they make long-term predictions within their domains of expertise. Figure 3.4 brings into sharp focus how pronounced that fox-hedgehog difference becomes when the hedgehogs are ideological extremists making long-term predictions within their domains of expertise.

Examining all three figures, we can take home four principal sets of conclusions:

1. The fox advantage on calibration is remarkably generalizable. It holds up across all dimensions of the data displayed—across experts versus dilettantes, moderates versus extremists, and short-term versus long-range forecasts—and it holds up across two additional

---

[9] The worst-performing professionals lose overall to the chimp because they win by too small a margin on discrimination to compensate for the size of their defeat on calibration. But they still dominate the briefly briefed undergraduates—a sign that, although we reach the point of diminishing predictive returns for knowledge quickly, well-informed hedgehog ideologues derive some predictive benefits from their impressive stores of knowledge.

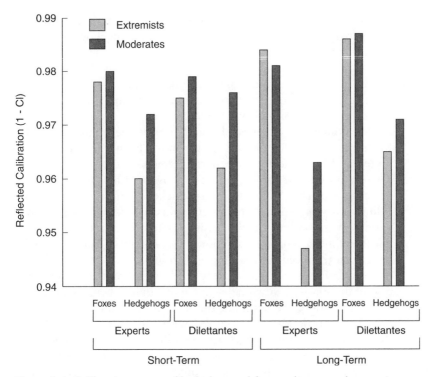

Figure 3.4. Calibration scores of hedgehog and fox moderates and extremists making short- and long-term predictions as either experts or dilettantes.

dimensions not displayed—across the zones of stability versus turbulence, and across domestic political versus economic versus national security outcomes.[10] The fox advantage fades only when fox forecasters become less foxy (among "fox-hogs") and when the hedgehog forecasters become foxier (among "hedge-foxes"). Here we find the largest cluster of "statistical ties" on calibration (in figure 3.2, data points 9, 10, 11, 12, 13, 15, 19, 20, 22, and 23).

[10] As noted in chapter 2 and the Technical Appendix, outcomes varied in the degree to which they could be predicted from knowledge of their own recent past or the recent past of other lagged variables in the dataset (squared multiple correlations from time series models ranging from .21 to .78). The generalizability of the fox advantage across outcomes casts doubt on the arguments that (a) foxes were merely more adept at picking the lowest-hanging predictive fruit (an argument that, even if true, hardly casts hedgehogs in a flattering light); (b) foxes "lucked out" and, because they were closer to being right on a few outcomes that were extensively connected to other outcomes, they enjoyed the benefits of cascading. It is worth emphasizing that our statistical tests avoid capitalizing on cascading by averaging across large numbers of observations and making highly conservative assumptions about degrees of freedom.

2. But the fox advantage on calibration is more pronounced for certain subgroups. The worst performers were hedgehog extremists making long-term predictions in their domains of expertise. From that valley (see especially figure 3.4), hedgehog performance improves as we move from experts to dilettantes, from long-term to short-term predictions, and from extremists to moderates. By contrast, the best performers were foxes making short-term predictions in their domains of expertise. From that peak (see again figure 3.4), fox performance deteriorates as we move from experts to dilettantes, and from short- to long-term predictions.

3. There is no support for the argument, advanced by some defenders of hedgehogs, that "foxes were just chickens" and their victory on calibration was as intellectually empty as the victory on the same variable as the chimp equal-guessing strategy in chapter 2. If foxes had been indiscriminately cautious, they—like the chimp—would have been trounced on the discrimination index. But the opposite happened. Foxes enjoyed a statistically significant advantage on discrimination—an advantage that fades only when, as occurred with calibration, we compare the least foxy foxes and the most foxy hedgehogs. Also, as occurred with calibration, we find that the worst-performing hedgehogs are still extremists making long-term predictions in their roles as experts. And the best-performing foxes are still moderates making predictions in their roles as experts. These results smash a critical line of defense for hedgehogs. Figure 3.2 underscores this point by showing that it was impossible to identify any plausible (monotonic) set of constant probability score curves consistent with the hypothesis that hedgehogs lost on calibration because they were making a prudent trade-off in which they opted to give up calibration for the sake of discrimination. Adding insult to injury, figure 3.2 shows it is easy to generate plausible indifference curves consistent with the hypothesis that hedgehogs and the dart-throwing chimp had equivalent forecasting skill and were simply striking different trade-offs between calibration and discrimination, with the chimp equal-guessing strategy "opting" for more calibration in return for zero discrimination and hedgehogs "opting" for less calibration in return for some discrimination.[11]

4. The patterning of fox-hedgehog differences has implications for the interpretation of the effects of other variables, especially expertise, forecasting horizon, and ideological extremism. For instance,

[11] The similar profile of correlates for calibration and discrimination should be no surprise given the substantial correlation, –.6, between the two indicators.

although expertise in chapter 2 had no across-the-board effect on forecasting accuracy, the null result is misleading. Foxes derive modest benefit from expertise whereas hedgehogs are—strange to say—harmed. And, although long-range forecasts were on average less accurate than short-term forecasts, the main effect was misleading. It was driven entirely by the greater inaccuracy of hedgehogs' long-term forecasts. Finally, although extremists were on average less accurate than moderates, this main effect too was misleading. It was driven almost entirely by the rather sharp drop in accuracy among hedgehog, but not fox, extremists.

To sum up, the performance gap between foxes and hedgehogs on calibration and discrimination is statistically reliable, but the size of the gap is moderated by at least three other variables: extremism, expertise, and forecasting horizon. These "third-order" interactions pass stringent tests of significance (probability of arising by chance [conditional on null hypothesis being true] less than one in one hundred), so it is hard for skeptics to dismiss them as aberrations.[12] And these interactions pose a profound challenge. We normally expect knowledge to promote accuracy (a working assumption of our educational systems). So, if it was surprising to discover how quickly we reached the point of diminishing returns for knowledge in chapter 2, it should be downright disturbing to discover that knowledge handicaps so large a fraction of forecasters in chapter 3.

The results do, however, fit comfortably into a cognitive-process account that draws on psychological research on cognitive styles and motivated reasoning. This account begins by positing that hedgehogs bear a strong family resemblance to high scorers on personality scales designed to measure needs for closure and structure—the types of people who have been shown in experimental research to be more likely to trivialize evidence that undercuts their preconceptions and to embrace evidence that reinforces their preconceptions.[13] This account then posits that, the more relevant knowledge hedgehogs possess, the more conceptual ammunition they have to perform these belief defense and bolstering tasks. By contrast, foxes—who resemble low scorers on the same personality scales—should be predisposed to allocate their cognitive resources in a more balanced fashion—in the service of self-criticism as well as self-defense.

---

[12] These statistical tests are based on mixed-design, repeated-measures analyses of variance that took the form of 4 (quartile split on cognitive-style scale) × 2 (expert versus dilettante) × 2 (moderate versus extremist) × (short-range versus long-range predictions) designs that allow for correlations between the repeated-measures variables. The tests rest on conservative assumptions about degrees of freedom (each short-term or long-term calibration or discrimination score is itself an average derived from, on average, thirty forecasts across two states).

[13] Kruglanski and Webster, "Motivated Closing of the Mind."

When fox experts draw on their stores of knowledge for judging alternative futures, they should pay roughly equal attention to arguments, pro and con, for each possibility. We should thus expect a cognitive-style-by-expertise interaction: there is greater potential for one's preferred style of thinking to influence judgment when one has a large stock of thoughts to bring to bear on the judgment task.

The next challenge for the cognitive-process account is to explain why the performance gap between fox and hedgehog experts should widen for longer-range forecasts. Most forecasters became less confident the deeper into the future we asked them to see. Understandably, they felt that, whereas shorter-term futures were more tightly constrained by known facts on the ground, longer-term futures were more "up for grabs." Linking these observations to what we know about hedgehogs' aversion to ambiguity, it is reasonable to conjecture that (a) hedgehogs felt more motivated to escape the vagaries of long-range forecasting by embracing cause-effect arguments that impose conceptual order; (b) hedgehogs with relevant subject matter knowledge were especially well equipped cognitively to generate compelling cause-effect arguments that impose the sought-after order. We should now expect a second-order cognitive style × expertise × time frame interaction: when we join the ability to achieve closure with the motivation to achieve it, we get the prediction that *hedgehog experts* will be most likely to possess and to embrace causal models of reality that give them too much confidence in their *long-range* projections.

The final challenge for the cognitive-process account is to lock in the fourth piece of the puzzle: to explain why the performance gap further widens among *extremists*. Laboratory research has shown that observers with strong needs for closure (hedgehogs) are most likely to rely on their preconceptions in interpreting new situations when those observers hold strong relevant attitudes (priors).[14] These results give us grounds for expecting a third-order interaction: the combination of a hedgehog style and extreme convictions should be a particularly potent driver of confidence, with the greatest potential to impair calibration and discrimination when forecasters possess sufficient expertise to generate sophisticated justifications (fueling confidence) and when forecasters make longer-range predictions (pushing potentially embarrassing reality checks on overconfidence into the distant future).

The cognitive-process account is now well positioned to explain the observed effects on forecasting accuracy. But can it explain the specific

---

[14] C-y Chiu, M. W. Morris, Y-y Hong, and T. Menon, "Motivated Cultural Cognition: The Impact of Implicit Cultural Theories on Dispositional Attribution Varies as a Function of Need for Closure," *Journal of Personality and Social Psychology* 78(2) (2000): 247–59; P. E. Tetlock, "Close-call Counterfactuals and Belief System Defenses: I Was Not Almost Wrong but I Was Almost Right," *Journal of Personality and Social Psychology* 75 (1998): 639–52.

types of mistakes that forecasters make? We have yet to break down aggregate accuracy. We do not know whether hedgehogs' more numerous mistakes were scattered helter-skelter across the board or whether they took certain distinctive forms: under- or overpredicting change for the worse or better.

To answer these questions, the Technical Appendix shows us we need indicators that, unlike the squared deviation formulas for calibration and discrimination, preserve direction-of-error information. These directional indicators reveal that, although both hedgehogs and foxes overpredict change (the lower base-rate outcome) and thus—by necessity—underpredict the status quo, hedgehogs make this pattern of mistakes to a greater degree than foxes. Relative to foxes, hedgehogs assign too high probabilities to both change for the worse (average subjective probabilities, .37 versus .29; average objective frequency = .23) and to change for the better (average subjective probabilities = .34 versus .30; average objective frequency = .28); and too low average probabilities, .29 versus .41, to perpetuation of the status quo (average objective frequency = .49). We can show, moreover, that the overprediction effect is not just a statistical artifact of regression toward the mean. A series of t-tests show that the gaps between average subjective probabilities and objective frequencies are statistically significant for both hedgehogs (at the .001 level) and foxes (at the .05 level). And the gaps for hedgehogs are consistently significantly larger than those for foxes (at the .01 level).

These asymmetries do suggest, though, there may be some, albeit limited, potential for hedgehogs to "catch up" via value adjustments that invoke the "I made the right mistake" defense (a point we revisit in chapter 6). For now, it must suffice to note that hedgehogs' tendency to assign too high probabilities to lower-frequency outcomes fits snugly within the emerging cognitive-process account of the data. We discover just how snugly when we explore the linkages between forecasting accuracy (either in aggregate or broken down into types of under- and overprediction) and the thought processes that forecasters reported when we called on them to explain their predictions.

We asked all participants twice (one inside and once outside their area of expertise): Why are you, on balance, optimistic, pessimistic, or mixed in your assessment of the future of *x*?" Our analyses of the resulting thought protocols targeted two properties of thinking styles that, if the cognitive-process account is correct, should distinguish foxes from hedgehogs and "explain" their differential forecasting performance. The key targets were as follows:

a. the evaluative differentiation index that taps into how often people use qualifying conjunctions such as "however," "but,"—and so on, that imply thoughts are in tension with one another.

b. the conceptual integration index that taps into how often people struggle to specify guidelines for resolving tensions among differentiated cognitions (e.g., grappling with trade-offs or acknowledging that sensible people, not just fools and scoundrels, could wind up viewing the same problem in clashing ways).

The Methodological Appendix provides coding details, as well as the rationale for combining the two measures into an integrative complexity index.[15]

Our analyses of forecasters' arguments reinforced the cognitive-process account of hedgehog-fox effects in several ways:

a. As one would expect if foxes and hedgehogs were equally knowledgeable but differed in their tolerance of dissonance and motivation to generate integrative cognitions, we find that (i) hedgehogs and foxes do not differ in the total number of thoughts they generate; (ii) they do differ on both evaluative differentiation and cognitive integration, each of which rises as we move from the "pure" hedgehog to the "pure" fox quartile of respondents. The composite-process measure, integrative complexity, correlated .38 with the hedgehog-fox scale.

b. As one would expect if these differences in styles of thinking were linked not only to the hedgehog-fox measure but also to forecasting skill, integrative complexity correlates with aggregate accuracy indicators, such as calibration (.32) and discrimination (.24), as well as with the directional indicator of tendency to overpredict change (.33).

c. As one would expect if these differences in styles of thinking partly mediate the connection between more foxlike cognitive styles and forecasting skill, the correlations between the hedgehog-fox scale and both calibration and overprediction of change take a significant tumble after we control for the overlap between these measures and integrative complexity (although the partial correlations remain significant).

d. As one would expect if there were an affinity between hedgehog styles of reasoning and ideological extremism, hedgehogs were more likely to be extremists (average $r = .31$ across the three content of belief system scales). Consistent with the notion that these affinities are rooted in hedgehogs' aversion to, and foxes' tolerance

[15] Suedfeld and Tetlock, "Cognitive Styles," in Tesser and Schwartz, *Blackwell International Handbook of Social Psychology*. To prevent my own biases from contaminating assessments of thinking styles, three additional coders—unaware of the hypotheses being tested and the sources of the material—applied the same coding rules to the texts. Depending on which variables and which subsamples of text were examined, interjudge reliability ranged between .76 and .89. Disagreements were averaged out for data analysis purposes.

of, dissonant combinations of ideas, extremists were also less integratively complex ($r = .32$).

e. As one would expect if hedgehog performance had been dragged down by forecasters with extreme convictions making extreme predictions that stray far from base rates, hedgehogs were more prone to use the high-confidence ends of the subjective probability scales. Relative to foxes, hedgehogs call significantly more things impossible or highly improbable (31.9 percent of judgments versus 24.3 percent) and more things certain or highly probable (7.4 percent of judgments versus 4.0 percent). And hedgehog extremists are the most prone of all subgroups to use these end point values: calling 34 percent of things impossible or nearly so and 9.4 percent of things certain or nearly so. To appreciate the magnitude of the performance drag, hedgehogs not only used the extreme end points more frequently, when they did, they also had higher miss rates (the "impossible" or "nearly impossible" happened almost 19.8 percent of the time compared to foxes' rate of 9.9 percent) and higher false alarm rates (sure things or nearly sure things failed to happen 31.5 percent of the time compared to foxes' rate of 20.8 percent).

f. Finally, some might try here to resurrect the "foxes are just chickens" hypothesis (which took a hammering when foxes beat hedgehogs on discrimination). Hedgehogs clearly do make braver forecasts— forecasts that will prove more embarrassing if the unexpected occurs. But the evidence is again consistent with the notion that the greater caution among foxes is rooted in balanced cognitive appraisals of situations, not a mindless clinging to the midpoints of the scales. The hedgehog-fox differential on extremity of predictions, once highly significant ($r = .35$), shrinks significantly when we control for the fact that foxes engage in more integratively complex thinking about problems than do hedgehogs (partial $r = .14$). It is hard to build up a lot of momentum for extreme predictions if one is slowed down by lots of buts and howevers.

Overall, these quantitative analyses yield a strikingly consistent portrait of good forecasting judgment. Figure 3.5 lays out a conceptual model that captures the pattern of correlations among key constructs. Good judges tend to be moderate foxes: eclectic thinkers who are tolerant of counterarguments, and prone to hedge their probabilistic bets and not stray too far from just-guessing and base-rate probabilities of events. However, the quantitative analyses give us only a vague picture of how foxes managed to outperform hedgehogs with such regularity in real-world settings. To get a richer sense for what transpired, we need to get behind the numbers, compare the reasoning strategies of hedgehogs and

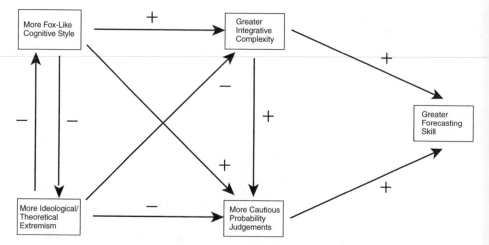

Figure 3.5. The foxes' advantage in forecasting skill can be traced to two proximal mediators, greater integrative complexity of free-flowing thoughts and a cautious approach to assigning subjective probabilities. These two mediators are, in turn, traced to broader individual differences in cognitive style (the hedgehog-fox scale) and in ideological extremism (scores on the three content-of-belief scales). Cognitive style and ideological extremity reciprocally influence each other: a fox style of reasoning encourages ideological moderation, and ideological extremism encourages a hedgehog style of reasoning.

foxes in particular domains, and trace the linkages between those strategies and forecasting triumphs and fiascoes.[16]

THE QUALITATIVE SEARCH FOR GOOD JUDGMENT

Isaiah Berlin argued that the fox-hedgehog distinction captured

> one of the deepest differences which divide writers and thinkers, and it may be, human beings in general. For there exists a great chasm between those, on one side, who relate everything to a single central vision, one system, more or less coherent or articulate, in terms of which they understand, think and feel . . . and, on the other side, those who pursue many ends, often unrelated and even contradictory, connected, if at all, only in some de facto way, . . . related to no moral or esthetic

[16] Readers unmoved by merely correlational evidence may be more persuaded by experimental evidence that forecasters forced to think in more complex ways (and to use multiple historical analogies) made more accurate predictions. See K. C. Green and J. S. Armstrong, "Structured Analogies for Forecasting," (Monash University Econometrics Working Paper 17/04, 2004), full text available at www.conflictforecasting.com.

principle. These last lead lives, perform acts and entertain ideas that are centrifugal rather than centripetal; their thought is scattered or diffused, moving on many levels, seizing upon the essence of a vast variety of experiences and objects for what they are in themselves, without, consciously or unconsciously, seeking to fit them into, or exclude them from, any one unchanging, all-embracing . . . inner vision. The first kind of intellectual belongs to the hedgehogs, the second to the foxes; and without insisting on a rigid classification, . . . Dante belongs to the first category and Shakespeare to the second; Plato, Lucretius, Pascal, Hegel, Dostoyevsky, Nietzsche, Ibsen, and Proust are, in varying degrees, hedgehogs; Herodotus, Aristotle, Montaigne, Erasmus, Molière, Goethe, Pushkin, Balzac, and Joyce are foxes.[17]

Berlin recognized that few fit the ideal-type template of fox or hedgehog. Most of us are hybrids, awkward hedge-fox and fox-hog amalgams. Indeed, Berlin suspected that his beloved Tolstoy was a fox who aspired to be a hedgehog. In the same vein, we should recognize that "hedgehogs" and "foxes" are defined here by arbitrary quartile cutoffs along a fuzzy measurement continuum. I met some participants whom formal measures classified as "foxes" but who admired the crisp, deductive style of reasoning of hedgehogs, and—imitation being the sincerest form of flattery—even sometimes snuck a bit of syllogistic certainty into their own cognitive repertoire. One "fox," by psychometric criteria, wistfully told me that it would be "nice to close an argument with QED." I also met participants whom the formal measures pigeonholed as "hedgehogs" but who grudgingly conceded that it may sometimes be futile to try to reduce the booming, buzzing confusion of this world into a single vision. One "hedgehog" feared that "God did give the damn physicists all the solvable problems." Another observed that "grown-ups understand the tragedy of knowledge: people do not fit into neat logical categories but neat logical categories are indispensable to the advance of knowledge."

Yet another respondent, who deserved his position near the midpoint of the continuum, offered the old chestnut: "There are two types of people—those who classify people into two types and those who don't." The remark was a pointed reminder that my participants were fully capable of thinking about thinking ("metacognition") and of transcending my procrustean categories by making midstream-of-consciousness adjustments when they suspect that they have gone too far in any one direction. I should not fall into the essentialist trap of viewing "hedgehogs" and "foxes" as distinct cognitive species. Reification leads only to quibbling: Are hedgehogs still hedgehogs when they engage in fox-style

---

[17] Berlin, "The Hedgehog and the Fox."

self-mockery? Are foxes still foxes when they pause to admire the elegance of a hedgehog framework?

Qualifications noted, it is still useful to inventory the distinctive attributes of the reasoning styles of hedgehogs and foxes that emerged from their free-flowing commentaries on how they went about forming and revising expectations. But we should approach the list in a foxlike spirit, as cognitive maneuvers that, when we look backward in time, worked well for some forecasters and not so well for others, but might well have worked out in the opposite manner save for quirky twists of fate. Acknowledging the tentativeness of our knowledge will protect us from disappointment when, looking forward in time, we discover how frequently extrapolations of past regularities into the future are upended. In this spirit, then, are six basic ways in which foxes and hedgehogs differed from each other. Foxes were more

a. skeptical of deductive approaches to explanation and prediction
b. disposed to qualify tempting analogies by noting disconfirming evidence
c. reluctant to make extreme predictions of the sort that start to flow when positive feedback loops go unchecked by dampening mechanisms
d. worried about hindsight bias causing us to judge those in the past too harshly
e. prone to a detached, ironic view of life
f. motivated to weave together conflicting arguments on foundational issues in the study of politics, such as the role of human agency or the rationality of decision making

Foxes Are More Skeptical of the Usefulness of Covering Laws for Explaining the Past or Predicting the Future

When senior hedgehogs dispense advice to junior colleagues, they stress the virtue of parsimony. Good judgment requires tuning out the ephemera that dominate the headlines and distract us from the real, surprisingly simple, drivers of long-term trends. They counsel that deep laws constrain history, and that these laws are knowable and lead to correct conclusions when correctly applied to the real world. They also endorse cognitive ideals that fit Berlin's characterization of the ideal-type hedgehog (hardly astonishing—a nonnegligible number had read Berlin's essay). They admire deductive reasoning that uses powerful abstractions to organize messy facts and to distinguish the possible from the impossible, the desirable from the undesirable.

But, agree though hedgehogs do on "how to think," they disagree, often fiercely, over what to think—over the correct content to insert into the logical machinery. To invoke the zoological metaphor, there are many ideological subspecies of hedgehogs, each with its own distinctive view of the fundamental drivers of events.

The propensity of hedgehogs to push their favorite first principles as far as possible, and sometimes beyond, arose on numerous occasions. For example, hedgehogs who stressed the primacy of ethnicity were among the first to suspect that the Soviet Union might not survive Gorbachev's policies that allowed "captive peoples" to express how miserable they were. Neorealist hedgehogs joined these "primordialists" in 1991–1992 in arguing that the demise of the USSR had now made Eastern Europe safe for conventional warfare among groups that had been compelled in the bipolar NATO–Warsaw Pact world to suppress their enmity. As a result, this combined camp scored impressive "hits." Even here, though, these hedgehogs did not reap much benefit in aggregate forecasting skill. They overpredicted conflict: war has yet to break out between Hungary and Romania, the divorce between the Czechs and Slovaks was as civilized as these things get, and Russia has not yet invaded the Baltics, the Ukraine, or Kazakhstan. Yugoslavia—which had already begun to unravel in 1991—was their "big hit."

These hedgehogs also went out on predictive limbs in 1992 with respect to the European Monetary Union (EMU) and NATO. They felt that the original driving force behind these organizations was the threat of Soviet aggression, and they now suspected that (a) Europeans would become more reluctant to sacrifice sovereign control over monetary and fiscal policy to transnational authorities; (b) Europeans would feel less grateful for the American nuclear umbrella and more irritated by the overbearing habits of the American hegemons. With respect to the European Monetary Union, some of these observers went all the way back to 1776 for the right historical analogy, noting that, notwithstanding their shared language and traditions, the thirteen colonies were wary after the Declaration of Independence to go beyond the weak linkages in the Articles of Confederation. The adoption of stronger central government was propelled by desire for common defense. These experts added that the emotional impetus toward the European Monetary Union was fear of repeating World War II. But, as time passes, the old folks die and the younger generation does not share their obsessions about German expansionism. Another camp of premature obituary writers for the EMU suspected that public support for the monetary union would evaporate when people appreciated the sacrifices needed to satisfy the stringent Maastricht convergence requirements for inflation, interest rates, and budget deficits.

Of course, every time hedgehogs of one persuasion suffered a setback, hedgehogs of another persuasion were well positioned to claim credit for their farsightedness. Hedgehog institutionalists were not surprised that the euro project survived currency crises, budgetary squeezes, close-call elections, and political scandals. Whether they grounded their cases in transaction cost economics or the evolving political self-images of Europeans, this camp bet on consolidation and gradual expansion of the transnational regime.

By contrast, foxes doubted that real-world problems could be squeezed, without serious distortion, into syllogistic templates.[18] The grounds for doubt included the following:

a. There is typically ambiguity about which laws apply. This is true, as one fox insisted, even when theory is "as good as it gets" in politics: modeling the vote-winning strategies of candidates. For instance, should we always expect the two major parties' platforms to converge on the preference profile of the median voter? Or should we back off: Have the conditions for applying the theorem been satisfied? Is the issue space one-dimensional? Do small third or fourth parties nullify all predictions? Is the system truly "winner take all?"

b. There is typically ambiguity about how to bridge the gap between ethereal abstractions and grubby facts on the ground. This is most true when we most need guidance. One fox brought up the problem of coping with adversaries. How much weight should policy makers give to deterrence theory (which stresses the dangers of pusillanimity) versus conflict spiral theory (which stresses the dangers of bellicosity)? When does conciliation become appeasement? When does deterrence grade into provocation? Another fox, who knew a lot about Northeast Asia, had a telling response to long lists of "bridging the gap" questions: "If you know the answers, you can read Kim Jong-il's and Jiang Zemin's minds a lot better than I can."

This uneasiness toward the "Hempelian" agenda to reduce history to social science mostly served foxes well. For example, although foxes did not assign as high a probability as hedgehogs to the Yugoslav conflagration, foxes did not overpredict wars: Czechs versus Slovaks, Hungarians versus Romanians, and Russians versus Ukrainians, Lithuanians, Latvians, Estonians, or Kazakhs, or—on a more global scale—civil wars in Nigeria, Pakistan, and South Africa.

---

[18] C. Hempel, "The Function of General Laws in History," in *The Philosophy of History*, ed. Patrick Gardiner (New York: Oxford University Press, 1942).

In the Yugoslav case, trumpeted as a forecasting coup by hedgehog primordialists, some foxes continued to distance themselves from deductive covering laws even *after the fact*. They stressed the complex confluence of events that made war likely but still far from inevitable: a legacy of interethnic hatred that Tito had temporarily suppressed, the power of economic threat to aggravate latent ethnic tensions, the collapse of the bipolar distribution of power on the continent (with the external Soviet threat gone, rival factions felt free to rekindle old hatreds), and the rise to leadership of ruthless populists in Serbia and Croatia. One fox posed a rhetorical counterfactual: "If Havel had been in charge of Serbia, would we have seen this butchery?" A lot of factors had to be in the right (wrong) position to produce this catastrophe.[19]

As a matter of cognitive policy, most foxes felt it foolish to be anchored down by theory-laden abstractions. They often tried, for example to blend opposing hedgehog arguments, such as those over the viability of the EMU. The net result was that they made less extreme predictions but leaned toward the view that the currency convergence project would lurch spasmodically forward, albeit with backsliding whenever satisfying the convergence criteria became too painful. In this unglamorous fashion, foxes wound up with the higher forecasting skill scores.[20]

Several foxes commented that good judges cultivate a capacity "to go with the flow" by improvising dissonant combinations of ideas that capture the "dynamic tensions" propelling political processes. For these self-conscious balancers, the status quo is often in precarious equilibrium and "seeing the truth" is a fleeting achievement for even the most Socratic souls.

---

[19] For conflicting postmortems on Yugoslavia, see "Ex-Yugoslavs on Yugoslavia: As They See It," *Economist* 338 (1996): 5–6; M. Glenny, *The Balkans: Nationalism, War, and the Great Powers, 1804–1999* (New York: Viking, 2000); J. Gowa, *Triumph of the Lack of Will: International Diplomacy and the Yugoslav War* (New York: Columbia University Press, 1997); D. Rieff, *Slaughterhouse: Bosnia and the Failure of the West* (New York: Simon & Schuster, 1995); P. Akhavaran and R. Howse, eds., *Yugoslavia, the Former and Future: Reflections by Scholars from the Region* (Washington: Brookings Institute, 1993); L. J. Cohen, *Broken Bonds: Yugoslavia's Disintegration and Balkan Politics in Transition* (Boulder, CO: Westview Press, 1995); L. J. Cohen, *The Serpent in the Bosom: The Rise and Fall of Slobodan Milosovic* (Boulder, CO: Westview Press, 2000).

[20] For conflicting views of the viability of the European Monetary Union, see Timothy G. Ash, "The European Orchestra," *New York Review of Books*, May 17, 2001, 60–65; P. Gowan and P. Anderson, eds., *The Question of Europe* (Verso, London, 1997); M. Feldstein, "Europe Can't Handle the Euro," *Wall Street Journal*, February 8, 2000; "A Survey of Europe: A Work in Progress," *Economist*, October 23, 1999; P. De Grauwe, *Economics of Monetary Union*, 4th ed. (Oxford: Oxford University Press, 2000); S. F. Overturk, *Money and European Union* (New York: St. Martin's Press, 1997); K. Dyson, ed., *The Road to Maastricht: Negotiating Economic and Monetary Union* (Oxford: Oxford University Press, 1999); B. Eichengreen, *The Political Economy of European Monetary Integration*

Foxes Are Warier of Simple Historical Analogies

Foxes saw kernels of truth in casual comparisons between Saddam Hussein and Hitler, F. W. de Klerk and Mikhail Gorbachev, de Gaulle and Yeltsin, Putin and Pinochet, and Saudi Arabia in the late 1990s and Iran in the late 1970s. But they were aware of the imperfections in each analogy: they looked at hypothesis-disconfirming mismatches as well as hypothesis-confirming matches. As the following examples show, foxes were more disposed than hedgehogs to invoke multiple analogies for the same case.

POST-COMMUNIST RUSSIA (EARLY 1992)

Pessimistic hedgehogs found many reasons to despair over Russia's future. One popular analogy was to Serbia—an analogy that warned of an irredentist Russia that would fight to reincorporate compatriots who suddenly found themselves on the wrong sides of new post-Soviet borders. An even more ominous analogy invoked the specter of Weimar Germany: it warned of total collapse followed by a ferocious pan-Slavic backlash. Imagine not a minor-league tyrant like Milosevic but a Russian Hitler.

The pessimists also generated—again in classic hedgehog fashion—a battery of reinforcing arguments. They warned of how the risks of irredentism were aggravated by the "political immaturity" of Russians: "Generations of Russians have been indoctrinated that private property is theft." They warned of how wrenching economic reform would be, of how low production would plummet and of how high inflation would soar, and of how ripe "Weimar Russia" would become for fascist demagoguery. And they pointed to the precarious legitimacy of democratic institutions and to the power of well-connected insiders to subvert privatization.

The pessimists also saw disturbing portents of the fragmentation of Russia itself, still a great nuclear power if nothing else, into regional fiefs. They noted that, within eighteen months of the collapse of the Soviet Union, the Russian army had fought brushfire ethnic wars in Georgia, Moldova, and Tajikistan (and two warned of looming horrors in Chechnya). The right analogy becomes pre-disintegration Yugoslavia or Austro-Hungary. One expert suggested that Russia by 1997 would control only half of the territory it controlled in 1992.

(Boulder, CO: Westview Press, 2000); J. Story and I. Walter, eds., *Political Economy of Financial Integration in Europe: The Battle of the Systems* (Cambridge: MIT Press, 1998); K. R. McNamara, *The Currency of Ideas: Monetary Politics in the European Union* (Ithaca, NY: Cornell University Press, 1998); J. Mills, *Europe's Economic Dilemma* (New York: Macmillan, 1998).

Optimists countered that Russia now had many attributes of a Western nation. They argued that, contrary to stereotype, Russians were not rabidly xenophobic or opposed to economic incentives. One optimist took heart from the growing use by Russians of the word "sovok" to describe their degradation under totalitarianism. Thoughtful Russians understood the need to change their own underlying psychology, to shift from thinking about "who will destroy whom" to thinking about compromise, persuasion, and mutual benefit.

By contrast, optimistic hedgehogs pointed to Deng Xiaoping or Pinochet as models of what ruthless leadership can accomplish. Although even the most optimistic did not claim Russia had the ingredients for "civil society," some believed that, after a bout of enlightened authoritarianism, Russia could emerge as a "normal European country" in the next ten years.

Foxes could also be divided into pessimistic and optimistic subspecies but, as usual, they shied away from extreme predictions. Most favored "muddling through" scenarios over the doomsday scenarios of harsh authoritarianism or civil war, or the rosy scenarios of free markets and democracy. Foxes appreciated the prescriptive power of the economic laws underlying shock therapy but also appreciated warnings that rapid change could produce nasty backlash and that, without proper legal infrastructure, privatization would just enrich the nomenklatura. One fox saw Russians as "profoundly ambivalent:" they admire the West but they resent it, they yearn for authoritarianism but they thirst for freedom, they dislike capitalism but hold its products in awe. The fence-sitting foxes covered their bets by expecting Russia to zigzag between advancing and retreating from Western ideas of progress.[21]

INDIA (MID-1988)

Pessimistic hedgehogs saw two principal threats to peace and prosperity: chaos induced by religious violence and economic stagnation induced

[21] For conflicting views of what went wrong in the first post-Communist decade in Russia, see R. L. Garthoff, "The United States and the New Russia: The First Five Years," *Current History* 96(612) (1997): 305–12; M. I. Goldman, "Russia's Reform Effort: Is There Growth at the End of the Tunnel?" *Current History* 96(612) (1997): 313–18; M. McFaul, "Democracy Unfolds in Russia," *Current History* 96(612) (1997): 319–25; G. Soros, "Who Lost Russia?" *New York Review*, April 2000, 10–16; T. E. Graham Jr., "The Politics of Power in Russia," *Current History* 98(630) (1999): 316–21; J. R. Millar, "The De-development of Russia," *Current History* 98(630) (1999): 322–27; R. P. Powaski, "Russia: The Nuclear Menace Within," *Current History* 98(630) (1999): 340–45; "Russia: Things Fall Apart; the Centre Cannot Hold," *The World in 1999 Economist* (2000): 60; "The Battle of Russia's Capitalisms," *Economist* 344 (1997): 14; Archie Brown, *Contemporary Russian Politics: A Reader* (Oxford: Oxford University Press, 2001); David D. Laitin, *Identity in Formation: The Russia-speaking Populations in the Near Abroad* (Ithaca, NY: Cornell University Press, 1998).

by overregulation. The gloomiest expected that a BJP (a Hindu fundamentalist party) electoral victory would reinvigorate Hindu-Muslim conflict in India and precipitate disputes with Pakistan that could escalate
into conventional or even nuclear war. They likened the BJP to the Nazi
Party in the dying days of the Weimar Republic (the Weimar analogy
makes an encore appearance).[22] One pessimist expanded on the comparison: "Sure, I see similarities: the BJP are Aryan supremists who direct
party thugs against an unpopular minority. That should ring a bell." Another pessimist characterized India as "geopolitically isolated and economically frail . . . , surrounded by an erratic Muslim adversary to the
west and a menacing Chinese adversary to the north, and fated to collapse into sectarian violence in the next decade."

Optimists countered that the BJP knows it must tone down the extremists in its ranks: "Although its leaders tactically stir up religious pas-
sions, they know violence will turn off the middle class whom they must
woo to win power." Some optimists even argued that India needed a BJP
government to break up the miasma of nepotism and inefficiency left in
the wake of the Congress Party's long hold on power. In 1993, in a five-
year follow-up assessment, another optimist maintained that, regardless
of who forms the government in Delhi, the economic reform program
started by Rao's government in 1991 is irreversible and will transform
India from a "shackled giant" into an economic powerhouse. India was
on the same economic trajectory as China ten years earlier (early 1980s).
His lament was that the residual ideology of the British Labor Party in
India's Congress Party had proven so much harder to shake off than Mao-
ism in China's Communist Party. Sometimes there is a benefit in being
"outlandishly wrong."

By 1998, foxes were closer to striking the right balance. The BJP did
take power and it did play a provocative nuclear card (a series of under-
ground tests that prompted retaliatory Pakistani tests). But the BJP did
not live up to its advance billing as proto-Nazi. It presided over a reasonably intact polity. And it edged India toward overdue economic reforms. The economy was growing but not as fast as China's and only
barely fast enough to keep pace with population.

KAZAKHSTAN (EARLY 1992)

One hedgehog pessimist—with a low threshold for warning of interethnic violence almost everywhere—characterized Kazakhstan as a
"Yugoslavia writ large, . . . a multiethnic cauldron on the verge of boiling

---

[22] Some influential historians argue that those who invoke the Weimar analogy fail to
appreciate how unlikely the Hitler outcome was even toward the very end of the Weimar
Republic. (H. Turner, *Hitler's 30 Days to Power* [New Haven, CT: Yale University Press,
1997].)

over." He feared nuclear weapons inherited from the Soviet Union falling into the hands of extremists. Nuclear civil war or proliferation to terrorists ranked among the most depressing of the downbeat scenarios.

Boomster hedgehogs saw Kazakhstan as a potentially rich country, endowed with massive oil and mineral reserves. One depicted President Nazarbayev as an Ataturk figure: a savvy, secular politician who knew how to mollify Kazakh anger and calm Russian fears and as a forceful autocrat capable of alternating between crushing and buying off domestic opposition.

The foxes leaned slightly toward the optimists, but they saw validity in both sets of arguments, and this habit of open-mindedness (or fence-sitting) served them well. The future of Kazakhstan was nowhere near as bleak as the pessimists had feared, but economic growth rates fell short of the optimists' projections and so did progress toward rule of law and democracy.[23]

POLAND (EARLY 1992)

Although shock therapy regimens varied in rigor of implementation and sensitivity to safety net concerns, the policies had enough in common to become the epicenter of heated debate in the post-Communism policy literature. Left-wing hedgehogs did not disguise their annoyance at purveyors of shock therapy advice to states struggling to manage the transition from state-controlled economies to free markets. They felt that the fiscal and monetary policies embraced by the Polish government would produce political instability, not economic prosperity. The inevitable backlash in response to the anticipated spikes in inflation and unemployment would pave the way for demagogues—"Polish Perons"—who would do for Poland what the original Peron did for Argentina: set it back by decades.

These observers overestimated the pain and instability that would be linked to transition not only for Poland but for several other economies, including the Czech Republic, Hungary, Estonia, and Lithuania. Peronist demagogues have yet to take power in these states. But these observers were right that there was some backlash and radically reconstructed Communist parties did sometimes regain power. These parties were socialist, though, in name only and were loath to tamper with an economic formula that seemed to be working.

[23] For contending views of the future of Kazakhstan, see R. C. Kelly, *Country Review, Kazakhstan 1998/1999* (New York: Commercial Data International, 1998); M. Alexandrov, *Uneasy Alliance: Relations between Russia and Kazakhstan in the Post-Soviet Era, 1992–1997* (Westport, CT: Greenwood Press, 1999); E. Gurgen, H. Sniek, J. Craig, and J. McHugh, eds., "Economic Reforms in Kazakhstan, Kyrgyz Republic, Tajikstan, Turkmenistan, and Uzbekistan" (Occasional Paper, International Monetary Fund No. 183).

Hedgehogs of the neoclassical economic persuasion were right that, properly implemented, their prescriptions would eventually breathe new life into moribund economies: "The same formula worked in Bolivia and it will work in Poland." However, these hedgehogs were insensitive to the intensity of resistance to reform from entrenched interests. One hedgehog noted: "I knew what they should do, but I couldn't tell you when it would dawn on them to do it."

Foxes made many of the aforementioned mistakes. On average, though, foxes who wove together dissonant analogies and covering laws were well positioned to reap a few of the forecasting successes, and to avoid some of the bigger failures, of both hedgehog camps.[24]

WAITING FOR THE LAST COMMUNIST "DOMINOES" TO FALL (1992)

After the collapse of the USSR, many "triumphalist" hedgehogs predicted the imminent collapse of Communist regimes beyond Eastern Europe. Some predictions were bull's-eyes (e.g., Ethiopia), but others have yet to come true (e.g., North Korea, Cuba).

The bleakest hedgehog visions for the Korean peninsula raised the specter of nuclear apocalypse. One Götterdämmerung, Hitler-in-the-bunker, scenario depicted a North Korean leadership that lashes out in deranged desperation at the South. A second scenario depicted a more rational leadership in Pyongyang that engages in calculated nuclear blackmail and, if need be, reinforces its threats by "lobbing a few radioactive artillery shells across the DMZ into downtown Seoul." A third scenario involved a Romanian-style meltdown of the North Korean polity, with pitched battles between rival military and security force units. The civil war could not last long—because resources are scarce—but hundreds of thousands would die of violence, starvation, and disease. South Korea would be left to clean up the irradiated ruins.

More optimistic scenarios assigned less rigidity to the top North Korean leadership. One argument held that Kim Jong-il was a closet reformer who, when his father died, would open North Korea up to foreign investment while simultaneously clamping down the political "lid," following Deng Xiaoping, not Gorbachev. The most optimistic scenario posited gradual liberalization and merging of the two Koreas, following the German model.

[24] For competing perspectives on how Poland and other East European economies should have managed the post-Communist transition to market economies, see H. Kierzkowski, M. Okolski, and W. Stanislaw, eds., *Stabilization and Structural Adjustment in Poland* (London: Routledge, 1993); F. Millard, *Politics and Society in Poland* (London: Routledge, 1999); K. Cordell, *Poland and the European Union* (London: Routledge, 2000); R. F. Starr, ed., *Transition to Democracy in Poland*, 2nd ed. (New York: St. Martin's Press, 1998); J. Adam, *Social Costs of Transformation to a Market Economy in Post-Socialist Countries* (New York: Palgrave, 2000).

Foxes straddled this divide. Most viewed the North Korean leadership as cunning psychopaths who understood the logic of power and the weakness of the hand they had to play, hence the need for lots of blustering. They also expected subtle nuclear blackmail to extort food, oil, and hard currency critical for maintaining the regime's "elaborate patronage network." They expected painfully slow movement toward opening the country to foreign investment because "more than anything the Kim dynasty fears destabilization."[25]

Turning to Cuba, hedgehogs on the right thought that, with the loss of Soviet subsidies, Castro's regime would fall quickly. Foxes warned that the simple puppet regime model underlying such forecasts was flawed in three ways: (1) The Cuban leadership was drawing lessons from the collapse of communism elsewhere. Castro would not liberalize, but he would purge deadwood in the party before compelled to do so; (2) Castro is "a quick study" and would "squelch any well-dressed technocrats of the sort who ousted the old guard in the Soviet Union." And "he won't repeat the mistakes of vain tyrants (in Nicaragua, Chile, etc.) who believed their own propaganda, called elections, and got crushed"; (3) Unlike the East European regimes, Castro is "an authentic revolutionary" who retains some legitimacy. "Although his disapproval ratings may be high (who really knows), there is no opposition to mobilize the discontent. And Castro can still blame the American embargo. It is a cliché but it is still true. With enemies like the United States, Castro may not need friends."

Foxes who foresaw a combination of economic misery and political stability, plus continued impasse with the United States and a frantic scramble for hard currency, were better forecasters. But foxes did not disagree with hedgehogs who defended their predictions of imminent collapse by arguing that they were just off on timing. Foxes agreed that "after Fidel, all bets are off. The two nations are destined—by geography and demography—to be close." At the same time, foxes were not impressed by the off-on-timing defense. One fox paraphrased Keynes: "Sure, they'll be right in the long run. But in the long run, even Fidel will be dead."[26]

[25] A RAND report of the period captures the range of possible futures deemed plausible by our specialists: Jonathan Pollack and Chung Min Lee, *Preparing for Korean Unification: Scenarios and Implications* (Santa Monica: RAND, 1999). For regional ramifications, see H. Chang, "South Korea: Anatomy of a Crisis," *Current History* 97(623) (1998): 437–41; T. Inoguchi and G. B. Stillman, eds., *North-East Asian Regional Security* (Tokyo: United Nations University Press, 1997); D. Levin, "What If North Korea Survives?" *Survival* 39 (1997–98): 156–74.

[26] For premature announcements of Castro's demise as well as analyses of how Castro outlasted his Soviet patrons, see A. Oppenheimer, *Castro's Final Hour: The Secret Story Behind the Coming Downfall of Communist Cuba* (New York: Simon & Schuster, 1993); D. J. Fernandez, *Cuba and the Politics of Passion* (Austin: University of Texas Press, 2000);

SAUDI ARABIA (1992)

Hedgehog observers who foresaw the demise of the ruling al-Saud family brought up the precedents of coups and revolutions that had deposed monarchies in the Middle East over the last five decades, putting special emphasis on the Islamic revolution that smashed the shah's regime in Iran. They also had no difficulty in generating reasons to bolster this prediction: the growing clamor among Wahhabi clerics for stricter enforcement of Islamic law, the growing corruption and declining legitimacy of the government, growing budget deficits that would eat away at the lavish welfare state, growing discontent among the well-educated elite who want democracy, and a growing sense of relative deprivation among lower-middle-class Saudis that would make them receptive to fundamentalist appeals. One pessimist mused: "The Saudis have a split personality: one part Islamic Vatican and one part gas station to the world." Another pessimist wrote off most Saudi princes as "Arab versions of the Beverly Hillbillies."

By now, we should have acquired the foxlike habit of being wary of the sound of one analogical hand clapping. Foxes listened to both hands but gave more weight to hedgehog experts who emphasized the enormous resources controlled by the king, the loyalty of the military and police, and the adroitness with which the opposition has in the past either been intimidated or co-opted. One fox, responding to the "hillbillies" remark, observed, "Maybe so, but that works to their advantage. Back in the 1970s the shah of Iran lectured King Fahd that he should follow the shah's example and modernize lest he lose his throne. Fahd responded that he appreciated the shah's advice but Reza Pahlavi should not forget that he is shah of Iran, not France. Sophistication can be fatal."

The foxes emerged relatively unscathed. They put more weight on the arguments for the perpetuation of the status quo (in the words of one fox, "Betting against governments is usually a bad bet"). But they conceded a risk that the "tiger" that the Saudi elite is feeding (puritanical clerics sympathetic to terrorism) might eventually "chew them to pieces and spit them out." Hedgehog performance was weighted down by those who prematurely consigned the Saudi royalty to the ash heap of history.[27]

E. A. Cardoso, *Cuba After Communism* (Cambridge: MIT Press, 1992); H. M. Erisman and J. M. Kirk, *Cuba's Foreign Relations in a Post-Soviet World* (Gainesville: University Press of Florida, 2000); D. E. Schulz, ed., *Cuba and the Future* (Westport, CT: Greenwood, 1994).

[27] For samplings from this rancorous debate: J. K. Aburish, *The Rise, Corruption and Coming Fall of the House of Saud* (St. Martin's Press, 1996); H. Khashan, *Arabs and the*

ANALOGICAL PERSPECTIVES ON THE ROOT CAUSES OF WAR AND PEACE

No discussion of analogical mapping would be complete without the two pivotal geopolitical analogies of the twentieth century: the Munich appeasement episode (the lodestar for deterrence theorists who fear that weakness will tempt ruthless adversaries to press harder) and the six-week crisis preceding World War I (the lodestar for conflict spiral theorists who fear that misunderstanding can lead to wars that no one wanted). Conflict spiral observers had lower thresholds for sending out strong warnings of the dangers of old enmities igniting into new wars (from Cyprus to Golan to Kashmir to the Taiwan Straits and the Korean DMZ) and of the dangers of new nuclear powers using their weapons against old adversaries. One hedgehog spiral theorist foresaw a nuclear war over Kashmir "that would grow out of a guerrilla skirmish that triggers an Indian retaliatory strike that, in turn . . ., and eventually Islamabad or Delhi becomes convinced that they are in a 'use them or lose-them' situation, that a preemptive strike is essential, and suddenly more people are dead than in World War II." He felt that the temptation to strike first will be strong for a dangerously long time too because neither side would have secure second-strike capabilities any time soon. He saw similarities to "the rigid mobilization schedules that locked the great powers of Europe into the escalatory cycle preceding World War I."

Hedgehog deterrence theorists did not dismiss the possibility of brush-fire wars, especially in areas where the deep-pocketed Americans have little interest in "incentivizing" good behavior. And they did not dispute that "rogue states" had active programs to procure weapons of mass destruction. But they saw the problems as manageable as long as the right deterrence messages are sent out: messages should begin with "develop" or "use these weapons" and end with "it will be the end of you, your regime, and possibly your country." Whether threats were predicated on "develop" or "use" hinged on judgments of rationality. Those inclined to preemption feared weapons falling into the hands of risk-seeking leaders or messianic movements. Those inclined to see containment and deterrence as stable saw no reason to suppose that "Kim Jong-il or Saddam Hussein harbors more of a death wish than Stalin or Mao" (both of whom had their fingers on the nuclear trigger). "These guys are consummate survivors." One deterrence theorist advanced the counterfactual that if Nazi Germany had existed in a world of mutual assured destruction, there would have been no second world war: "Even Hitler, the

Crossroads: Political Identity and Nationalism (Gainesville: University Press of Florida, 2000); G. L. Simmons, *Saudi-Arabia: The Shape of a Client Feudalism* (New York: Palgrave, 1999); N. Safran, *Saudi Arabia: The Senseless Quest for Security* (Cambridge, MA: Belknap Press of Harvard University Press, 1985).

twentieth century's poster boy of malign irrationality, would have behaved more cautiously."

Foxes clustered around more middle-of-the-road analyses. They conceded that peace requires deftly managing balance-of-power relationships and implementing credible deterrence commitments. But they also saw real risks of provoking desperate states and setting off conflict spirals that could be avoided by adopting a more empathic posture. These foxes made mental room for two contradictory propositions: (a) nuclear proliferation is not as dangerous as supposed because such weapons (coupled with secure second-strike capabilities) induce caution; (b) nuclear proliferation is every bit as dangerous as widely supposed because, absent 100 percent confidence in the leadership and command and control of each new nuclear power, each instance of proliferation has the net effect—after subtracting out the benefits of mutual deterrence—of increasing the likelihood of nuclear war.[28] One fox gets the last word: "I'm not smart enough to know who is right. I'm not sure anyone is. We don't have a lot of experience with nuclear war."

Foxes are Less Likely to Get Swept Away in Their Own Rhetoric

Hedgehogs reminded one fox of Churchill's definition of a fanatic: someone who cannot change his mind and will not change the subject. This was, of course, unfair: most hedgehogs were not fanatics. But it was true that, once many hedgehogs boarded a train of thought, they let it run full throttle in one policy direction for extended stretches, with minimal braking for obstacles that foxes took as signs they were on the wrong track. We see this phenomenon most clearly when hedgehogs launch into arguments with self-reinforcing feedback loops that, left unchecked, lead to predictions of radical change. For instance, pessimistic hedgehogs readily constructed loops in which "bad causes" like hatred, poverty, and environmental degradation produced bad effects that, in turn, became bad causes that led to more of the same. Optimistic hedgehogs were equally adept at working in the opposite direction: "good causes" like the rule of law, freedom of inquiry, and market competition produced good effects that, in turn, became good causes that led to more of the same.[29]

The downside risk was that when hedgehogs were wrong, they were often very wrong. The long list of predictions gone awry includes the disintegration of nation-states that are still with us (Canada, Nigeria,

[28] S. Sagan and K. Waltz, *The Spread of Nuclear Weapons: A Debate* (New York: W. W. Norton, 1995).

[29] For a rich analysis of systems thinking in world politics, see R. Jervis, *Systems Effects* (Princeton, NJ: Princeton University Press, 1997).

India, Pakistan, Indonesia, Iraq, etc.), the collapse of powerful political parties (such as the Swedish Social Democrats, the British Labor and later the Conservative parties, the Cuban Communist Party and the Republican Party in the United States), a global depression precipitated by meltdowns of equity markets in the leading economies and debt defaults by less developed economies, and nuclear wars in the Indian subcontinent triggered by the Kashmir conflict and in the Korean peninsula by the enigmatic personality cult regime in Pyongyang.

But there was also upside potential in this aggressive intellectual style, which will be explored more in chapter 6. Hedgehogs made many mistakes, but when they were right, they were very right. When stunning discontinuities took almost everyone by surprise, it was a good bet that a few hedgehogs would be left standing to take credit for anticipating what no one else did. The trade-off here should be familiar to baseball fans. Home run hitters know that they need to swing hard at a lot of pitches. They also know they will strike out frequently, but they judge the price acceptable if they can hit enough home runs. Experts who in 1988 predicted the collapse of the USSR in 1993 might be forgiven for "overpredicting" the collapse of other regimes.

To resist the conformity pressures of conventional opinion as tenaciously as some hedgehogs do, self-confidence is essential—and self-reinforcing feedback loops are powerful confidence generators. Hedgehogs often intuitively appreciated this point. The more senior ones reported that, in their mentoring, they stressed the dangers of "analysis-paralysis" and the benefits of taking bold stands that do not bend with the changing winds of intellectual fashion.

Foxes Are More Worried about Our Judging Those in the Past Too Harshly (and Less Worried about Those in the Future Judging Us Harshly for Failing to see the Obvious)

Many hedgehogs were skilled at convincing not just others, but themselves. Some even talked themselves into the curious mental state of "anticipatory hindsight."[30] After generating a battery of reasons that made his predicted outcome seem foreordained by a divinity with whom he was on intimate terms ("from God's lips to my ears"), one hedgehog paused to ponder how today's concerns will look to tomorrow's chroniclers: "Historians will wonder how so many smart people could have been so myopic." The psycho-logic is straightforward. What the future holds in store is, from his point of view, already obvious. It will therefore be even more obvious to historians of the future. It will

---

[30] See Fischhoff, "Hindsight," for the classic experimental demonstration of the effect.

also be obvious to those historians that it should have been obvious to us. The warning signs were too plain for all but the obdurately obtuse to ignore.

A sampling of conflicting hedgehog arguments bearing on possible futures facing the United States in 1992–93 conveys the flavor of the anticipatory hindsight effect. Back then, it was not unusual for pessimistic hedgehogs to pronounce on the inevitability of American decline, with rhetorical flourishes such as "Decline, like fog, creeps up on civilizations on little cat's feet" and "It has not yet dawned on most Americans, but our decline is well under way." Indeed, any doomster worth his or her salt could (and some still can) generate a list of reasons why decline was inevitable. One left-of-center hedgehog argued: "The government spends far more than it raises in taxes. We consume more than we produce. We borrow more than we save. We import more than we export. We are on the fast track to second-class status." He compared "free-market ideologues" to the "sailor on the *Titanic* who declared that God Almighty could not sink this ship. Every great power before us thought itself immune from decline, and none was right." We should learn from the base-rate fate of previous great powers.

Optimistic hedgehogs expected the opposite with equal conviction. One opined that "future generations will laugh at the neurotic pessimism of today's pundits, with their hand-wringing about global warming and Western decline." The dominant forces in the twenty-first century will converge into a self-amplifying virtuous circle in which "economic development stimulates democracy, instantaneous cross-border communications undercut oppressive governments, and democracy lays the foundation for the rule of law necessary for markets to flourish." Early twentieth-century optimists, like Norman Angell who thought the great powers had become too interdependent to go to war again, were merely premature. Humanity is moving fitfully but inexorably toward a peaceful capitalist global order. Only the pedantic would split hairs over whether humanity reaches its destination in the twenty-first or twenty-second centuries. This preemptive off-on-timing defense gives forecasters a century's worth of wiggle room.

Whereas hedgehogs were preoccupied with the dangers of underplaying their intellectual hand, foxes frequently expressed mirror-image concerns. One respondent captured in an introspective moment a defining marker of the fox temperament: "Whenever I start to feel certain I am right . . . a little voice inside tells me to start worrying." Self-criticism had been elevated to declaratory cognitive policy. Confidence beyond a certain point became a sign not that one is right but rather that one may be wrong, and that the time had come to brake the train of thought driving confidence into the zone of hubris.

The thought protocols yielded numerous such examples. The fate of the American economy in the late 1990s—in particular, its high-tech sectors—offers an instructive reversal of the dour "declining empire" talk of the 1980s. Although it is difficult to re-create emotional atmospherics in the wake of the NASDAQ crash in 2000, it is worth recalling that many forecasts were beyond upbeat. They were euphoric: Dow 36,000, telecommuting eliminating rush-hour traffic jams, Web retailers driving brick-and-mortar stores out of business, interactive televisions allowing couch potatoes to alter plots from their armchairs, universities swept away by on-line learning, and near-instantaneous electronic flows of capital making borders obsolete.

The errant predictions were driven by unchecked momentum. If a proposal passed the low-hurdle "can I believe this" test, boomster technophiles did not pause to ponder potential resistance from flesh-and-blood humans who have deep-rooted social needs and work within remarkably durable social systems. Of course, the boomster technophiles can argue that they were "just off on timing" and that variants of all their predictions will still come true. But a dose of foxlike prudence would have spared this group considerable embarrassment.[31]

A final example of the perils of not knowing when to apply the mental brakes comes from the 1992 Ukrainian forecasts. In a debriefing interview, I gave one easy-to-spot fox the explanations that an equally easy-to-spot hedgehog had given for his pessimism. The hedgehog had argued: "Things did not have to be this awful. The Ukraine was once a wealthy part of the Russian empire. . . . But the current leadership is hopeless. These party chieftains don't have the faintest idea why they can't just print money. As for rule of law, they play by Brezhnevist rules. So we have Mafia-style cronyism, a bad-joke currency and the squandering of resources on value-subtractive state enterprises. I see hyperinflation and massive unemployment in the next few years and a debt-to-GDP ratio going through the roof." This expert had an accurate bead on Ukrainian economic performance in the 1990s, but he went overboard in predicting war and border change. He foresaw growing tensions with Russia that would culminate in interethnic violence, a Russian energy embargo and military intervention to protect Russians, and the forced ceding of territory to mother Russia.

The fox replied: "I don't disagree with anything he said. But he did not allow for the chance the Ukrainians will come to their senses. The formula for recovery will become undeniable in the next five years: just

---

[31] For perhaps the shortest-lived boomster predictions: Joel Kurtzman and Glenn Rifkin, *Radical E: from G. E. to Enron, Lessons on How to Rule the Web* (New York: John Wiley & Sons, 2001).

look west." The fox also doubted the "tightness" of the connection between economic implosion and violent conflict with Russia. He suspected that the Ukrainian leadership would not recklessly provoke the Russians and that the Russians were not spoiling for a fight. Wariness of facile generalizations helped this fox forge an integrative set of economic and political expectations that were more accurate than that of most other specialists.[32]

I also asked several foxes to comment on the phenomenon of anticipatory hindsight. Some thought it possible that we, the inhabitants of the present, might be deemed dumb by inhabitants of the future for failing to see beyond our noses. But most found the mirror-image error more worrisome: the danger that we, the inhabitants of the present, are unfairly blaming the inhabitants of the past for failing to predict the unpredictable. One fox waxed metaphysical: "Sure, we now know what happened. But before we scold the imbeciles back then for their stupidity, let's imagine how many other things could have happened and, if one of them had, how that would transform the grand lessons we draw from history." (Chapter 5 multiplies these examples of foxes' greater sensitivity to "close-call counterfactuals.") Another fox was sensitive to the power of the mind to play tricks on us: "We forget how clueless everyone was about how things were going to work out in the Soviet Union in 1988. . . . It feels good to lord over those saps who could not see beyond their noses." Good judges retain memory traces of their prior opinions even after they know what needs to be explained. It encourages humility.

Foxes See More Value in Keeping "Political Passions Under Wraps"

Many participants hailed from academic fields regularly roiled by accusations of politicized scholarship—fields in which critics on the right accuse the left of serving as chronic apologists for Soviet tyranny or Latin American corruption or Islamic terrorism, whereas critics on the left

---

[32] For possible futures of the Ukraine, see P. D'Anieri, *Politics and Society in Ukraine (Westview Series on the Post-Soviet Republics)* (Boulder, CO: Westview Press, 1999); K. Dawisha and B. Parrott, preface to *Democratic Changes and Authoritarian Reactionism in Russia, Ukraine, Belarus and Moldova* (Cambridge: Cambridge University Press, 1997); T. Kuzio, R. S. Kravchuk, and P. D'Anieri, eds., *State and Institution Building in Ukraine* (New York: Palgrave, 2000); P. D'Anieri, *Economic Interdependence in Ukranian-Russian Relations* (New York: State University of New York Press, 1999); I. Prizel, *National Identity and Foreign Policy: Nationalism and Leadership in Poland, Russia, and Ukraine* (New York: Cambridge University Press, 1998); G. K. Bertsch and W. C. Potter, eds., *Dangerous Weapons, Desperate States: Russia, Belarus, Kazakhstan, and Ukraine* (London: Routledge, 1999); A. Wilson, *The Ukrainians: Unexpected Nation* (New Haven, CT: Yale University Press, 2001); R. Szporluk, *Russia, Ukraine and the Breakup of the Soviet Union* (Stanford: Hoover Institution, 2001).

portray the right as chronic apologists for American imperialism and multinational corporations.

Foxes, as usual, saw some merit in the accusations leveled by each side. But they did not mindlessly split the differences. Most foxes could identify academic fields that they felt had become so suffused with bias that only a vocal minority dared to state obvious but unpleasant truths. One conservative fox observed: "Too many of my colleagues have a "hear no evil, see no evil" attitude toward groups that have gotten a raw deal from the West. So they worry about the feelings of poor Soviet apparatchiks being insulted by Reagan's evil-empire talk, or poor finance ministers from sub-Saharan Africa being insulted by International Monetary Fund (IMF) technocrats who impose so many onerous conditionalities on loans that you might think the ministers themselves were thieves." A second, more liberal, fox thought the key to good judgment was the capacity to distinguish between explanations (which require seeing the world from the other's perspective) and excuses (which require recognizing that just because the other has thoroughly rationalized a policy does not oblige you to embrace the rationalization). A second, quite liberal, fox made a similar point: "It is an admirable human trait to sympathize with the underdog, but it is stupid not to recognize that underdogs can be rabid and vicious." We set ourselves up for nasty surprises when we ignore repugnant characteristics of groups that we believe have been "shafted" by the reigning hegemon. He feared that this "willful blindness" explained why many experts on the Middle East were blindsided by the ferocious repressiveness of the Iranian revolution in the late 1970s and why "the same crew" glossed over the potential for terrorism in the late 1990s. There was no logical reason why one could not simultaneously take the position that the shah of Iran was a corrupt despot whom the Americans inflicted on the Iranian people in 1953 and that Khomeini's brand of Shi'ite fundamentalism had been in many ways worse. Or why one could not simultaneously believe that the Saudi monarchy was abhorrent but that its clerical critics would impose an even worse "Talibanish" regime if they got the chance. A self-described neo-Marxist fox saw a "depressing relationship" between how strongly observers opposed the old white-minority government in South Africa and how reluctant they now are to acknowledge ominous signs of "moral drift" in the new black-majority government ("endemic corruption, a stupid and cruel AIDS policy, and a cowardly unwillingness to condemn Mugabe's tyranny").

Foxes worried about colleagues who had "little stomach for unpalatable truths." A liberal fox pointed to the "hyperventilating" that greeted Huntington's clash of civilizations thesis that "the great source of conflict in the post–cold war world will be cultural." Rather than addressing the argument on its merits, "too many colleagues started slinging epithets—calling Sam a 'racist essentialist.'" A conservative fox thought that his "ideological allies" should be more honest about how unsavory many of America's cold war and post–cold-war allies were. "Would it kill them to admit that Iran is more democratic than Saudi Arabia?" A third fox lamented the reluctance of "idealists" to admit that "America had good balance-of-power reasons during the cold war" for embracing "mind-bogglingly corrupt" dictators such as Mobutu (Zaire/Congo) and Suharto (Indonesia), for supporting the mujahedeen struggle against the Soviet occupation of Afghanistan, for tilting toward Iraq when Iran seemed close to prevailing, and for permitting Saddam to stay in power (after Gulf War I) by massacring Shi'ite rebels in southern Iraq. But this fox also lamented the reluctance of realists to admit that, good though the reasons once were for such policies, there are "blowback risks" in adopting a purely Realpolitik stance: chaos in the Congo and Indonesia, transnational Islamic terrorist networks headquartered in Afghanistan, and the uncertainty over Iraqi weapons of mass destruction. Moral purity takes a toll in predictive accuracy. Ignoring the vices of our friends and the virtues of our enemies sets us up for nasty surprises.[33]

Foxes Make More Self-conscious Efforts to Integrate Conflicting Cognitions

Open-mindedness is no guarantee that one will strike the right balance between the competing arguments that dominate the debate at any moment. Judges who are indiscriminately complex—who enter whatever arguments come to their attention in an automatic balancing act—would be all too easy prey for forceful agenda setters. Good judges need to be judicious: they need to be discerning consumers of the massive flows of information and misinformation circulating through the marketplace of ideas.

Can we say anything more specific about these balancing acts? Did foxes give more weight to certain ideas over others? The answer is usually no. Foxes were not especially likely to endorse particular substantive positions on rationality, levels of analysis, macroeconomics, or foreign policy. Their advantage resided in how they thought, not in what they thought.

It is still instructive, however, to consider foxes' integrative tactics up close. Foxes thought that the propensity of hedgehogs to stake out strong

[33] See R. A. Packenham, *The Dependency Movement: Scholarship and Politics in Development Studies* (Cambridge: Harvard University Press, 1992); Martin Kramer, *Ivory Towers on Sand: The Failure of Middle Eastern Studies in America* (Washington, DC: Washington Institute for Near East Studies, 2001).

positions on "unresolvable foundational issues"—such as the role of human agency in history or the rationality of decision making—was silly. They gravitated instead toward split-the-difference judgments. As the next series of examples underscore, these split judgments were not always right but few were totally wrong and many were spookily prescient.

INTEGRATIVE RESOLUTIONS TO "WHEN DO LEADERS MATTER?"

Although there was wide consensus that leaders are constrained by powerful societal forces, foxes usually balked at the "actor dispensability thesis" that treats leaders as mere conveyor belts. They insisted that sometimes it matters who is in charge and that we should not fall into the trap of either idolizing or demonizing leaders. Good judges are attuned to the power of their own personal predilections to bias their assessments. They recognize that whether leaders ascend to greatness or descend into pettiness depends on complicated match-ups between the inner machinations of leaders' minds and the external machinations of the social system.[34]

USSR (1988). The greater emotional detachment of foxes proved helpful during the endgame phase of the glasnost and perestroika period. Some foxes had a remarkable flair for piecing together discordant arguments that deeply divided the academic and intelligence communities. On the one hand were liberal Sovietologists, who quickly picked up on the significance of Gorbachev (indeed, consistent with the broken-clock theory of forecasting, a few had been predicting the "Moscow spring" that arrived in 1985 for decades). These observers felt that the Soviet system could be both reformable and viable. On the other hand were conservatives, who worked with an "essentialist" view of the Soviet Union and who had a visceral dislike for "Steve Cohen pluralistic Communism" scenarios. Some subscribed—right through the 1980s—to peredyshka or breathing-spell arguments that portrayed Gorbachev "as a neo-Stalinist in Gucci garb."

Certain foxes were well positioned to integrate these contradictory assessments. They agreed with the left that Gorbachev was an earnest reformer and with the right that the Soviet Union was an old-fashioned empire with virtually no legitimacy outside Russia and dubious legitimacy inside Russia. These observers in 1988 foresaw that liberalization

---

[34] Many writers on leadership have reached similar conclusions about the importance of personality-context matches in determining whether leadership styles deliver desired results: D. K. Simonton, *Genius Creativity and Leadership* (Cambridge: Harvard University Press, 1984); D. K. Simonton, *Greatness: Who Makes History and Why* (New York: Guilford Press, 1994); B. Kellerman, ed., *Political Leadership: A Source Book* (Pittsburgh: University of Pittsburgh Press, 1986).

would release pent-up forces that would eventually tear apart the Soviet Union (or lead to a desperate coup by orthodox Communists to stave off disintegration). Great improvement though Gorbachev was over his predecessors, he was doomed to fail. Now that the genie of liberalization had been unbottled, it would be impossible for the top-down liberators in the Kremlin to achieve legitimacy in the eyes of populations that had for decades felt like prisoners of the Soviet Union. Gorbachev was trying, in Yeltsin's words, to square the circle. One farsighted fox opined that perhaps, if Andropov had possessed stronger kidneys, "he might have been able—like Deng—to pull off economic reform and keep the political lid on. But if you wanted to dismantle the Soviet Union cleanly and quickly, you could not have found a better General Secretary than Gorby if you had called up central casting in Langley (CIA headquarters). Small wonder that the Kryuchkov gang thought he was a spy."[35]

Overall, foxes were more open than hedgehogs to psychological analyses of leaders. They felt most leaders had considerable wiggle room. Preferring explanatory closure, hedgehogs found this insistence cloying. It opens the door to butterfly effects—cancerous tumors, love affairs, and assassins' bullets—likely to trick ordinary folks who know firsthand the power of tiny causes to alter the courses of human lives, but who do not possess the professionals' bag of theoretical tricks for bringing history back on track with higher-order what-ifs (see chapter 5).

South Africa (1988).   Many foxes wove optimistic and pessimistic themes into their assessments of South Africa. They mostly concurred with optimists that white-minority rule was doomed. The new generation of Afrikaner leadership—the "verligte" (enlightened) faction within

---

[35] The literature on the disintegration of the Soviet Union includes contributions not just by scholars but by many of the original players who have commented on what they think was or was not possible. In addition to the memoirs of Gorbachev and Ligachev, see Anatoly S. Chernyaev, *My Six Years with Gorbachev* (University Park, PA: Pennsylvania State University Press, 2000). For more detached commentary, see W. Wohlforth, ed., *Witnesses to the End of the Cold War* (Baltimore: Johns Hopkins University Press, 1996); R. Garthoff, *The Great Transition* (Washington, DC: Brookings, 1994); D. Oberdorfer, *The Turn* (New York: Touchstone, 1992). For the argument that Reagan made the cold war last longer, see R. N. Lebow and J. Stein, *We All Lost the Cold War* (Princeton, NJ: Princeton University Press, 1994). For an analysis of internal forces contributing to collapse, see Vladislav Zubok, "The Collapse of the Soviet Union: Leadership, Elites, and Legitimacy," in *The Fall of the Great Powers*, ed. Geir Lundestad (New York: Oxford University Press, 1994). For perspectives that assign credit to Reagan's policies, see Fareed Zakharia, "The Reagan Strategy of Containment," *Political Science Quarterly* (Fall 1990); Peter Schweizer, *Victory: The Reagan Administration's Secret Strategy That Hastened the Collapse of the Soviet Union* (City: Atlantic Monthly Press, 1994); P. Rutland, "Sovietology: Notes for a Post-Mortem," *National Interest* (1993): 109–22; for the role of personal relations in revising Soviet perceptions of Reagan, see William D. Jackson, "Soviet Reassessment of

the National Party—was not nearly as prickly and combative as the old P. W. Botha generation. The new generation could read the writing on the wall: the differential growth rates of the white and black populations, the burgeoning black townships brimming with resentment, and the mounting international pressures for an end to minority rule.

Foxes discounted—although they did not assign zero likelihood to—then influential forecasts of a white backlash that declared: "As soon as de Klerk comes close to an agreement with the African National Congress [ANC], hardliners will stonewall and raise the specter of black Bolsheviks establishing another banana republic." The backlash pessimists foresaw an impasse, with a gradual partitioning of the country into zones of influence accompanied by violence, "the kind of low-grade civil war all too common in sub-Saharan Africa."

Foxes assigned less likelihood to the bleakest scenarios because they had reasons for thinking that moderates in both the ANC and National Party had the political clout to prevent events from sliding into the Hobbesian abyss. Some reasons were structural: the end of the cold war and the waning of Soviet strength made concerns about "black Bolsheviks" sound shrilly anachronistic. Other reasons were interpersonal: the can-do technocrats in the National Party would strike a deal with the Mandela wing of the ANC that would contain enough constitutionally mandated assurances to the white community to marginalize the extremists.

Seeing through the endgame of white-minority rule, in rough outline, was an achievement.[36] In passing, it is worth noting though that the foxes' optimism was characteristically tentative: they shared some of the pessimists' fears about the future—fears that, in contrarian fashion, they expressed even in the happy transitional year of 1994. One fox opined: "If Nelson had Winnie's personality, South Africa under ANC rule would look like Nigeria in fifteen years, maybe less." The foxes worried that, after Mandela, corruption would deepen, white flight would ramp up from trickle to flood, business confidence would erode, and the ANC would resort to "Mugabean" demagoguery to solidify its base. These foxes also

---

Ronald Reagan, 1985–1988," *Political Science Quarterly* (Winter 1998–99): 617–44. For arguments about the Bush administration's missed opportunity of 1989, see Robert Legvold, "Lessons from the Soviet Past," in *Reversing Relations with Former Adversaries: U.S. Foreign Policy after the Cold War,* ed. C. R. Nelson and K. Weisbrode (Gainesville: University Press of Florida, 1998), 17–43.

[36] For conflicting views of what could have happened in South Africa and of what might yet happen, see *Economist,* "The End of the Miracle" (December 13, 1997): 117–19; G. Boynton, *Last Days in Cloud Cuckooland: Dispatches from White Africa* (New York: Random House, 1999); A. Heribert, F. van Zyl Slabbert, and Kogilan Moodley, *Comrades in Business: Post-liberation in South Africa* (Ultrecht: International Books, 1998); "South Africa's Uncertain Future," *Economist* 345 (1997): 17–21.

worried about the fraying of law and order and about public health collapsing under the AIDS epidemic.

Sharp regime changes are rare events. Although foxes were more open to the potential for transformational leadership to produce sharp change in the Soviet Union and South Africa, they were not clairvoyant: they did not always assign high probabilities to what happened, just higher than many others assigned. It also merits note that in other contexts, such as Japan and Nigeria, foxes shifted toward the other side of the opinion continuum and stressed the risks of "more of the same," of policy drift in leadership vacuums.

Japan (1992–1993). The big question was whether the stock market collapse and recession marked the end of the Japanese miracle. The modal answer was no. Most experts expected that Japan would recover, but the majority was thin and it should not mask deep divisions between optimistic and pessimistic hedgehogs, or the more subtle distinctions among foxes who occupied their customary centrist positions.

Pessimists insisted that Japan had reached a turning point. From 1950 to 1990, it had grown richer at a 7.6 percent annual average rate, a record still unsurpassed in the economic history of the world. Slowing growth was to be expected with the narrowing income gap between Japan and other rich countries. One respondent observed: "Japan is no longer playing catch-up: it faces the challenges of economic maturity. . . . Adaptation of foreign technology can no longer be the principal engine of growth. There are too many low-cost competitors, and things are only going to get worse." This pessimist argued that politicians would soon start meddling with policy prerogatives of the technocrats in the hallowed Ministry of International Trade and Industry. "The politicians acquiesced when the technocrats delivered the goods. But this arrangement will unravel as growth slows and the population ages." A blunter observer announced: "The special-interest pigs are jostling at the budgetary trough. The competition for scraps will get nasty."

The ultra-pessimists feared that the real estate and equity bubbles were far from deflated and that bad debts would drive the banking system into bankruptcy, Japan into depression, and the world into recession. They foresaw policy paralysis. "The Liberal Democratic Party [LDP] will be held responsible for this debacle. But no other party will be strong enough to pick up the pieces."

Optimists countered that the secrets of Japan's success were cultural. Japan would not grow as quickly as before, but it would still outperform big industrial economies over the long term. The optimists also believed that Japanese policy makers had "deflated the speculative bubble that had enveloped its financial markets." In 1990, the land prices in Tokyo were reputedly so high that the grounds of the Imperial Palace were worth more than all the real estate in Los Angeles. By 1992, these prices began falling, although even optimists felt not far enough.

As usual, the foxes carved out their niches in the crevices of the grand canyon separating pessimistic and optimistic hedgehogs. On the bright side, they felt that Japan in 1992 still did many things right: high rates of saving, low levels of public spending and taxation, a moderate amount of state intervention, and a pro-business ethos. But they recognized the severity of the crisis. This analysis led to the modal prediction of an unusually protracted recession and Nikkei slump, numerous changes in leadership (probably not, though, triggering the collapse of the LDP in the ten-year range), and a reluctance to impose beneficial reforms that inflicted pain on potent constituencies—a reluctance that could only be overcome if "things get really bad" and a "charismatic leader rises out of the rubble with a mandate to change the old ways of doing business." Foxes knew that strengths can quickly become weaknesses: the cohesive keiretsu networks that worked well in the booming sixties and seventies were now big obstacles to the restructuring demanded by the nineties. By decade's end, pessimistic foxes looked pretty prescient.[37]

Nigeria (1992).   Everyone agreed that Nigeria's problems were severe and traceable to ethnic and religious conflict, bad leadership, and institutionalized thievery on a breathtaking scale. Opinion ran between those anticipating full descent into Hobbesian hell and those expecting continued repression, corruption, and factionalism in the ruling oligarchy.

The most pessimistic hedgehogs believed that Nigeria had been doomed from the start. One expert dismissed Nigeria as being "nothing more than a geographical expression" that, like most nations constructed by colonial powers in the nineteenth century, has "boundaries ridiculously mismatched with the languages and religions of the people who live there." He felt it a minor miracle that the country survived its brush with death during the war of Biafran secession: "The Ibos from the east could have won if two groups that do not get along—the Yorubans from the west and the Hausa from the north—had not joined forces." Other pessimists identified more proximal causes, including the influx of $200 billion of oil money into Nigeria between 1972 and 1992: "This was a

---

[37] M. M. Weinstein, "The Timid Japanese Banking Bailout Just Might Do the Job," *New York Times*, October 22, 1998, C2; "Business in Japan: No More Tears," *Economist* (November 27, 1999): 4–18; "Three Futures for Japan: Views from 2020," *Economist* (March 21, 1998): 25–28; T. L. Friedman, "Japan's Nutcracker Suite," *New York Times*, April 30, 1999, A31; T. J. Pempel, "Japan's Search for a New Path," *Current History* 97(623) (1998): 431–36; "Reality Hits Japan," *Economist* 345 (1997): 15–16; "Japan's Unhappy Introspection," *The World in 1999, Economist* (1998): 33.

mixed blessing. Nigeria was a new nation struggling to leapfrog from feudal fiefdoms to parliamentary democracy. Is it surprising that politicians used public moneys to feather their private nests? The top job meant you and your buddies had hit the jackpot." Another commentator added: "It did not even feel wrong to military and civilian elites. Just the opposite: Their first duty was to look after their own." Far from immoral, nepotism was a communal-sharing obligation.[38]

The optimists could summon only a few feeble counterarguments. Some hoped that the 1992 elections might usher in democracy (a hope quickly dashed). And some hoped that Nigerians have learned from their civil war and other episodes of mass violence to step back from the precipice. These observers added that there has been a lot of internal migration and mixing of groups and that the Nigerian elite now has a strong interest in preserving the country.

Foxes tilted toward the pessimists. They did not expect any transition to democracy soon. More military rule was in Nigeria's near-term future. But foxes qualified their pessimism and this helped them to avoid false alarming on the apocalyptic scenarios endorsed by some hedgehogs.[39] Foxes did not assign zero likelihood to genocidal civil war; they gave it, on average a one in five chance in the ten-year range from 1992, and they thought the likelihood of "something really vicious" would only grow larger the longer the leadership vacuum persisted ("the exasperating unwillingness of elites to rein in the kleptocracy"). Foxes also hedged their bets on the consequences of return to military rule: "It depends on how the coup dice roll." One fox's best bet was that the next cohort of generals would overlap a lot with the previous cohort. The lower-probability outcomes were that the new generals would be worse ("greedier and nastier") or better ("tentative commitment to rule of law"). Again, foxes believed that which future we are funneled into hinges on unpredictable micromediators: the predilections of a small military clique.

HEDGE BETS ON THE RATIONALITY OF LEADERS

Most participants found it unlikely, given the hardscrabble struggle to gain high office, that the upper echelons of leadership would be populated with "idiots." Their first-order assumption was that high-level decision

---

[38] For a bleak, but not unusually so, account of the Nigerian economy and polity, see K. Maier, *This House has Fallen: Midnight in Nigeria* (New York: Public Affairs, 2000). On cross-cultural variation in what constitutes an appropriate exchange, see A. Fiske and P. E. Tetlock, "Taboo Trade-offs: Reactions to Transactions That Transgress Spheres of Justice," *Political Psychology* 18 (1997): 255–97.

[39] A sign of the hedgehogs' intensity of conviction here: in the five-year 1997 follow-up, hedgehogs who judged the disintegration of Nigeria to be the most likely class of possible futures in 1992 were in no mood to back off: "OK, so it did not happen in that time frame

makers are "smart," by which they meant adept at using "interactive knowledge" to anticipate the reactions of key players in the domestic and international power games that determine whether posterity labels them successes or failures. Foxes differed from hedgehogs, though, in how quickly they modified this first-order assumption when decision makers behaved unexpectedly "irrationally." The foxes more promptly did one of two things: (1) scaled down their estimates of rationality and looked for mind-sets blinkering perceptions of reality at the top; or (2) changed their assessments of the two-level-game constraints within which decision makers had to work.[40]

Persian Gulf War I (1990–1991). Observers familiar with the relative military capabilities of the antagonists, and with local geography and climate, dismissed dire estimates in the fall of 1990 that the land war would last years and claim between twenty thousand and fifty thousand American casualties: "Doves are picking numbers out of thin air to scare Congress and public opinion. They are wrong. This is no Vietnam." These observers included an even mixture of foxes and hedgehogs and they recognized that, if there were to be war, it would be a quick American win. But hedgehogs who worked from rational actor premises frequently took the argument further: "Saddam is as smart as I am and recognizes that he will hang, and not just metaphorically, if he fails to loosen the alliance noose tightening around his neck." This analysis led many hedgehog rational actor theorists to the incorrect surmise that Saddam would in the next few months preemptively withdraw from part or all of Kuwait.

Foxes did not dismiss this possibility—they rarely assign zero probabilities—but they gave greater weight to the possibilities either that Saddam had not correctly sized up the military predicament ("He thinks he can bloody up the weak-kneed Americans in the ground war so they will retreat") or that Saddam had compelling political reasons for refusing to retreat ("Saddam may think it better to be a rooster for a day than a chicken for all eternity. Being a chicken for all eternity is not an option in Ba'ath politics. Chickens get slaughtered"). Foxes also suspected that Saddam might have been outfoxed and that, once the Western alliance had made a massive military investment in the Saudi desert, the alliance

---

but be patient and you are going to see an explosion of ghastly proportions: take the Rwandan genocide and multiply by 20 or, if you are the Eurocentric, take Bosnia and multiply by 200".

[40] On balancing domestic and foreign policy imperatives, see Peter B. Evans, Harold K. Jacobson, and Robert D. Putnam, eds., *Double-edged Diplomacy: International Bargaining and Domestic Politics* (Berkeley: University of California Press, 1993).

would not allow Saddam a face-saving retreat so that he could attack again at a more opportune moment ("when there is a Dukakis Democrat in the White House," one conservative moaned). The net result was that foxes assigned higher probabilities to the combination of war and Iraqi rout than did hawkish hedgehogs who feared peace because they thought the Iraqis could foresee they would be routed, or than did dovish hedgehogs, who feared war because they exaggerated its costs.[41]

Macroeconomic Policies in Latin America (1988–1992). The intellectual agility of foxes was also apparent going in the opposite direction: when the prevailing expectation was not of rationality but inertia, that elites would keep on repeating the same old "mistakes" either because they just "didn't get it" or were locked into suboptimal policies by political constraints. Latin Americanist foxes did not disagree with their hedgehog colleagues that there would be sharp resistance in Brazil, Argentina, and Mexico to long-overdue reform. They did though sense a palpable fear among elites in those countries about "missing the bus." The conspicuous success of the Chilean economy rankled local elites, and so did the view of international financial institutions that the locals were either incorrigibly corrupt or "dependencia dunces." The failure of socialist economics, and of Cuban-style caudillo worship, had left leading leftists so dispirited that some had begun embracing Friedmanite policy nostrums. Foxes did not pretend that imposing fiscal and monetary discipline would be easy, or that backsliding would not be common, but they were better positioned to expect the wave of pro-market policy change that swept through the region and to anticipate the improvements in debt-to-GDP ratios, GDP growth, unemployment, and inflation through much of the 1990s.

Of course, the foxes' predictions that key countries would finally start listening to the IMF and World Bank could be—and indeed were—reached by other paths of reasoning. Boomster hedgehogs embraced globalization arguments with characteristically greater enthusiasm than most foxes. They saw inexorable trends toward economic interdependence that would encroach on national sovereignty and limit the freedom of decision makers to pursue "dumb policies that produce short-term highs but impoverish people in the long term." This reasoning led them to much the same conclusion as the foxes about Argentina, Brazil, and Mexico. The difference was that the boomster hedgehogs drew more

[41] No forecasters scored the forecasting equivalent of a trifecta: assigning their highest likelihood values to war, to Iraqi rout, and to both Iraq and Saddam Hussein surviving such a military debacle. The conceptual ingredients for each correct prediction could be identified in the sample as a whole, but no single individual had all the necessary mental pieces.

sweeping conclusions, making similar predictions for the sophisticated economies of Canada and Scandinavia as well as for the emerging economies of eastern Europe, the Middle East, South Asia, and sub-Saharan Africa. Foxes saw some truth in the globalization arguments but were more alert than the boomster hedgehogs to (a) the danger of egalitarian backlash and the opportunities that rapid economic change creates for demagogues to stir up old antipathies and inspire mayhem; (b) the power of entrenched interests—be they French or Japanese farmers or American truckers or steel manufacturers—to delay and sometimes reverse cross-border economic integration; (c) the destabilizing effects that unrestricted flows of capital can have on developing countries with limited currency reserves and weak regulatory institutions.[42] Many foxes acknowledged uncertainty about which causal forces would prevail, and this cushioned them for setbacks in Mexico in the mid-1990s and Argentina in 2002.[43]

Role reversal exercises came more naturally to foxes who recognized that what looks rational to us might look foolish or unfair to them, and that what looks irrational to us might seem honorable or necessary to them. Foxes tended to see the world as a shifting mixture of self-fulfilling and self-negating prophecies: self-fulfilling ones in which success breeds success and failure, failure but only up to a point, and then self-negating prophecies kick in as people recognize that things have gone too far. Foxes saw wisdom in the old adage that we never know we have had enough until we have had more than enough, and they agreed with skeptics that it is impossible to predict the moment of epiphany—the "magic moment" when, on an evening stroll, a Gorbachev will turn to a Shevardnadze and say, "We can't go on living like this anymore."

China (1992). Optimists thought that China could sustain annual growth rates of 10 percent indefinitely. But they split on the implications of that growth. Some foresaw an easing of repression and emergence of democracy. Others thought growth would prop up hardliners and subsidize the military apparatus that keeps the Communists in power. The preponderance of sentiment, however, favored the former view: economic pluralism and rising living standards would lead to political pluralism just as it had in South Korea, Taiwan, and Singapore. The burgeoning middle class would in due course topple the tyrants who brought them prosperity.

[42] P. Krugman, *Currency and Crises* (Cambridge: MIT Press, 1992); P. Krugman, *Pop Internationalism* (Cambridge: MIT Press, 1996); Jagdish Bhagwati, *The World Trading System at Risk* (Princeton, NJ: Princeton University Press, 1991); Jagdish Bhagwati, *Protectionism* (Cambridge: MIT Press, 1998).

[43] Friedman, "The Lexus and the Olive Tree."

Hedgehog optimists dwelled on the parallels between China and the miracle economies of the "Asian Tigers," parallels they justified by pointing to cultural and political commonalities: a Confucianist legacy of respect for education, thrift, and duty and an authoritarian legacy of single-party rule.

Hedgehog pessimists replied that big improvements were "easier" earlier because the baseline of comparison was so low and inefficiency so blatant. The pessimists focused on rampant corruption, on the risk of chaos in future power struggles and on the lack of political legitimacy. Some even thought China might fall apart. Invoking the specters of the British, French, and Soviet empires, one characterized China as the "last of the great multiethnic empires" encompassing "Buddhist Tibet, Muslim Xinjiang, Korean cities in Manchuria, Cantonese Guangdong, and cosmopolitan Hong Kong." China's early twenty-first-century future would resemble its early twentieth-century past: "a patchwork of fiefdoms under rival warlords." Another observer compared Chinese Communism to a "decrepit mansion held together by shoddy repair jobs. . . . [Its] leaders are scrambling to keep up with deferred maintenance. But they will eventually have to justify their existence. When the economy stalls, and it must, the government will resort to the last refuge of scoundrels [patriotism]. . . . China has boundary disputes not just with Taiwan but also with Vietnam, Russia, and India. In the next decade, the Asian equivalent of NATO will arise with the purpose of containing China."

The foxes warned against overreacting. One noted in fortune-cookie fashion: "Things are rarely as bad as they look in the troughs or as good as they look at the peaks. There was despair after the Tiananmen massacre. There will be more causes for despair." Foxes also split over how wisely the Chinese leadership would cope with coming crises. The dominant view was that Deng Xiaoping was "awesomely shrewd" ("he had thirty IQ points on Mao") and had picked successors who shared his game plan. The dominant prediction was therefore "repressive stability," "robust growth," and occasionally tense but mostly businesslike relations with the United States. Foxes reserved the right to change their minds if reactionaries seized control, reversed movement toward free markets, and picked fights that galvanized an alliance against China. The foxes also agreed with pessimists that, as the income gap grows between rural and urban dwellers, a vast migratory labor class from the countryside will start demanding jobs in the cities, producing a surge in crime and unrest ("Mao's revenge"). On its path to world-power status, China might pass "through several Tiananmen-magnitude crises. It will be a bumpy ride but China can stay on the trajectory toward superpower status if the post-Deng leadership keeps an even policy keel."[44] This fox paraphrased former U.S. Treasury secretary Larry Summers: "When the history of the twentieth century is written one hundred years from now, the most significant event will be the revolutionary changes in China. . . . For more than a century, the United States has been the world's largest economy. The only nation with a chance of surpassing it in the next generation in absolute scale is China." Indeed, if China were to hit Taiwan's per capita income, its economy would be larger than all industrialized countries in the world combined. It would be "like the rise of Japan, except China has nuclear weapons and ten times the population."

A fox, sympathetic to hegemonic transition theory, gets the last word: "If Deng's successors play their cards right, we are heading into a Sinocentric world by the mid-twenty-first century, at least a world in which China is America's principal rival. Managing such power transitions is a delicate task that many statesmen have failed, leaving wars in their wake. The Beijing leadership could set back the clock for the rise of China by decades, even centuries, if they throw around their weight carelessly. . . . My guess is that they will be too smart to pass up this historical opportunity by picking unnecessary fights." Here is the trademark eclecticism of foxes. The speaker applied a macrotheory (hegemonic transition) in a way that allowed for microvariables (leadership decisions) to gate us into alternative futures. The conversation closed with another fox trademark: the hedge. "Of course, there are elements of chance. . . . Deng's successors might revert through regression toward the mean to the average intelligence of politicians."

CLOSING OBSERVATIONS

Quantitative and qualitative methods converge on a common conclusion: foxes have better judgment than hedgehogs. Better judgment does not

---

[44] "China's Communism, 50 Years On," *The World in 1999, Economist* 31 (1998): 56–58; *Current History* 96(611) (September 1997), special issue on China; D. Burstein, *Big Dragon: China's Future: What It Means for Business, the Economy, and the Global Order* (New York: Simon & Schuster, 1998); Xiaobo Lu, *Cadres and Corruption: The Organizational Involution of the Chinese Communist Party (Studies of the East Asian Institute)* (Stanford, CA: Stanford University Press, 2000); W. W. Lam, *China after Deng Xiaoping: The Power Struggle in Beijing Since Tiananmen* (Singapore: John Wiley & Sons, 1995); G. Murray, *China: The Next Superpower: Dilemmas in Change and Continuity* (New York: St. Martin's Press, 1998); S. S. Kim, ed., *China and the World: Chinese Foreign Policy Faces the New Millennium* (Boulder, CO: Westview Press, 1998); Lau Chung-Ming and Shen Jianfa, eds., *China Review 2000* (Hong Kong: Chinese University Press, 2001); N. D. Kristof and S. Wudunn, *China Wakes: The Struggle for the Soul of a Rising Power* (New York: Vintage Books, 1995); T. G. Carpenter and J. A. Dorn, eds., *China's*

mean great judgment. Foxes are not awe-inspiring forecasters: most of them should be happy to tie simple extrapolation models, and none of them can hold a candle to formal statistical models. But foxes do avoid many of the big mistakes that drive down the probability scores of hedge-hogs to approximate parity with dart-throwing chimps. And this accomplishment is rooted in foxes' more balanced style of thinking about the world—a style of thought that elevates no thought above criticism.

By contrast, hedgehogs dig themselves into intellectual holes. The deeper they dig, the harder it gets to climb out and see what is happening outside, and the more tempting it becomes to keep on doing what they know how to do: continue their metaphorical digging by uncovering new reasons why their initial inclination, usually too optimistic or pessimistic, was right. Hedgehogs are thus at continual risk of becoming prisoners of their preconceptions, trapped in self-reinforcing cycles in which their initial ideological disposition stimulates thoughts that further justify that inclination which, in turn, stimulates further supportive thoughts.[45]

There are intriguing parallels between the evidence on how foxes outperformed hedgehogs and the broader literature on how to improve forecasting. We learn from the latter that (a) the average predictions of forecasters are generally more accurate than the majority of forecasters from whom the averages were computed; (b) trimming outliers (extremists) further enhances accuracy; (c) one can do better still by using the Delphi technique for integrating experts' judgments in which one persuades experts to advance anonymous predictions and arguments for those predictions, one then circulates everyone's predictions and arguments to everyone else (so everyone has a chance to reflect but no one has a chance to bully), and one continues the process until convinced the process has reached the point of diminishing returns.[46] These results dovetail with the cognitive interpretation of the fox-hedgehog performance

---

Future (Washington, DC: Cato Institute, 2000); B. Gilley, "Jiang Zemin: On the Right Side of History?" *Current History* 98(629) (1999): 249–53; P. H. B. Godwin, "China's Nuclear Forces: An Assessment," *Current History* 98(629) (1999): 260–65; M. Yahuda, "China's Search for a Global Role," *Current History* 98(629) (1999): 266–70; E. S. Steinfeld, "Beyond the Transition: China's Economy at Century's End," *Current History* 98(629) (1999): 271–75; J. Fewsmith, "Jiang Zemin Takes Command," *Current History* 97(620) (1999): 250–56; M. M. Pearson, "China's Emerging Business Class: Democracy's Harbinger?" *Current History* 97(620) (1999): 268–72; N. R. Lardy, *China's Unfinished Economic Revolution* (Washington, DC: Brookings Institution Press, 1998); R. Bernstein and R. H. Munro, *The Coming Conflict with China* (New York: Alfred A. Knopf, 1997).

[45] Tesser, "Attitude Polarization," A. H. Eagly and S. Chaiken, *The Psychology of Attitudes* (Fort Worth, TX: Harcourt Brace Jovanovich, 1993); A. H. Eagly and S. Chaiken, *The Psychology of Attitudes* (Fort Worth, TX: Harcourt Brace Jovanovich, 1993).

[46] J. S. Armstrong, *Principles of Forecasting: A Handbook for Researchers and Practitioners* (Boston: Kluwers, 2001).

gaps: foxes do better because they are moderates who factor conflicting considerations—in a flexible, weighted-averaging fashion—into their final judgments.[47]

Overall, chapter 3 makes a strong case that the foxes' "victory" was a genuine achievement. We looked for good judgment and found it—mostly among the foxes. And, interestingly, this does not appear to be where most of the media are looking. Hedgehog opinion was in greater demand from the media, and this was probably for the reason noted in chapter 2: simple, decisive statements are easier to package in sound bites. The same style of reasoning that impairs experts' performance on scientific indicators of good judgment boosts experts' attractiveness to the mass market–driven media.

It is premature, though, to segue into social commentary. Not everyone is ready to concede that foxes do better because they are better cognitively equipped for making sense of the world. One pocket of resistance is concentrated among psychologists who subscribe to the argument that fast-and-frugal heuristics—simple rules of thumb—perform as well as, or better than, more complex, effort-demanding algorithms.[48] Another pocket of resistance is concentrated among policy makers who prefer one-handed advisers—and among political scientists and historians who defend that preference.[49] But, whatever the roots of the resistance, the resisters—if they are to engage the scientific debate—need to identify logical or empirical flaws in the arguments advanced here—flaws sufficiently severe that they justify dismissing the consistently large performance gaps between hedgehogs and foxes as illusory.

Some pro-hedgehog reviewers of this manuscript have attempted to identify such flaws—and compelled me to sharpen my own case (our most relentless critics sometimes teach us the most).[50] One critique maintains

[47] This argument foreshadows one of the last-ditch defenses of hedgehogs in chapter 6. As one would expect if foxes were already doing intuitively what averaging does statistically, and what hedgehogs were failing to do (blending perspectives with nonredundant predictive power), hedgehogs benefit more from averaging: the average hedgehog forecast surpasses the average hedgehog forecaster by a far greater margin than the average fox forecast surpasses the average fox forecaster.

[48] G. Gigerenzer and P. M. Todd, *Simple Heuristics That Make Us Smart* (New York: Oxford University Press, 2000); P. Suedfeld and P. E. Tetlock, "Psychological Advice about Political Decision Making: Heuristics, Biases, and Cognitive Defects," in *Psychology and Social Policy*, ed. P. Suedfeld and P. E. Tetlock (Washington, DC: Hemisphere, 1991).

[49] For an expanded discussion of individual differences among executive decision makers on the relative utility of more versus less complex decision procedures, see P. E. Tetlock, "Cognitive Biases and Organizational Correctives: Do Both Disease and Cure Depend on the Politics of the Beholder?" *Administrative Science Quarterly* 45 (2000): 293–326.

[50] Chapter 3 challenges the influential but often overstated argument that fast-and-frugal heuristics are adaptively superior to more time- and effort-consuming methods of making up our minds. The evidence, reviewed in Suedfeld and Tetlock "Psychology and

that we will discover that hedgehogs are every bit as discerning observers as foxes when we factor in the different error-avoidance priorities of the two groups (hence the need for value-adjusted probability scores). Another critique complains about an uneven playing field: hedgehog experts "lost" because they specialized in more unpredictable regions of the world and were dealt tougher assignments (hence the need for difficulty-adjusted forecasting scores). Yet a third critique calls for giving more weight to the defenses that forecasters offered when the unexpected occurred—credit for being almost right (hence the need for fuzzy-set adjustments). Fairness requires giving all appeals a hearing, but we defer the hearing until chapter 6, where defenders of hedgehogs have the chance to rebut not just the evidence in this chapter, but also that in chapters 4 and 5.

Social Advocacy," and Gigerenzer and Todd "Simple Heuristics," was never sufficient to sustain more than the weak claim that simple decision rules can—under some conditions—produce outcomes as good as, or better than, complex decision rules. Moreover, there are good reasons for supposing that politics poses an especially tough test of fast-and-frugal heuristics. Political observers often latch onto simple heuristics that point in opposite predictive directions. This may be why—as we discover in chapter 6—weighted averages of forecasts (an inherently complex strategy) typically perform better than the majority of individual forecasters (especially the hedgehog extremists among them). Chapter 3 also challenges over-stated claims that overconfidence is an artifact of either regression toward the mean or biased sampling of questions (G. Gigerenzer, "Fast and Frugal Heuristics," in *Blackwell Handbook of Judgment and Decision Making*, ed. D. Koehler and N. Harvey [Oxford: Blackwell, 2004]). We tested the former claim and found it wanting. But we could not decisively rule out the latter, more elusive, claim. No one, frankly, knows how to sample questions in an unbiased fashion from the conceptual universes of issues covered in our forecasting exercises. Virtually everyone, however, knows that when the stakes are high enough—the fates of regimes, nations and economies hang in the balance—it is thin consolation to be told that over-confident experts might have done better if we had posed more "representative" questions (see also Chapter 6).

CHAPTER 4

Honoring Reputational Bets

FOXES ARE BETTER BAYESIANS THAN HEDGEHOGS

> When the facts change, I change my mind. What do you
> do, sir?
>
> —JOHN MAYNARD KEYNES

CHAPTERS 2 AND 3 measured expert performance against correspondence benchmarks of good judgment. The test was "getting it right": affixing realistic probabilities to possible futures. The spotlight shifts in chapters 4 and 5 to coherence and process benchmarks of good judgment. The focus is on "thinking the right way": judging judgment on the logical soundness of how we go about drawing inferences, updating beliefs, and evaluating evidence. These alternative conceptions of good judgment are more complementary than competitive. It would be odd if people who think the right way failed to get more things right in the long run. Indeed, if they did not, should we not—before questioning common sense—question our measures?

Chapter 4 relies on logical-coherence and process tests of good judgment derived from Bayesian probability theory. The coherence tests are static. They require single carefully aimed snapshots to capture the extent to which belief systems hang together in logically consistent ways. The process tests—which play the more central role here—are dynamic. They require at least two snapshots of forecasters' belief systems, one before and one after they learn what happened. Good judges should be good hypothesis testers: they should update their beliefs in response to new evidence and do so in proportion to the extremity of the odds they placed on possible outcomes before they learned which one occurred. And good judges should not be revisionist historians: they should remember what they once thought and resist the temptation of the hindsight or "I knew it all along" bias.

We shall discover that (a) even accomplished professionals often fail these tests of good judgment; (b) the same people who fared poorly against the correspondence tests in chapter 3 fare poorly against the coherence and process tests in chapter 4; (c) similar psychological processes underlie performance deficits on both correspondence and coherence tests of good judgment.

A LOGICAL-COHERENCE TEST

If I labored under any illusion that people are natural Bayesians, that illusion was dispelled well before I could check whether people are good belief updaters. The Bayesian framework rests on logical identities, and we can tell whether those identities are satisfied from single snapshots of belief systems at isolated slices of time. Imagine an observer who distinguishes only two possible interpretations of the world: his own and a rival's. We can deduce the likelihood that observer should attach to an outcome (X_1) from knowledge of (a) how confident the observer is in his own versus his rival's reading of reality; (b) how likely the observer believes X_1 to be if his versus his rival's reading of reality is correct:

$$P(X_1) = P(X_1 \mid \text{Observer's hypothesis})P(\text{Observer's hypothesis}) \\ + P(X_1 \mid \text{Rival hypothesis})P(\text{Rival hypothesis})$$

When we asked experts to make predictions in eleven regional forecasting exercises by filling in values for each variable on the left and right sides of this equation (see Methodological Appendix), it rarely dawned on anyone to base their likelihood-of-x estimates on anything beyond their conditional likelihood estimates of x that were predicated on their own view of the world. Their answers to these two questions were almost interchangeable $(r = .83)$. It was as though experts were 100 percent confident that they were right and everyone else wrong. Therefore, the probability of x given their construal of the forces at work must be the same thing as the probability of x.

A charitable view chalks this "mistake" up to linguistic confusion. People understandably think that, when we ask them about the likelihood of an event, we want their point of view, not someone else's. But the results hold up even when we press the issue and, just prior to asking about the likelihood of an outcome, we solicit separate judgments of the likelihood of the rival perspective being true *and* of the likelihood of the outcome if the rival perspective were true. In estimating the likelihood of x, experts do not compute weighted averages of the likelihood of x conditional on various interpretations of the world being correct, with the weights proportional to experts' confidence in each interpretation. They consult a gut-level intuition anchored around one point of view, their own, which they treat as an existential certainty.[1]

---

[1] From the standpoint of work on conversational norms, the order of questioning used in this study—posing the questions about alternative perspectives right before the bottom-line probability assessment—constitutes a particularly tough test of the notion that forecasters are oblivious to alternative perspectives. Recency is often a cue in conversations that the speaker considers the just-discussed information to be relevant (H. P. Grice,

There would also be nothing logically wrong with considering only one's own view of the world if one were totally confident one was right. The second half of the right-hand side of the identity equation would fall to zero. But most participants—including hedgehogs—were not that sure of themselves. When we asked forecasters about the likelihood that other points of view might be correct, they assigned values substantially greater than zero (average .27). There would also be nothing wrong with considering only one's own point of view if one believed that other perspectives made precisely the same predictions. But when we asked forecasters about the likelihood of their "most likely futures" conditional on other views being correct, they assigned values substantially lower than those they assigned conditional on their own view being correct (average gap of .46). The net result—as shown in figure 9.6 in the Technical Appendix—was an "egocentricity gap": the probability that experts assigned their most likely futures was consistently higher than the value they should have assigned those futures if they were good Bayesians who took other points of view into account.

This slighting of alternative perspectives is no harmless technicality. If forecasters had been better Bayesians, their forecasts would have been better calibrated. They would have assigned more realistic probability estimates to their most likely futures, shrinking probability-reality gaps by up to 26 percent. Both foxes and hedgehogs would have benefited, with estimated reductions up to18 percent for foxes and 32 percent for hedgehogs (for details, see Technical Appendix).

The pattern of results is an early warning that experts are not natural Bayesians who routinely treat experience as an opportunity for adjusting the odds ratios of competing hypotheses. A more plausible model is that we are naturally egocentric. In sizing up situations, we have difficulty taking other points of view seriously. Few of us spontaneously factor other views into our assessments—even points of view that, on second thought, we acknowledge have a nonnegligible likelihood of being right.[2]

"Logic and Conversation," in *Syntax and Semantics*, vol. 3, *Speech Acts*, ed. P. Cole and J. L. Morgan [New York: Academic Press, 1975], 41–58).

[2] This result converges with several lines of experimental research, including (a) work on pseudo-diagnosticity that shows that people give too little weight to the denominator of likelihood ratios; (b) work on egocentricity biases. See H. R. Arkes and M. Rothbart, "Memory, Retrieval, and Contingency Judgments," *Journal of Personality and Social Psychology* 49 (1985): 598–606; B. Fischhoff and R. Beyth-Marom, "Hypothesis Evaluation from a Bayesian Perspective," *Psychological Review* 90 (1983): 239–60; L. Ross and D. Griffin, "Subjective Construal, Social Inference, and Human Misunderstanding," in *Advances in Experimental Social Psychology*, vol. 24, ed. M. Zanna (New York: Academic Press, 1991), 319–59; R. E. Nisbett and L. Ross, *Human Inference: Strategies and Shortcomings of Social Judgment* (Englewood Cliffs, NJ: Prentice-Hall, 1980).

A Dynamic-process Test: Bayesian Updating

Giving short shrift to other points of view proves a recurring theme when we turn to process tests that probe forecasters' willingness to change their minds in response to new evidence. Bayes's theorem again sets the gold standard. Once we learn what happened in a forecasting exercise, the theorem tells us how much confidence we should retain in the hypotheses that underlie accurate and inaccurate forecasts. That final confidence ratio (the posterior odds ratio) should be a function of the confidence we initially had in the clashing hypotheses about the drivers of events (the prior odds ratio) multiplied by the beliefs we once held about the likelihood of the observed outcome assuming the correctness of either our own or other points of view (the likelihood ratio):

$$\frac{P(\text{your hypothesis} \mid X_1 \text{ occurs})}{P(\text{rival hypothesis} \mid X_1 \text{ occurs})} = \frac{P(X_1 \mid \text{your hypothesis})}{P(X_1 \mid \text{rival hypothesis})} \times \frac{P(\text{your hypothesis})}{P(\text{rival hypothesis})}$$

Posterior odds = Likelihood Ratio × Prior Odds

Applying this framework was straightforward in early laboratory studies of belief updating. Researchers would tell participants that there was an unknown proportion of red and blue poker chips in a bag (thus, prior odds were 50/50) and then randomly sample ten chips from the bag, x of which turn out to be red and y blue. Researchers would compare how much people would change their minds about the color ratio to how much Bayes's theorem says they should have changed their minds (posterior odds).[3]

We lose this precision when we gauge experts' reactions to unfolding real-world events, such as market meltdowns and mass murder. The dividing line between the rational and irrational, between the defensible and indefensible, becomes blurrier to the degree there is room for our prior beliefs to bias our assessments of whether we were right or wrong: there is little such room for judging the color of poker chips but a lot when it comes to judging movement toward political or economic freedom. That said, though, studies of judgments of real-world events are far from irrelevant. Such studies still speak volumes on how difficult it is for experts to concede that they were wrong. We discover how much we can discover by examining the regional forecasting studies in which we reduced forecasters' wiggle room by eliciting ex ante commitments on the probative value of possible outcomes. Forecasters' answers to the following questions gave us the inputs we needed for computing—to a crude first order of approximation—whether they were good belief updaters:

[3] Fischhoff and Beyth-Marom, "Hypothesis Evaluation from a Bayesian Perspective."

1. How likely do you estimate each possible future if your under-standing of the underlying forces at work is correct? In belief-updating equations, we designated these variables as $p(x_1|$your hypothesis), $p(x_2|$your hypothesis) ... where x_1, x_2 ... refer to sets of possible futures and your hypothesis refers to "your view of the underlying forces at work."
2. How much confidence do you have in your understanding of the underlying forces at work? We designated this variable p (your hy-pothesis).
3. Think of the most influential alternative to your perspective on the underlying forces. How likely is that perspective to be correct? We designated this variable as p (rival hypothesis).
4. How likely do you think each possible future if this alternative perspective is correct? We designated these variables $p(x_1|$rival hypothesis), $p(x_2|$rival hypothesis). ... We used this format in seven forecasting domains, including the Soviet Union (1988), South Africa (1988), the Persian Gulf War of 1991, Canada (1992), Kaza-khstan (1992), the U.S. presidential election of 1992, and the Euro-pean Monetary Union (1992), as well as a different format in four other domains, including the European Monetary Union (1998), China (1992), Japan (1992), and India (1992).[4]

These exercises are "reputational bets": they ask experts to specify, as exactly as would an odds-setting bookie, predictions predicated on com-peting views of reality. After we have learned what happened, we can compute the posterior odds: the "correct" Bayesian answer to the ques-tion of how much experts should have increased or decreased their con-fidence in their prior worldviews. We can also recontact experts and pop the big question: Given your earlier reputational bet and the course of subsequent events, how much do you wish to change your confidence in your understanding of the forces at work? We can then see how well ex-perts as a whole, or subgroups such as hedgehogs and foxes, stack up against Bayesian benchmarks of good judgment.

Reactions to Winning and Losing Reputational Bets

There are good reasons for expecting smart people to be bad Bayesians. Decades of laboratory research on "cognitive conservatism" warn us

---

[4] This alternative format "depersonalized" hypothesis testing by no longer pitting experts against their "rivals." For example, in addition to asking experts on Western Europe in 1998 to judge the likelihood of various countries adopting the euro in the next three to five years, we asked them to judge the truth or falsity or the hypothesis "there is a long-term process

that even highly educated people tend to be balky belief updaters who admit mistakes grudgingly and defend their prior positions tenaciously.[5] And decades of research on cognitive styles warn us that this problem will be more pronounced among thinkers who fit the hedgehog rather than the fox profile.[6] Chapter 3 showed that hedgehogs are attracted to grand schemes that promise to explain a lot but that do not translate into a lot of forecasting successes. Hedgehogs should thus be more disappointed by disconfirmation, and delighted by confirmation, than foxes. Assuming no more than a common desire to maintain a positive-mood equilibrium, it follows that hedgehogs should try harder to neutralize disconfirming data by subjecting it to withering scrutiny and to savor confirming data by taking it at face value.

Figure 4.1 shows that hedgehogs made bolder reputational bets and put more professional esteem on the line by emphatically differentiating their conditional expectations from those of rival perspectives. But their timing was bad: they made more of these dramatic predictions when they were dramatically wrong (their most likely futures failed to materialize) than when they were dramatically right (their most likely futures materialized). Thus, when hedgehogs lost, the Bayesian-prescribed confidence "hit" they suffered was larger than that for foxes; but when they

---

of economic and political integration at work in Europe," and then make two sets of conditional-likelihood judgments: (a) assume for sake of argument that the hypothesis is definitely (100 percent) true and judge the conditional likelihood of various countries adopting the euro by January 2001 or 2008; (b) assume the opposite and then make the same conditional likelihood judgments. The results from the two different formats were sufficiently similar to justify pooling the data.

[5] Some researchers have concluded that people are such bad Bayesians that they are not Bayesians at all (Fischhoff and Beyth-Marom, "Hypothesis Evaluation from a Bayesian Perspective"). Early work on cognitive conservatism showed that people clung too long to the only information they initially had—information that typically took the form of base rates of variously colored poker chips that defined judges' "priors." See L. D. Phillips and D. Edwards, "Conservatism in a Simple Probability Inference task," *Journal of Experimental Psychology* 54 (1966): 346–54. But later work showed that people often ignored base rates when they could construct plausible causal stories from case-specific information (Nisbett and Ross, *Human Inference*). This confusion is readily resolved here. Our forecasters did cling too long to their prior hypotheses (replicating "cognitive conservatism"), but those hypotheses were grounded in strong beliefs about political causality at work in specific cases, not in statistical summaries of how often outcomes occur in specified regions or periods. Indeed, these ideological schemata often cause experts to overpredict low-frequency outcomes, as noted in chapter 3, and this can be viewed as a form of base-rate neglect. My experience is that base rates shape political judgments mostly when people have no other information or have imbued the base rate with causal potency (e.g., sweeping stereotypes about Russians or Islam).

[6] A. W. Kruglanski and D. M. Webster, "Motivated Closing of the Mind: 'Seizing' and 'Freezing,'" *Psychological Review* 103 (1996): 263–68.

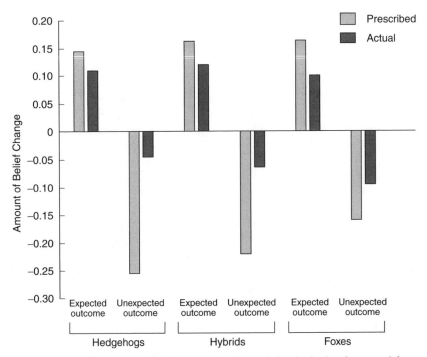

Figure 4.1. The relative willingness of hedgehogs, hybrids (hedge-foxes and fox-hogs), and foxes to change their minds in response to relatively expected or unexpected events, and the actual amounts of belief adjustment compared to the Bayesian-prescribed amounts of belief adjustment.

won, the prescribed boost they enjoyed was only roughly equal to that for foxes.[7]

But betting is one thing, paying up another. Focusing just on reactions to losing reputational bets, figure 4.1 shows that neither hedgehogs nor foxes changed their minds as much as Reverend Bayes says they should have. But foxes move more in the Bayesian direction than do hybrids and hedgehogs. And this greater movement is all the more impressive in light of the fact that the Bayesian updating formula demanded less movement

[7] The average likelihood ratio for hedgehogs was 3.2:1, whereas the ratio for foxes was 2.3:1. Hedgehogs were also twice as likely as foxes to assign a zero likelihood to competing prior hypotheses (approximately 9 percent versus 4 percent of the time). This created a technical problem. Belief-updating equations become undefined whenever forecasters assign a hypothesis a value of zero (hence the need for recoding zero as .01 and 1.0 as .99). Once someone commits to the view something is impossible, no amount of evidence— within a Bayesian framework—can move them. One can view this outcome as a failure of the framework or as a failure of respondents to appreciate how closed-minded they are when they use zero on the subjective probability scale.

from foxes than from other groups. Foxes move 59 percent of the pre-scribed amount, whereas hedgehogs move only 19 percent of the pre-scribed amount. Indeed, in two regional forecasting exercises, hedgehogs move their opinions in the opposite direction to that prescribed by Bayes's theorem, and nudged up their confidence in their prior point of view after the unexpected happens. This latter pattern is not just contra-Bayesian; it is incompatible with all normative theories of belief adjustment.[8]

Shifting to reactions to winning reputational bets, figure 4.1 shows that everyone—hedgehogs, foxes, and hybrids—seems eager to be good Bayesians when that role requires reaffirming the correctness of their prior point of view. Belief adjustments now hover in the vicinity of 60 percent of the prescribed amount for foxes and 80 percent of the pre-scribed amount for hedgehogs.

Taken together, these results replicate and extend two classic psycho-logical effects. One is cognitive conservatism: the reluctance of human beings to admit mistakes and update beliefs.[9] The other is the "self-serving" attribution bias: the enthusiasm of human beings for attributing success to "internal" causes, such as the shrewdness of one's opinions, and failure to external ones, such as task difficulty, unfair testing condi-tions, or bad luck.

Psychologists find it reassuring when their laboratory effects hold up so well in the messy real world. These effects are not, however, reassur-ing to those who believe the world would be a better place if people ad-hered to Bayesian canons of rationality. From this latter standpoint, it is critical to understand how experts manage to retain so much confidence in their prior beliefs when they "get it wrong." Which belief system de-fenses do they switch on to take the sting out of disconfirmation? Do hedgehogs rely more on these defenses than foxes? And, most intriguing, are the contours of a theory of good judgment emerging: a theory that posits a self-reinforcing virtuous circle in which self-critical thinkers are better at figuring out the contradictory dynamics of evolving situations, more circumspect about their forecasting prowess, more accurate in

[8] For an experimental demonstration of an analogous effect, see C. Lord, M. Lepper, and E. Preston, "Considering the Opposite: A Corrective Strategy for Social Judgement," *Journal of Personality and Social Psychology* 46 (1984): 1254–66; C. Lord, L. Ross, and M. Lepper, "Biased Assimilation and Attitude Polarization: The Effects of Prior Theories on Subsequently Considered Evidence," *Journal of Personality and Social Psychology* 37 (1979): 2098–2109.

[9] "Conservatism" carries no ideological connotation here. It refers to conserving exist-ing mental structures, regardless of content. Liberals can be, and often are, as "guilty" of cognitive conservatism as conservatives. Some researchers find cognitive conservatism ef-fects to be ideologically symmetrical: Nisbett and Ross, *Human Inference*; Z. Kunda, *So-cial Cognition: Making Sense of People* (Cambridge: MIT Press, 1999); P. E. Tetlock and A. Levi, "Attribution Bias: On the Inconclusiveness of the Cognition-Motivation Debate,"

recalling mistakes, less prone to rationalize those mistakes, more likely to update their beliefs in a timely fashion, and—as a cumulative result of these advantages—better positioned to affix realistic probabilities in the next round of events?

Belief System Defenses

Forecasters embraced a variety of ingenious arguments for reneging on reputational bets, but we reduce all of them here to seven categories of "belief system defenses": challenging whether the logical conditions for hypothesis testing were satisfied, invoking the exogenous-shock, close-call counterfactual, and off-on-timing arguments, declaring politics hopelessly indeterminate, defiantly insisting they made the right mistake (and would do it again), and making the metaphysical point that unlikely things sometimes happen.

We used both qualitative and quantitative research methods to explore how forecasters who got it wrong managed to preserve so much confidence they were right. Qualitative methods—to which we turn first—shed light on how forecasters interpret outcomes and why they frequently feel justified in not changing their minds. Listening to forecasters' arguments reminds us why we should not write off all resistance as ego-defensive whining. Determining whether people are good Bayesians in real-world settings proves more than a matter of arithmetic. "Belief system defenses" may often be defensible efforts to redefine the likelihood ratios that determine how much belief change is warranted (a point we revisit in chapter 6).

Quantitative methods—to which we turn second—remind us that, however justified forecasters' arguments may be, there is strong statistical evidence of a self-serving bias operating in the overall pattern of argumentation. Experts invoke arguments from the list of seven only when they make big mistakes and virtually never when they "get it right." There is also a strong statistical connection between how often experts invoke arguments from the list and how far short they fall as Bayesians.

QUALITATIVE ANALYSIS OF ARGUMENTS

Challenge whether the Conditions for Hypothesis Testing were Fulfilled. Each forecast was conditional on the correctness of the expert's understanding of the underlying forces at work. One does not need to be

---

Journal of Experimental Psychology 18 (1982): 68–88. Other researchers, however, find that ideological conservatives tend to be more cognitively conservative. See P. E. Tetlock, "Cognitive Structural Analysis of Political Rhetoric," in *Political Psychology: A Reader,* ed. S. Iyengar and W. J. McGuire (Durham, NC: Duke University Press, 1992), 380–407.

a logician to appreciate the complexity of this "conditionality." Experts are free to affix responsibility for errors on the least ego-threatening mistake they made in sizing up situations. Consider three examples:

1. A panel of prominent political scientists announced in August 2000 that their models of presidential elections foretold the outcome of the upcoming Bush-Gore contest. With confidence estimates ranging from 85 percent to 97 percent, they declared Gore would win—and win big with at least 52 percent and perhaps as much as 60 percent of the vote.[10] There was no need to pay attention to campaign trivia or polling blips. The incumbent party could not lose: the economy was too strong, the country too secure, and presidential approval too high. Of course, the modelers were wrong. After the election, we found that, the more sympathetic forecasters were to the modelers, the more they argued that the basic premise of the enterprise was still sound: the models had just been fed misleading macroeconomic numbers. The crumbling of the NASDAQ, and a net loss in personal wealth in 2000, had heralded a slowdown in the heady growth rates of the late 1990s. People were already feeling pain.

2. The Persian-Gulf conflict of 1990–1991 also illustrates how experts can rescue core assumptions by tracing their mistakes to "theoretically trivial" misspecifications of antecedent conditions. Observers who expected Saddam to do the "rational thing" and fracture the American alliance by withdrawing from Kuwait frequently insisted they were right: Saddam did do the rational thing. But the rational response changed with changing circumstances. Preemptive withdrawal had ceased to be a face-saving option for Iraq because the United States had blocked it. The geopolitical definition of rationality that inspired the original forecast had been superseded by a domestic political one. Of course, as in the "guess the number" game in chapter 2, it is unclear where to halt this infinite regress of game-theoretic inferences. Why not suppose that Saddam could have blocked the effort to block a face-saving withdrawal? Indeterminacy arises when we do not know where to draw the boundaries on bounded rationality.

3. More generally, it is common in political debates to hear one side complain that it has been stuck with an idiotic prediction. The

[10] For wider ranging analyses of what went wrong for these models: L. Bartels and J. Zaller, "Presidential Vote Models: A Recount," *Political Science and Politics* 34 (2001): 9–20; C. Wlezien, "On Forecasting the Presidential Vote," *Political Science and Politics* 34 (2001): 25–32; J. Campbell, "The Referendum That Didn't Happen: The Forecasts of the 2000 Presidential Election," *Political Science and Politics* 34 (2001): 33–38; R. Erikson, "The 2000 Presidential Election in Historical Perspective," *Political Science Quarterly* 116 (1) (2001): 29–52.

"wronged" side insists that they were not mistaken about the efficacy of basic strategies of diplomatic influence or basic instruments of macroeconomic policy. They "merely" failed to anticipate how maladroitly the policy would be implemented. Thus, experts insisted at various points in the 1990s that "if NATO had sent the Serbs the right mix of signals, we could have averted this new bloodshed" or "if Yeltsin had practiced real shock therapy, Russia could have avoided this new bout of hyperinflation." This belief system defense transforms a conditional forecast (if x is satisfied, then y will occur) into a historical counterfactual (if x had been satisfied, then y would have occurred). Counterfactual history becomes a convenient graveyard for burying embarrassing conditional forecasts.

The Exogenous-shock Defense. All hypothesis testing presupposes a ceteris paribus or "all other things equal" clause. In principle, forecasters can always argue that, although the conditions for activating the forecast were satisfied—their understanding of the underlying forces was correct—key background conditions took on unforeseeably bizarre forms that short-circuited the otherwise reliably deterministic connection between cause and effect.

Theorists also find this defense convenient. It gives them license to explain away unexpected events by attributing them to forces outside the logical scope of their theory. One realist, surprised by how far Gorbachev went in making concessions on arms control issues, commented: "I study interstate relations. I am not a Sovietologist. Has a theory of marriage failed if it predicts that a couple will stay unhappily married, the couple toughs it out for decades, and suddenly the husband has a fatal heart attack? Of course not, the failure lies in not checking with the cardiologist. Well, my failure was not recognizing how sick the Soviet state was."

In the same vein, some modelers of presidential elections attributed Gore's defeat to an "out of the blue" variable. As a result of Clinton's effort to cover up his sexual dalliance with Monica Lewinsky, and his subsequent impeachment, a substantial segment of the public had become more attuned to the moral rather than the economic health of the nation. There is no room in parsimonious models for promiscuous presidents and perjury traps.

Exogenous shocks can range from the ridiculous (e.g., a White House intern flashing her underwear at a president with limited capacity to delay need gratification) to the sublime (e.g., the unusual maturity of a political prisoner soon to become president in his country's first multiracial election) to the tragic (e.g., the assassination of a prime minister of a bitterly divided nation trying to make peace with a longtime foe). And exogenous shocks need not be measured on the micro scale. They can be big: the crumbling of the Soviet economy or financial panics in East Asia, Mexico, and Wall Street, or droughts, earthquakes, and other natural disasters. In effect, anything that falls outside the expert's framework can qualify. Of course, once "shocked," experts can choose either to continue excluding the shock from their models (relegating it to irreducible error variance) or to incorporate it ("messing up" their models but also increasing the future absorptive capacity of those models).

The Close-call Counterfactual Defense ("I was almost Right"). This strategy takes the exogenous-shock defense to its natural extreme by explicitly arguing that, although the predicted outcome did not occur, it "almost did" and would have but for trivial and easily-imagined-undone contingencies. Such "close-call counterfactuals" popped up in several forecasting arenas:

1. Observers of the former Soviet Union who, in 1988, thought the Communist Party could not be driven from power by 1993 or 1998 were especially likely to believe that Kremlin hardliners almost overthrew Gorbachev in the 1991 coup attempt, and they would have if the conspirators had been more resolute and less inebriated, or if key military officers had obeyed orders to kill civilians challenging martial law or if Yeltsin had not acted so bravely.

2. Experts who expected the European Monetary Union to collapse argued that the event almost happened during the currency crises of 1992 and would have but for the principled determination (even obstinacy) of politicians committed to the euro and but for the interventions of sympathetic central bankers. Given the abiding conflict of interest between states that have "solid fundamentals" and those that "resort to accounting gimmicks to shrink their budget deficits," and given "burbling nationalist resentment" of a single European currency, these experts thought it a "minor miracle" that most European leaders in 1997 were still standing by monetary union, albeit on a loophole-riddled schedule.

3. Observers of the U.S. scene who expected Bush to be reelected in 1992 found it easier to imagine a world in which Clinton never became president than did those who foresaw a Clinton victory. All they needed to do was to posit a more compliant Federal Reserve Board (cutting interest rates earlier in 1991 "as it should have done in a recession anyway") and a deft campaign of negative advertising aimed at Clinton's character ("strip off the mask and reveal the rogue underneath—the campaign was too gentlemanly").

4. Experts who expected Quebec to secede from Canada noted how close the second separatist referendum came to passing ("well within sampling error, if a fraction of a percentage point more of the electorate had voted *oui*, confederation would have unraveled") and how a more deftly managed campaign could have tipped the outcome ("if a savvier politician, Bouchard rather than Parizeau, had spearheaded the cause, Quebec would be a nation today").

5. Experts who expected Saddam Hussein to withdraw from Kuwait after the balance of power had tipped against him often claimed that Saddam would have acted as they predicted if he had only understood the situation as clearly as they did. They were also inclined to trace the tragedy to Saddam's pathological personality, which predisposed him to act far more recklessly than most heads of state. One expert complained: "Who knows what sets him off? Perhaps he thought it better to be a rooster for a day than a chicken for all eternity. But judging from his record, he could have latched on to another proverb and convinced himself that it was better— like Saladin—to retreat in order to fight another day." In this opinion, we were just a synaptic connection in Saddam's brain away from averting that war.

6. Observers of South Africa who expected continued white-minority rule from 1989 to 1994 were especially likely to believe that were it not for the coincidental conjunction of two key individuals—de Klerk and Mandela—in leadership roles, South Africa could easily have gone down the path of increasing repression, polarization, and violence.

7. Observers who viewed Kazakhstan as "several Yugoslavias waiting to erupt into interethnic violence" attributed the nonoccurrence to the shrewdness of the Kazakh leadership as well as to the lack of interest among the current crop of Russian leaders in playing the "ethnic card," something that could easily change as soon as "Yeltsin's heart finally gives out" and it becomes politically expedient to champion the cause of diaspora Russians.

8. The beleaguered modelers of presidential elections also raised the close-call defense. At first glance, this defense seems a slam dunk. The election will go down as history's flukiest, hinging on butterfly ballots, hanging chads, and judicial whims. But the macro modelers who projected decisive or even landslide Gore victories should not get off so easily. They need to invoke potent forces to close several-million-vote gaps between their predictions and reality. To this end, they summoned up a variety of close-call scenarios, including "if Nader had not been so appealing or so narcissistic or so stubborn . . . ," "if Gore had not been such an abysmal debater . . . ,"

"if the election had been a few days later, the trend line would have . . . ," and "if Clinton had not been so incorrigibly self-indulgent. . . ."

The "Just-off-on-Timing" Defense. This strategy moves us from the realm of counterfactual worlds back into the actual world. Experts often insist that, although the predicted outcome has yet to occur, we just need to be patient: it will eventually. This defense is limited, of course, in its applicability to political games in which the predicted outcome has not yet been irreversibly foreclosed. No one expected Al Gore to take George W. Bush's place in the White House in 2001. Some deals are done deals. But experts did often argue that a trend they deemed likely has merely been delayed and that Canada still will disintegrate (the Parti Québecois will prevail on its third attempt), that Kazakhstan will ultimately fall into a Yugoslav-style conflagration of interethnic warfare (demagogues will seize on the opportunities for ethnic mobilization that Kazakhstan presents), that the European Monetary Union's misguided effort to create a common currency will someday end in tears and acrimony (the divergent interests of members will trigger crises that even determined leadership cannot resolve), and that nuclear war will eventually be the tragic fate of South Asia or the Korean peninsula. In effect, these experts admitted that they may have been wrong within my arbitrary time frames but they will be vindicated with the passage of time.

The "Politics is Hopelessly Cloudlike" Defense. Experts also have the philosophical option of arguing that, although all preconditions were satisfied and the predicted outcome never came close to occurring and now never will, this failure should not be held against the forecaster. Forecasting exercises are best viewed as lighthearted diversions of no consequence because everyone knows, or else should know, that politics is inherently indeterminate, more cloudlike than clocklike.[11] As Henry Kissinger wryly wrote Daniel Moynihan after the fragmentation of the Soviet Union, "Your crystal ball worked better than mine."[12] Here is a concession that concedes nothing.

A variant of this defense warns of the dangers in "stochastic environments" of anointing false prophets (those who got it right were just "lucky") and of the perils of hastily rejecting sound points of view (those who got it wrong were just unlucky). Some forecasters who thought they could say quite a bit about the future at the onset of our exercise, who

[11] Robert Jervis, "The Future of International Politics: Will It Resemble the Past?" *International Security* 16 (1992): 39–73; G. Almond and T. Genco, "Clouds, Clocks, and the Study of Politics," *World Politics* 29 (1977): 489–522.

[12] D. Moynihan, *Pandemonium* (New York: Oxford University Press, 1993).

certainly thought they had more to offer than a dart-throwing chimpanzee, sounded like radical skeptics by the end of our exercise—a transformation that raises the suspicion that some of the radical skeptics in chapter 2 were bold forecasters who had yet to recover from recent muggings by reality.

The "I made the Right Mistake" Defense. This sixth strategy concedes error but, rather than minimizing the gap between expectation and reality, it depicts the error as the natural by-product of pursuing the right political priorities. As one conservative defiantly declared, "Overestimating the staying power of the Soviet Communist Party was a wise thing to do, certainly wiser than underestimating it." Some liberals invoked a mirror image of this defense in defense of International Monetary Fund (IMF) loans to Russia in the 1990s. Much of the money may have been misdirected into Swiss bank accounts but, given the risks of allowing a nuclear superpower to implode financially, issuing the loans was, to paraphrase the number 2 decision maker at the IMF, Stanley Fischer, the "prudent thing to do."[13]

Experts resorted to the "we made the right mistake" defense in many policy arenas, including nuclear proliferation, ethnic cleansing, and financial contagion. There is, moreover, a common theme running through these examples. In each case, experts possessed value systems that allowed them to portray "false alarms" of change for the worse as less serious than "misses." As one expert replied a tad testily, "Crying wolf is the price of vigilance." In the aftermath of the terrorist assaults on New York and Washington, D.C., in September 2001, this expert added: "Americans now understand that far-fetched threats can suddenly materialize and that if you want safety, you better be paranoid."

The Low-probability Outcome Just Happened to Happen. Our listing of belief system defenses would be incomplete if we did not acknowledge those hardy souls who insisted that their initially low-likelihood estimate of x was not in error and that we need to come to existential terms with living in a low-likelihood world. This defense overlaps a lot with other defenses, such as exogenous-shock and close-call counterfactual arguments, that portray the observed outcome as fluky. But there is a distinction. One could argue that we wound up inhabiting a low-likelihood world without offering any extenuation (such as the higher-likelihood world almost occurred) or excuse (unpredictable forces blew history off course). Decision makers are constantly spinning the roulette wheel of

[13] "No. 2 Official of the IMF to Step Down at Year's End, *New York Times*, May 9, 2001, C5."

history, so we should not be astonished when the silver ball stops occasionally not in the black or red slots that make up more than 90 percent of the wheel, but in one of the few green slots.

We now shift from listening to arguments to counting them. Our goal is to document how often various groups of forecasters advanced various categories of arguments in various contexts. The closer we look, the stronger the grounds become for characterizing the arguments in aggregate as belief system defenses that experts deployed in largely self-serving ways to justify refusing to change their minds when they lost reputational bets that they themselves once endorsed.

The case for a self-serving bias in argumentation rests on several lines of evidence:

1. The suspicious selectivity with which forecasters advanced arguments that trivialized earlier reputational bets. Experts were far more likely to endorse such arguments when something unexpected occurred. In thirty-nine of sixty comparisons, t-tests revealed that experts who had just lost reputational bets (their most likely future failed to materialize) endorsed arguments from the list of seven more enthusiastically ($p < .05$) than experts who had just won such bets. By contrast, experts who had won their bets *never* showed more enthusiasm for "defensive" cognitions than experts who had just lost them.

2. The linkage between the size of mistakes and the activation of defenses. The psychologic is straightforward: the more confident experts were in the original forecast, the more threatening the disconfirmation and the more motivated experts will be to neutralize the troublesome evidence. All else equal, an expert who in 1988 was 90 percent confident that Soviet hardliners would reassert control between 1988 and 1993 should be more unsettled by intervening events than an expert who attached only slightly more than "guessing" confidence to the same forecast. To test this prediction, we created a composite defensiveness index by summing the six measured belief system defenses. The predicted pattern emerged. Among less accurate forecasters, the correlations between ex ante confidence and the composite defensiveness index are always positive, ranging from 0.26 to 0.42 across domains; among more accurate forecasters, the same correlations hover near zero, between $-.05$ and $+0.08$.

3. The linkage between reliance on defenses and retention of confidence in prior opinions. If belief system defenses cushion the blow of unexpected events, then experts whose most likely scenarios do

not materialize but who endorse "defensive" cognitions should re-tain more confidence in their original forecasts after they learn what happened (ex post confidence). But there should be no such correlation among experts whose forecasts were borne out and who should therefore not have experienced any threat to the core tenets of their belief systems. As predicted, among inaccurate fore-casters, the defensiveness index is correlated with ex post confi-dence across domains (correlations ranging from .29 to .59). By contrast, among accurate forecasters, there is almost no relation-ship between defensiveness and ex post confidence (correlations again hovering near zero, between − .01 and .06).

4. The linkages among reliance on defenses, failures of belief updating, and cognitive style. We find that (a) the more "losers" resisted revis-ing their prior opinions, the more defenses they embraced ($r = .49$); (b) hedgehog losers (who resisted changing their minds more than fox losers) embraced roughly twice as many defenses as did fox losers; (c) the larger the gap between the amount of belief change prescribed by Bayes's theorem and the amount of belief change that losing experts conceded, the more defenses experts endorsed ($r = .31$); (d) when we control for the frequency with which experts endorse belief system defenses, there ceases to be a relationship be-tween being a hedgehog and being a bad loser of reputational bets.[14]

In sum, the belief system defense hypothesis ties together many strands of evidence. Defensive cognitions are activated when forecasters most need them. And endorsement of defensive cognitions—in aggregate—distinguishes better from worse Bayesian belief updaters. But it is worth stressing that our focus has been psychological, not epistemological. We postpone a thorough discussion of the defensibility of defenses until chapter 6.[15]

HINDSIGHT EFFECTS: ARTIFACT AND FACT

When we recontacted experts to gauge their reactions to the confirma-tion or disconfirmation of their predictions, we frequently ran into an awkward problem. Our records of the probability judgments made at the beginning of forecast periods often disagreed with experts' recollections

---

[14] See D. Kenny, *Correlation and Causality* (New York: Wiley-Interscience, 1979).

[15] On the perils of "naive falsificationism" and the frequent justifiability of refusing to abandon hypotheses that have run aground awkward evidence, see I. Lakatos, ed., *Criticism and the Growth of Knowledge* (Cambridge: Cambridge University Press, 1972), 9–101; F. Suppe, *The Structure of Scientific Theories* (Urbana: University of Illinois Press, 1974).

of what they predicted. There was, moreover, a systematic bias in these recollections. Experts claimed that they assigned higher probabilities to outcomes that materialized than they did. From a narrowly Bayesian perspective, this 20/20 hindsight effect was a methodological nuisance: it is hard to ask someone why they got it wrong when they think they got it right. But from a psychological perspective, the hindsight effect is intriguing in its own right. What counts as fact or artifact depends on the goals of inquiry.[16]

For purposes of assessing Bayesian belief updating, it was necessary to remind experts, as delicately as possible, of their original predictions. Only then could we pose the question: given your earlier position and given subsequent events, do you want to change your mind? But the opportunity to build on psychological work on hindsight bias was irresistible,[17] so we decided, in six cases, to ask experts to recollect their positions prior to receiving the reminder from our records. Those cases were the Soviet Union/Russia (1988–1993), South Africa (1988–1989, 1993–1994), Canada (1993–1998), China (1992–1997), European Monetary Union (1992–1997, 1998–2001), and the Korean peninsula (1992–1997).

Figure 4.2 shows that we replicated two well-established laboratory effects: (a) widespread susceptibility to the hindsight bias; (b) more pronounced hindsight bias among hedgehogs.[18] When we asked experts to recall their original likelihood judgments, experts, especially hedgehogs, often claimed that they attached higher probabilities to what subsequently happened than they did. Figure 4.2 also adds a new wrinkle. Experts shortchanged the competition. When experts recalled the probabilities they once thought their most influential rivals would assign to the future that materialized, they imputed lower probabilities after the fact than before the fact. In effect, experts displayed both the classic hindsight effect (claiming more credit for predicting the future than they deserved) and the mirror-image hindsight effect (giving less credit to their opponents for anticipating the future than they deserved).

[16] See W. J. McGuire, "A Contextualist Theory of Knowledge: Its Implications for Innovation and Reform in Psychological Research," *Advances in Experimental and Social Psychology* 16 (1983): 3–87.

[17] S. Hawkins and R. Hastie, "Hindsight: Biased Judgment of Past Events after the Outcomes Are Known," *Psychological Bulletin* 107 (1990): 311–27.

[18] J. Campbell and A. Tesser, "Motivational Interpretations of Hindsight Bias: An Individual Difference Analysis," *Journal of Personality* 51 (1983): 605–20; some also argue that hindsight distortion will be most pronounced when better possible worlds fail to occur because people are motivated to avoid disappointment by portraying such worlds as impossible. See O. E. Tykocinski, D. Pick, and D. Kedmi, "Retroactive Pessimism: A Different Kind of Hindsight Bias," *European Journal of Social Psychology* 32(4) (2002): 577–88. We did not find support for this argument.

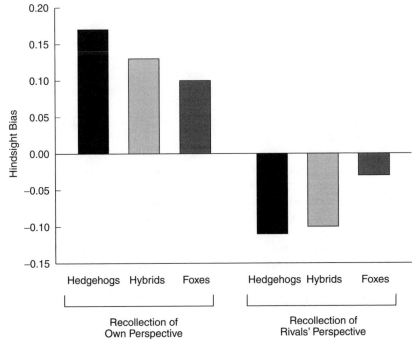

Figure 4.2. The relative magnitude of the hindsight bias when experts try to recall: (a) the probabilities that they themselves once assigned to possible futures (own perspective); and (b) the probabilities that they once said intellectual rivals would assign the same possible futures. Positive scores on the y-axis mean a "knew it all along" or positive hindsight bias; negative scores mean a "never would have known it" or negative hindsight bias. Hedgehogs show stronger "I know it all along" bias as well as the complementary "They never would have known it all along" bias.

Hindsight effects are undoubtedly partly rooted in the simple human desire to portray oneself as smarter, and to portray rivals as dumber, than is the case. In the most cynical variant of this view, people knew what their prior positions were and dissembled. This explanation cannot, however, explain all the evidence. Experimenters find the memory-distortion effect even when, as was the case here, people know the researcher has access to the correct answers and can detect false self-promotion.

A fuller explanation must trace hindsight bias to a deeper cause capable of producing genuine self-deception: the largely unconscious cognitive processing that is automatically activated whenever we learn what has happened and that allows us to rapidly assimilate the observed outcome into our network of beliefs about what makes things happen. People manage to convince themselves, sometimes within milliseconds, that they knew it all along. This explanation dovetails nicely with the greater propensity of hedgehogs to exhibit the effect. Hedgehogs should place a higher value on cognitive continuity, on minimizing gaps between their current and past opinions. Hedgehogs should thus be more predisposed—by dint of their cognitive and emotional makeup—to assimilate outcomes, as soon as they become known, into their favorite explanatory categories.

This explanation also helps to account for why the hindsight bias was so selective, inflating the powers of foresight only of like-minded, right-thinking observers and deflating those of one's rivals. The world did not become retrospectively foreseeable for everyone. The clarity of ex post determinism was reserved for those with the correct worldviews.[19]

Discerning readers might, however, sense a contradiction between two results: the greater susceptibility of hedgehogs to hindsight effects and the greater interest of hedgehogs in invoking close-call counterfactuals that rescue forecasts from disconfirmation. Hindsight bias portrays what happened as, in retrospect, inevitable: hence, something one should have foreseen. By contrast, close-call counterfactuals portray what happened as highly contingent: hence, unforeseeable. How could the same people invoke such contradictory defenses?

The short answer is that the same people did not usually invoke these two defenses. Although the correlation between being a hedgehog and endorsing close-call counterfactuals is statistically significant (.36), as is the correlation between being a hedgehog and hindsight bias (.29), the correlation between endorsing close-call counterfactuals and susceptibility to hindsight bias is a meager .11.[20]

The pieces of the puzzle now fit together. The hindsight bias and belief system defenses are complementary strategies of reinforcing our self-images as rational beings: hindsight bias pumps up the likelihood we

[19] In chapter 6, defenders of hedgehogs try to trivialize the hindsight bias by arguing that, cognitive resources being finite, it is adaptive to wipe the mental slate clean after we have learned what happened.

[20] Although the two defenses are weakly correlated, some observers displayed both effects. This is possible if beliefs serve shifting mixtures of functions over time. Close-call counterfactuals may initially serve as shock absorbers that cushion disconfirmation bumps as we travel through history: "Oops, my most likely scenario of a hard-liner coup to save the USSR did not materialize, but it almost did." Gradually, though, these close-call arguments become integral parts of our mental models of the world with which we must come to terms: "Mulling it over, I guess the USSR was doomed and the coup that tried to stave off the inevitable was fated to fail." Such revised mental models build on and subtly modify the cause-effect reasoning that led to the original off-base forecast. This restructuring is often so seamless that observers feel as though they "knew all along" both why the outcome had to occur roughly as it did and why the future they once thought likely was fated not to occur. What happened can feel inevitable even though it was unexpected and the unexpected initially had to be explained away as an aberration.

recall attaching to futures that materialized, whereas the belief system defenses stress the reasonableness of the opinions that once led us to think other things would happen. Why change one's mind in response to the unexpected when one can convince oneself that one saw it coming all along, and to the degree one must concede an element of surprise, one can still argue that one's earlier expectations were at least "almost right"?

LINKING PROCESS AND CORRESPONDENCE CONCEPTIONS OF GOOD JUDGMENT

We can close the circumstantial circle of correlational evidence. Chapter 3 used a variety of indicators to show that foxes attached more realistic probability estimates to possible futures than did hedgehogs. The best-fitting explanation traced the performance differential to the different reasoning styles of foxes and hedgehogs. The fox advantages in forecasting accuracy disappeared when we controlled for the influence of styles of reasoning—the tendency of foxes to report thoughts that were both self-critical in content and dialectical in structure, alternating between advancing reasons for expecting an outcome, then shifting into critiques of that reasoning and generating arguments for expecting opposing outcomes, and finally shifting into self-reflective efforts to forge viable syntheses of the clashing considerations. Foxes were, in psychological jargon, more "integratively complex" than hedgehogs.[21]

Chapter 4 has shown that, although foxes were far from perfect belief updaters by Bayesian standards, they were more likely to change their minds in the right direction and to the right degree when the unexpected happened, as often it did. The best-fitting explanation traced the performance differential to two factors: (a) the greater reliance of hedgehogs on belief system defenses such as close-call counterfactuals and off-on-timing that gave them intellectual cover for arguing that no serious mistake had been made and for refusing to abandon prior positions; (b) the greater susceptibility of hedgehogs to hindsight bias that allowed them to maintain with conviction the fiction that their original predictions were not all that far off the mark.

In both chapters, the root cause of hedgehog underperformance has been a reluctance to entertain the possibility that they might be wrong. This interpretation ties together additional loose ends. The integrative-complexity index, the measure of self-critical reasoning that predicted correspondence indicators of good judgment in chapter 3, also predicted the tendencies to resist changing probability estimates in response to the

---

[21] Suedfeld and Tetlock, "Individual Differences."

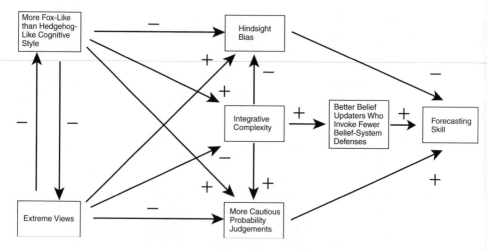

Figure 4.3. A conceptual framework that builds on figure 3.5. It inserts what we learned in chapter 4 about the tendency of integratively complex foxes to be better Bayesian belief updaters. It posits that integratively complex thinkers enjoy advantages in forecasting skill, in part, because they are more willing to change their minds in response to the unexpected, in part, because they are more likely to remember past mistakes (reduced hindsight bias), and in part, because they are more likely to see the case for expecting opposing outcomes and thus make cautious probability estimates. Those quicker to acknowledge past mistakes are less prone to make future mistakes.

unexpected, to mobilize belief system defenses that justify those prior estimates, and to exhibit the hindsight bias in recall of past positions (r's = .26, .35, and .27). The same, self-justifying, hedgehog style of reasoning that translated into poorer forecasting performance translated into poorer belief-updating performance. Inspection of correlation matrices also reveals that better belief updaters had better forecasting records, especially calibration scores. These correlations are also not stunningly large—ranging between .25 and .36—but they are consistently significant. When we formally factor the fallibility of our measures into the equation by correcting for attenuation of correlations due to unreliability, the convergence of evidence is all the more impressive.

Figure 4.3 integrates these new findings into the conceptual framework for good judgment laid out in Figure 3.6. The effects of a foxlike, integratively complex style of reasoning on forecasting skill are now mediated by the tendencies both to hedge probability bets and to be better belief updaters.

But have we learned anything surprising about good judgment in the late twentieth century? Here we run into the defining dilemma of the social scientist: the choice between being judged either obvious or obviously wrong. Intellectual foxes will see the current results as a rather unsurprising, although still welcome, vindication of what they have been saying all along. These scholars have repeatedly traced the psychological roots of intelligence failures to an unwillingness to be sufficiently self-critical, to reexamine underlying assumptions, to question dogma, and to muster the imagination to think daringly about options that others might ridicule.[22] Political observers are well advised to heed Oliver Cromwell's (unintentionally ironic but intentionally ominous) advice to his foes in 1650: "I beseech you, in the bowels of Christ, think it possible you may be mistaken."[23]

Hedgehog commentators will not be so welcoming. They will see the current results as deeply misleading, for reasons laid out in chapter 6: policy and intelligence failures can more often be traced to paralysis and self-doubt induced by excessive self-criticism. To paraphrase Dean Acheson's admonition to Richard Neustadt during the Cuban missile crisis, "I know your theory, professor. You think the president should be warned. But you are wrong. He needs confidence." So-called biases such as overconfidence and belief perseverance put sorely needed backbone in policy.

Arguments over the right process prescriptions are rooted as much in temperament as in evidence. Still, evidence is not irrelevant. The data tell us something that one camp suspected was true, another camp suspected was false, but neither camp had investigated systematically because both camps were convinced of the blindingly obvious truth of their positions. It must be left to posterity to judge whether the results to this point are obvious or obviously wrong.

[22] Many academics have endorsed these prescriptions (for a review, P. E. Tetlock, "Social Psychology and World Politics"). And so have many intelligence analysts—foremost among them, Sherman Kent, who was famous for admonishing his colleagues to be skeptical of favorite sources and alert to the power of prejudices to bias assessments of evidence (S. Kent, *Collected Essays*, U.S. Government: Center for the Study of Intelligence, 1970, http://www.cia.gov/csi/books/shermankent/toc.html).
[23] E. R. May, *Lessons of the Past: The Use and Misuses of History in American Foreign Policy* (New York: Oxford University Press, 1973).

CHAPTER 5

Contemplating Counterfactuals

FOXES ARE MORE WILLING THAN HEDGEHOGS
TO ENTERTAIN SELF-SUBVERSIVE SCENARIOS

> The historian must . . . constantly put himself at a point in the past at which the known factors will seem to permit different outcomes. If he speaks of Salamis, then it must be as if the Persians might still win; if he speaks of the coup d'état of the Brumaire, then it must remain to be seen if Bonaparte will be ignominiously repulsed.
>
> —JOHAN HUIZINGA

> The long run always wins in the end. Annihilating innumerable events—all those which cannot be accommodated in the main ongoing current and which therefore are ruthlessly swept to one side—it indubitably limits both the freedom of the individual and even the role of chance.
>
> —FERNAND BRAUDEL

> Men use the past to prop up their prejudices.
>
> —A.J.P. TAYLOR

THERE IS SOMETHING disturbing about the notion that history might turn out to be, as radical skeptics have indefatigably insisted, one damned thing after another. And there is something reassuring about the notion that people can, if they look hard enough, discover patterns in the procession of historical events and these patterns can become part of humanity's shared endowment of knowledge. We need not repeat the same dreadful mistakes ad nauseam and ad infinitum. Here is a bedrock issue on which hedgehogs and foxes can agree: good judgment presupposes some capacity to learn from history.

The agreement does not last long, however. The strikingly different intellectual temperaments that shaped thinking about the future in chapters 3 and 4 shape thinking about the past in chapter 5. Hedgehogs are still drawn to ambitious conceptual schemes that satisfy their craving for explanatory closure. And foxes are still wary of grand generalizations: they draw lessons from history that are riddled with probabilistic loopholes and laced with contingencies and paradoxes.

Chapter 5 works from the premise that underlying all lessons that experts extract from history are implicit counterfactual assumptions about how events would have unfolded if key factors had taken different forms. If we want to understand why experts extract one rather than another lesson from history, we need to understand the preconceptions they bring to the analysis of what was possible or impossible at particular times and places. Chapter 5 also provides an array of evidence that suggests how powerful these preconceptions can be. We can do a startlingly good job of predicting how experts judge specific historical possibilities from broad ideological orientations. And these prediction coefficients are especially large among hedgehogs who are unembarrassed about approaching history in a top-down fashion in which they deduce what was plausible in specific situations from abstract first principles.

Chapter 5 does not, however, confuse correlation with causality. It also relies on turnabout thought experiments—that manipulate the content of fresh discoveries from historical archives—to gauge experts' willingness to change their minds. Reassuringly, most are prepared, in principle, to modify their counterfactual beliefs in response to new facts. But the effect sizes for facts are small and those for preconceptions large. Hedgehogs and foxes alike impose more stringent standards of proof on dissonant discoveries (that undercut pet theories) than they do on consonant ones (that reinforce pet theories). Moreover, true to character type, hedgehogs exhibit stronger double standards and rise more unapologetically to the defense of those standards.

JUDGING THE PLAUSIBILITY OF COUNTERFACTUAL REROUTINGS OF HISTORY

Learning from the past is hard, in part, because history is a terrible teacher. By the generous standards of the laboratory sciences, Clio is stingy in her feedback: she never gives us the exact comparison cases we need to determine causality (those are cordoned off in the what-iffy realm of counterfactuals), and she often begrudges us even the roughly comparable real-world cases that we need to make educated guesses. The control groups "exist"—if that is the right word—only in the imaginations of observers, who must guess how history would have unfolded if, say, Churchill rather than Chamberlain had been prime minister during the Munich crisis of 1938 (could we have averted World War II?) or if, say, the United States had moved more aggressively against the Soviet Union during the Cuban missile crisis of 1962 (could we have triggered World War III?).[1]

But we, the pupils, should not escape all blame. A warehouse of experimental evidence now attests to our cognitive shortcomings: our willingness to jump the inferential gun, to be too quick to draw strong conclusions from ambiguous evidence, and to be too slow to change our minds as disconfirming observations trickle in.[2] A balanced apportionment of blame should acknowledge that learning is hard because even seasoned professionals are ill-equipped to cope with the complexity, ambiguity, and dissonance inherent in assessing causation in history. Life throws up a lot of puzzling events that thoughtful observers feel impelled to explain because the policy stakes are so high. However, just because we want an explanation does not mean that one is within reach. To achieve explanatory closure in history, observers must fill in the missing counterfactual comparison scenarios with elaborate stories grounded in their deepest assumptions about how the world works.[3]

That is why, cynics have suggested, it is so easy to infer specific counterfactual beliefs from abstract political orientations. The classic example is the recurring debate between hawks and doves over the utility of tougher versus softer influence tactics.[4] Hawkish advocates of deterrence are convinced that the cold war would have lasted longer than it did if, instead of a Reagan presidency, we had had a two-term Carter presidency,[5] whereas doveish advocates of reassurance are convinced that the cold war would have ended on pretty much the same schedule. Surveying the entire cold war, hawkish defenders of nuclear deterrence argue that nuclear weapons saved us from ourselves, inducing circumspection and sobriety in superpower policies. But doveish critics reply that we were extraordinarily lucky and that, if a whimsical deity reran cold war history one hundred times, permitting only minor random variations in starting conditions, nuclear conflicts would be a common outcome.[6] The confidence with which observers of world politics announce such counterfactual opinions is itself remarkable. Whatever their formal logical status, counterfactual beliefs often feel factual to their holders. It is almost

---

[1] J. Fearon, "Counterfactuals and Hypothesis Testing in Political Science," *World Politics* 43 (1991): 169–95, 474–84; P. E. Tetlock and A. Belkin, *Counterfactual Thought Experiments in World Politics: Logical, Methodological, and Psychological Perspectives* (Princeton, NJ: Princeton University Press, 1996).

[2] S. Fiske and S. Taylor, "Social Cognition."

[3] N. J. Roese, "Counterfactual Thinking," *Psychological Bulletin* 121 (1997): 133–48.

[4] A.J.P. Taylor, *The Struggle for Mastery in Europe, 1848–1918* (Oxford: Clarendon, 1954).

[5] Pipes.

[6] On the "theoretical implications" of the Cold War: J. L. Gaddis, "International Relations Theory and the End of the Cold War," *International Security* 17 (1992): 5–58.

as though experts were telling us: "Of course, I know what would have happened. I just got back from a trip in my alternative-universe teleportation device and can assure you that events there dovetailed perfectly with my preconceptions."

Our first order of business was therefore to determine to what degree counterfactual reasoning is a theory-driven, top-down affair in which observers deduce from their worldviews what was possible at specific times and places. Is the appropriate mental model the covering-law syllogism in which the major premise is "this generalization about societies, economies, or international relations is true," the minor premise is "this generalization covers this case," and the conclusion is "this generalization tells me what would have happened if details of the case had been different"? Or is counterfactual reasoning a messy bottom-up affair in which observers often surprise themselves and discover things in the hurly-burly of history that they never expected to find? Do they often start out thinking an outcome inconceivable but, in the light of new evidence, change their minds?

Common sense tells us that each hypothesis must capture some of the truth. If we did not rely on our preconceptions to organize the past, we would be hopelessly confused. Everything would feel unprecedented. And if we relied solely on our preconceptions, we would be hopelessly closed-minded. Nothing could induce us to change our minds. Common sense can only take us so far, though. There is no substitute for empirical exploration of how the mix of theory-driven and data-driven reasoning varies as a function of both the cognitive style of the observer and the political content of the counterfactual.

This chapter tests two key hypotheses. First, hedgehogs should be drawn to more top-down, deductive arguments, foxes to more bottom-up inductive arguments. It should thus be easier to predict hedgehogs' reactions to historical counterfactuals from their ideological orientation than to predict foxes' reactions from theirs. Second, counterfactual arguments are logically complex. One can agree with some parts of subjunctive conditionals and disagree with others. Consider: "If Stalin had survived his cerebral hemorrhage in March 1953, but in an impaired state of mind, nuclear war would have broken out soon thereafter." An observer could concede the mutability of the antecedent (Stalin could have survived longer if his medical condition had been different) but still insist that even a cowed Politburo would have blocked Stalin from acting in ways guaranteed to kill them all. Hence the observer would disagree with the implicit connecting principles that bridge antecedent and consequent. This analysis suggests that counterfactual reasoning is a two-stage affair in which the first stage is sensitive to historical details bearing on the mutability of antecedents (is there wiggle room at this juncture?) and the second stage is dominated by theory-driven assessments of antecedent-consequent linkages and long-term ramifications (what would be the short- and long-term effects of the permissible wiggling?).

To test these hypotheses, we needed to satisfy an array of measurement preconditions in each historical domain investigated. The Methodological Appendix itemizes these preconditions, including reliable and valid measures of cognitive style, of ideological or theoretical convictions, and of reactions to specific counterfactual scenarios that tap into each possible line of logical defense against dissonant counterfactual scenarios. The next section summarizes the historical laws at stake in each domain, the counterfactual probes selected for provoking irritated rejection from believers in those laws, and the principal findings.

History of the USSR

Competing Schemas. Conservative observers viewed the Soviet state, from its Bolshevik beginnings, as intrinsically totalitarian and oppressively monolithic. Stalinism was no aberration: it was the natural outgrowth of Leninism. Liberal observers subscribed to more pluralistic conceptions of the Soviet polity. They dated cleavages between doctrinaire and reformist factions of the party back to the 1920s and they saw nothing foreordained about the paths taken since then.[7] These observers suspected that the system had some legitimacy and that dissolution was not the inevitable result of Gorbachev's policies of glasnost and perestroika.

Counterfactual Probes. The competing schemas carry starkly different implications for the acceptability of specific close-call scenarios. Once the Soviet Union comes into existence in 1917, conservatives see far less flexibility than do liberals for "rewriting" history by imagining what might have happened had different people been in charge of the party apparatus: counterfactuals such as "If the Communist Party of the Soviet Union had deposed Stalin in the early 1930s, the Soviet Union would have moved toward a kinder, gentler version of socialism fifty years earlier than it did," or "If Malenkov had prevailed in the post-Stalin succession struggle, the cold war would have ended in the 1950s rather than the 1980s," or "If Gorbachev had been a shrewder tactician in his pacing of reforms, the Soviet Union would exist today." Conservatives tend to believe only powerful external forces can make a difference and are thus receptive only to counterfactuals that front-load big causes: "Were it not for the chaos and misery of World War I, there would have been no

[7] Stephen F. Cohen, Alexander Rabinowitch, and Robert Sharlet, *The Soviet Union Since Stalin* (Bloomington: Indiana University Press, 1985).

TABLE 5.1

Correlations between Political Ideology and Counterfactual Beliefs of Area Study Specialists

Counterfactual	Antecedent	Antecedent/ Consequent Linkage
About Soviet Union		
No WWI, no Bolshevik Revolution	.25	−.57
Longer life to Lenin, no Stalinism	.13	.68
Depose Stalin, kinder, gentler Communism	.66	.70
Malenkov prevails, early end to cold war	.17	.71
No Gorbachev, CPSU has conservative shift	−.16	.30
No Reagan, no early end to cold war	−.30	−.74
A shrewder Gorbachev, Soviet Union survives	.11	.51
About South Africa		
No de Klerk, still white-minority rule	.15	−.42
No Mandela, still white-minority rule	.08	−.10
No Western sanctions, still white-minority rule	.06	.48
No demographic pressures, still white-minority rule	.11	.15
No Soviet collapse, fewer white concessions	.18	−.51

Note: Larger positive correlations, stronger liberal endorsement.

Bolshevik Revolution" or "Were it not for Reagan's hard-line policies, the cold war would not have ended as peacefully and quickly as it did."

Findings. Table 5.1 shows that ideology proved a potent predictor of resistance to dissonant close-call counterfactuals, but it was primarily a predictor of resistance grounded in the more abstract, "theoretical" belief system defenses that either challenged connecting principles or invoked second-order counterfactuals. Sovietologists who subscribed to opposing images of the Soviet Union rarely disagreed over the mutability of antecedents: whether Malenkov could have won enough Politburo support in 1953 to prevail or whether Gorbachev could have failed to win enough support to prevail in 1985. To get a good brawl going among Sovietologists, it was usually necessary to put the spotlight on the large-scale historical consequences of these small-scale modifications of antecedent conditions: whether Malenkov would have brought about a more rapid end to the cold war or an alternative to Gorbachev could have done a better job of holding the Soviet Union together.[8]

Discussion. Historical observers draw on different criteria in judging different components of counterfactual arguments. The initial "decision" of how to evaluate the "if" premise of what-if scenarios often appears to be under the control of strong narrative expectations grounded in assessments of particular historical players confronting particular challenges. People find it hard to resist being lured into what-if thoughts when this narrative coherence is violated by something surprising: when they learn the result of a close-call vote or learn that unusually tolerant or paranoid leaders have come to power or that commanding figures have fallen from grace or that healthy people have suddenly dropped dead. Our natural response to these violations of our expectations is to "undo" the aberration mentally, to wonder how things would have unfolded but for. . . . However, once people have been lured into counterfactual cogitation, they need to rely on increasingly abstract, ideology-laden beliefs about cause and effect to figure out the longer-term significance of these developments.[9]

The big exception to these generalizations was Stalin. Liberals and conservatives strongly disagreed over the plausibility of the antecedent as well as over the conditional linkage for the Stalinism counterfactual. Conservatives had a harder time than liberals imagining that the Soviet Communist Party could have purged, or would have wanted to purge, Stalin in the early 1930s. From a conservative perspective, which views Stalinism (not just Stalin) as the natural next step of Leninism, the deletion-of-Stalin counterfactual violates the minimal-rewrite rule. But this counterfactual may well pass the minimal-rewrite test for those with a more liberal perspective on Soviet polity.

Liberals and conservatives also disagreed on what would have happened if Stalin had been deposed. Like most historical counterfactuals, this one does not spell out the complex connecting principles necessary for

[8] This differential predictability was not due to statistical artifacts such as differential reliability of measures or restriction-of-range artifacts.

[9] N. J. Roese, "Counterfactual Thinking," *Psychological Bulletin* 121 (1997): 133–48; P. E. Tetlock and P. Visser, "Thinking about Russia: Possible Pasts and Probable Futures," *British Journal of Social Psychology* 39 (2000): 173–96.

bridging the logical gap between antecedent and consequent. To hold the counterfactual together, it is necessary to posit that advocates of Gorbachev-style socialism in the Communist Party of the Soviet Union (CPSU) would have seized the reins of power and guided the Soviet state toward social democracy. Conservatives regard such arguments as fanciful.

Taken as a whole, these data are open to two rival interpretations. One hypothesis asserts that those on the left view history as more fluid, contingent, and indeterminate than those on the right. The other asserts that liberals and conservatives do not have fundamentally different philosophies of history but there is something special about the Soviet Union that motivates wistful perceptions of lost possibilities on the left and angry accusations of inevitable repression and expansion on the right. If we could identify a state that excites fear and loathing on the left comparable to that once excited by the Soviet Union on the right, we would observe a sign reversal of the correlation coefficients between ideological sympathies and counterfactual beliefs. South Africa was the ideal case for teasing these hypotheses apart.

Demise of White-minority Rule in South Africa

Competing Schemas. Observers on the left now leaned toward essentialism. The incorrigibly racist, white-minority regime would cede power only under enormous pressure. Observers on the right favored a more pluralistic view of politics inside Pretoria. They sensed that "verligte" or enlightened factions were eager to enter into flexible power-sharing arrangements.

Counterfactual Probes. This disagreement was as close to a mirror image of the controversy over the Soviet Union as nature was going to provide. We therefore hypothesized a reversal in relative openness to close-call counterfactuals: the right would now embrace counterfactuals that assign a key role to political personalities within the regime (e.g., "If no de Klerk, then continued impasse"), and the left would now embrace counterfactuals that assign a key role to external pressure (e.g., "If no Western sanctions, then continued minority rule"). The operative principle is dissonance reduction: the more we hate a regime, the more repugnant it becomes to attribute anything good to redemptive dispositions of the regime (such as a capacity for self-correction).

Findings. Consistent with the two-stage model of counterfactual inference, political ideology was again an anemic predictor of the mutability of historical antecedents but a robust predictor of antecedent-consequent linkages. Conservatives assigned more credit to de Klerk and to the collapse of Soviet-style Communism, whereas liberals gave more credit to Western sanctions.

The debate over the impact of sanctions on South Africa does indeed closely mirror the debate over the impact of Reagan's defense buildup on the Soviet Union. Paraphrasing sentiments some Western liberals attributed to the Soviet elite at the dawn of the Gorbachev period, one conservative argued that the momentum for change inside South Africa had become irresistible because white elites had concluded from the township revolts and demographic trends that they "could not go on living this way." Another conservative argued that credit for ending white-minority rule should go to Reagan, whose policies precipitated the implosion of Soviet Communism, allowing de Klerk to convince his followers that negotiating with the ANC was not tantamount to surrender to the Kremlin. We thus come full circle. The observer refuted the argument that "even if you conservatives were right about the Soviet Union, you were wrong about South Africa" by arguing that "it was because we conservatives were right about the Soviet Union that we were also right about South Africa."

Discussion. Conservatives' openness to the de Klerk counterfactual in the South African case parallels liberals' openness to the Stalin, Malenkov, and Gorbachev counterfactuals in the Soviet case; liberals' skepticism toward the Reagan-pressure counterfactual in the Soviet case parallels conservatives' skepticism toward the economic sanctions counterfactual in the South African case. These data undermine the sweeping claim that liberals subscribe to a more contingent view of philosophy of history than conservatives. Much hinges on whose "policy ox" is being gored.

Taken together, the two studies show that beliefs about specific counterfactual possibilities were rather tightly coupled to overall ideological outlooks. But neither study was well equipped to test the cognitive-style hypothesis that hedgehogs are more likely than foxes to reject close-call counterfactuals that undercut their pet theories. And both studies were conducted when the policy debates had only recently been rendered moot (1992 in the Soviet case, 1995 in the South African case), leaving open the question of what happens when scholars contemplate counterfactuals that undo events further removed from current controversies. Does temporal distance reduce the iron grip of our preconceptions on our judgments of what could have been? The next four studies address these issues.

Rerouting History at Earlier Choice Points

UNMAKING THE WEST

Competing Schemas. Historians have long puzzled over how a small number of Europeans, and their colonial offshoots, came between 1400 and 1700 C.E. to exert such disproportionate influence around the globe. The resulting debate has polarized scholars. In one camp are determinists who view Western geopolitical ascendancy as having been inevitable for a long time. Western culture possessed critical advantages in the Darwinian struggle for societal survival: more deeply rooted traditions of private property and individual rights, a religion that encouraged achievement in this world, and a fractious multistate system that prevented any single power from dominating all others and bringing all innovation to a grinding halt whenever reactionary whims struck the ruling elite. In the other camp are the radical antideterminists who believe, to adapt Gould's famous thought experiment, that if we were to rerun world history repeatedly from the same conditions that prevailed as recently as 1500 C.E., European dominance would be a rare outcome. The European achievement was a precarious one that can be easily unraveled.

Counterfactual Probes. Antideterminists have generated a long list of close-call counterfactuals designed to puncture "Eurocentric triumphalism": South Asia, East Africa, and perhaps the Americas might have been colonized by an invincible Chinese armada in the fifteenth century if there had been more support in the imperial court for innovation and expansion; Europe might have been conquered and Islamicized in the eighth century if the Moors had cared to launch a serious invasion of southern France and Italy; and European civilization might have been devastated by Mongol armies in the thirteenth century but for the fortuitous timing of Genghis Khan's death.

Findings. Table 5.2 shows that the more experts embraced deterministic explanations for Western dominance, the more dismissive they were of counterfactuals that implied that the West was just luckier than the Rest and the more prone they were to reject counterfactuals that implied that other civilizations could have blocked Western hegemony or achieved dominance themselves. The hypothesized interaction also emerged: the power of preconceptions to predict reactions to counterfactuals was greater among the hedgehogs who—as one might expect by now—struggled harder to squeeze history into their ideological frameworks. By contrast, foxes were more tolerant of counterfactuals that poked holes in their ideological frameworks. This cognitive-style-by-ideological-worldview interaction also held in the final three studies, which explored reactions to rewrites of twentieth-century history.

THE OUTBREAK OF WORLD WAR I

Competing Schemas. Some scholars believe that war among the Great Powers of Europe in the early twentieth-century was inevitable. This thesis

TABLE 5.2
Predicting Resistance to Close-call Counterfactuals

Covering Law	β	SE	t	p
Neorealist balancing	0.96	0.30	3.18	.001
Cognitive style	0.35	0.29	1.20	NS
Balancing × style	0.74	0.36	2.07	.01
$n = 87$				
$R^2 = 0.47$				
Nuclear deterrence	0.89	0.34	2.65	.01
Cognitive style	0.33	0.31	1.07	NS
Deterrence × style	0.69	0.33	2.06	.01
$n = 86$				
$R^2 = 0.43$				
Adaptive advantage of West	0.82	0.36	2.27	.01
Cognitive style	0.23	0.28	0.83	NS
West × style	0.73	0.36	2.01	.05
$n = 63$				
$R^2 = 0.41$				

Note: This table presents the results of multiple regressions that treat resistance to close-call counterfactuals as the dependent variable and treat as independent variables experts' commitment to theoretical schools of thought (neorealist balancing, robustness of nuclear deterrence, adaptive advantage of West), cognitive style (need for closure/reflected version of hedgehog-fox scale), and a cross-product term for capturing whether resistance is greatest when both theoretical commitment and need for closure are highest.

is often grounded in causal arguments that stress the inherent instability of multiethnic empires and multipolar balances of power, as well as the "cult of the offensive" (the widespread perception among general staffs that the side that struck first would gain a decisive advantage).

Counterfactual Probes. The more experts endorse these "macro" causal arguments, the more ill-disposed they should be toward counterfactuals that imply that war could have been avoided by undoing one of the bizarre coincidences preceding the assassination of Archduke Ferdinand or by permitting minor alterations of the content or timing of diplomatic messages exchanged among the Great Powers in the six weeks preceding the outbreak of war.

THE OUTCOMES OF WORLD WARS I AND II

Competing Schemas. Neorealist balancing, a profoundly influential framework in world politics, asserts that when one state threatens to dominate the international system, other states coalesce to preserve the balance of power.[10] It is no accident that would-be world conquerors such as Philip II, Napoleon, and Hitler failed: their failures were predetermined by this fundamental law of world politics.

Counterfactual Probes.   The more experts endorse neorealist balancing, the more ill-disposed they should be to close-call counterfactuals that imply that the Germans could easily have emerged victorious in either of the two world wars and achieved at least continental hegemony if they had made better strategic-military decisions at key junctures.

WHY THE COLD WAR NEVER GOT "HOT"

Competing Schemas.   Some scholars believe in the robustness of nuclear deterrence and mutual assured destruction: rational actors do not commit suicide.[11] When these scholars look back on the cold war, they find it hard to imagine that crises could have escalated out of control (just as they have a hard time getting agitated about future dangers of nuclear proliferation).

Counterfactual Probes.   These scholars should be dismissive of close-call counterfactuals in which the United States and USSR slip into nuclear war at various junctures in the cold war (e.g., if Kennedy had heeded the advice of his hawkish advisers and launched air strikes against Soviet missile sites in Cuba in October 1962, or if Eisenhower had followed through on his threat to use nuclear weapons to break the stalemate in the Korean War).

Aggregated Findings.   In all three twentieth-century contexts, the more committed scholars were to a generalization undercut by a counterfactual, the more dismissive they were of that counterfactual. And in all three contexts, hedgehogs were especially likely to dismiss counterfactuals that undercut their theoretical commitments. As table 5.2 underscores, counterfactuals were viewed as a nuisance at best, and a threat at worst, to analysts on the prowl for ways of achieving explanatory closure by assimilating past events into favorite theories of history.

Also, again, we observe far tighter links between theoretical orientations to world politics and the more historically transportable belief system defenses (challenging connecting principles and generating second-order

[10] J. A. Vasquez, "The Realist Paradigm and Degenerative versus Progressive Research Programs: An Appraisal of Neotraditional Research on Waltz's Balancing Proposition," *American Political Science Review* 91 (1997): 899–913; K. N. Waltz, *Theory of International Politics* (Reading, MA: Addison-Wesley, 1979).

[11] S. Sagan and K. Waltz, *The Spread of Nuclear Weapons: A Debate* (New York: W. W. Norton, 1995).

counterfactuals) than we do with the most historically rooted defense (challenging the mutability of the antecedent). There is no reason why one's position on the macro causes of war should predict whether one believes the assassination of Archduke Ferdinand could have been thwarted if his carriage driver had a better sense of direction or why one's position on the robustness of nuclear deterrence should predict whether one believes Stalin could have survived his cerebral hemorrhage.

Curiously though, the strategy of resisting close-call counterfactuals by challenging the mutability of the antecedent was not completely decoupled from abstract beliefs. Ideological orientations predicted significant (8 percent to 12 percent) proportions of the variance in judgments of the mutability of antecedents. These results suggest that even the most apolitical facts—the reconnaissance capabilities of U-2 aircraft on partly cloudy days or the cerebrovascular health of an aging dictator— can quickly be politicized as soon as rival schools of thought discover an advantage in showing a downstream outcome to be either easy or hard to undo.

Taken in their entirety, the results might appear at odds with those in chapter 4 in which hedgehogs endorsed more close-call counterfactuals than did foxes. Context, however, matters. In chapter 4, hedgehogs showed more interest in only those close-call counterfactuals that protected their forecasts from disconfirmation, that let them save face by invoking the "I was almost right" defense. The contradiction vanishes when we consider how hedgehogs could most efficiently achieve the same face-saving goal in settings, like those here in chapter 5, in which close-call counterfactuals undermine their favorite deterministic accounts of the past. Protecting one's belief system now requires invoking the "I was not almost wrong" defense, demonstrating that, although it might look easy to derail a historical process, on close inspection it is remarkably difficult: as soon as one cuts off one pathway to the observed outcome, other pathways arise, hydralike, in second-order counterfactuals. There is nothing stylistically inconsistent in rejecting close-call counterfactuals that challenge one's preferred explanations of the past and embracing close calls that buffer one's expectations about the future from refutation.

Assessing Double Standards in Setting Standards of Evidence and Proof

These data raise a worrisome question: What is to stop politically motivated observers from positing counterfactuals that justify whatever causal assertions they find it expedient to make? Tetlock and Belkin answer this question by specifying criteria for winnowing out specious counterfactuals.[12] They argue that, although counterfactual claims are strictly speaking about empirically inaccessible possible worlds (no one can hop into a time machine, undo key events, and document what would have happened), it is often possible to test the implications of such claims in this world. Indeed, there is a voluminous literature on the logical, statistical and historical criteria that scholars should use in judging counterfactuals.[13] Most of us suspect that some counterfactuals are more compelling than others, and this literature suggests that there are good grounds for holding to this suspicion. But there is a cognitive catch: to prevent speculation from sliding into the solipsistic abyss, experts must be willing to change their minds about possible worlds in response to real-world evidence. As we shall now see, many are reluctant.

Let us revisit the sharply contested counterfactual "If the Communist Party of the Soviet Union had deposed Stalin in the late 1920s, the USSR would have moved toward a kinder, gentler form of Communism fifty years earlier." As a thought experiment, suppose that historical sleuths in the Kremlin archives claim to discover documents that reveal rising resistance to Stalin in the late 1920s and that, given the chance, the most likely successors would have constructed a kinder, gentler Communism. How should experts respond? It seems a trifle dogmatic to refuse even to consider changing one's mind. But such a response might be justifiable if overwhelming evidence from other credible sources pointed to the contrary conclusion. Many scientists justify their dismissal of evidence for "far-out claims" such as extrasensory perception on the ground that such findings violate too many well-established physical and biological laws. In Bayesian terms, it seems presumptuous for nonexperts to tell experts how "diagnostic" particular evidence is with respect to particular causal hypotheses.

It is possible, however, to design a better mousetrap for documenting the impact of theory-driven thinking about counterfactual history. Imagine that we transform our thought experiment into an actual experiment that holds evidence constant—say, documents recently discovered in Kremlin archives—but manipulates findings—say, whether the documents contain revelations favorable either to those who view Stalinism as an aberration or to those who view it as a natural outgrowth of Leninism. Insofar as observers deem evidence compelling *only* when it reinforces their prior beliefs, the experiment would reveal a disturbing

[12] P. E. Tetlock and A. Belkin, *Counterfactual Thought Experiments in World Politics: Logical, Methodological, and Psychological Perspectives* (Princeton, NJ: Princeton University Press, 1996).

[13] J. Elster, *Logic and Society: Contradictions and Possible Worlds* (New York: John Wiley & Sons, 1978).

double standard in judgments of the probative value of evidence. To the degree that scholars keep two sets of books for scoring knowledge claims—one set for consonant claims and the other for dissonant ones—the risk grows that their beliefs about historical causality will ossify into brittle tautologies in which they alternate between invoking ideological preconceptions to justify their claims about what could have been and invoking claims about what could have been to justify their preconceptions.

To explore this idea, we transformed the turnabout thought experiment into an actual experiment by asking respondents how they *would react if* a research team working in the Kremlin archives announced the discovery of evidence that shed light on three choice points in Soviet history: whether Stalinism could have been averted in the late 1920s, whether the cold war could have been brought to an end in the mid-1950s, and whether the Politburo in the early 1980s could just as easily have responded to Reagan's policies in a confrontational manner.[14]

The Methodological Appendix presents the details of the sample, research procedures, and research design which took the form of a $2 \times 2 \times 3$ mixed-design factorial, with two between-subjects independent variables—liberal or conservative tilt of evidence discovered by hypothetical research team and the presence or absence of methodological checks on ideological bias—and one repeated-measures factor representing the three historical "discoveries." In the liberal-tilt condition, participants imagined that a team uncovers evidence that indicates Stalinism was avertable in the late 1920s, the cold war could have ended in the mid-1950s, and Reagan almost triggered a downward spiral in American-Soviet relations in the early 1980s that could have ended in war. In the conservative-tilt condition, participants imagined that the evidence indicates that history could not have gone down a different path at each of these three junctures. In the high-research-quality condition, participants are further asked to imagine that the team took special precautions to squelch political bias. In the unspecified-quality condition, participants received no such assurances. After reading about each discovery, participants judged the credibility of the research conclusions as well as of three grounds for impugning the team's credibility: dismissing the motives of the researchers as political rather than scholarly, disputing the authenticity of documents, and arguing that key documents were taken out of context.

Table 5.3 shows that, although there was a weak effect of methodological precautions, that effect was eclipsed by the effects of ideological preconceptions. Regardless of announced checks on bias, both liberals and conservatives rated consonant evidence as highly credible and dissonant

---

[14] For a more extensive discussion of the utility of turnabout thought experiments, see P. E. Tetlock, "Political Psychology or Politicized Psychology: Is the Road to Scientific Hell Paved with Good Moral Intentions?" *Political Psychology* 15 (1994): 509–30.

TABLE 5.3

Average Reactions to Dissonant and Consonant Evidence of Low- or High-quality Bearing on Three Controversial Close-call Counterfactuals

a. Low-quality Evidence					
Archival Data Suggest:	Ideology of Respondents	Overall Credibility	Impugn Motives	Question Authenticity	Question Interpretation
Purging Stalin (never close / nearly happened)	Liberals	3.0 / 6.6	6.2 / 2.9	6.8 / 3.8	7.1 / 3.5
	Conservatives	7.1 / 3.1	3.5 / 6.9	4.0 / 7.2	3.2 / 6.9
Ending cold war in 1950s (never close / nearly happened)	Liberals	2.8 / 5.7	5.9 / 3.5	6.5 / 3.7	7.2 / 4
	Conservatives	7.0 / 4.1	4.2 / 6.6	3.3 / 6.8	2.9 / 7.2
Confrontational Soviet response to Reagan (never close / nearly happened)	Liberals	3.4 / 6.5	7.0 / 3.9	6.8 / 3.1	6.9 / 3.6
	Conservatives	6.7 / 2.6	3.4 / 7.0	3.9 / 7.4	3.4 / 6.7
b. High-quality Evidence					
Archival Data Suggest:	Ideology of Respondents	Overall Credibility	Impugn Motives	Question Authenticity	Question Interpretation
Purging Stalin (never close/ nearly happened)	Liberals	2.8 / 5.2	5.4 / 2.5	6.1 / 3.2	7.3 / 4.2
	Conservatives	6.1 / 2.9	3.6 / 6.4	3.7 / 5.9	4.4 / 7.1
Ending cold war in 1950s (never close/ nearly happened)	Liberals	3.0 / 5.5	5.2 / 2.6	5.8 / 3.1	7 / 4.4
	Conservatives	5.7 / 4.0	3.8 / 6.0	3.1 / 6.4	4.7 / 7
Confrontational Soviet response to Reagan (never close/ nearly happened)	Liberals	3.1 / 6.1	6.8 / 2.8	6.2 / 2.7	7 / 4.3
	Conservatives	6.0 / 2.5	3.5 / 5.5	3.7 / 7.1	4.3 / 6.9

Note: Higher scores, high credibility (col. 1); greater resistance (cols. 2–4)

evidence as relatively incredible. When reacting to dissonant data discovered by a team that did not implement precautions, experts used all three belief system defenses: challenging the authenticity of the archival documents, the representativeness of the documents, and the competence and the motives of the unnamed investigators. The open-ended data underscore this point. The same tactics of data neutralization were almost four times more likely to appear in spontaneous comments on dissonant than on consonant evidence (62 percent of the thought protocols produced by experts confronting dissonant data contained at least one evidence-neutralization technique versus 16 percent of the protocols produced by experts confronting consonant data, with the size of the double standard about equal for experts on opposite sides of the ideology scale). When we measure the tendency to endorse all three tactics of data neutralization, this composite scale consistently predicts rejection of the conclusions that the investigators want to draw from their "discovery" (correlations from .44 to .57 across scenarios).[15]

Hedgehogs were also more likely than foxes to deploy double standards in evaluating evidence. Far from changing their minds in response to dissonant discoveries, hedgehogs increased their confidence in their prior position, whereas foxes at least made small adjustments to the new evidence.[16] Moreover, hedgehogs were defiant defenders of double standards. In debriefing, we asked experts how much their evaluations of the study were affected by the study's results. Foxes were reluctant to acknowledge that they kept two sets of epistemological books and maintained their reactions would have been similar. By contrast, hedgehogs acknowledged that their reactions would have been strikingly different and defended a differential response. We return to these defenses in chapter 6 when we give hedgehogs an opportunity to respond to the whole battery of allegations of cognitive bias.[17]

The key point of the turnabout experiment is the pervasiveness of double standards: the tendency to switch on the high-intensity searchlight for

[15] For similar results in other experimental work on belief perseverance, see C. Lord, L. Ross, and M. Lepper, "Biased Assimilation and Attitude Polarization: The Effects of Prior Theories on Subsequently Considered Evidence," *Journal of Personality and Social Psychology* 37 (1979): 2098–2109.

[16] For parallel results in the more general literature on cognitive styles, see Kruglanski and Webster, "Need for Closure"; C. Y. Chiu, M. W. Morris, Y. Y. Hong, and T. Menon, "Motivated Cultural Cognition: The Impact of Implicit Cultural Theories on Dispositional Attributions Varies as a Function of Need for Closure," *Journal of Personality and Social Psychology* 78 (2001): 247–59.

[17] Experts were far more responsive to the manipulation of empirical findings than to that of research quality, ignoring the latter altogether when the data reinforced ideological preconceptions and giving only grudging consideration to high-quality data that challenged their preconceptions. Before issuing a blanket condemnation, however, we should consider three qualifications. First, not all experts ignored disagreeable evidence; some were swayed by high-quality dissonant evidence. Second, the greater effect sizes for "empirical findings" than for "research procedures" might merely reflect that we manipulated the former in a more compelling fashion than the latter. Comparisons of effect sizes across such different independent variables are notoriously problematic. Third, the data do not demonstrate that experts are too slow to accept dissonant evidence. It may be prudent to ask sharp questions of unexpected results.

flaws only in disagreeable results. Whether we trace the problem to excessive skepticism toward dissonant data or insufficient skepticism toward consonant data, our beliefs about what could have been can easily become self-perpetuating, insulated from disconfirming evidence by a thick protective belt of defensive maneuvers that attribute dissonant evidence to methodological sloppiness or partisan bias. It is telling that no one spontaneously entertained the possibility that "I guess the methodological errors broke in my direction this time."

Closing Observations

This chapter underscores the power of our preconceptions to shape our view of reality. To the previous list of judgmental shortcomings—overconfidence, hindsight bias, belief underadjustment—we can add fresh failings: (a) the alacrity with which we fill in the missing control conditions of history with agreeable scenarios and with which we reject dissonant scenarios; (b) the sluggishness with which we reconsider these judgments in light of fresh evidence. It is easy, even for sophisticated professionals, to slip into tautological patterns of historical reasoning: "I know x caused y because, if there had been no x, there would have been no y. And I know that, 'if no x, no y' because I know x caused y." Given the ontological inadequacies of history as teacher and our psychological inadequacies as pupils, it begins to look impossible to learn anything from history that we were not previously predisposed to learn.

These results should be unsettling to those worried about our capacity to avoid repeating the mistakes of the past. But they are reassuring to psychologists worried about the generalizability of their findings to real people judging real events. Surveying the findings laid out in chapters 2 through 5, we find several impressive points of convergence with the larger literature.

First, researchers have shown that experts, from diverse professions, can talk themselves into believing they can do things that they manifestly cannot.[18] Experts frequently seem unaware of how quickly they reach the point of diminishing marginal returns for knowledge when they try to predict outcomes with large stochastic components: from recidivism among criminals to the performance of financial markets. Beyond a stark minimum, subject matter expertise in world politics translates less into forecasting accuracy than it does into overconfidence (and the ability to spin elaborate tapestries of reasons for expecting "favorite" outcomes).[19]

[18] Dawes, "Behavioral Decision Theory."

[19] H. N. Garb, *Studying the Clinician: Judgment Research and Psychological Assessment* (Washington, DC: American Psychological Association, 1998).

Second, like ordinary mortals, seasoned professionals are reluctant to acknowledge that they were wrong and to change their minds to the degree prescribed by Reverend Bayes. Experts judging political trends were as slow to modify their opinions as ordinary people have been to modify their views in laboratory experiments on belief perseverance. Reviewing the cognitive strategies experts used to justify holding firm, we discover a formidable array of dissonance-reduction strategies tailor-made for defusing threats to professional self-esteem.[20]

Third, like ordinary mortals, experts fall prey to the hindsight effect. After the fact, they claim they know more about what was going to happen than they actually knew before the fact. This systematic misremembering of past positions may look strategic, but the evidence indicates that people do sometimes truly convince themselves that they "knew it all along."[21]

Fourth, like ordinary mortals, experts play favorites in the hypothesis-testing game, applying higher standards of proof for dissonant than for consonant discoveries. This finding extends experimental work on theory-driven assessments of evidence[22] as well as work on shifting thresholds of proof in science.[23]

Fifth, individual differences in styles of reasoning among experts parallel those documented in other populations of human beings. Whatever label we place on these individual differences—Isaiah Berlin's classification of hedgehogs and foxes or the more prosaic taxonomies of psychologists who talk about "need for closure or structure or consistency" and "integrative simplicity-complexity"—a pattern emerges. Across several samples and tasks, people who value closure and simplicity are less accurate in complex social perception tasks and more susceptible to overconfidence, hindsight, and belief perseverance effects.[24]

In all five respects, our findings underscore that laboratory-based demonstrations of bounded rationality hold up in a more ecologically representative research design that focuses on the efforts of trained specialists (as opposed to sophomore conscripts) to judge complex, naturally occurring political events (as opposed to artificial problems that the experimenter has concocted with the intent of demonstrating bias).

[20] P. E. Tetlock, "Prisoners of our Preconceptions."

[21] S. Hawkins and R. Hastie, "Hindsight: Biased Judgment of Past Events after the Outcomes Are Known," *Psychological Bulletin* 107 (1990): 311–27.

[22] C. Lord, L. Ross, and M. Lopper, "Considering the Opposite: A Corrective Strategy for Social Judgement," *Journal of Personality and Social Psychology* 47 (1984): 1231–43.

[23] Timothy D. Wilson, Bella M. DePaulo, D. G. Mook, and K. G. Klaaren, "Scientists' Evaluations of Research: The Biasing Effects of the Importance of the Topic," *Psychological Science* 4 (September 1993): 322–25.

[24] Suedfeld and Tetlock, "Individual Differences."

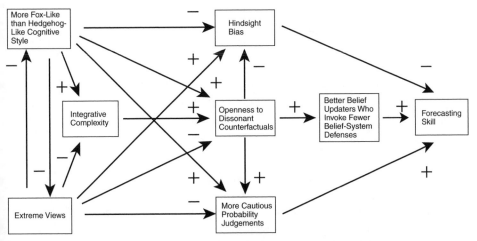

Figure 5.1. This figure builds on figures 3.5 and 4.3 by inserting what we have learned about the greater openness of moderates, foxes, and integratively complex thinkers to dissonant historical counterfactuals. This greater willingness to draw belief-destabilizing lessons from the past increases forecasting skill via three hypothesized mediators: the tendencies to hedge subjective probability bets, to resist hindsight bias, and to be better Bayesians.

This chapter rounds out the normative indictment. Since we introduced the hedgehog-fox distinction in chapter 3, hedgehogs have repeatedly emerged as the higher-risk candidates for becoming "prisoners of their preconceptions." Figure 5.1 integrates the key findings from chapter 5 into the conceptual model of good forecasting judgment that has been evolving through the last three chapters. In this revised scheme, moderate foxes have a new advantage over extremist hedgehogs—their greater tolerance for dissonant historical counterfactuals—in addition to their already established network of mutually reinforcing advantages: their greater capacity for self-critical integratively complex thinking, their greater flexibility as belief updaters, and their greater caution in using probability scales.

But have hedgehogs been run through a kangaroo court? Are many alleged errors and biases normatively defensible? Chapter 6 makes the case for the defense.

CHAPTER 6

The Hedgehogs Strike Back

There are two sides to every argument, including this one.
— ANONYMOUS

IT REQUIRES better defense counsel than the author to get the hedgehogs acquitted of all the charges against them. Too many lines of evidence converge: hedgehogs are poor forecasters who refuse to acknowledge mistakes, dismiss dissonant evidence, and warm to the possibility that things could have worked out differently only if doing so rescues favorite theories of history from falsification.

That said, any self-respecting contrarian should wonder what can be said on behalf of the beleaguered hedgehogs. Fifty years of research on cognitive styles suggests an affirmative answer: it does sometimes help to be a hedgehog.[1] Distinctive hedgehog strengths include their resistance to distraction in environments with unfavorable signal-to-noise ratios;[2] their tough negotiating postures that protect them from exploitation by competitive adversaries;[3] their willingness to take responsibility for controversial decisions guaranteed to make them enemies;[4] their determination to stay the course with sound policies that run into temporary difficulties;[5] and their capacity to inspire confidence by projecting a decisive, can-do presence.[6]

---

[1] Suedfeld and Tetlock, "Individual Differences," G. Gigerenzer and P. M. Todd, *Simple Heuristics That Make Us Smart* (New York: Oxford University Press, 2000).

[2] On the risks of looking too hard for signals in "noisy" data, see R. E. Nisbett, H. Zukier, and R. Lemley, "The Dilution Effect: Nondiagnostic Information," *Cognitive Psychology* 13 (1981): 248–77; P. E. Tetlock and R. Boettger, "Accountability: A Social Magnifier of the Dilution Effect," *Journal of Personality and Social Psychology* 57 (1989): 388–98.

[3] P. E. Tetlock and A. Tyler, "Winston Churchill's Cognitive and Rhetorical Style: The Debates over Nazi Intentions and Self-government for India," *Political Psychology* 17 (1996): 149–70.

[4] P. E. Tetlock and R. Boettger, "Accountability Amplifies the Status Quo Effect When Change Creates Victims," *Journal of Behavioral Decision Making* 7 (1994): 1–23.

[5] Suedfeld and Tetlock, "Individual Differences"; G. Gigerenzer and P. M. Todd, *Simple Heuristics That Make Us Smart* (New York: Oxford University Press, 2000).

[6] B. M. Staw and J. Ross, "Commitment in an Experimenting Society: A Study of the Attribution of Leadership from Administrative Scenarios," *Journal of Applied Psychology* 65 (1980): 249–60.

There is little doubt then that there are settings in which one does better heeding hedgehog rather than fox advice. But to dispel the cloud of doubt hovering over hedgehogs that has built up over the last three chapters, any spirited defense cannot shirk the task of rebutting the evidence in those chapters. A well-prepared hedgehog's advocate should raise a veritable litany of objections:

1. "You claim we are flawed forecasters, but you messed up the grading by overrelying on a simplistic method of probability scoring." We need sophisticated scoring systems that incorporate value, difficulty, and other adjustments that will even the score.
2. "You claim we are poky belief updaters, but you overrelied on simplistic Bayesian scoring rules that gave no weight to the valid arguments that experts invoked for not changing their minds.
3. "You claim to have caught us applying double standards in judging agreeable versus disagreeable evidence, but you forget that some double standards are justifiable."
4. "You claim we use counterfactual history to prop up our prejudices, but you do not appreciate the wisdom of adopting a deterministic perspective on the past.
5. "You think you caught us falling prey to the hindsight bias, but you do not grasp how essential that 'bias' is to efficient mental functioning."
6. This defense shifts from defending the answers hedgehogs gave to attacking the questions hedgehogs were asked. It concedes that there were systematic, difficult-to-rationalize biases running through hedgehog judgments but insists that if I had posed more intelligent questions, performance deficits would have disappeared.
7. This defense grants that hedgehogs made many mistakes but tries to deflect negative conclusions about their cognitive styles by (a) positing that the experts studied here did not have the right credentials or were not properly motivated or (b) chalking up failures to the turbulent character of late twentieth-century history.
8. The final defense attributes performance differentials to a misunderstanding. I judged participants by the standards of my world—an academic subculture that values empirical accuracy and logical coherence—whereas many participants judged themselves by the standards of their worlds—partisan subcultures in which the game of "gotcha" requires denying one's own mistakes and pinning as many mistakes as possible on the other side.

Each defense gets a fair hearing, but not a free pass. When appropriate, the prosecution will attach skeptical rejoinders. In the end, we shall see that the case against the hedgehogs is neither as solid as their detractors declare nor as flimsy as their defenders hope. Qualified forms of the earlier indictments remain standing.

It would, however, be a mistake to read this chapter solely as an effort to give hedgehogs a fair shake. Each defense raises issues that arise whenever we confront the claim "Members of group x have 'better judgment' than members of group y." Indeed, taken together, the eight defenses reveal the extraordinary complexity of the assumptions underlying all judgments of good judgment—a point reinforced by the Technical Appendix, which details the computational implementation of these defenses.

Really Not Such Bad Forecasters

In chapter 3, foxes bested hedgehogs on basic indicators of forecasting accuracy. But defenders of hedgehogs argue that the victory was a false one. Foxes did "better" not because they have better judgment but because (a) hedgehogs have more skewed error-avoidance priorities and either tolerate lots of false alarms to avoid misses or tolerate many misses to avoid false alarms; (b) hedgehogs used the probability scale more aggressively and swung harder for forecasting "home runs" by assigning zeroes to non-events and 1.0's to events; (c) hedgehogs were dealt tougher forecasting assignments; (d) our coding of forecasts as right or wrong was biased in favor of foxes; (e) our reality checks were predicated on the "naïve" assumption that forecasts could be coded as either right or wrong and, when we adopt a more nuanced scoring system, performance differentials vanish. In the end, we make a curious discovery rooted in an old levels-of-analysis paradox. Even though it is a great statistical struggle to raise the average accuracy of individual hedgehogs to parity with the average accuracy of individual foxes, it is easy to show that the accuracy of the average forecast of all hedgehogs is almost identical to that of all foxes.

THE NEED FOR VALUE ADJUSTMENTS

Some defenders of hedgehogs dismiss the foxes' advantage as illusory—a by-product of our rigidly value-neutral probability-scoring rules that treat all errors equally. Hedgehogs get worse scores because they are less concerned with maximizing overall accuracy and more with minimizing those mistakes they deem really serious, even if at the expense of making many less consequential mistakes. Perhaps some hedgehogs subscribe to a "better safe than sorry" philosophy that puts a premium on being able to say, "I was never blindsided by change for the worse." And perhaps other hedgehogs subscribe to a "don't cry wolf" philosophy that puts a premium on avoiding false alarms of change for the worse that could undercut their long-term credibility.

The Technical Appendix describes the basic idea behind value-adjusting probability scores: to give experts some benefit of the doubt that the mistakes they make are the right mistakes in light of their own value priorities. Thus, if hedgehogs overpredict change for the worse, one value adjustment solves for a value of k that brings their forecasts into line with the observed base rate for change for the worse. Insofar as hedgehogs are more prone than foxes to this error, the value adjustment helps them "to catch up" on this task.

But rescuing hedgehogs via k-style value adjustments proves futile for a simple reason: foxes make fewer errors of both under- and overprediction. Figure 6.1 shows there are no constant probability score "indifference" curves consistent with the hypothesis that foxes and hedgehogs are equally good forecasters with different tastes for under- and overprediction. Foxes are consistently to the "northeast" of hedgehogs. Adding insult to injury, figure 6.1 shows how easy it is to postulate constant-probability-score indifference curves consistent with the hypothesis that hedgehogs and dart-throwing chips had equivalent forecasting skill and just "opted" for different blends of mistakes. Lastly, figure 6.1 shows that, even after introducing the k adjustment, hedgehogs "lose" to foxes, regardless of whether the forecasting focus was on identifying change for the better, change for the worse, or change in either direction.[7]

Hedgehogs can never catch up via across-the-board k-style adjustments. To produce performance parity, we have to tailor value adjustments to specific types of mistakes using the a_0/a_1 method (see Technical Appendix). But when do we decide we have gone too far in contorting scoring rules in pursuit of parity? Figure 6.2 shows that crossover is possible only if we define the forecasting objective in a very particular way—distinguishing change (regardless of direction) from the status quo—and when we treat underpredicting change as at least seven times more serious than overpredicting change. Crossover occurs for two reasons: (a) aggregate hedgehog performance is dragged down by two subgroups—extreme optimists who exaggerate the likelihood of change for the better and extreme pessimists who exaggerate the likelihood of

---

[7] Figure 6.1 reveals that errors of underprediction dwarf those of overprediction. This result, is however, "forced" by the logical structure of the forecasting task. In three-possible-future tasks, the probabilities assigned to each possible future—status quo, and change in the direction of either less or more of something—were usually constrained to add to 1.0 and thus average to a grand mean of .33. The actual averages for these futures hovered between .25 and .40, and these values are obviously further from 1.0 (the value taken by reality when the target event occurs and the only possible error is underprediction) than from zero (the value taken by reality when the target event does not occur and the only possible error is overprediction).

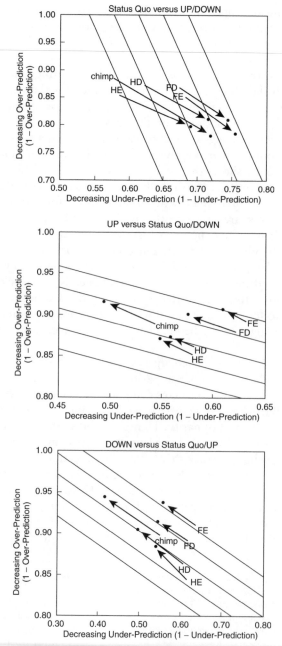

Figure 6.1. The impact of *k*-value adjustment on performance of hedgehog and fox experts and dilettantes (HE, HD, FE, FD) and chimps in three different forecasting tasks: distinguishing status quo from change for either better or worse (panel 1 in which everyone benefits from reducing underprediction of the status

change for the worse; (b) the adjustments give lots of credit for the aggressive predictions of change by each subgroup that prove correct but trivialize the aggressive predictions by each subgroup that prove off the mark.

There is no rule that tells us how far to take value adjustments: we could, in principle, tailor them to each forecaster's probability estimate of each state of the world (say, correcting for overpredicting unemployment but underpredicting inflation). But such special-purpose value adjustments almost certainly give forecasters too much benefit of the doubt. Such adjustments make the null hypothesis of cognitive parity nonfalsifiable (they can make even the dart-throwing chimp perfectly calibrated). My own inclination is therefore not to go far beyond adjustments of the generic k sort. Hedgehogs lose too consistently to foxes—across outcome variables, time frames, and regional domains—to sustain the facile hypothesis that all performance differentials can be attributed to different value priorities.

THE NEED FOR PROBABILITY-WEIGHTING ADJUSTMENTS

Hedgehogs may also have been unfairly penalized because they tried harder to hit the forecasting equivalent of home runs: assigning the extreme values of zero (impossible) and 1.0 (sure thing) more often than foxes who were content with the forecasting equivalent of base hits (assigning low, but not zero, probabilities to things that did not happen and high, but not 1.0, probabilities to things that did happen). In this view, hedgehogs should get credit for their courage. People take notice when forecasters say something will or will not happen, with no diluting caveats. But impact falls off steeply as forecasters move from these endpoints of the probability scale into the murkier domain of likely or unlikely, and falls off further as we move to "just guessing."

Defenders of hedgehogs argue for scoring adjustments that capture this reality. And they point to recent empirical revelations of how people actually use subjective probabilities in decision making. Expected utility theory traditionally treated a shift in probability from .10 to .11 as exactly as consequential a determinant of the final choice that people made as a shift from .99 to 1.0; by contrast, cumulative prospect theory posits

---

quo), distinguishing change for better from either status quo or change for worse (panel 2 in which everyone benefits from reducing overpredicting change for the worse), and distinguishing change for worse from either status quo or change for better (panel 3 in which everyone benefits from reducing overpredicting change for the better). K-value adjustments improve the overall performance of all groups but fail to produce hedgehog-fox performance parity.

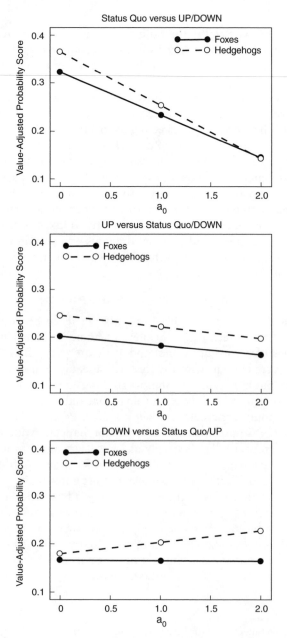

Figure 6.2. The gap between hedgehogs and foxes narrows, and even disappears, when we apply value adjustments, a_0, that are increasingly tough on false alarms (over-predicting status quo [top panel], change for better [middle panel], and change for worse [bottom panel]). Crossover occurs with sufficiently extreme adjustments when we define the prediction task as distinguishing the status quo from change in either direction (up or down).

that people use subjective probabilities in strikingly nonlinear ways.[8] People are willing to pay much more to increase the probability of winning a lottery ticket from .99 to 1.0 than they are from .10 to .11. And they are willing to pay much more to reduce the likelihood of disaster from .0001 to zero than they are from .0011 to .001. In the spirit of these observations, we introduced probability-weighting adjustments of probability scores that (a) assign special positive weights to home run predictions that gave values of 1.0 to things that happen and values of zero to things that do not; (b) assign special negative weights to big strike-out predictions that gave values of 1.0 to things that do not happen and values of zero to things that do happen; (c) count movement in the wrong direction at the extremes as a more serious mistake (when x happens, moving from 1.0 to .8; when x does not happen, moving from zero to .2) than movement in the wrong direction in the middle of the probability scale (say, from, .6 to .4 or from .4 to .6).

Hedgehogs benefit from these scoring adjustments. As noted in chapter 3, they benefit, in part, because they swing for home runs more often than foxes: they call outcomes inevitable (1.0) 1,479 times in comparison to the foxes' 798 times, and they call outcomes impossible (zero) 6,929 times in comparison to foxes' 4,022 times. And hedgehogs benefit, in part, from the fact that most of the occasions when they assign extreme values, they were right: roughly 85 percent of the outcomes they labeled "impossible" never materialize and roughly 74 percent of the outcomes they label "sure things" do materialize. Hedgehogs must, by logical necessity, be "very right" more often than foxes: foxes could not catch up on this dimension even if they never made mistakes.

But here the good news ends for hedgehogs. Major hedgehog misses (declaring something impossible that subsequently happens) vastly outnumber major fox misses (14 percent versus 4 percent), and major hedgehog false alarms vastly outnumber fox false alarms (26 percent versus 14 percent). These big mistakes slow the rate at which hedgehogs can catch up to foxes via probability-weighting adjustments. As figure 6.3 shows, the catch-up point occurs only when the weighting parameter, gamma, takes on an extreme value (roughly .2), so counterintuitively extreme, in fact, that it treats

[8] In prospect theory, the shape of the probability-weighting function reflects the psychophysics of diminishing sensitivity: marginal impact diminishes with distance from reference points. For probability assessments, there are two reference points: impossibility (zero) and certainty (1.0). Diminishing sensitivity implies an S-shaped weighting function that is concave near zero and convex near 1.0. The weight of a probability estimate decreases with its distance from the natural boundaries of impossibility and certainty. This weighting function helps to explain the well-established fourfold pattern of risk attitudes: overweighting low probabilities (risk seeking for gains and risk averse for losses), and underweighting high probabilities (risk averse for gains and risk seeking for losses). See A. Tversky and D. Kahneman. "Advances in Prospect Theory: Cumulative Representation of Uncertainty. *Journal of Risk and Uncertainty*, 5, 297–323(1992).

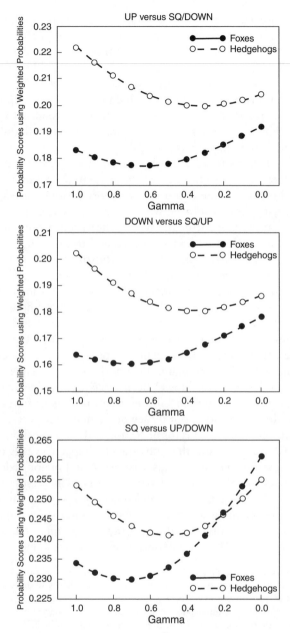

Figure 6.3. The gap between foxes and hedgehogs narrows, but never closes in the first and second panels and even eventually reverses itself in the third panel, when we apply increasingly extreme values of gamma to the weighted probabilities entered into the probability-scoring function. Extreme values of gamma treat all mistakes in the "maybe zone" (.1 to .9) as increasingly equivalent to each other.

big errors (Judge A says x is highly likely [.9] and x does not occur) as only slightly more severe than small errors (Judge B says x is highly unlikely [.1] and x does not occur). Adjustments of this magnitude violate the intuition most of us have that the two cases are far from equivalent: we feel that Judge A was almost wrong and Judge B almost right. Adjustments of this magnitude also imply that, if our goal is to produce catch-up effects, we need a much more sharply inflected S-shaped weighting function than the more psychologically realistic one in prospect theory. Finally, even when we implement adjustments this extreme, catch-up only occurs when we define the forecasting goal as distinguishing the status quo from either change for the better or the worse (not when we look for directional accuracy—the ability to predict whether change will be for the better or the worse).

THE NEED FOR DIFFICULTY ADJUSTMENTS

Hedgehogs may also look worse because they specialize in more volatile regions of the world and, thus, when they made predictions in their roles as experts, they more often wound up trying to predict the unpredictable. Table 6.1 shows there is a degree of truth to this objection. Although the similarities between hedgehog and fox forecasting environments were more pronounced than the differences—in both the short- and long-term forecasting exercises for foxes and hedgehogs, the status quo was the right answer more often than either change for the better (always coming in second) and change for the worse—there were still differences. Hedgehogs were dealt marginally tougher forecasting tasks (where tougher means closer to the 33/33/33 breakdown one would expect if all possible outcomes—the status quo, change for either the better or the worse—were equiprobable).

The Technical Appendix makes the case for difficulty-adjusted probability scores that level the playing field by taking into account variation in environmental variability. Figure 6.4 shows the results: difficulty-adjusted scores replicate the hedgehog-fox performance gaps observed with unadjusted probability scores. The results reinforce the notion that hedgehogs play a steep price for their confident, deductive style of reasoning. Difficulty-adjusted probability scores below zero signify lower forecasting accuracy than could have been achieved by just predicting the base rate. And the steepest decline into negative territory occurs among hedgehogs making long-term forecasts outside their specialties.

But, just as there is legitimate disagreement about how far to take value adjustments, so there is about how far to take difficulty adjustments.[9] The "right" base rate for computing difficulty adjustments hinges on judgment

---

[9] Indeed, there is so much ambiguity that Robert Jervis has argued that the cognitive bias of base-rate neglect is not a bias in world politics. See R. Jervis, "Representativeness in Foreign Policy Judgments," *Political Psychology* 7 (1986): 483–505.

TABLE 6.1

How often "Things" Happened (Continuation of Status Quo, Change in the Direction of More of Something, and Change in the Direction of Less of Something.

	Short-term Forecasts			Long-term Forecasts		
	SQ	More	Less	SQ	More	Less
Experts						
Hedgehogs	49.60%	29.00%	21.46%	44.06%	28.06%	27.88%
Foxes	53.47%	27.97%	17.79%	46.21%	28.84%	25.65%
Dilettantes						
Hedgehogs	48.09%	31.33%	20.58%	42.82%	30.21%	26.96%
Foxes	53.30%	26.03%	20.67%	41.09%	30.64%	27.61%

This table summarizes the percentage frequency of occurrence of possible futures (status quo and change for better or for worse) when hedgehogs and foxes made short- and long-term predictions inside and outside their domains of expertise.

calls. For instance, the base rate of nuclear proliferation falls off quite rapidly to the degree we expand the set of usual suspects to encompass not just immediate-risk candidates (such as Pakistan, North Korea, and Iran) but longer-term risks (Brazil, Argentina, Libya, Taiwan, Japan, South Korea, etc.). Similarly, regime change is rare in the zone of stability but occurs with moderate frequency in longer time spans in the zone of turbulence and with high frequency if we confine comparisons to the former Soviet bloc in the late 1980s and early 1990s. Much the same can be said for cross-border warfare, genocidal violence within borders, debt default, and so on.

Unfortunately for defenders of hedgehogs, figure 6.4 shows that hedgehogs lose to foxes across a range of plausible assumptions about base rates, with values ranging from 50 percent lower to 50 percent higher than the base rate for the entire dataset. The confidence bands reveal that increasing the base rate generally improved the forecasting skill scores of both hedgehogs and foxes and that decreasing the base rate generally impaired these scores. We can also see that, although hedgehogs benefit more than foxes from increasing the base rates, hedgehogs still receive worse difficulty-adjusted scores. Hedgehogs catch up only when we give them the most favorable possible assumptions about the base-rates of target events and foxes the least favorable—hardly a leveling of the playing field.[10]

[10] One could also argue that, although the fox and hedgehog environments may have been roughly equally difficult to predict—as gauged by overall variability and percentage of that variability that can be captured in formal statistical models—the foxes may have won merely because they were better at picking out variables with large autocorrelations (and thus could be predicted by extrapolating from the past) or because they were more attuned to intercorrelations among outcome variables (and thus aware of the implications of change in one variable for other variables). The Technical Appendix shows this is not true. The fox advantage holds up, reasonably evenly, across variables with the smallest to the largest squared multiple

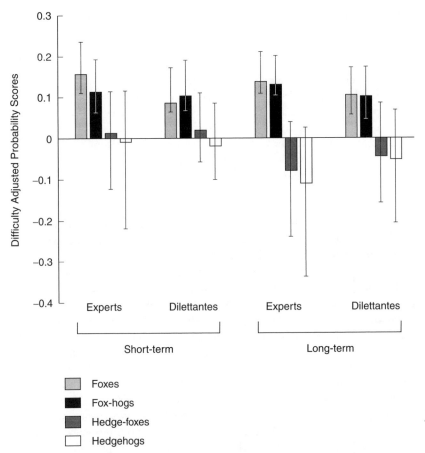

Figure 6.4. The difficulty-adjusted forecasting skill of hedgehogs and foxes making short or long-range forecasts inside or outside their specialties. Higher scores indicate better performance and confidence bands show how forecasting skill shifts with estimated base rates (lower bands corresponding to lower estimates, higher bands to higher estimates). Hedgehogs and foxes gain or lose in similar ways from base rate adjustments and never converge in performance.

THE NEED FOR CONTROVERSY ADJUSTMENTS

Defenders of hedgehogs can argue that some mistakes attributed to hedgehogs should have been attributed to us. Although we tried to pose only questions that passed the clairvoyance test, disputes still arose over which possible futures materialized. Did North Korea have the bomb in

---

correlations. But, even if this objection were true, it hardly counts as a compelling defense that hedgehogs were so committed to their theories that they missed such obvious predictive cues.

1998? Did the Italian government cook the books to meet the Maastricht criteria? How much confidence should we have in Chinese economic growth statistics? Who was in charge in China as Deng Xiaoping slowly died?

Controversy adjustments show how the probability scores of forecasters shift when we heed "I really was right" protests and make alternative assumptions about what happened. Hedgehogs, however, get little traction here. Neither hedgehogs nor foxes registered a lot of complaints about reality checks. They challenged roughly 15 percent of the checks and were bothered by similar issues. Hedgehogs and foxes thus benefited roughly equally from adjustments.

THE NEED FOR FUZZY-SET ADJUSTMENTS

Defenders of hedgehogs can argue that, although hedgehogs were not as proficient at predicting what actually happened, they catch up when we give them credit for things that nearly happened. As we saw in chapter 4, inaccurate forecasters often insisted that their forecasts should be classified as almost right rather than clearly wrong—almost right because, although the expected future did not materialize, it either almost did (Quebec almost seceded) or soon will (South Africa has not yet had its tribal bloodbath, but it will). Fuzzy-set adjustments take such protests seriously by shrinking gaps between ex ante probability judgments and ex post classifications of reality whenever experts mobilized one of three belief system defenses (the close-call-counterfactual, off-on-timing and exogenous-shock).

Of all the possible ways to tinker with probability scores, fuzzy-set adjustments most polarized reviewers of this book. Positivists warned of opening Pandora's box. We can never conclude that anyone ever made a mistake if we lower the bar to the point where we accept at face value all rationalizations that smart people concoct to save face. By contrast, constructivists saw fuzzy-set adjustments as a welcome break from the "naïve" practice of coding reality into dichotomous on/off, zero/one, categories. We live in a world of shades of gray. Sometimes it makes sense to say that things that did not happen almost did or that things that have not happened still might or that exogenous shocks have thrown off the predictions of a sound theory.

Our probability-scoring procedures are flexible enough to transform an irreconcilable philosophical feud into a tractable measurement problem. As the Technical Appendix describes, we drew on fuzzy-set theory to transform binary variables into continuous ones.[11] With no adjustment,

[11] Fuzzy sets are not the product of fuzzy math. See L. Zadeh, "A Fuzzy-Set-Theoretic Interpretation of Linguistic Hedges," *Journal of Cybernetics* 2 (1972): 4–34. On the implications for social science of fuzzy-set concepts, see C. Ragin, *Fuzzy-Set Social Science* (Chicago: University of Chicago Press, 2000).

the probability score for an expert who assigned a .6 likelihood to a future that did not occur would be .36 (higher scores indicate worse fits between judgments and reality). But with adjustments that shrink reality-probability gaps in proportion to the frequency with which different groups of experts invoked belief system defenses and in proportion to the credibility weights we assign those defenses, the probability scores can be cut in half or more.

Can generous fuzzy-set adjustments eradicate the stubborn performance gap between hedgehogs and foxes? It depends on how defensible one views the belief system defenses. Hedgehogs gain ground from fuzzy-set adjustments for three reasons: first, the gaps between probability judgments and reality were bigger for hedgehogs (hence, hedgehogs benefit more in absolute terms from percentage-shrinkage, fuzzy-set adjustments); second, these initial probability-reality gaps were larger because hedgehogs more consistently exaggerated the likelihood of change for both better and worse (hence hedgehogs catch up only when we define the forecasting goal as distinguishing the status quo from change in either direction); third, hedgehogs resorted roughly twice as often as foxes to belief system defenses that triggered fuzzy-set adjustments (hence hedgehogs get the benefit of roughly twice as many adjustments). Figure 6.5 shows the predictable result: the advantage foxes enjoyed on forecasting skill disappears when we focus on distinguishing the status quo from change and assign large credibility weights to belief system defenses (greater than .6).

This "victory" for hedgehogs is purchased, though, at a price many see as prohibitive. Positivists suspect that I have now made the transition from collegial open-mindedness to craven appeasement of solipsistic nonsense. Fuzzy-set adjustments mean that, when we take at face value the rationalizations that poor forecasters offer for being off the mark, these forecasters look as accurate as their less defensive and more accurate colleagues. Positivist critics also remind us of how selectively experts, especially hedgehogs, advanced close-call counterfactual, exogenous-shock, and off-on-timing interpretations of political outcomes. Chapter 4 showed these interpretive strategies became most popular when experts had embarrassingly large gaps between subjective probabilities and objective reality that needed closing. Experts rarely gave intellectual rivals who bet on the wrong outcome the same benefit of the close-call doubt. Large fuzzy-set adjustments thus reward self-serving biases in reasoning. If we reduce the adjustments in proportion to the selectivity with which belief system defenses were invoked (thus punishing self-serving reasoning), the performance gaps in forecasting skill reappear.

What role remains for fuzzy-set adjustments? The answer is, fittingly, fuzzy. Constructivists are right: there is a certain irreducible ambiguity

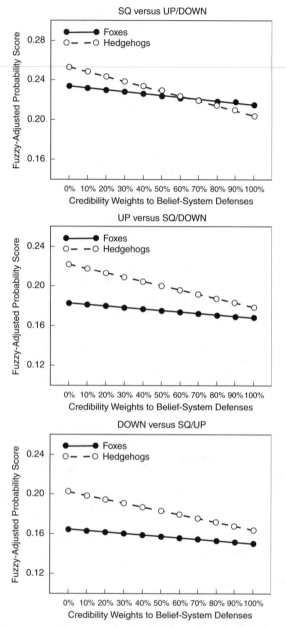

Figure 6.5. The gap between hedgehogs and foxes narrows, and even disappears, when we apply fuzzy-set adjustments that give increasingly generous credibility weights to belief system defenses. Crossover occurs with sufficiently extreme adjustments when we define the forecasting task as distinguishing continuation of the status quo from change in either direction (up or down). Lower scores on y axis are better scores.

about which rationales for forecasting glitches should be dismissed as rationalizations and which should be taken seriously. But the positivists are right: hedgehogs can only achieve cognitive parity if we permit implausibly large fuzzy-set adjustments that reflect the greater propensity of hedgehogs to explain away mistakes.

A PARADOX: WHY CATCH-UP IS FAR MORE ELUSIVE FOR THE AVERAGE
INDIVIDUAL THAN FOR THE GROUP AVERAGE

The previous defenses tried, rather futilely, to raise the average hedgehog forecaster to parity with the average fox forecaster. But all scoring adjustments were applied at an individual level of analysis. There may be a better way to salvage hedgehogs' collective reputation in the forecasting arena.

It is an intriguing mathematical fact that the inferiority of the average forecaster from a group need not imply the inferiority of the average forecast from that group.[12] With respect to the current dataset, for instance, Jensen's inequality tells us that, for quadratic variables such as probability scores, the average accuracy of individual forecasters will typically be worse than the accuracy of the average of all their forecasts. Jensen's inequality also implies that this gap between the average forecaster and the average forecast will be greater for groups—such as hedgehogs—that make more extreme (higher variance) forecasts. Consistent with this analysis, we find that, whereas the probability score for the average of all fox forecasts is only slightly superior to that of the average fox forecaster (.181 versus .186), the probability score for the average for all hedgehog forecasts is massively superior to that of the average hedgehog forecaster (.184 versus .218). The average fox forecast beats about 70% of foxes; the average hedgehog forecast beats 95% of hedgehogs.

Why do we finally find catch-up here? The political-psychological intuition behind this result is that, relative to the congenitally balanced foxes, the intellectually aggressive hedgehogs make more extreme mistakes in all possible directions and thus derive disproportionate benefit when we let their errors offset each other in composite forecasts. Foxes do intuitively what averaging does statistically, and what hedgehogs individually largely fail to do: blend perspectives with nonredundant predictive information. Defenders of hedgehogs could take this as a vindication of sorts: national security advisers do not do appreciably worse relying on the average predictions of hedgehog analysts than on those of fox analysts. But it seems more reasonable to the author to take this result as reinforcing the analysis in chapter 3 of why hedgehogs performed consistently

---

[12] For a popularization of this argument, see J. Surowiecki, *The Wisdom of Crowds: Why the Many Are Smarter than the Few and Collective Wisdom Shapes Business, Economies, Societies, and Nations* (New York: Doubleday, 2004).

more poorly than foxes. Hedgehogs lost because their cognitive style was less well suited for tracking the trajectories of complex, evolving social systems.

Really Not Incorrigibly Closed-minded Defense

The focus shifts here from "who got what right" to "who changed their minds when they were wrong." Defenders of hedgehogs can try to parry the charge that their clients are bad Bayesians by arguing that the indictment rests on bad philosophy of science. Drawing on "post-positivist philosophy of science," they warn us of the perils of "naïve falsificationism" and admonish us that all hypothesis testing rests on background assumptions about what constitutes a fair test.[13] We can justify *modus tollens*, the inference from "if hypothesis p is true, then q" to "$\sim q$ therefore $\sim p$," only if we can show that the conditions for applying hypothesis p to the world have been satisfied and q truly did not occur.

But this challenge too ultimately stands or falls on the defensibility of the belief system defenses that losers of reputational bets invoke to sever *modus tollens*. These bets asked forecasters to estimate the probabilities of possible futures conditional on the correctness of their perspective on the underlying drivers of events at work and then conditional on the correctness of a rival perspective. If I say that the survival of the Soviet Union is likely given my view of the world (.8) but unlikely given your view of the world (.2), and the Soviet Union collapses, I am under a Bayesian obligation to change my mind about the relative merits of our worldviews and to do so in proportion to the extremity of the odds I originally offered (4:1).

But should I change my mind if the necessary conditions for applying "my theory" to the world were not fulfilled, if exogenous shocks undercut the ceteris paribus requirement for all fair tests of hypotheses, if the predicted event almost occurred and still might, and if I now believe prediction exercises to be so riddled with indeterminacy as to be meaningless? Each defense provides a plausible reason for supposing that, whatever experts thought the odds were years ago, they now see things in a different light that justifies their refusals to change their minds.

---

[13] On falsification and the methodology of scientific research programs, see Suppe, "Scientific Theories," and Lakatos, "Research Programs." Objections of this sort played a role in persuading philosophers to abandon simple (Popperian) falsificationism in favor of more complex variants of the doctrine (Suppes). It is not necessary here to stake out a detailed position on falsificationism. It is sufficient to specify a procedural test of bias that, if failed, would convince even forgiving falsificationists that something is awry. This *de minimis* test asks: Do judges who "got it wrong" display vastly greater interest than judges who "got it right" in challenging the probity of the exercise? If so, we still cannot determine who is biased (incorrect forecasters may be too quick to complain or correct forecasters too quick to accept the test), but we can say that bias exists.

There is endless room for wrangling over the merits of specific applications of specific defenses. But there is still no avoiding the observation in Chapter 4 that experts activated defenses in a curiously asymmetrical fashion. They almost never mobilized defenses to help out adversaries whose most likely scenarios failed to materialize. Virtually no one says: "Don't hold the nonoccurrence of y against those who assigned steep odds in favor of the proposition 'if x, then y' because the conditions for x were never satisfied." The inescapable conclusion is that experts are far fussier about signing off on the background conditions for testing their own pet ideas than they are for testing those of their opponents.

In a similar vein, one virtually never hears forecasters try to spare their rivals embarrassment by insisting that, although the predicted outcome did not occur in the specified time frame, it almost did (close-call defense) and perhaps soon will (off-on-timing defense). These defenses acknowledge that, although technically, y failed to occur, it almost did and those who said it would deserve credit for being almost right, not blame for being wrong by so whisker thin a margin. Hypothesis testing can be easily thrown off by lustful presidents, drunken coup plotters, determined assassins, and the exact timing of the puncturing of market bubbles—as long as the hypothesis at stake is one's own.

How should we weigh these arguments? On the one hand, we can exonerate hedgehogs of charges of reneging more often on reputational bets if we allow generous fuzzy-set adjustments that assign large credibility weights (.7 or higher) to the close-call, off-on-timing, or exogenous-shock defenses. On the other hand, we also know that experts in general, and hedgehogs in particular, invoked these defenses in suspiciously self-serving ways. A balanced appraisal is that, although the normative verdicts reached in chapters 3 and 4 may need more case-specific qualifications, the overall verdicts stand.

Rebutting Accusations of Double Standards

Chapter 5 showed that experts, especially hedgehogs, advanced three reasons for dismissing dissonant evidence that they rarely applied to congenial evidence: challenging the authenticity and representativeness of documents, and the motives of investigators. Follow-up interviews revealed that hedgehogs saw little need to apologize for upholding a lenient standard for congenial evidence and a tough standard for disagreeable evidence. Their attitude was: "The more ludicrous the claim, the higher the hurdle its promoters should jump." Claims that contradict established knowledge merit sharp scrutiny.[14]

---

[14] Suppe, "Scientific Theories."

By contrast, foxes were more flustered by the unveiling of their own double standards and quicker to sense the risks of the hedgehog defense of double standards: one will never change one's mind if one always accepts poor research with agreeable conclusions and hammers away at good research with disagreeable conclusions. The question becomes: When do double standards become unacceptable? Many philosophers of science argue that one reaches that point when one becomes insensitive to variations in research quality and attends only to the agreeableness of the results.[15] One's viewpoint then becomes impregnable to evidence. Using this standard, reanalysis of the Kremlin archives study reveals that, although foxes and hedgehogs were both more inclined to accept discoveries that meshed with their ideological preconceptions, foxes were at least moderately responsive to the quality of the underlying research, whereas hedgehogs were seemingly oblivious. This finding is a warning that, although setting higher standards for dissonant claims is sometimes defensible, hedgehogs risk taking the policy too far.

Rebutting Accusations of Using History to Prop Up One's Prejudices

Chapter 5 showed that experts, especially hedgehogs with strong convictions, used a number of lines of logical defense to neutralize close-call counterfactuals that undercut pet theories. We also saw that hedgehogs saw no need to apologize for their dismissive stance toward close-call counterfactuals. They felt that learning from history would become impossible if we paid attention to every whimsical what-if that might stray through the minds of dreamy observers. Confronted with comparisons to foxes' greater openness to close-call scenarios, hedgehogs saw the contrast in a light favorable to themselves: "We (hedgehogs) know how to follow through on the historical implications of an argument" and they (foxes) "tie themselves up in self-contradictory knots." Foxes, of course, saw things differently: they suspected hedgehogs of being "heavy-handed determinists" ("How can they be so confident about things no one could know?") Foxes thought that they knew when to rein in the impulse to generalize.

Lacking definitive correspondence standards for assessing how re-routable history was at given junctures, some say we are left with utterly subjective judgment calls.[16] Logic and evidence cannot, however, be

---

[15] Ibid.

[16] For illustrations of how easy it is to put conflicting spins on low and high ends of cognitive style dimensions, see P. E. Tetlock, R. Peterson, and J. Berry, "Flattering and Unflattering Personality Portraits of Integratively Simple and Complex Managers," *Journal of Personality and Social Psychology* 64 (1993): 500–511; P. E. Tetlock, D. Armor, and R. Peterson, "The Slavery Debate in Antebellum America: Cognitive Style, Value Conflict, and

completely shunted out. A higher-order inconsistency bedevils both many hedgehogs and foxes, but especially hedgehogs: the tendency to fit the distant past into neat deterministic patterns coupled with the tendency, especially right after forecasting failures, to portray the recent past as riddled with contingency. Inasmuch as there is no compelling reason to suppose that the recent past is more stochastic than the distant past, this pattern is suggestive of cognitive illusion.

Defending the Hindsight Bias

Chapter 4 also showed that hedgehogs were more susceptible to hindsight effects: to exaggerate the degree to which "they saw it coming all along." Defenders of hedgehogs can, however, challenge the characterization of hindsight bias as cognitive defect. Hindsight may be an adaptive mechanism that "unclutters our minds by tossing out inaccurate information—a kind of merge/purge for the mind . . . a mental bargain, a cheap price for a much larger cognitive gain: a well-functioning memory that can forget what we do not need—such as outdated knowledge—and that constantly updates our knowledge, thereby increasing the accuracy of our inferences."[17] As one exasperated expert commented, "We all once believed in Santa Claus. You don't think I keep track of every screwy belief I once held."

Granting that the hindsight effect is cognitively convenient does not, however, alter its status as a mistake in the strictest correspondence meaning of the term—a deviation from reality that makes it difficult to learn from experience. Hindsight bias forecloses the possibility of surprises, and surprises—because they are hard to forget—play a critical

---

the Limits of Compromise," *Journal of Personality and Social Psychology* 66 (1994): 115–26. These conflicting spins also tie into old debates between cognitive consistency theorists over how tightly integrated belief systems tend to be. Minimalists such as Robert Abelson stressed the wispy connections among idea-elements, whereas maximalists such as William McGuire posited more constraints. See R. Abelson, "Psychological Implication," in *Theories of Cognitive Consistency: A Source Book* ed. R. Abelson, E. Aronson, W. McGuire, T. Newcomb, M. Rosenberg, and P. Tannenbaum (Chicago: Rand McNally, 1968), 112–39; W. J. McGuire, "Theory of the Structure of Human Thought," in Abelson et al., *Theories of Cognitive Consistency.*

[17] U. Hoffrege, R. Hertwig, and G. Gigerenzer, *Journal of Experimental Psychology: Learning, Memory, and Cognition* 26 (2000): 303–20. Curiously, psychologists who mostly disagree over the adaptive value of certainty of hindsight agree on the processes underlying the effect. They agree that when people cannot remember their original judgment—which often happens—they reconstruct the judgment based on what they know about the situation. They agree that people automatically use outcome feedback to update their knowledge about the situation. And they agree that people reconstruct their original judgments using this updated knowledge.

role in learning when and where our beliefs failed us. Indeed, neuroscientists have begun to pinpoint the mechanisms involved: surprise and learning are both linked to neural activation in the dorsolateral prefrontal cortex. The key point should not, though, require magnetic resonance imaging of brain functions. Aesop's fables warn us of the dangers of a smug "knew it all along" attitude toward the world.

We Posed the Wrong Questions

Imperfect though they may be, there are still standards for judging replies to forecasting and belief-updating questions. But it gets progressively harder to tease out testable implications from the sixth, seventh, and eighth hedgehog defenses: "The researchers asked the *wrong questions* of the *wrong people* at the *wrong time*." The only response is sometimes: "Well, if you think you'd get different results by posing different types of questions to different types of people, go ahead." That is how science is supposed to proceed.

In fairness to hedgehogs, though, some offered the "wrong questions" protest well before we knew who got what right. They told me from the outset that their province is the long view, measured not in months or years but rather in decades, generations, and occasionally centuries.[18] One hedgehog expressed the view of many: "I cannot tell you what will happen tomorrow in Kosovo or Kashmir or Korea. These idiotic squabbles will go on until exhaustion sets in. But I can tell you that irreversible trends are at work in the world today."

We noted in chapter 3 that hedgehogs found comprehensive worldviews congenial and were drawn to three major offerings from the late twentieth-century marketplace of ideas: optimistic-rationalist positions that predict that states will be compelled by competitive pressures to become increasingly democratic and capitalistic, more pessimistic identity politics–neorealist positions that predict that peoples, and the nation-states they inhabit, will be forever divided by bitter in-group–out-group distinctions, and still more depressing neo-Malthusian views that predict ever-nastier ecocatastrophes and conflicts between the haves and the have-nots.

---

[18] It is useful to distinguish moderate from extreme proponents of this defense. My differences with the moderates are a matter of degree: I preferred shorter time frames and more precisely defined outcome variables. But my differences with the extremists—those more at home with prophecy than prediction—are unbridgeable. One hedgehog asked whether my "tidy scheme" left room for visionaries such as Nietzsche or Marx. Would I count Nietzsche's "God is dead" pronouncement as wrong because religion still thrives in the late twentieth century? Could I concede that Nietzsche had anticipated that totalitarian movements would fill the spiritual void left by the death of God? My view is that the God-is-dead prediction might be resuscitated via the off-on-timing defense, but it currently looks like a loser and that

Each school of thought spun elaborate justifications for its profoundly different view of the long-term future. And although it will take a long time to sort out which predictions will prove prophetic, there is no reason to believe that the relative performance of hedgehogs would improve even if we waited decades. Hedgehogs are ideologically diverse. Only a few of them can be right in each long-term competition. The best bet thus remains on the less audacious foxes.

We Failed to Talk to Properly Qualified and/or Properly Motivated People at the Right Time

The first prong of this three-pronged defense questions the professional qualifications of forecasters. Perhaps I recruited "unusually dumb hedgehogs" and "unusually smart foxes." I cannot respond by offering IQ data (or by lifting the veil of anonymity promised participants). I cannot even claim representative samples of "experts" (my samples are samples of convenience). But I can point to the summary profile data in the Methodological Appendix that show most participants had postgraduate degrees and, on average, twelve years of professional experience. And I can point to the analyses in chapter 3 that reveal negligible relations between (a) professional status, seniority, and field of specialization and the key correspondence and coherence measures of good judgment; (b) cognitive style and professional specialization or status. These arguments do not eliminate the possibility that another, more "elite" cohort of hedgehogs would have bested foxes, but they do shift the burden of proof to challengers.

The second prong of the three-pronged defense questions how motivated participants were to display good judgment. Here it is necessary to cede a bit more ground. Many of the judgments we elicited were undoubtedly top-of-the-head opinions that experts knew they would never have to justify. This raises the possibility that experts might have done better if the stakes had been higher and they had been more motivated to get it right. There is some truth in this objection. Accountability and incentives do sometimes "de-bias" judgment. But they also often have either no effect or the effect of amplifying, not attenuating, bias and error.[19] And it is a stretch to argue that either incentives or accountability pressures would

---

Nietzsche should not get credit for anticipating Stalinism or Nazism given there is scant evidence that these phenomena arose because people had stopped believing in God and scanter evidence that Nietzsche came remotely close to predicting when, where, and how these phenomena would arise. We might as well credit Nostradamus with predicting World War II.

[19] C. F. Camerer and R. M. Hogarth, "The Effects of Financial Incentives in Experiments: A Review and Capital-Labor-Production Framework," *Journal of Risk and Uncertainty* 19 (1999): 1–3, 7–42.

have helped only hedgehogs. Indeed, if accountability motivates experts to do their cognitive best, and if hedgehogs and foxes have different views on what their cognitive best is, one can make a good case that accountability pressures would widen the performance gap by making hedgehogs even more hedgehogish and foxes even more foxish.[20]

The last prong of the three-pronged defense declares that experts look far worse than they normally would because we picked an unusually turbulent period of twentieth-century history in which to study good judgment. This objection has little merit. First, it misses a key argument of this book. Of course, experts can predict more accurately in periods of tranquility. But the data show that, even in quiescent times, hedgehogs suffer a performance deficit (relative to both foxes and simple extrapolation algorithms). Second, this objection underestimates how turbulent other fifteen-year slices of the twentieth century have been. World War I astonished those who thought that the major powers were too financially interdependent to go to war. The Great Depression startled economists who thought that boom-bust cycles were passé. And the threat posed by the Nazis was recognized by only an opinionated minority until late in the game. The transformations wrought by the advent of nuclear weaponry and later ballistic missiles were mostly unanticipated (and continue to provoke controversy as experts offer radically discrepant estimates of both the feasibility and long-term effects of ballistic missile defense). The dramatic turn of events in China in the 1970s—Maoist extremism evolving into pragmatic reformism—may have an illusory retrospective inevitability, but few foresaw them. The case that experts got stuck with an unusually unpredictable decade is weak.

Misunderstanding What Game Is Being Played

Hedgehogs can play a final card. They can argue that epistemic criteria do not apply to them: their real goal is political impact. As one hedgehog resident of a "think tank" patiently explained, "You play a publish-or-perish game run by the rules of social science. . . . You are under the misapprehension that I play the same game. I don't. I fight to preserve my reputation in a cutthroat adversarial culture. I woo dumb-ass reporters who want glib sound bites." In his world, only the overconfident survive, and only the truly arrogant thrive.

---

[20] This influential hypothesis holds that accountability and other possible motivators of cognitive work have the net effect of increasing the likelihood of dominant or overlearned responses. P. E. Tetlock and J. Lerner, "The Social Contingency Model: Identifying Empirical and Normative Boundary Conditions on the Error-and-Bias Portrait of Human Nature," in *Dual Process Models in Social Psychology*, ed. S. Chaiken and Y. Trope (New York: Guilford Press, 1999).

Another hedgehog stressed the need—if one wants to be remembered—to make bold claims that "run against the grain of the conventional wisdom." One needed considerable gumption in the mid-1930s to tell the influential appeasers in the governments of the major democracies that Nazi Germany was a gangster state with which it was impossible to do business, or to announce in the late 1970s that China, staggered by the convulsions of the Cultural Revolution, was about to take off economically, or that OPEC, riding high from having repeatedly multiplied the price of oil, would soon get its comeuppance, or to declare in the early 1980s that the Soviet Union was marching straight into the ash heap of history.

It is tough to gauge whether this objection is a flimsy excuse or compelling alternative explanation. But the evidence tips toward "excuse." In debriefing interviews, we asked nearly half of the participants whether they saw themselves more as "neutral observers whose primary goal is figuring out what is going on" or "promoting a point of view." We found only the slightest of tendencies for self-professed neutral observers to be either foxes ($r = .10$) or better forecasters ($r = .08$). It is thus hard to argue that hedgehogs lost to foxes as consistently as they did because they were playing a policy-advocacy game.

CLOSING OBSERVATIONS

Even the formidable combination of defenses mobilized in this chapter fails to acquit hedgehogs of all allegations of error and bias leveled against them. But the defense objections took some sting out of certain allegations. Hedgehogs narrow the performance gap when we introduce big value adjustments (giving them the benefit of the doubt that their mistakes were the right mistakes), big probability-weighting adjustments (giving them credit for making courageous predictions) and big fuzzy-set adjustments (giving them some credit for being "almost right"). Defenders of hedgehogs are also right that endorsing a belief system defense does not automatically make one defensive, that some double standards are justifiable, and that openness to close-call counterfactuals is not presumptive evidence of open-mindedness (it may be a sign that one has not thought things through). Most important, defenders of hedgehogs do us a service by calling our attention to the elaborate matrix of assumptions on which attributions of "better" or "worse" judgment must rest. Claims of the form "members of group X have better judgment than members of group Y" are not purely scientific; they are complex amalgams of empirical generalizations, value priorities, and even metaphysical sentiments.

In sum, chapter 6 reminds us of the provisional character of judgments of good judgment. It transforms what has heretofore been a cognitive morality play, populated with well-defined good and bad guys, into a murkier tale, populated by characters attired in varying shades of grey. Chapter 7 takes us still further in this anti-Manichaean direction.

CHAPTER 7

Are We Open-minded Enough to Acknowledge the Limits of Open-mindedness?

> The impossible sometimes happens and the inevitable sometimes does not.
>
> —KAHNEMAN

> Like the measured length of a coastline, which increases as the map becomes more specific, the perceived likelihood of an event increases as its description becomes more specific.
>
> —TVERSKY AND KOEHLER 1994

> These observations suggest an image of the mind as a bureaucracy in which different parts have access to different data, assign them different weights, and hold different views of the situation.
>
> —KAHNEMAN AND TVERSKY 1982

CHAPTER 6 revealed considerable canniness in what looked like incorrigible closed-mindedness. It failed, however, to exonerate experts of all the cognitive indictments against them. In this chapter, therefore, let us assume a lingering problem: all too often experts, especially the hedgehogs among them, claim to know more about the future than they actually know (chapter 3), balk at changing their minds in the face of unexpected evidence (chapter 4), and dogmatically defend their deterministic explanations of the past (chapter 5).

The diagnosis implies a cure: observers would stack up better against our benchmarks of good judgment if only they were a tad more open-minded. We should not be glib, though, in our prescriptions. Careless cures can cause great harm. Promoters of "debiasing" schemes should shoulder a heavy burden of proof. Would-be buyers should insist that schemes that purportedly improve "how they think" be grounded in solid assumptions about (a) the workings of the human mind and—in particular—how people go about translating vague hunches about causality into the precise probabilistic claims measured here; (b) the workings of the external environment and—in particular—the likely impact of proposed correctives on the mistakes that people most commonly make in coping with frequently recurring challenges.

Chapter 7 reports the first systematic studies of the impact of a widely deployed debiasing tool, scenario exercises, on the judgmental performance of political experts in real-world settings.[1] Such exercises rest on an intuitively appealing premise: the value of breaking the tight grip of our preconceptions on our views of what could have been or might yet be. I am also convinced from personal experience that such exercises, skillfully done, have great practical value in contingency planning in business, government, and the military. But the data reported in this chapter make it difficult to argue that such exercises—standing alone—improve either the empirical accuracy or logical coherence of expert's predictions. For scenario exercises have no net effect on the empirical accuracy and logical coherence of the forecasts of roughly one-half of our sample (the hedgehogs) and an adverse net effect on the accuracy and coherence of the forecasts of the other half (the foxes). The more theory-driven hedgehogs find it easier to reject proliferating scenario branching points summarily, with a brusque "It just ain't gonna happen." The more open-minded foxes find it harder to resist invitations to consider strange or dissonant possibilities—and are thus in greater danger of being lured into wild goose chases in which they fritter away scarce resources contemplating possibilities they originally rightly dismissed. For the first time in this book, foxes become more susceptible than hedgehogs to a serious bias: the tendency to assign so much likelihood to so many possibilities that they become entangled in self-contradictions.

The Power of Imagination

In the last fifteen years, there has been an intriguing convergence between experimental efforts to correct judgmental biases and the entrepreneurial efforts of scenario consultants to improve contingency planning in business and government. Experimental psychologists have found that many judgmental shortcomings can be traced to a deeply ingrained feature of human nature: our tendency to apply more stringent standards to evidence that challenges our prejudices than to evidence that reinforces those prejudices. These psychologists have also stressed the value of busting up this cozy arrangement. And they have had some success in correcting overconfidence by asking people to look for reasons that cut against the

---

[1] "Judgmental performance" here refers only to those most readily measurable aspects of good judgment: the empirical accuracy and logical coherence of subjective probability forecasts. This chapter does not test the claim—central to the livelihoods of scenario consultants but notoriously difficult to quantify—that scenario exercises stimulate contingency planning that more than compensates for the transaction costs of the scenario exercises.

grain of their current expectations,[2] in correcting belief perseverance by highlighting double standards for evaluating evidence,[3] and in correcting hindsight bias[4] by asking people to imagine ways in which alternative outcomes could have come about. Of course, these demonstrations have all been in controlled laboratory conditions. The results tell us little about the mistakes people make in natural settings or about the adverse side effects of treatments.

Reassuringly, scenario consultants—who cannot be quite so readily dismissed as detached from reality—hold strikingly similar views on the causes of, and cures for, bad judgment.[5] They appeal to clients to stretch their conceptions of the possible, to imagine a wider range of futures than they normally would, and then to construct full-fledged stories that spell out the "drivers" that, under the right conditions, could propel our world into each alternative future. Scenario writers know that it is not enough to enumerate pallid possibilities. They must make it easy "to transport" ourselves into possible worlds, to get a feeling for the challenges we would face. They urge us to abandon the illusion of certainty: to adopt the stance "I am prepared for whatever happens."[6]

Scenario consultants should not, of course, be the final judges of their own effectiveness. When pressed for proof, the consultants have thus far offered only anecdotes, invariably self-promoting ones, drawn from a massive file drawer that holds an unknown mix of more or less successful test cases. Their favorite success story is Royal Dutch Shell in the early 1970s. The Shell group was looking for factors that could affect the future price of oil. They suspected that the Arabs would demand higher prices for their oil, but they could not say when. But they needed the ability to read the mind of Anwar Sadat, or a spy in the Egyptian high command, to predict the Yom Kippur war in October 1973. They knew only that storm clouds loomed on the horizon. The United States was exhausting its known reserves. American demand for oil was growing. And OPEC was flexing its muscles. A large fraction of the world reserves was controlled by Middle Eastern regimes that bitterly resented Western support for Israel. One of their scenarios now sounds eerily

[2] Koriat, Fischhoff, and Lichtenstein, "Over-Confidence"; P. E. Tetlock and J. Kim, "Accountability and Overconfidence in a Personality Prediction Task," *Journal of Personality and Social Psychology* 52 (1987): 700–709.

[3] C. Anderson, "Inoculation and Counter-explanation: Debiasing Techniques in the Perseverance of Social Theories," *Social Cognition* 1 (1982): 126–139.

[4] Hawkins and Hastie, "Hindsight."

[5] The *Economist* in October 2001 characterized scenario planning as the most popular approach to protecting big organizations from nasty surprises lurking in the ill-defined future.

[6] Schwartz, "Long View."

prescient: massive price shocks that transformed the oil business and contributed to the "stagflation" of the 1970s. Schwartz claims that mentally preparing Shell managers for this medium-term future gave them a critical advantage against their less imaginative competitors.[7]

Although scenario writers eschew prediction, they take parental pride when one of their progeny proves prophetic. In addition to the bull's-eye OPEC scenario, the Shell group advertises its success in anticipating, in 1983 when U.S.-Soviet tensions were running high, radical reform inside the Soviet Union. The Shell futurists persuaded top executives to consider the possibility that the Soviet Union would open its massive untapped resources for development by multinational companies, that the cold war would thaw, and that Europeans would be willing to buy most of their natural gas from the soon-to-be-former Soviet Union. The Shell team also advanced a scenario in which OPEC unity fractured as new supplies came on-line and as demand for oil remained flat. They can thus claim to have foreseen not only the rise of OPEC in the 1970s but also its partial fall in the 1980s.

These bull's-eyes are less impressive, however, when we remember that consultants write so many scenarios that they are guaranteed to be right once per gig. For instance, James Ogilvy and colleagues constructed three scenarios for China in 2022 that covered a broad waterfront of possibilities.[8] The first envisioned a prosperous, democratic China that becomes, in absolute terms, the world's largest economy and boasts of a per capita income equivalent to today's Taiwan. The second depicted a China that is dominated by an oligarchic network of extended families and is so beset by regional factions that it teeters on the edge of civil war. A third anticipated corruption and inequitable distribution of wealth becoming so pervasive that a populist military leader seizes control (after conquering oil-rich territory in Russia's Far East). The authors advised investors to test the viability of their business plans against each scenario because none could be ruled out.

There are good reasons to be wary here. Portfolio diversification theory in finance would not command such wide professional acclaim if it had not advanced beyond the folk aphorism "Don't put all your eggs in one basket." And scenario consultants cannot expect more than fleeting fame if their advice reduces to "anything is possible" so "be prepared for anything." There is also the concern that advocates of scenario methods make good livings hawking their wares and have little incentive to explore the negative side effects of leading people down too many

---

[7] Schwartz, "Long View."

[8] J. A. Ogilvy, P. Schwartz, and J. Flower, *China's Futures* (San Francisco, CA: Jossey-Bass, 2000).

overembellished paths. Absent the regulatory equivalent of the Food and Drug Administration to set standards for cognitive self-improvement products, it is hard to say whether consumers are wasting their hard-earned dollars on scenario snake oil.[9]

There is, then, a need for a disinterested assessment. The starting point for our assessment is support theory, the final work of the extraordinary psychologist, Amos Tversky. Support theory posits the likelihoods people attach to outcomes to be monotonic functions of the relative strength of the arguments people can muster for those outcomes. If I feel that the arguments for one set of possibilities are five times more powerful than those for another, that 5:1 ratio will translate into a higher subjective probability (how much higher must be estimated empirically). More controversially, the theory also posits that people are quite oblivious to the complex possibilities implicit in characterizations of events and, as a result, prone to violate a core assumption of formal probability theory: the "extensionality" principle. Odd though it sounds, the expectation is that people will often judge the likelihood of a set of outcomes to be less than the sum of the likelihoods of each member of that set. "Unpacking" stimulates us to imagine sub-possibilities, and arguments for those sub-possibilities, that we would have otherwise overlooked. Thus, unpacking a set of events (e.g., victory in a baseball game) into its disjoint components, $A_1 \cup A_2$ (e.g., victory by one run or victory by more than one run), typically increases both its perceived support and subjective probability.[10]

Support theory raises a warning flag: people should quickly become discombobulated, and routinely violate extensionality, when they do what scenario consultants tell them to do: decompose abstract sets of

[9] Moreover, there is a good chance, given the capacious capacity of human beings to rationalize choices and the stingy feedback history provides, that consumers themselves are not "in the know." If we had relied in this project on experts' self-assessments of whether they were overconfident or self-justifying—instead of assessing their performance—we would have concluded that "all's well because the experts tell us so." Even now, it is a safe bet that few readers think of themselves as systematically biased thinkers.

[10] These imagination-driven biases are fueled by dramatizing scenarios in ways that, on the one hand, make it easier to transport ourselves into the fictional universe but, on the other, make the overall scenario increasingly improbable by any logical standard. As a result of this perverse inverse relationship between the psychological impact of stories and the cumulative likelihood of their event linkages, more imaginative thinkers become more susceptible to making self-contradictory judgments that violate basic precepts of probability theory. They find themselves endorsing oxymoronic assertions such as "I believe that by this point outcome x was inevitable but alternatives to x were still possible." They also assign higher likelihoods to vividly embellished scenarios than they would have to the abstract sets of possibilities from which scenarios were derived and thus constitute subsets. The result is exactly what Amos Tversky's support theory predicts: reverse Gestalt effects in which people judge the probability of the whole to be *less* than the sum of its exclusive and exhaustive parts.

possibilities—say, all possible ways a leader might fall—into increasingly specific and easily imagined sub-possibilities that specify in scenario-like detail the various ways in which that outcome might happen.[11] According to Daniel Kahneman and Amos Tversky, such confusion derives from the difficulty that people have in reconciling the tension between "inside" and "outside" approaches to forecasting.[12] Unpacking scenarios encourages people to adopt an inside view: to immerse themselves in each case and judge the plausibility of pathways to outcomes by drawing on their detailed case-specific knowledge of the forces at work. People usually find more support for these case-specific predictions than they would have if they had based their judgments on an outside view, if they had stepped back from the details of individual cases and grouped them into summary categories (base rates). This is because the outside view is anchored in external referents that stop people from being swept away by "good stories." For example, revolutions are rare events even in the "zone of turbulence," and the outside view reminds us that, no matter how good a story one can tell about impending regime collapse in North Korea or Saudi Arabia, one should adjust one's inside perspective likelihood estimates by outside perspective base rates for comparable outcomes in sets of comparable cases.

Of course, in the end we might decide that confusion is a price worth paying if scenario exercises shield us from cognitive biases such as overconfidence and belief perseverance. The best way to combat powerful theory-driven biases could be by activating countervailing biases rooted in our imaginative ability to suspend disbelief and to mobilize support for even far-fetched possibilities.[13]

DEBIASING JUDGMENTS OF POSSIBLE FUTURES

In the 1990s, we conducted a series of small-scale experiments designed to assess whether the hypothesized benefits of scenario exercises outweighed

[11] Support theory has held up in many samples—from undergraduates to options traders to physicians—so presumably it also applies to professional observers of the political scene.

[12] A. Tversky and D. Kahneman, "Extensional vs. Intuitive Reasoning: The Conjunction Fallacy in Probability Judgment," *Psychological Review* 90 (1983): 293–315.

[13] P. E. Tetlock, "The Logic and Psycho-logic of Counterfactual Thought Experiments in the Rise-of-the-West Debate," in *Unmaking the West: What-If Scenarios That Rewrite World History*, ed. P. E. Tetlock, R. N. Lebow, and G. Parker (Ann Arbor: University of Michigan Press, 2006); M. C. Green and T. C. Brock, "The Role of Transportation in the Persuasiveness of Narratives," *Journal of Personality and Social Psychology* 79(5) (2000): 701–21; A. Tversky and C. Fox, "Weighting Risk and Uncertainty," *Psychological Review* 102(2) (1995): 269–83.

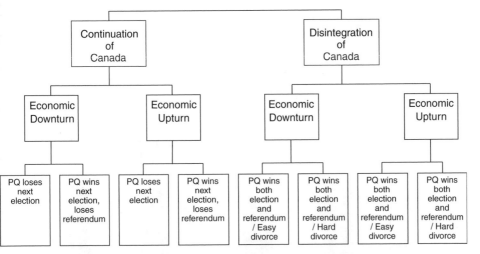

Figure 7.1. The set of possible futures of Canada unpacked into increasingly differentiated subsets. In the control condition, experts assigned probabilities to the two (exclusive and exhaustive) futures at the top of the figure. In the experimental unpacking condition, experts assigned probabilities to each of the eight exclusive and exhaustive futures at the bottom of the figure.

the hypothesized costs. The largest two of these experiments drew participants from the forecasting exercises on Canada and Japan (for details, see Methodological Appendix).

Canadian Futures Scenarios

This experiment compared the likelihood judgments that expert and dilettante, fox and hedgehog, forecasters made before they did any scenario exercises, after they completed scenario exercises, and finally, after they completed "reflective equilibrium" exercises that required reconciling logical contradictions between their pre- and postjudgments by ensuring their probabilities summed to 1.0. Figure 7.1 lays out the scenarios that were judged (a) possible futures involving either a continuation of the status quo (federal and provincial governments agree to continue disagreeing over constitutional prerogatives) or a strengthening of Canadian unity (in which agreements are reached); (b) possible futures in which a secessionist referendum in Quebec succeeds, and controversy shifts to the terms of divorce.

Figure 7.2 shows that we replicated the well-established finding that "merely imagining" outcomes increases the perceived likelihood of those outcomes: pre-scenario judgments of probability were uniformly smaller

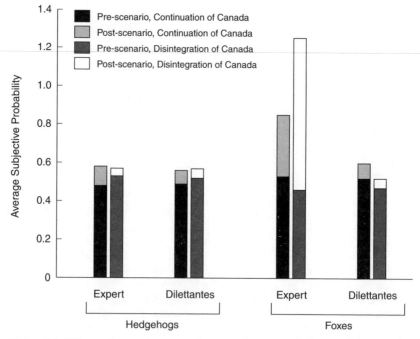

Figure 7.2. Effects of scenario-generation exercises on hedgehog and fox, expert and dilettante, forecasters of possible five- and ten-year futures on Canada (1992–1997–2002).

than post-scenario judgments.[14] We also broke new ground. We discovered that the imagination effect was greatest under three conditions: (a) forecasters were experts rather than dilettantes; (b) forecasters were imagining departures from the status quo (the breakup of Canada) rather than continuation of the status quo; (c) forecasters were foxes rather than hedgehogs. These results took us a bit aback. Our guess had been that expertise would make it easier to winnow out far-fetched scenarios. But the net effect of expertise—especially expertise coupled to an imaginative cognitive style—was to make it easier to get swept away by "change scenarios" that prime rich networks of cause-effect associations.

It is hard to make a convincing correspondence or coherence case that these scenario exercises improved judgment. If we adopt the correspondence definition that good judges assign higher probabilities to things

[14] J. S. Carroll, "The Effect of Imagining an Event on Expectations for the Event: An Interpretation in Terms of the Availability Heuristic," *Journal of Experimental Social Psychology* 14 (1978): 88–96; L. Ross, M. R. Lepper, F. Strack, and J. Steinmetz, "Social Explanation and Social Expectation: Effects of Real and Hypothetical Explanations on Subjective Likelihood," *Journal of Personality and Social Psychology* 35 (1997): 817–29.

that happen than to things that do not, the exercises clearly led forecasters astray. Before the exercise, experts judged continuation of Confederation more likely than disintegration; afterward, they flipped. If we adopt the coherence definition that good judges must be logically consistent, it gets even harder to discern the benefits of scenario exercises. Before the exercise, binary complementarity held: the judged probability of Canada holding together plus that of Canada falling apart summed to nearly exactly 1.0 for both experts and dilettantes. After the exercise, the average probability of these futures summed to 1.58 for all experts and 2.09 for fox experts. Probability judgments became increasingly sub-additive and in violation of the "extensionality" norm of probability theory.

Why do we find this? Unpacking is mentally disruptive and scenarios are extreme forms of unpacking. One takes a vague abstraction, all possible paths to Canada's disintegration, and explores increasingly specific contingencies. Quebec secedes and the rest of Canada fragments: the Maritimes—geographically isolated—clings to Ontario, but Alberta flirts with the United States rather than bonding with the other western provinces that have broken with Ontario. One knows in the back of one's mind that the cumulative likelihood of all these contingent linkages holding true is vanishingly small. But the images are vivid, the plotlines plausible, and it becomes increasingly taxing to keep all the other logical possibilities in focus.

Mediational analyses underscore this account. "Imaginability" appears to drive the inflation of subjective probabilities. Participants judged easier-to-imagine futures more likely (average $r[58] = .46$, $p < .05$). And, after controlling for variation in the imaginability of scenarios, the power of scenario exercises to inflate subjective probabilities disappears, as does the greater susceptibility of experts and foxes to scenario effects.

In the closing phase of the experiment, it seemed only fair to give defenders of the scenario method a final shot at showing that, although incoherence may be the temporary price of exploring alternative futures in depth, experts encouraged to reflect on their clashing probability estimates would produce "better" judgments than experts not so encouraged. We brought to experts' attention, as diplomatically as possible, the logical impossibility of the subjective probabilities they had assigned scenarios. As a "consistency check" we asked experts to add the probabilities that they had assigned across "classes of scenarios." (These sums exceeded 1.0 for 85 percent of respondents.) We then asked them to adjust their estimates so that the sums would equal the mandated ceiling on probabilities of 1.0, and to approach this adjustment process in pursuit of what philosophers call "reflective equilibrium." "It is well known," we informed participants, that "different methods of posing questions about complex events frequently elicit different answers. For this reason, we routinely ask participants how they would prefer to reconcile any potential conflicts among their responses."

We are now in uncharted territory. One conjecture was that, although scenario exercises puffed up probabilities across the board, they puffed up some more than others, and experts would preserve the new proportional relations among probabilities that emerged from the scenario exercises. So, if an expert judged the continuation-of-Canada and the disintegration-of-Canada scenarios as having the same cumulative likelihood of .70 each (summing to 1.4), he should "normalize" around the values of .5 and .5, regardless of what the expert thought earlier. The second conjecture was that experts would conclude that they had been led down the primrose path, recognize that their estimates had been artificially inflated by the "imaginability" of scenarios, and correct themselves by returning to their pre-scenario estimates. The second conjecture was closest to the mark for hedgehogs who were the most outspokenly skeptical of the scenario exercises at the beginning and remained so at the end; the first conjecture captured the foxes who were the most open to scenarios at the outset and remained convinced the exercises had some lasting value.

Cynics might say that the scenario exercise was a circuitous journey into incoherence that brought us back to roughly where we started. Although scenarios changed some minds, they did not change many by much after we pressured people to integrate their conflicting intuitions into a coherent stand. And those changes in perspective that did persist through the reflective equilibrium exercise had the net effect of reducing accuracy: assigning higher probabilities to things that did not happen and lower probabilities to things that did.

Japanese Futures Scenario Experiment

Defenders of the scenario method could argue that the Canadian results are peculiar to the country, time period, and experts examined. Anticipating this objection, we ran a parallel experiment on forecasters who had already, without scenario assistance, attached probability estimates to the possible futures of Japan. Figure 7.3 shows that the "stories about possible futures for the Japanese economy" fell into three categories: possible futures featuring a continuation of the status quo, a substantial improvement on the status quo, and a substantial deterioration. We "unpacked" each economic future into three subclasses of scenarios that specified possible political pathways to each future.

Figure 7.4 shows that scenario exercises again puffed up probability estimates beyond the bounds of reason. Pre-scenario estimates of each possible future summed roughly to 1.0, whereas the post-scenario estimates (produced by adding the likelihoods of sub-scenarios), substantially

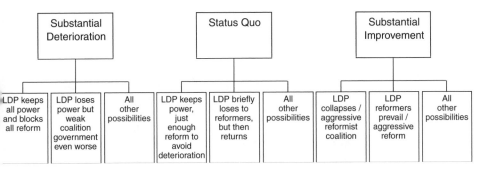

Figure 7.3. The set of possible Japanese futures unpacked into increasingly differentiated subsets.

surpassed 1.0. Scenario thinking encouraged sub-additive estimates in which the judged likelihood of the whole consistently fell short of the sum of its parts. Overall, the results paralleled those of the Canadian study in several key respects: (1) scenario exercises had more pronounced effects on experts than on dilettantes, especially experts with foxlike cognitive styles; (2) the power of scenarios to inflate subjective probabilities was greater for departures from the status quo, either upward or downward, than for the status quo; (3) when participants performed the "reflective equilibrium" task of reconciling logical contradictions and disciplining probability estimates to sum to 1.0, they mostly split the difference between their pre- and post-scenario estimates.

Summing Up the Scenario Experiments

Scenario exercises are promoted in the political and business worlds as correctives to dogmatism and overconfidence. And by this point in the book, the need for such correctives should not be in question. But the scenario experiments show that scenario exercises are not cure-alls. Indeed, the experiments give us grounds for fearing that such exercises will often fail to open the minds of the inclined-to-be-closed-minded hedgehogs but succeed in confusing the already-inclined-to-be-open-minded foxes—confusing foxes so much that their open-mindedness starts to look like credulousness.[15]

[15] The greater susceptibility to scenario generation effects of foxes is a result that holds up well in this chapter, regardless of whether experts were contemplating possible futures or possible pasts. These results nicely parallel those of experimental work that demonstrates the greater susceptibility of low-need-for-structure (or closure) respondents to divergent-thinking manipulations. See E. Hirt, F. Kardes, and K. Markman, "Activating a Mental-simulation Mindset through Generation of Alternatives: Implications for De-biasing in Related and Unrelated Domains," *Journal of Experimental Social Psychology* 40 (2004): 374–83.

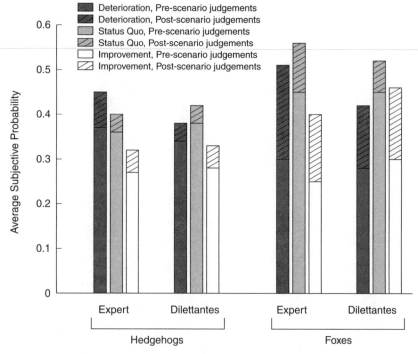

Figure 7.4. Effects of scenario-generation exercises on hedgehog and fox, expert and dilettante, forecasters of five- to ten-year futures of Japan (1992–1997–2002).

Attentive readers will notice here a mirror image of the expertise-by-cognitive-style interaction that drove down the forecasting accuracy of hedgehogs in chapter 3. Back then, hedgehog accuracy suffered most when hedgehogs made predictions in domains where they were most knowledgeable—and thus had the cognitive resources to construct convincing stories for their favorite future. In chapter 7, fox coherence suffered most when foxes worked through scenario exercises in domains where they were most knowledgeable—and thus had the cognitive resources to construct convincing stories for widely divergent possible futures. In each case, cognitive style moderated how forecasters used their expertise: for self-justifying ends among hedghogs and for self-subversive ends among foxes. Or, if we flip the interaction, we could say that expertise moderated the magnitude of the cognitive-style effect: without a rich knowledge base, the cognitive style effect was anemic; with one, it was powerful.

Two scenario experiments are obviously not a massive database, but the results are sufficiently similar that it is worth posing a thought experiment. Suppose that participants in all forecasting domains had worked through scenario exercises and the effects were identical to the Canadian and Japanese experiments. We could then extrapolate what the effects of scenario exercises would have been across the board by replacing the probabilities that various subgroups of forecasters assigned with the hypothetical probabilities they would have assigned if they had done scenarios exercises. We know, for example, that the biggest increases were concentrated among foxlike experts contemplating change from the status quo. We also know that scenario effects were larger for low and middle probability categories (0.1 to 0.6) and smaller at the end points of zero (impossible) and 1.0 (sure thing), where forecasters were presumably more confidently settled in their judgments. What happens when we perform these value substitutions: pumping up low and moderate probabilities and merging probability categories whenever a lower-likelihood class of events (say, .2) rises so fast that it overtakes an adjacent category (say, .3)?

Figure 7.5 shows the impact on two key indicators—calibration and discrimination—of the forecasting accuracy of foxes and hedgehogs making predictions in their roles as experts or dilettantes. Even when we impose the reflective equilibrium constraint that scenario-inflated probabilities must add to 1.0, the projected effects on performance are uniformly negative. And when we relax the constraint that probabilities must add to 1.0, the projected effects are worse, with foxes taking a bigger hit than hedgehogs. The causal mechanisms are not mysterious. Scenarios impair accuracy because they embolden forecasters to attach excessive probabilities to too many possibilities, and this is especially true of foxes judging dramatic departures from the status quo. Indeed, returning to the catch-up theme of chapter 6, we find that hedgehogs who refuse scenario exercises are at performance parity with foxes who embrace the exercises.

It would be foolish to conclude from this extrapolation exercise that the scenario method can *never* help anyone. It is possible that we did not calibrate our scenario manipulations correctly and thus failed to produce the optimal blend of analytical and imaginative thinking that would open hedgehogs to new possibilities but not overwhelm foxes with too many possibilities. It is also possible that there are conditions under which the scenario method—even as operationalized here—could enhance accuracy. But those conditions are strikingly restrictive. Scenarios should most reliably help when (a) the reigning consensus favors continuation of the status quo; (b) big surprises lie in waiting and will soon produce sharp departures from the status quo; (c) the scenario script writers have good hunches as to the direction that change will take and skew the scenario elaboration exercises accordingly. Unfortunately, the data in earlier chapters make it hard to argue that experts (scenario writers included) can do much better than chance in anticipating big surprises

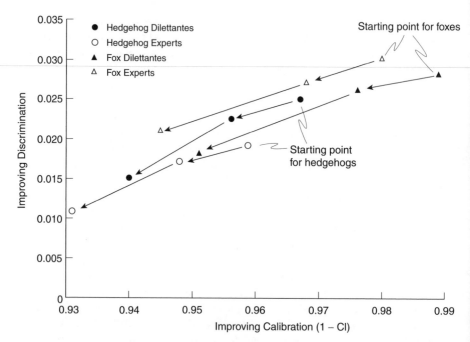

Figure 7.5. The performance of hedgehogs and foxes (H and F), making predictions inside or outside of their domains of expertise (E and D), deteriorates when we replace their original forecasts (the starting points at the origin of each set of arrows) with best estimates of the forecasts they would have made if they had disciplined their scenario-based thinking with reflective equilibrium exercises that required probabilities to sum to 1.0 (downward arrow from first to second data point) or if they had not so disciplined their scenario-based thinking (downward arrow from second to third data point). Lower scores on both the *x*- and *y*-axes signify worse performance. Both hedgehog and fox performance suffers, but fox performance suffers more.

for either the better or the worse. And the data on scenario effects in this chapter make it hard to argue that hiring scenario consultants is a prudent expenditure of resources unless the writers can do better than chance in targeting which futures to embellish and which to "pass on."

Debiasing How We Think about Possible Pasts

One might despair over the utility of the scenario method for improving probability judgments about possible futures but still hope the method will check biases in how people judge possible pasts. The first two studies in this section examine the power of thinking about counterfactual scenarios to check the well-known hindsight bias in which, once people learn of a historical outcome, they have difficulty recalling how they thought things would work out prior to learning of the outcome. To study this bias, we need to compare experts' ex ante states of mind to their ex post recollections of those states of mind. The second set of studies assesses the impact of counterfactual scenario thinking on perceptions of historical events that occurred long before contemporary observers were born. We obviously can no longer measure the accuracy of ex post recollections of ex ante states of mind. But we can assess the degree to which counterfactual scenarios sensitize observers to contingencies that they previously downplayed and to hitherto latent logical inconsistencies in their probabilistic reasoning.

Hindsight Bias

The hindsight bias is a promising candidate for correction. As readers of chapter 4 may recall, in two of the certainty-of-hindsight studies conducted in 1997–1998, we asked specialists who had made predictions for North Korea and China in 1992–1993 to reconstruct the subjective probabilities that they had assigned to possible futures five years earlier. These studies revealed a hindsight bias: experts exaggerated the likelihood that they had assigned to the status quo options (in both cases, the correct "correspondence" answer). Experts originally set average probabilities of .38 for continuation of the political status quo in China and of .48 for continuation of the status quo in North Korea; five years later, experts recalled assigning subjective probabilities of .53 and .69 respectively.

Normally, at this juncture, the researcher would reveal, as diplomatically as possible, our records of experts' original expectations and proceed to measure the belief system defenses that were a major focus of chapter 4. In these two cases, however, we altered the interview schedule by asking experts to make another judgment: "Looking back on what has happened in China/North Korea over the last five years, we would value your expert opinion on how close we came to experiencing alternative outcomes—alternative outcomes that are either significantly better politically or economically than the current situation or significantly worse." To create a social atmosphere in which participants felt they would not lose face if they changed their minds but also did not feel pressured to change their minds, we informed participants that "sometimes thinking about these what-if scenarios changes our views not only of the past but also our recollections of what we ourselves once thought possible or impossible. And sometimes these what-if exercises have no effect whatsoever. In light of the exercise you just did, do you want to

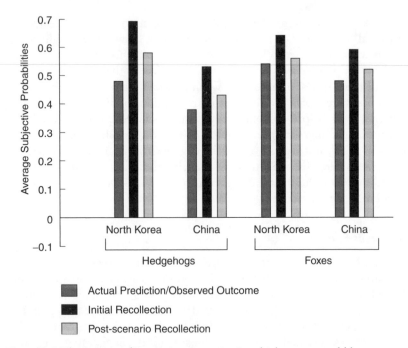

Figure 7.6. The impact of imagining scenarios in which events could have unfolded differently on hindsight bias in 1997–1998 recollections of predictions made in 1992–1993 for China and North Korea. Reduced hindsight effects can be inferred from the smaller gap between post-scenario recollections and actual predictions than between immediate recollections and actual predictions.

modify any of your earlier estimates of the subjective probabilities that you assigned five years ago?"[16]

Figure 7.6 shows that encouraging forecasters to generate scenarios of alternative outcomes reduced the hindsight bias in both the North Korean and Chinese exercises. The reduction was roughly of equal magnitude for hedgehogs and foxes—which meant it was substantial enough to cut hindsight down to nearly zero for foxes and to halve the effect for hedgehogs. "Imaginability" largely drove those effects. The power of scenarios to attenuate bias disappears when we control for the fact that, the more elaborate experts' scenarios of alternative pasts, the less prone experts were to the hindsight effect.

These results are strikingly similar to those obtained in laboratory research on debiasing hindsight via "imagine alternative outcome"

[16] This manipulation bears a strong similarity to those employed in laboratory work on debiasing. See Hawkins and Hastie, "Hindsight."

manipulations. Stimulating counterfactual musings helps to check smug "I knew it all along" attitudes toward the past. These results also dovetail with theoretical accounts that attribute the hindsight effect to the "automaticity" of theory-driven thought: the rapidity with which people assimilate known outcomes into their favorite cause-effect schemas, in the process demoting once possible, even probable, futures to the status of implausible historical counterfactuals. One mechanism via which scenario manipulations may be checking hindsight is by resurrecting these long-lost possibilities and infusing them with "narrative life." Ironically, though, this resurrection is possible only if people fall prey to an opposing-process cognitive bias: the human tendency to attach higher probabilities to more richly embellished and thus more imaginable scenarios—the exact opposite of what we should do if we appreciated the basic principle that scenarios can only fall in likelihood when we add contingent details to the narrative.

The successful use of scenario exercises to check hindsight bias provides reassurance that the failure of scenario exercises to improve foresight was not just a by-product of the feebleness of our experimental manipulations. But this should be faint consolation for the consultants. There is not nearly as much money in correcting judgments of possible pasts as of possible futures. It is hard to envision hordes of executives clamoring for assistance in recalling more accurately how wrong they once were. Future work should address the possibility, however, that shattering the illusion of cognitive continuity (the "I knew it all along" attitude) is a necessary first step in transforming observers into better judges of the limits of their own knowledge (better confidence calibration) as well as more timely belief updaters (better Bayesians). Cultivating humility in our assessments of our own past predictive achievements may be essential to cultivating realism in our assessments of what we can do now and in the future.

Sensitizing Observers to Historical Contingency

Hindsight bias is a failing of autobiographical memory. When we examine historical thinking about events further back in time, however, we lose the valuable "what did you really think earlier" benchmark of accuracy. We cannot travel back in time to reconstruct how likely observers thought (prior to learning of outcomes) that the Cuban missile crisis of October 1962 would be resolved peacefully or that the July 1914 crisis preceding World War I would culminate in such carnage. Nonetheless, chapter 5 offers grounds for suspecting the operation of a more generic form of hindsight bias, a failure of historical imagination that limits our appreciation of possibilities that once existed but have long since been foreclosed. Observers in general, and hedgehogs in particular, often seem overeager to achieve explanatory closure and, in this quest, adopt a heavy-handedly deterministic stance toward history that portrays what is as something that had to be, as the inevitable consequence of the operation of favorite covering laws on well-defined antecedent conditions. One gauge of "how close to inevitable" those perceptions can become is the degree to which observers summarily reject close-call counterfactuals that imply history could easily have been rerouted. Close-call scenarios have the potential to mess up our understanding of the past, to riddle grand generalizations, such as "neorealist balancing" and "the robustness of nuclear deterrence," with probabilistic loopholes.

Ned Lebow, Geoffrey Parker, and I conducted two experiments that assessed the power of unpacking scenarios to open observers' minds to the possibility that history contains more possibilities than they had previously supposed.[17]

CUBAN MISSILE CRISIS EXPERIMENT

One experiment examined retrospective judgments of experts on the inevitability of the Cuban missile crisis—a crisis that, as we saw in chapter 5, believers in the robustness of nuclear deterrence have difficulty imagining working out all that differently from how it did. In the control condition, experts fielded two questions that, on their face, look totally redundant. The inevitability curve question imposed a factual framing on the historical controversy over why the Cuban missile crisis ended as it did. It began by asking experts: At what point between October 16, 1962, and October 29, 1962, did some form of peaceful resolution of the crisis become inevitable (and thus deserve a probability of 1.0)? Then, after experts had specified their inevitability points, they estimated how the likelihood of some form of peaceful resolution waxed or waned during the preceding days of the crisis. The fourteen daily judgments, spanning October 16 to 29, defined the "inevitability" curve for each expert.

The impossibility curve question is the logical mirror image of the inevitability curve question. It imposes a counterfactual framing on the historical controversy. It asks: At what point during the crisis, between October 16, 1962, and October 29, 1962, did all alternative, more violent endings of the Cuban missile crisis become impossible (and thus deserve to be assigned a subjective probability of zero)? After identifying their impossibility points, experts estimated how the likelihood of alternative, more violent endings waxed or waned during the preceding fourteen days of the crisis. These judgments defined the impossibility curve for each expert.

---

[17] P. E. Tetlock, R. N. Lebow, and G. Parker, eds., *Unmaking the West: What-If Scenarios That Rewrite World History* (Ann Arbor: University of Michigan Press, 2006); Tetlock and Lebow, "Poking Counterfactual Holes."

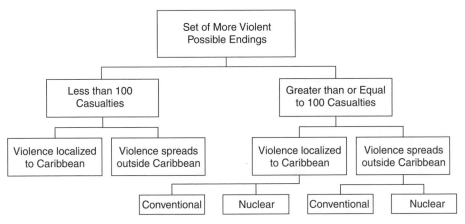

Figure 7.7. Unpacking alternative, more violent endings of the Cuban missile crisis.

In the "intensive unpacking" experimental condition, experts responded to the same questions with one key difference: the impossibility curve question now asked experts to judge the likelihood of alternative, more violent endings that had been decomposed into exhaustive and exclusive subsets. As Figure 7.7 shows, this set of counterfactual scenarios was initially decomposed into subsets with fewer than one hundred casualties or with one hundred or more casualties, that, in turn, were broken into sub-subsets in which violence was limited to the Caribbean or violence extended outside the Caribbean. Finally, all subsets with more than one hundred casualties were broken down still further into those scenarios in which only conventional weaponry was used and those in which nuclear weaponry was used. After presenting these possibilities, we asked experts to perform the same inevitability—and impossibility—curve exercises as in the control condition but to do so for each of the six subsets that appear at the bottom of figure 7.7.

We did not expect experts to be blatantly inconsistent. Our working hypothesis was that, when experts completed the two measures back to back, their judgments of the retrospective likelihood of some form of peaceful outcome would mirror their judgments of the retrospective likelihood of alternative, more violent, outcomes. Logic and psychologic should coincide when experts can plainly see that the summed probabilities of x and its complement, $\sim x$, are 1.0. But we did not expect logic and psychologic always to coincide. Factual framings of historical questions invite experts to search for potent forces that create an inexorable momentum toward the actual outcome. To answer this question, analysts must convince themselves that they know roughly when x had to happen. By contrast,

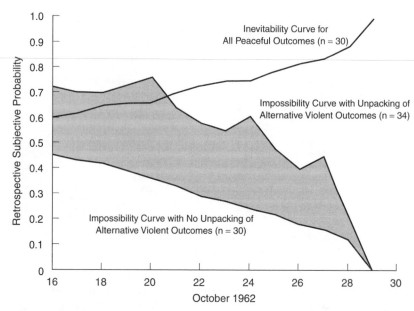

Figure 7.8. Inevitability and impossibility curves for the Cuban missile crisis. The inevitability curve displays gradually rising likelihood judgments of some form of peaceful resolution. The lower impossibility curve displays gradually declining likelihood judgments of the set of all alternative more violent endings. The higher impossibility curve was derived by adding the experts' likelihood judgments of six specific subsets of these alternative violent possible endings. Adding values of the lower impossibility curve to the corresponding values of the inevitability curve yields sums only slightly above 1.0. But inserting values from the higher impossibility curve yields sums well above 1.0. The shaded area between the two impossibility curves represents the cumulative impact of unpacking on the subjective probability of counterfactual alternatives to reality.

counterfactual framings of historical questions invite analysts to look for causal candidates that have the potential to reroute events down different paths. And when we unpack the counterfactual possibilities into detailed sub-scenarios, the invitation is all the stronger. Accordingly, we expected anomalies in retrospective likelihood judgments, such as sub-additivity, when we compared the judgments of two groups of experts, one of which had completed the inevitability curve exercise first, and the other of which had completed the impossibility curve exercise first, but neither of whom had yet responded to the exercise just completed by the other.

Figure 7.8 demonstrates that logical anomalies do indeed emerge. Three findings stand out: (a) the power of unpacking ~x counterfactual alternatives to reality to inflate subjective probabilities beyond reason. Observers consistently judged the whole set of alternative violent outcomes to be less likely than the sum of its exclusive and exhaustive parts. The shaded area between the two impossibility curves represents the magnitude of this effect: the cumulative increase in the judged probability of counterfactual possibilities when experts generated impossibility curves not for the whole set of more violent outcomes (lower curve) but rather for each of the six unpacked subsets of more violent outcomes (higher curve). When we sum the values on the higher impossibility curve with corresponding dates on the inevitability curve, the sums routinely exceed 1.0; (b) the tendency of unpacking effects to grow gradually smaller as we move toward the end of the crisis. Experts who were unpacking ~x possibilities saw less and less wiggle room for rewriting history as the end approached; (c) the power of unpacking to mess up our understanding of the past. In the no-unpacking control group, simple linear equations captured 82 percent of the variance in judgments of the undifferentiated sets of peaceful outcomes and more violent alternatives. The past looks like a smooth linear progression toward a predestined outcome. In the unpacking condition, the past looks more like a random walk, albeit around a discernible trend, with three noticeable shifts in direction (violations of monotonicity). A fourth-order polynomial equation is necessary to explain 80 percent of the variance in these retrospective likelihood judgments.

Although figure 7.8 does not display it, foxes who unpacked counterfactual possibilities exhibited the strongest sub-additivity effects (probability judgments exceeding 1.0). Averaging across dates, their combined inevitability and impossibility judgments summed to 1.38, significantly greater than foxes in the control group ($\overline{x} = 1.07$), or hedgehogs in either the unpacking ($\overline{x} = 1.18$) or control conditions ($\overline{x} = 1.04$). Foxes were also more prone to twilight-zone effects in which self-contradiction became particularly flagrant. There were periods of time for 85 percent of foxes, but only about 60 percent of hedgehogs, during which peace seemed inevitable (modal inevitability date = Oct. 27) but war still possible (modal impossibility date = Oct. 28).

A final sign of the power of unpacking comes from cross-condition comparisons of correlations between theoretical beliefs, such as the robustness of nuclear deterrence, and reactions to close-call counterfactuals raising the specter of nuclear war. The correlation is greater in the control than in the unpacking condition, ($r[28] = 0.61$ versus $r[32] = 0.27$). This drop-off is consistent with the notion that, under unpacking, observers shift from an abstract, covering-law mode of thinking to a more idiographic, case-by-case mode.

UNMAKING THE WEST EXPERIMENT

A second experiment replicated the previous results but on a grander measurement canvas. Experts drawn from the World History Association judged possibilities that stretched over one thousand years, not just fourteen days. The target issue was the rise of the West: How did it come to pass that a small number of Europeans, working from unpromising beginnings one thousand years ago, came to wield such disproportionate geopolitical influence? We saw in chapter 5 that hedgehogs who believe in the survival-of-the-fittest civilizations tended to see this mega-outcome as the product of deep and immutable causes and to be dismissive of close-call counterfactuals that implied otherwise.

There were two experimental conditions. In the control condition, experts received no encouragement, one way or the other, to think about alternative historical outcomes. We merely presented two measures. The starting question for the inevitability curve exercise was: At what point did some form of Western geopolitical domination become inevitable? The starting point for the impossibility curve exercise was: At what point did all possible alternatives to Western geopolitical domination become impossible? After identifying their inevitability and impossibility points, experts estimated how the likelihood of each class of historical outcome waxed or waned prior to those points. By contrast, the intensive-unpacking condition broke the set of all possible alternatives to Western domination into more refined subsets of scenarios in which either no civilization achieves global dominance or a non-Western civilization achieves global dominance. It then broke the no-hegemon world into subsets in which this outcome is brought about by either enfeebling the West (e.g., more lethal plagues, deeper Mongol incursions) or by empowering one of the Rest (e.g., Islam, China) and it broke the alternative-hegemon world into subsets in which Islam, China, or some other civilization achieves global power projection capabilities. Experts then judged the likelihood of each subset by plotting inevitability and impossibility curves.

The results replicated the missile crisis study in several key respects: (a) unpacking counterfactual alternatives to reality again inflated subjective probabilities beyond reason. As figure 7.9 shows, observers consistently judged the whole set of alternatives to Western domination to be less likely than the sum of its exclusive and exhaustive parts. The shaded area between the two impossibility curves captures the cumulative magnitude of this effect; (b) unpacking effects again grow smaller as we move to the end of the historical sequence; (c) unpacking again had the power to mess up our understanding of the past, transforming a smooth progression toward a foreordained outcome into a far more erratic journey. We need a fifth-order polynomial equation to capture 80 percent of the variance in the zigzaggy perceptions of the likelihood of unpacked outcomes, whereas a simple linear equation does the same work in the no-unpacking control condition; (d) unpacking again cut into the power of covering-law beliefs to constrain perceptions of the possible, with correlations dropping from .63 in the control condition to .25 in the unpacking condition; (e) foxes

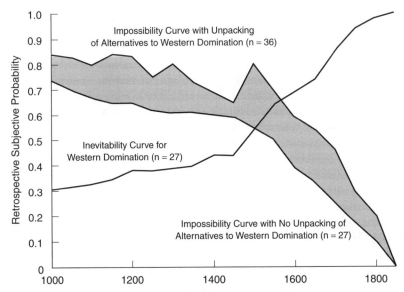

Figure 7.9. Inevitability and impossibility curves for the Rise of the West. The inevitability curve displays rising likelihood judgments of Western geopolitical dominance. The lower impossibility curve displays declining likelihood judgments of all possible alternatives to Western dominance. The higher impossibility curve was derived by adding experts' likelihood judgments of six specific subsets of alternative historical outcomes. Adding values of the lower impossibility curve to the corresponding values of the inevitability curve yields sums only slightly above 1.0. Inserting values from the higher impossibility curve yields sums well above 1.0. The shaded area between the two impossibility curves represents the cumulative impact of unpacking on the subjective probability of counterfactual alternatives to reality.

were again more susceptible to unpacking effects and made more sub-additive probability judgments. Their inevitability and impossibility curve judgments averaged 1.41, markedly greater than for foxes in the control group ($\bar{x}$ = 1.09), or hedgehogs in either the control ($\bar{x}$ = 1.03) or unpacking groups ($\bar{x}$ = 1.21); (f) foxes who unpacked counterfactual possibilities again displayed longer twilight-zone periods. In the control group, foxes and hedgehogs did *not* disagree by a significant margin: the twilight zone period was roughly eighteen years long (they judged Western domination to be inevitable by 1731, on average, but considered alternatives to be still possible as late as 1749). But in the unpacking condition, the fox twilight zone stretched for forty-seven years compared to the hedgehogs' twenty-five years (foxes judged Western domination to be inevitable by 1752 but alternatives to be still possible as late as 1799).

Thoughts on "Debiasing" Thinking about Possible Pasts

Chapters 5 and 7 bring into sharp relief the strengths and weaknesses of fox and hedgehog styles of historical reasoning. Chapter 5 showed that hedgehogs wove tighter mental connections between their abstract theoretical beliefs and specific opinions about what was possible at particular times and places. Their trademark approach was deductive. For example, if I believe the neorealist theory of balancing is correct, and that the historical context under examination is one in which a would-be hegemon (Philip II, Napoleon, Hitler, etc.) was squelched by a coalition of nervous rivals, then I can confidently rule out close-call counterfactuals that imply that, with minor tweaking of background conditions, the bid to achieve hegemony could have succeeded.

There was not much room in chapter 5 to contest the facts: the repeated demonstrations of the joint effects of cognitive style and theoretical beliefs on resistance to dissonant close-call scenarios. But there was room to contest how to "spin" those facts. In postexperimental conversations, many hedgehogs defended their deductive orientation toward history on the grounds of parsimony. A few hedgehogs also remarked on the foolishness of treating "things that perhaps almost happened" as serious arguments against an otherwise robust generalization. "Open-mindedness" here shaded into "credulousness." As one participant commented: "I'll change my mind in response to real but not imaginary evidence. Show me actual cases of balancing failing. Then we can talk about when the proposition holds." Hedgehogs also saw nothing commendably open-minded about endorsing a generalization at one moment and at the next endorsing close-call counterfactuals that poked so many holes in the generalization as to render it "practically useless." Thinking of that sort just looked "flip-floppy" to them.

When it came to invidious intellectual stereotyping, however, the foxes gave as good as they got. Some foxes were "appalled by the breathtaking arrogance" of the deductive covering-law approach, which they derogated as "pseudoscience," "conjecture that capitalizes on hindsight," and—the capstone insult—"tone-deaf to history." They saw tight linkages between abstract theoretical beliefs and specific historical ones not as a strength ("nothing to brag about") but rather as a potential weakness (an ominous sign of a "dogmatic approach to the past"). They saw looser linkages between general and specific beliefs not as a weakness (muddled and incoherent) but rather as a potential strength (a mature recognition of how riddled with coincidence and exceptions history is).

In chapter 7, we see similar disagreements over the right normative "spin" to put on the facts. But chapter 7 offers the first evidence of systematic bias more pronounced among foxes than among hedgehogs.

Foxes were markedly more affected by the "unpacking of scenario" manipulations going both forward and backward in time. Some hedgehogs found the foxes' predicament amusing. Shown the aggregate data in a debriefing, one participant quipped: "I'll bet they're good talkers, but let them try to talk their way out of the knots that they have tied themselves into here." The greater susceptibility of foxes to "sub-additivity" effects reinforced the suspicion of hedgehogs that there was something sloppy about the fox approach to history. It looks disturbingly easy to lure foxes into the inferential equivalent of wild goose chases that cause them to assign too much likelihood to too many scenarios.

The foxes' reaction to their falling short was both similar to and different from the hedgehogs' reactions to their falling short on correspondence and coherence measures in chapters 3 and 4. Like the hedgehogs, the first response was to challenge the messenger. "You set us up" was a common refrain—although that begged the question of why foxes were easier to set up and raised the counter that, if foxes could be led astray by so simple a manipulation as scenario proliferation, then surely the experiments reveal a threat to good judgment in their professional lives. Like hedgehogs caught in earlier epistemic predicaments, many foxes tried to defend what they had done. No one put it exactly this way but they said, in essence, that foolish consistency is the hobgoblin of little minds. Do not worry that unpacking possibilities creates or reveals contradictions within belief systems. Preserving formal logic is not nearly as important as appreciating that life is indeterminate and full of surprises.

Unlike hedgehogs, though, the more introspective foxes showed considerable curiosity about the mental processes underlying the scenario effect and the potential implications of the effect. One fox quickly connected two observations: on the one hand, the debiasing studies of hindsight showed that encouraging experts to imagine alternatives to reality "made things better" by one standard (more accurate recall of past states of mind) and on the other hand, the Cuban missile crisis and "Unmaking the West" studies showed that unpacking alternatives to reality "made things worse" by another standard (more incoherent probability judgments). Anticipating my own preferred value spin on the results, he observed: "Well, you have two offsetting sources of error. We need to figure out how to manage them."

CLOSING OBSERVATIONS

Chapter 7 does not tell us whether, in any given case, observers struck the right balance between theory and imagination-driven thinking. But the findings do sharpen our understanding of the criteria we use to make attributions of good judgment. On the one hand, scenario exercises can check hindsight bias and occasionally improve forecasting accuracy by stretching our conceptions of the possible. On the other hand, it is easy to overdo it when we start imagining "possible worlds." Taking too many scenarios too seriously ties us into self-contradictory knots. Balancing these arguments, we might say that scenario exercises check theory-driven biases by activating countervailing imagination-driven biases, the cognitive equivalent of fighting fire with fire. And, though imagination-driven biases have not loomed large in this book as threats to good judgment, one could argue that people who make sub-additive probability judgments are as at risk of making flawed decisions as people who are overconfident and poky belief updaters.

Indeed, if we were to design correctives to imagination-driven biases, they would look like mirror images of the scenario generation exercises that we designed to correct theory-driven biases. To check runaway unpacking effects, people need plausibility pruners for cutting off speculation that otherwise grows like topsy over the bounds of probability. And people naturally rely on their preconceptions about causality to figure out where to start pruning, where to start saying "That couldn't happen because. . . . "

These tensions capture a metacognitive trade-off. Whether we know it or not, we are continually making decisions about how to decide, about how best to mix theory-driven and imagination-driven modes of thinking. Theory-driven thinking confers the benefits of closure and parsimony but desensitizes us to nuance, complexity, contingency, and the possibility that our theory is wrong. Imagination-driven thinking sensitizes us to possible worlds that could have been but exacts a price in confusion and even incoherence.

Hedgehogs and foxes disagree over how to manage this trade-off. Hedgehogs put more faith in theory-driven judgments and keep their imaginations on tighter leashes than do foxes. Foxes are more inclined to entertain dissonant scenarios that undercut their own beliefs and preferences. Insofar as there are advantages to be accrued by engaging in self-subversive thinking—benefits such as appropriately qualifying conditional forecasts and acknowledging mistakes—foxes will reap them. Insofar as there are prices for suspending disbelief—diluting one's confidence in sound predictions and being distracted by ephemera—foxes will pay them. To link this argument to nature-versus-nurture debates over the heritability of cognitive styles—admittedly a stretch—it would be surprising from a population genetics perspective if both cognitive styles were not well represented in the human genome today. Foxes were better equipped to survive in rapidly changing environments in which those who abandoned bad ideas quickly held the advantage. Hedgehogs were better equipped to survive in static environments that rewarded persisting with tried-and-true formulas. Our species—homo sapiens—is better off for having both temperaments and so too are the communities of specialists brought under the cognitive microscope in this volume.

It would be a mistake, however, to depict theory- and imagination-driven cognition as equally powerful forces in mental life. Most of the time, theory-driven cognition trumps imagination-driven cognition for foxes and hedgehogs alike. The differences that arise are matters of degree, not reversals of sign. We all do it, but theory-driven hedgehogs are less apologetic about applying demanding "Must I believe this?" tests to disagreeable evidence. Just how overwhelming evidence must be to break this barrier is illustrated by the ridiculously high thresholds of proof that partisans set for conceding their side did something scandalous. It required the Watergate recordings to force Nixon defenders to acknowledge that he had obstructed justice, and it required DNA testing of Monica Lewinski's dress to compel Clinton defenders to concede that something improper had occurred in the Oval Office (at which point the defenders shifted into another belief system defense—trivialization). And we all do it, but theory-driven hedgehogs are also less apologetic about applying lax "Can I believe this?" tests to agreeable evidence. Just how easy it is to break this barrier is illustrated by the ridiculously low thresholds of proof that partisans set for rustling up evidence that supports their side or casts aspersions on the other. When we use this standard, we risk becoming the mental repositories of absurdities such as "Extraterrestrials are warning us to be better custodians of our planet: vote for Gore in 2000" or "Bill Clinton is an agent of the People's Republic of China."

Good judgment, then, is a precarious balancing act. We often learn we have gone too far in one direction only after it is too late to pull back. Executing this balancing act requires cognitive skills of a high order: the capacity to monitor our own thought processes for telltale signs of excessive closed- or open-mindedness and to strike a reflective equilibrium faithful to our conceptions of the norms of fair intellectual play. We need to cultivate the art of self-overhearing, to learn how to eavesdrop on the mental conversations we have with ourselves as we struggle to strike the right balance between preserving our existing worldview and rethinking core assumptions. This is no easy art to master. If we listen to ourselves carefully, we will often not like what we hear. And we will often be tempted to laugh off the exercise as introspective navel-gazing, as an infinite regress of homunculi spying on each other . . . all the way down. No doubt, such exercises can be taken to excess. But, if I had to bet on the best long-term predictor of good judgment among the observers in this book, it would be their commitment—their soul-searching Socratic commitment—to thinking about how they think.

CHAPTER 8

Exploring the Limits on Objectivity and Accountability

> "When I use a word," Humpty Dumpty said, in a rather scornful tone, "it means just what I choose it to mean—neither more nor less." "The question is," said Alice, "whether you can make words mean so many different things." "The question is," said Humpty Dumpty, "which is to be master—that's all."
>
> —LEWIS CARROLL

> You never know you have had enough until you have had more than enough.
>
> —WILLIAM BLAKE

OBJECTIVITY was the bedrock principle on which professional societies of historians and social scientists were founded in the nineteenth century. The disciplinary mandate was to move closer, by successive imperfect approximations, toward the truth, a truth unadorned by mocking quotation marks. Well before the twentieth century's end, however, scholars started chiseling at this foundation, raising doubts about the positivist project and the feasibility of sharp distinctions between observer and observed, fact and value, and even fact and fiction.[1] Constructivist and relativist epistemologies—which depicted "truth" as perspectival and demanded to know "whose truth"—garnered considerable respectability.

My own sympathies should not be in doubt. This research program has been unabashedly neopositivist in conception and design. In study after study, I exhorted experts to translate inchoate private hunches into precise public assertions that I classified as accurate or inaccurate, defensible or indefensible, and duly entered into my expandable correlation matrix of indicators and predictors of good judgment. From a neopositivist perspective, it is tempting to close on a defiant note, to declare that until someone comes up with something demonstrably better, these imperfect measures are reasonable approximations of an elusive construct.

I divide this final chapter into two sections. The first section grapples with the philosophical objections raised in chapter 1 against this entire

---

[1] For a historical account of the ups and downs of the concept of objectivity in twentieth-century scholarship, see P. Novick, *That Noble Dream: The Objectivity Question and the American Historical Profession* (New York: Cambridge University Press, 1988).

enterprise. It is organized around a Socratic exchange among rival perspectives on what the behavioral and social sciences have to offer. Constructivist and postmodernist critics of objectivity remind us that, as they
prophesied, the pursuit of objectivity did occasionally bog down. "Truth"
is to some degree perspectival and socially constructed: what counts as
good judgment hinges on judgment calls on the "right" value, probability weighting, and controversy adjustments to probability scores, on the
"best" estimates of base rates for difficulty adjustments, and on the
"correct" credibility weights to assign experts' rationales for refusing to
change their minds when the unexpected occurs. Positivist proponents of
objectivity remind us of the dangers of cutting experts too much slack by
permitting too many adjustments. It is possible to define empirical and
logical standards of accountability that transcend partisan wrangling and
that allow us to gauge the judgmental performance of experts, from diverse points of view, on common metrics.

If there is a grand moral here, it is that there is no quick measurement
fix to the traditional tension between subjectivist and objectivist approaches to human judgment. The significance of this effort does not lie in
the exact balance struck between conflicting views of good judgment; it
lies in the broader precedent of using objectivist methods to factor difficult
to quantify, subjectivist objections into the measurement process. The criss-
crossing epistemological divisions of our day—qualitative versus quantitative, subjective versus objective, constructivism versus positivism—are not
as irreconcilable as some suppose.

The second section of the chapter grapples with the policy implications
of this effort to objectify standards for judging judgment. The motivation
for the project was not solely a basic science one: the opportunity to test
hypotheses about the political-psychological correlates and determinants
of susceptibility to judgmental biases. The motivation was also, in part, an
applied science one. I suspected at the outset that we as a society would be
better off if we held experts—be they pundits in the public arena or intelligence analysts behind the scenes—systematically accountable to standards
of evidence that command broad assent across the spectrum of reasonable
opinion. Subsequent findings from this project—as well as events over the
last twenty years—have reinforced my suspicion that there is something
wrong with existing mechanisms for getting to the truth both in the media-
driven marketplace of ideas and in the top-secret world of intelligence
analysis. Indeed, one of the more disconcerting results of this project has
been the discovery of an inverse relationship between how well experts do
on our scientific indicators of good judgment and how attractive these experts are to the media and other consumers of expertise. The same self-
assured hedgehog style of reasoning that suppresses forecasting accuracy
and slows belief updating translates into compelling media performances:
attention-grabbing bold predictions that are rarely checked for accuracy

and, when found to be wrong, that forecasters steadfastly defend as "soon to be right," or "almost right" or as the "right mistakes" to have made given the available information and choices.

From a broadly nonpartisan perspective, the situation cries out for remedy. And from the scientific vantage point offered by this project, the natural remedy is to apply our performance metrics to actual controversies: to pressure participants in debates—be they passionate partisans or dispassionate analysts—to translate vague claims into testable predictions that can be scored for empirical accuracy and logical defensibility. Of course, the resistance would be fierce, especially from those with the most to lose—those with grand reputations and humble track records. But I do still believe it possible to raise the quality of debate by tracking the quality of claims and counterclaims that people routinely make about what could have been (if you had had any sense, you would have listened to us!) or might yet be (if you have any sense, listen now!). The knowledge that one's forecasting batting average and reputation for honoring reputational bets are at stake may motivate even the most prone-to-self-justification hedgehogs, and the most prone-to-groupthink groups, to try harder to distinguish what they really know about the future from what they suspect, hope, or fear might be the case.[2]

Clashing Philosophical Perspectives

Relativists have doubted this undertaking from the start.[3] I find it useful, though, to distinguish degrees of doubt. Adamant relativists give no

---

[2] This policy recommendation is grounded in the now large research literature on the effects of accountability on judgment and choice. Accountability by itself is no panacea. But the right types of accountability can help. In engineering accountability systems to promote more self-critical and reflective styles of thinking, one is well advised to ensure that forecasters believe they must answer for judgments they have yet to make to audiences whose own views forecasters cannot readily infer (closing off the option of telling people what they want to hear) and whose respect forecasters value (encouraging sober second thought). For a review, see P. E. Tetlock and J. Lerner, "The Social Contingency Model: Identifying Empirical and Normative Boundary Conditions on the Error-and-Bias Portrait of Human Nature," in *Dual Process Models in Social Psychology*, ed. S. Chaiken and Y. Trope (New York: Guilford Press, 1999).

The psychologic underlying this proposal bears some similarities to explanations that have been offered for the well-documented power of prediction markets to produce aggregate forecasts that are more accurate than the vast majority of individual forecasters. These explanations often stress the power of competitive interaction among forecasters, driven by a mix of financial and social-image motives, to encourage more flexible, rapid-fire belief updating in response to new evidence (see J. Wolfers and E. Zitzewitz, "Prediction Markets," *Journal of Economic Perspectives* 18 [2004]: 107–26).

[3] Relativists and their constructivist allies in political science stress the multiplicity of meanings people attach to each other's actions, and the contestability of those meanings in

ground. Look at chapter 6, they chortle, and count the dubious assumptions and scoring adjustments that the author had to make in gauging whether hedgehogs are worse forecasters or pokier belief updaters than foxes. Look at chapter 7 and enumerate the judgment calls the author had to make in weighing the mind-opening benefits of scenario exercises against the costs of cognitive chaos. Good judgment, the harsh indictment runs, is a quicksilver concept forever slipping from our positivist grasp. Less doctrinaire relativists give some ground: they concede we may have learned something useful about the linkages between styles of reasoning and good judgment variously conceived, but reaffirm their antipathy toward any effort to "objectify" anything as profoundly "intersubjective" as good judgment.

I also find it useful to array neopositivist replies to these complaints along a conciliatoriness continuum. At the confrontational end are hardliners who believe I made too many concessions to the "thinly disguised whining" of sore losers who refuse to admit their mistakes. At the conciliatory end, where I place myself, are more accommodating responses to relativists: "Yes, we do live in a controversy-charged, ambiguity-laden world that maps imperfectly onto right-wrong classification schemes" and "Yes, the assumptions underlying our measures of good judgment are open to moral, metaphysical, and historical challenges." But even we "accommodationists" are willing to give up only so much to those who insist on the futility of all efforts to objectify good judgment. We have to draw the line somewhere.

Let us then populate our "Socratic dialogue" with four speakers: unrelenting and reasonable relativist critics as well as accommodating and hard-line neopositivist defenders. Readers can judge for themselves who proves the most incisive interlocutor.

Unrelenting Relativist

Occasionally, the author comes tantalizingly close to grasping the self-contradictions in which he has ensnared himself. He tried to capture a value-laden construct with a net of value-neutral measures and, not surprisingly, he came up empty. We have to wait until chapter 6, though, for the author finally to recognize that his centerpiece correspondence mea-

---

rough-and-tumble encounters in which people jostle to claim desirable identities for themselves and to "cast" rivals into less desirable ones. Moderate forms of relativism and constructivism are easy for students of human cognition to accept: they warn us of the power of mind-sets to shape how we pose questions and go about answering them. See F. Suppe, *The Structure of Scientific Theories* (Chicago: University of Chicago Press, 1974). The hard-core forms are another matter: they cast doubt not only on the possibility of understanding the world but also on the wisdom of even trying.

sure of good judgment, the probability score, is flawed in a multitude of ways. And even here, he refuses to acknowledge the key implication of these flaws: the impossibility of developing a theory-free, value-free measure of "getting it right." Instead, the author resorts to desperate patch-ups: difficulty adjustments to cope with variation in the unpredictability of forecasting tasks, value adjustments to cope with variation in the priorities that forecasters attach to avoiding different mistakes, controversy adjustments to cope with variation in views on what really happened, and fuzzy-set adjustments to cope with variation in views on what almost happened or might yet happen. The author is delusional if he thinks these patch-ups bring him closer to "Platonic true" scores on a good-judgment continuum.

Each patch-up raises more questions than it answers. Consider the challenge of computing the "correct" base rate for difficulty-adjusted probability scores. Which time frames should we use to ascertain how often there is leader turnover or shifts in central government expenditure or . . .? Which comparison cases should we use for Ethiopia in the early 1990s: "sub-Saharan African countries" or "former Soviet bloc nations transitioning from Communism" or "dictatorships transitioning to democracy"? Is it even meaningful to talk about base rates for many outcomes? There was only one Soviet Union. What do we learn by lumping it with other multiethnic empires (a small set populated by diverse entities that resist all but the most circumscribed comparisons)?

Base rates represent inappropriate intrusions of probability theory into domains where well-defined sets of comparison cases do not exist. As one defiant participant declared: "This ain't survey research." And I am not swayed by the author's tinkering with alternative base-rate estimates in difficulty adjustments. These pseudoscientific "sensitivity analyses"— raising or lowering arbitrary estimates by arbitrary fudge factors—are fig leaves for ignorance.

Or consider the daunting problems of value-adjusting probability scores. It requires only glancing familiarity with the political scene to guess where true believers will line up. Those on the left have traditionally tried to avoid false alarms that treat status quo states as expansionist or that push harsh austerity measures on developing countries. Those on the right have harbored the mirror-image concerns. But, of course, more nuanced thinkers are less predictable. Their error-avoidance priorities take different forms in different circumstances—judgments that require the "excessively generous value adjustments" the author explicitly abjures.[4]

---

[4] Value priorities are also not immutable. Positions can shift quickly in response to shocking events. An example is the metamorphosis in American attitudes toward false-alarm detentions of suspected terrorists in the wake of the 9/11 attacks.

The author is too stingy in granting value adjustments. But I have a more fundamental objection. Like difficulty adjustments, value adjustments are utterly arbitrary. In both cases, the author tries to conceal the capriciousness of the process under the scientific rhetoric of "gauging robustness" and "assessing boundary conditions." Tinkering with alternative value adjustments—shrinking or expanding gaps between subjective probabilities and "objective reality" by plucking coefficients from the air—is just another fig leaf.

And that brings us to the most desperate of all the patch-ups—controversy and fuzzy-set adjustments—where we can no longer dodge the intersubjective character of objectivity. Underlying all of the author's correspondence and belief-updating measures of good judgment is the naïve assumption that things either did or did not happen and, once we know the truth, we can code reality as zero or 1.0, and then assess forecasting accuracy (by computing deviations between subjective probabilities and objective realities) or appropriate belief updating (by computing deviations between observed change and that required by earlier reputational bets).

Research participants, fortunately, had the temerity to challenge these accuracy criteria. Sometimes they argued that what they predicted really did happen and that the author's reality checks were flawed, hence the need for controversy adjustments to probability scoring. Sometimes they conceded that the predicted outcome did not occur but that it almost occurred and might still occur, hence the need for fuzzy-set adjustments.

These objections highlight the need to rethink the objectivist ontology underlying this project. The world is better viewed through a more pluralistic prism that allows for shades of grey between the real and unreal, for clashing perspectives on what is real or unreal, and even for the possibility that what we call the actual world is but one of a multiplicity of possible worlds, some of which may have once been considerably more likely than our world. The author's house-of-cards argument crumbles when we replace his "naïve" objectivist framework with a sophisticated one that leaves room for legitimate differences of opinion on what is, what could have been, and what might yet be.

The epicyclical complexities of scoring "adjustments" are proof that the author's initial fears were sound: he did show bad scientific judgment in trying to objectify good political judgment. The author fell prey to a linguistic illusion. He inferred that, because people casually talk about something—good judgment—as though it were a unitary thing that we possess to varying degrees, that thing must exist in some quantifiable form. This project is the by-product of excessive literalism.

Hard-line Neopositivist

If the point of this project had been to derive a single numerical estimate of good judgment, a political IQ score that would rank experts along an ordinal scale, these criticisms might sting. But the author backed off from that reductionist goal at the outset. Indeed, he retreated too fast and too far: he bent over backward to accommodate virtually every self-serving protest that floundering forecasters advanced. In the process, he came close to doing exactly what his relativist critic just did: slip off the solipsistic precipice into the cloud-cuckoo land of relativism where no one need acknowledge mistakes because they can invoke value adjustments that give them credit for making the right mistake or, most ridiculous of all, fuzzy-set adjustments that give them credit for being almost right. The author narrowly dodged this fate in chapter 6 by placing at least some limits on how precisely tailored value adjustments can be to forecasters' mistakes and on how generously fuzzy-set adjustments could be extended whenever forecasters cover up their mistakes with "I was almost right" exercises.

The burden of proof now properly falls on relativists who want even more extravagant scoring adjustments. The time has come to put up or shut up: to propose schemes for assessing the accuracy and defensibility of real-world judgments that do not simply defer to every excuse experts offer.

Moderate Neopositivist

My hard-line ally draws sharper dichotomies than I do. But we agree that relativists take the greatest strength of the neopositivist framework—its flexible capacity to absorb "principled" objections and transform them into "technical" adjustments—and depict it as a fatal weakness. The gradual "complexification" of the author's measures of good judgment does not nullify the entire approach. If anything, it brings the advantages of the neopositivist approach into focus. Hopelessly vague arguments about "who got what right" can take more tractable forms. We can say that the pragmatic foxes outperform the theory-driven hedgehogs, within certain ranges of difficulty, value, controversy, and even fuzzy-set adjustments, but if you introduce sufficiently extreme adjustments, then the differences between the two cognitive-stylistic groups disappear. We gain a framework for thinking about thinking that tells us the boundary conditions we should place on the generalization that experts with certain styles of thinking outperform experts with other styles of thinking.

Reasonable Relativist

Neopositivists can, if they wish, treat the "complexification" of measures of good judgment as progress. But note how much they have had to acknowledge the "perspectival" character of good judgment. Eventually, they may even recognize that disagreements over definitions of good judgment should not be relegated to measurement error; such disagreements should be the central focus of inquiry.

Moderate Neopositivist

Different phenomena are of interest for different purposes. My quarrel with the gentle relativist critic reduces to whether we should view the glass as partly full or still mostly empty. Relativists are too pessimistic because they adopt too tough a baseline of comparison. They ask: Have we created perfectly theory-free and value-free indicators of good judgment? And the answer is, "Of course not." But a more reasonable baseline is whether we know more about good judgment variously conceived than we did before. Intellectual progress is sometimes possible only if we are prepared to jettison traditional ways of doing things, to experiment with new formats for expressing judgments (like subjective probability scales) and new methods of scoring judgments for accuracy and defensibility (like probability scoring—with adjustments, or reputational bets—with weighting of belief system defenses).

Unrelenting Relativist

Let the moderates meet at the mushy middle if they wish. But it is a mistake to forget that, in the end, this "objectivist" project reduces to a power grab: a bid by one scholarly community to impose its favorite analytical categories on other communities. After we strip away the highfalutin rhetoric, it comes down to a high-handed effort to tell people how to think. If you don't think the way the self-appointed arbiters of good judgment say you should think, you can't qualify as a good judge.

Such high-handedness is all the more insufferable when it comes from pseudoscientists whose quantitative indicators rest on nothing more substantial than their opinion versus someone else's. Whose value priorities in forecasting should we use: those who fear false alarms but are tolerant of misses or those who dread misses but are indulgent toward false alarms? Whose estimates of the base rates to enter into difficulty adjustments should we use: those who define the reference population of coup-prone states broadly or those who define the population narrowly? And what should we do when forecasters argue that the events they predicted really did happen (controversy adjustments) or that the events they predicted almost happened or will eventually happen (fuzzy-set adjustments)? Should we scold these forecasters for being bad Bayesians or congratulate them for having the courage of their convictions?

So-called belief system defenses are justified acts of intellectual rebellion against arbitrary neopositivist strictures for classifying answers as right or wrong. Close-call counterfactuals pose a metaphysical challenge. Who is the author to rule out the possibility that futures once widely deemed possible almost came into being and would have but for inherently unforeseeable accidents of fate? What privileged access to the counterfactual realm gives him warrant to announce that experts were wrong to have assigned an 80 percent or 90 percent probability to futures that never materialized? How does he know that we don't happen to live in an unlikely, extremely unlikely world? The off-on-timing defense poses a similar challenge. Who appointed the author God: the epistemological umpire who calls forecasters "out" if a predicted outcome does not happen in the designated time range?

Hard-line Neopositivist

If we took the aggressive-relativist critique seriously, we would commit ourselves to a brand of cognitive egalitarianism in which it is bad manners to challenge anyone else's conception of good judgment. Everything would reduce to Humpty Dumpty's question: "Who is to be master?" As soon as someone raises a protest, we must either accommodate it or stand indicted of intellectual imperialism—of trying to reduce vast areas of political science to the status of disciplinary colonies of psychologists who study judgment and choice.

That might not be such a bad thing. There is plenty of evidence of cognitive biases among political observers that the usual academic quality-control mechanisms are not up to correcting. But let's follow the thread of the strong-relativist argument. If we all get to keep our own scorecards and to make whatever post hoc adjustments we want to our probability scores and belief-updating equations, we wind up back in the subjectivist swamp we vowed to escape in chapter 1. Relativists not only refuse to help; they try to push us back into the quagmire every time we try to lift ourselves out. Anytime anyone proposes a trans-ideological standard for evaluating claims, relativists deride the effort as a power grab.

The reductio ad absurdum is, of course, that strong relativism is self-refuting. It too can be dismissed as a power grab—a power grab by radically egalitarian intellectuals who are skeptical of science and hostile to modernity. Indeed, it is hard to imagine a doctrine that is more polar opposite to the author's agenda. Radical relativists transform scientific debates into ideological ones; the author transforms ideological debates into scientific ones.

It is tempting to end this exchange by returning to Dr. Johnson's famous rebuke of Bishop Berkeley "I refute him thus," where "thus" involved kicking a stone to dispel doubts about the existence of the external world. Here the stone-kicking involves pointing to errors so egregious that no one with any sense rises to their defense. We don't have to look long. The death of the most famous strong relativist of recent times, Michel Foucault, offers just such an object lesson. In *The Lives of Michel Foucault*, David Macey tells a chilling tale of the consequences of acting on the postmodern doctrine that truth is a social construct. Foucault argued there are no objective truths, only truths promoted by dominant groups intent on preserving their dominance. In the early 1980s Foucault was infected with the AIDS virus. Like many others then, he dismissed the mounting evidence that a lethal epidemic was sweeping through the gay community. The "gay plague" was rumormongering by homophobes.

Die-hard relativists might insist that Foucault will be posthumously vindicated. Or, upping the ante, they might argue that Thabo Mbeki, president of South Africa, will yet be vindicated for flirting with conspiracy theories of AIDS and denying poor pregnant women antiretroviral drugs. History will not be kind to this school of thought.

Moderate Neopositivist and Reasonable Relativist

The debate has again become unnecessarily polarized. Relativists are right that there is a certain irreducible ambiguity about which rationales for forecasting glitches should be dismissed as rationalizations and which should be taken seriously. And neopositivists are right that the objectivist methods used here are well suited for identifying double standards and giving us a precise sense of how much persuasive weight we must give to rationalizations for forecasting failures to close the gap in forecasting performance between hedgehogs and foxes, or any other groups.

Unrelenting Relativist

Neopositivist social scientists like to wrap themselves in the successes of their big brothers and sisters in the biological and physical sciences. And exploiting a personal tragedy to undercut a scholar's posthumous reputation is a low blow. Rather than dignify demagoguery with a response, let's shift to topics where there is limited potential for agreement. In chapter 7, neopositivist research methods—experiments that explored the effects of question framing and unpacking—yielded results consistent with both the author's theory and core tenets of constructivism. The results repeatedly showed that the answers historical observers reach hinge on the questions they posed. History looks slightly more contingent when we pose the query "At what point did alternative outcomes become impossible?" than when we pose the logically equivalent query

"At what point did the observed outcome become inevitable?" And history looks massively more contingent when we unpack questions about alternative counterfactual outcomes into more specific sub-scenarios. Where we begin inquiry can thus be a potent determinant of where we end it. And inasmuch as there is a large set of "reasonable" starting points, there is an equally large set of reasonable termination points. Truth is perspectival, and the cognitive research program infuses this postmodern insight with deeper meaning by specifying exactly how our existing perspective refracts our view of possible pasts and futures.

Unfortunately, although we can agree that historical observers do "construct" historical knowledge, this brief convergence of views breaks down when the author settles back into his habit of passing judgment on whether people were up to snuff on this or that correspondence or coherence "test" of good judgment. The author fixates on an apparent paradox: the admittedly odd phenomenon of sub-additive probabilities in which experts wind up judging entire sets of possibilities to be *less* than the sum of their exclusive and exhaustive components. Using formal logic and probability theory as benchmarks for good judgment, the author's first instinct is to portray the framing and unpacking effects as evidence of incoherence. After all, he reasons, how can the likelihood of a set of possible futures be *less* than the sum of its subsets? How can we possibly justify subjective probabilities that sum to more than unity?

By contrast, when we relativists "see" smart people doing something "stupid," our first instinct is to ask whether we are imposing an inappropriate mental framework on those we observe. Relativists are epistemological pluralists, and we suspect that neopositivists make a "category mistake" when they label sub-additivity an error. Jerome Bruner's brand of epistemic pluralism helps us to see why. His theory of knowledge allows for two distinct modes of ordering experience: the logico-scientific and the narrative-humanistic. "Efforts to reduce one mode to the other or to ignore one at the other's expense inevitably fail to capture the rich diversity of thought."[5]

The author's category mistake was to apply the standards of formal logic to thinking organized around storytelling—and organized this way for good reasons. Philosophers of history have noted that narrative explanations are more flexible and thus better suited than cumbersome covering laws to making sense of quirky concatenations of events that unfold only once and that force us to rely on what-if guesswork to infer causality.[6] Narratives are so compelling, in this view, because they are so lifelike: they capture contingencies that so frequently arise in

---

[5] J. Bruner, *Actual Minds, Possible worlds* (Cambridge: Harvard University Press, 1995).

[6] For a thoughtful analysis of the debate over covering laws in history, see C. Roberts, *The Logic of Historical Explanation* (University Park: Pennsylvania State University Press, 1995).

daily life. There should be no mystery why storytelling predates probability theory by several millennia: stories map more readily onto human experience.

To preempt another cheap shot by the hard-line neopositivist, I stress that I am not trying to defend sub-additivity in the court of formal logic; rather, I seek to move the normative case to a jurisdiction governed by "narrativist" norms. The standards in this new court stress thematic coherence and imaginative evocativeness. It is no more surprising that storytellers fail coherence tests of subjective probabilities than that musicians flunk tests in acoustical engineering or that painters don't know the wave/particle theory of light.

Here is the soft methodological underbelly of this project: the misbegotten notion that it makes sense to rely on benchmarks of good judgment derived from probability theory. The probability calculus is inappropriate. Questions posed in probabilistic terms require experts to shift into an unnatural discourse: to abandon a free-flowing storytelling mode that traces the rich interconnections among events and to adopt a logical mode that requires affixing artificially precise probabilities to arbitrarily restrictive hypotheses about states of nature.

Hard-line Neopositivist

Sub-additivity is so flagrant a violation of formal rationality, not to mention common sense, that I thought only the lunatic fringe would challenge its status as an error. So, it is revealing that the strong relativist chose to take a stand even here.

Let's scrutinize the claim that sub-additivity ceases to be an error when we evaluate expert judgment not against the canons of logic but against those of good storytelling. This live-and-let-live complementarity argument treats the two modes of knowing as if they existed in qualitatively different realms and as if contradictions between them were the inventions of confused souls who make the "category mistake" of plugging standards appropriate to one arena of life into arenas properly governed by other standards. We should thus judge narrativists and scientists by separate standards: those of good storytelling and good hypothesis testing.

As a formula for academic civility between the humanities and sciences, this approach is commendable. But as a formula for coping with everyday life, the complementarity thesis is inadequate.[7] One can sympathize with the separate-but-equal sentiment but still be stuck with the practical problem of when to be guided by one or the other account.

---

[7] L. Cederman, *Emergent Actors in World Politics: How States and Nations Develop and Dissolve* (Princeton, NJ: Princeton University Press, 1997).

Consider how easy it is to tell engrossing, completely true, tales of air-plane accidents that overinflate our probability estimates of the risk of flying. It is hard, moreover, to allay these anxieties, once aroused, with dispassionate recitals of statistics on the true risk per passenger mile of different modes of transportation. People who are swayed by the stories and drive rather than fly across the United States will wind up injured or dead in greater numbers than those who heed the statistical evidence. In-deed, in the long run, the 9/11 attacks may well claim their largest num-ber of victims by diverting people into automobile travel.[8] Sometimes there are right answers: sub-additivity is an error, no matter how franti-cally relativists try to spin it into something else.

Let's also scrutinize the claim that it is somehow unnatural to think probabilistically about the events under examination here. It implies that we can do away with efforts to quantify uncertainty and judge judgment by reference to other (conveniently unspecified) benchmarks.

Like Molière's good doctor who discovered that he spoke prose, rela-tivist critics may be astonished to discover that even they—as well as the experts they defend—have been speaking "probabilities" for most of their sentient existence on this planet. From roughly the age of five years on-ward, people begin deploying linguistic expressions for quantifying their uncertainty about both possible pasts and possible futures. Initially, the lexicon is impoverished: a "maybe" here or a "not sure" there. Over time, though, educated people become quite adept at distinguishing degrees of confidence in outcomes: "absolute certainty," or "virtual certainty" or "probably," or "slightly better than even odds" or "50/50," or "a bit worse than even odds," or "somewhat improbable," or "quite unlikely," or "bad bet," or "only the remotest chance," or "not a snowball's chance in hell." Such everyday expressions do not have precise probability refer-ents, but people can, with moderate reliability, translate them into numer-ical probability estimates.[9] And these implicit quantifiers play fundamental roles in life: they capture—albeit crudely—the strength of the underlying expectancies that guide decision making.

In a nutshell, the notion that people do not reason probabilistically—indeed, the notion they can avoid such reasoning in a stochastic world—is silly.

Moderate Neopositivist and Reasonable Relativist

Again, the debate has become overheated. Relativists are right that the question-framing and unpacking effects demonstrate the elusiveness of

---

[8] G. Gigerenzer, "Dread Risk, September 11, and Fatal Traffic Accidents," *Psychological Science* 15 (2004): 286–87.

[9] For examples of such work: T. Amer, K. Hackenbrack, and M. Nelson, "Between Audi-tor Differences in the Interpretation of Probability Phrases," *Auditing: A Journal of Practice*

the Rankean goal of a theory-neutral data language in which we can tell history "as it really was." Experimental manipulations of starting points—factual versus counterfactual—do leave an indelible imprint on the conclusions that we draw about what was or was not inevitable or impossible. But neopositivists see nothing odd or ironic about using the scientific method to detect sources of bias in inquiry. Objectivity may be unattainable in its pure Platonic form, but that does not mean we should stop trying to move in that direction (no more than we should stop trying to translate poetry). Identifying systematic biases in human cognition is as an integral part of the Enlightenment project of extending the reach of reason. The only way scientists can improve their measurement instruments—be they almost infallible atomic clocks or highly fallible human observers—is to be vigilant for sources of error.

The constructive question is neither relativist nor neopositivist in character. It is pragmatic: when are we better off translating our vague verbal conceptions of probability into a quantitative metric governed by restrictive conventions? If we leave things undisturbed, it will continue to be distressingly difficult to determine which of our intuitions are right or wrong, consistent or inconsistent. The correspondence and coherence benchmarks of rationality used in this book will remain beyond our measurement reach. But if we cross the qualitative-quantitative Rubicon, and get into the habit of affixing exact numbers where once there was only vague verbiage, we gain the opportunity to assess how well rival schools of thought "stack up" against each other as well as against fundamental standards of logical consistency and empirical accuracy. The comparisons will sometimes be uncomfortable, and there will be room for reasonable people to disagree over what the numbers mean. But we will have a framework for learning more about ourselves, about what we do well and what stands in need of correction.

IMPROVING THE QUALITY OF DEBATE IN POLICY CONTROVERSIES

I have made so many concessions in this project to moderate brands of relativism that I no longer know whether I am better pigeonholed as an "epistemologically liberal neopositivist" or an "epistemologically

and Theory 13 (1994): 126–36; K. H. Teigen, "When Equal Chance-Good Chances: Verbal Probabilities and Equiprobability Effect," *Organizational Behavior and Human Decision Processes* 85 (2000): 77–108; K. H. Teigen and W. Brun, "Ambiguous Probabilities: When Does $p = 0.3$ Reflect a Possibility, and When Does It Reflect a Doubt?" *Journal of Behavioral Decision Making* 13 (2000): 345–62; K. H. Teigen and W. Brun, "Verbal Probabilities: A Question of Frame?" *Journal of Behavioral Decision Making* 16 (2003): 53–72.

conservative relativist."[10] Whatever the correct classification, and it scarcely matters, the resulting hybrid position straddles a deep divide. On the one hand, it acknowledges an irreducible pluralism of perspectives on good judgment. There will always be wiggle room for arguing over who got it right. On the other hand, it directs us to hold rival perspectives accountable to fundamental tests of good judgment that, imperfect though they are, permit stark comparisons of relative performance.

This hybrid framework has guided us through seven chapters, but it does not tell us what to do next. The cautious scientific response would be to wait for the full peer-review verdict on this project and its follow-ups. We would then execute the Humean handoff: remind readers of David Hume's famous fact-value distinction, declare we have reached the limits of science, and assign you, the readers, the role of ultimate arbiters of what use to put the evidence as you do your citizens' duty of deciding who in the public arena does or does not have the right cognitive stuff, of deciding whether to risk being too tough (and punishing pundits for errors that should have been forgiven) or too lenient (and "forgiving" them for errors that deserved punishment). This division of intellectual labor might look like buck-passing, but it is rooted in the principled neopositivist conviction that scientists should not mix their roles as fact gatherers and analysts, where they have a comparative advantage, and their roles as policy advocates, where their opinions merit no greater weight than those of their fellow citizens.

We could end here. But my preference in the final section of this final chapter is to speak as a citizen, not a social scientist. I will provisionally assume the soundness of the approach to good judgment taken here and make the case that we as a society would be better off if participants in policy debates stated their beliefs in testable forms, monitored their forecasting performance, and honored reputational bets.

Making this case, however, is impossible without establishing how well off we are now: how effective are existing quality control mechanisms? The traditional answers—from liberal democratic theory—have been reassuring. We can count on open marketplaces of ideas to be self-correcting. Political partisans do not need to be naturally honest scorekeepers of their predictive track records if they know that if they fail to rein in their self-promotional puffery, rival factions will pillory them as dogmatic dunces. We humans do not need to be perfect as long as we are flawed in offsetting ways. In the long term, market forces will winnow out the truth.

I have long resonated to classical liberal arguments that stress the efficacy of free-for-all exchanges in stimulating good ideas and screening

---

[10] Or, mirror imaging Clifford Geertz's ploy of proclaiming himself an anti-anti-relativist, I might proclaim myself an anti-anti-positivist.

out bad ones.[11] But I now see many reasons why the routine checks and balances—in society at large as well as in the cloisters of academe—are not up to correcting the judgmental biases documented here. The marketplace of ideas, especially that for political prognostication, has at least three serious imperfections that permit lots of nonsense to persist for long stretches of time.[12]

First, vigorous competition among providers of intellectual products (off-the-shelf opinions) is not enough if the consumers are unmotivated to be discriminating judges of competing claims and counterclaims. This state of affairs most commonly arises when the mass public reacts to intellectuals peddling their wares on op-ed pages or in television studios, but it even arises in academia when harried, hyperspecialized faculty make rapid-fire assessments of scholars whose work is remote from their own. These consumers are rationally ignorant. They do not think it worth their while trying to gauge quality on their own. So, they rely on low-effort heuristics that prize attributes of alleged specialists, such as institutional affiliation, fame, and even physical attractiveness, that are weak predictors of epistemic quality. Indeed, our data—as well as other work—suggest that consumers, especially the emphatically self-confident hedgehogs among them, often rely on low-effort heuristics that are negative predictors of epistemic quality. Many share Harry Truman's oft-quoted preference for one-armed advisers.[13]

Second, the marketplace of ideas can fail not because consumers are unmotivated but rather because consumers have the "wrong" motives. They may be less interested in the dispassionate pursuit of truth than they are in buttressing their prejudices. John Stuart Mill—who coined the marketplace of ideas metaphor—was keenly aware that audiences

[11] A casual glance over twentieth-century history—Hitler's Germany, Stalin's Russia, Mao's China, Pol Pot's Cambodia, the Taliban's Afghanistan, and the institutionalized insanity that is still North Korea—should remind us of how oppressively surreal things can get when tiny cliques enforce monopoly claims on truth. The superiority of democratic regimes over totalitarian ones should not count, however, as evidence that there is no room for improvement. Even in relatively open societies, it is far more difficult than it need be for attentive consumers of information to sort out which points of view have proven more prescient on which points of contention.

[12] Richard A. Posner, *Public Intellectuals: A Study of Decline: A Critical Analysis* (Cambridge: Harvard University Press, 2001); for a pioneering study of the criteria that ordinary people use in judging whether an idea is worth keeping alive in the marketplace of ideas, see C. Heath, C. Bell, and E. Sternberg, "Emotional Selection in Memes: The Case of Urban Legends," *Journal of Personality and Social Psychology* 81 (2002): 1028–41.

[13] For a review of work that suggests integratively simple rhetoric often has a political-psychological advantage over more complex forms of rhetoric, see P. E. Tetlock, "Cognitive Structural Analysis of Political Rhetoric: Methodological and Theoretical Issues," in *Political Psychology: A Reader*, ed. S. Iyengar and W. J. McGuire (Durham, NC: Duke University Press, 1992), 380–407.

like listening to speakers who articulate shared views and blast opposing views more compellingly than the audience could for itself. In his chronicle of the decline of public intellectuals, Richard Posner notes that these advocates specialize in providing "solidarity," not "credence," goods. The psychological function being served is not the pursuit of truth but rather enhancing the self-images and social identities of co-believers: "We right-minded folks want our side to prevail over those wrongheaded folks." The psychology is that of the sports arena, not the seminar room. These observations also fit well with our data. Fans should find it much easier to identify with the brave hedgehogs who, unlike the equivocating foxes, do not back off in ideological combat and do not give the other side the satisfaction of savoring their mistakes. Even though we might disavow the sentiment if put too baldly, many of us seem to subscribe to the implicit theory that real leaders do not admit mistakes.[14]

Third, even granting that consumers are properly motivated, they can still fail because of either cognitive constraints or task difficulty constraints. Cognitive constraints are rooted in human nature: even smart people have limited mental capacity and make elementary errors of reasoning that are surprisingly resistant to correction by exhortations to "think harder."[15] Task difficulty constraints are rooted in the political environment: no matter how smart people are, it may be impossible to determine—even ex post—which pundits were closer to the truth. There are three intertwined reasons for suspecting this is true of many political controversies: (a) the propensity of partisans to make vague-to-the-point-of-oracular predictions that can be rendered consistent with a wide range of contradictory outcomes and thus never falsified; (b) the ingenuity of partisans, especially hedgehogs, in generating justifications and excuses whenever a respected member of their camp is so rash as to offer a prediction that can be falsified; (c) the inscrutability of the environment, which makes it easy for partisans to pick and choose convenient what-if scenarios in which the policies favored by one's side always lead to better outcomes than would have otherwise occurred and the policies favored by the other side always lead to worse outcomes.

This combination of arguments gives ample reasons for fearing that the marketplace for political prognostication will be far from infallibly self-correcting. Figuring out our next move is not, however, easy. The prognostication market is not like that for goods or services in which the consumer can readily gauge or sellers guarantee quality (how often do

[14] For a review, Tetlock, "Cognitive Structural Analysis."

[15] C. F. Camerer and R. M. Hogarth, "The Effects of Financial Incentives in Experiments: A Review and Capital-Labor-Production Framework," *Journal of Risk and Uncertainty* 19 (1999): 1–3, 7–42.

pundits declare they will forswear punditry if they get it wrong). The market for political prognostication is also not like those for medical or legal services in which, although consumers cannot readily gauge quality, public anxieties about quality control (abetted by insiders' less-than-altruistic desire to limit competition) have led to strict oversight of who can offer opinions. The First Amendment should override laws mandating that only state-licensed persons can voice opinions on public policy.

The obvious corrective to these market imperfections is a collective commitment to furnish public intellectual goods that make it easier to distinguish lower- from higher-quality political speculation. And academia is the obvious place to look for quality control guidance and precedents. Its elaborate systems of peer review represent a concerted effort to enforce norms of epistemic accountability that transcend allegiances to quarreling schools of thought. To obtain grants and to be published in scholarly journals—to get one's voice heard in the marketplace of ideas among specialists—one must pass through a rigorous gauntlet of anonymous reviewers tasked with checking the soundness of one's arguments.

The good news is that such systems do filter out a lot of "noise." The bad news is that the key filtering mechanism—severely restricting access to publication outlets—is neither constitutionally feasible nor desirable in the broader marketplace of ideas. The added bad news is that existing journals in the social sciences are oriented around highly abstract theoretical controversies in which contributors virtually never stake their reputations to explicit predictions about the types of messy real-world outcomes so central to our forecasting exercises. These contributors are, moreover, right to be reticent given the game they are playing: the ceteris paribus requirement for theory testing can never be satisfied when so many uncontrolled variables are at work and so little is known about how those variables interact.

In this age of academic hyperspecialization, there is no reason for supposing that contributors to top journals—distinguished political scientists, area study specialists, economists, and so on—are any better than journalists or attentive readers of the *New York Times* in "reading" emerging situations. The data reported in chapters 2, 3, and 4 underscore this point. The analytical skills undergirding academic acclaim conferred no advantage in forecasting and belief-updating exercises. If these null-hypothesis results capture the true state of nature, it is not surprising there is so much disdain among high-ranking academics for forecasting exercises (the opposite of the attitude I would expect if they thought they held some advantage). One social science colleague told me with ill-concealed contempt: "We leave that for the media mavens."

Caveats to the side, my own public-intellectual-goods proposal builds on the principle of rigorous review that prevails in top-ranked academic journals. These journals, like this project in miniature, are offspring of the Enlightenment quest to identify correspondence and coherence benchmarks for judging claims that transcend clashing schools of thought and establish criteria by which civilized people can agree to resolve disagreements—or at least agree on terms for disagreeing. To achieve legitimacy within a political or scholarly community, it is necessary for aspiring, public-intellectual-goods providers not only to maintain high evidentiary standards but also to honor basic norms of procedural fairness, including (a) equality of treatment so that representatives of opposing views perceive that the same epistemic ground rules apply to everyone; and (b) responsiveness to protests about the application of standardized rules in cases in which special circumstances allegedly arise.[16]

Unlike the precedent of academic journals, however, the proposal advanced here is not centered around evaluating the explanatory strengths and weaknesses of abstract theoretical accounts; the focus is on the capacity of flesh-and-blood observers, drawing on whatever mix of street smarts and academic knowledge they deem optimal, to decode real events unfolding in real time. To this end, observers would be subject to the same bottom-line correspondence and coherence tests of their judgments in this book. The only permissible deviations from standardization would be those necessary to assure participants from diverse viewpoints that the norms of procedural fairness are being respected. For example, at the beginning of the forecasting exercise, all participating observers would be given the option of specifying whether they wish to avail themselves of difficulty and value adjustments to their forecasting accuracy scores; at the end of the exercise, observers would be given the option of revising those adjustments as well as given the opportunity to accept additional modifications such as controversy adjustments (for residual uncertainty over what really happened) and fuzzy-set adjustments (for residual uncertainty over what nearly happened (close-call counterfactuals) or what might yet happen (off-on-timing). Observers could also opt either to keep their results private (and use the resulting feedback purely for cognitive self-improvement) or to go public (demonstrating their willingness to put their reputations on the line).

Observers would not, however, have infinite wiggle room for covering up mistakes. The performance feedback results would always include—in addition to whatever adjustments observers added—standardized baseline measures of forecasting accuracy and timeliness of belief updating that represent an ideologically balanced panel's sense of what actually

---

[16] T. R. Tyler and H. J. Smith, "Social Justice and Social Movements," in *The Handbook of Social Psychology*, ed. D. T. Gilbert, S. Fiske, and G. Lindzey (New York: McGraw-Hill, 1998).

happened, with no moral or metaphysical second-guessing. Consumers of political prognostication could thus decide for themselves whether to rely on the objective forecasting accuracy and belief-updating performance statistics or to be more charitable and accept some or all of the adjustments to those scores proposed either ex ante or ex post by the forecasters themselves. Prudent consumers should become suspicious when they confront big gaps between objective performance indicators and subjectively adjusted indicators. Unadjusted ex ante forecasting performance tells consumers in the media, business, and government what most want to know: how good are these guys in telling us what will happen next? Ex post adjustments to forecasting accuracy tell us how good a job forecasters do, after the damage is done, in closing the gap between what they said would happen and what subsequently did happen.[17]

Of course, we have yet to confront the most daunting of all the barriers to implementation: the reluctance of professionals to participate. If one has carved out a comfortable living under the old regime of close-to-zero accountability for one's pronouncements, one would have to be either exceptionally honest or masochistic to jeopardize so cozy an arrangement by voluntarily exposing one's predictions to the rude shock of falsification. Powerful inertial forces keep the current system in place. However collectively suboptimal it may be, entrenched incumbents have a big interest in preserving it.

Big incentives will therefore be required to induce people to work through the sorts of arduous, frequently humbling, cognitive exercises that are the methodological backbone of this book—just as surely as big

[17] One could argue that much the same end could be achieved by mandating that those offering advice on futures—be they pundits in the public eye or intelligence analysts behind the scenes—regularly participate in prediction markets that require testing their wits against a wide range of fellow experts as well as dilettantes. There is indeed much to recommend this idea. I see the growing interest in prediction markets as a hopeful sign that the era of close-to-zero-accountability-for-predictive-track-records may slowly be coming to a close (see S. Weber and P. E. Tetlock, "New Economy: The Pentagon's Plan for Futures Trading," *New York Times*, August 11, 2003, C3).

A task for future work will be to sort the commonalities and differences underlying four approaches that have shown promise in improving political and business forecasting: prediction markets, the Delphi method of integrating divergent perspectives, the power of simple consensus forecasts, and the superior forecasting skill of more self-critical and flexible forecasters. One common theme is that useful information for predicting complex outcomes is typically spread across diverse sources and there is a price to be paid for narrow-mindedness. A second theme is that there is often a price to be paid for extremism, for betting heavily on long shots (R. Thaler and W. Ziemba, "Anomalies: Pari-mutuel Betting Markets: Racetracks and Lotteries," *Journal of Economic Perspectives* 2 [1988]: 161–74). A third theme running through three of the four approaches—prediction markets, the Delphi method, and cognitive styles—is that information processing systems generate more accurate forecasts to the degree that competing ideas—all of them—are subject to critical assessment.

incentives have been necessary to induce people to surmount the formidable cognitive barriers to entry into every other prestigious profession in our society. To motivate would-be doctors and lawyers to acquire demonstrable competence, we have state licensing boards that aggressively pursue charlatans who offer medical and legal advice without passing through grueling professional hurdles. To motivate providers of other goods and services, society has instituted other protections, including laws on truth in advertising and fraud. But, again, none of these solutions applies here for obvious constitutional reasons.

I suspect the incentive problem is insuperable without concerted action by the big buyers of political prognostication in media, business, and government. The best hope of breaking the status quo is by publicizing that demand for public intellectuals has become partly conditional on their proven track records in drawing correct inferences from relevant real-world events unfolding in real time, and that the buyers are no longer automatically relying on the "Rolodex" or prestigious affiliation or ideological compatibility heuristics. Smart newcomers would then see the new regime as a means of more rapid ascent in the media star or consulting hierarchy than might otherwise be available. And insofar as upstarts began to claim serious market shares, even comfortably ensconced incumbents might feel compelled to rethink how they think.

Resistance would naturally be fierce, especially from influential hedgehogs who would have the most to lose, and we had a foretaste of the forms it is likely to take in the strong relativist objections to this entire project. Few of us look pretty under the cognitive microscope. And one does not need to buy fully into George Bernard Shaw's definition of professions (conspiracies to defraud the public) to recognize that no profession welcomes in-depth scrutiny of its collective claim to expertise. Sociologists have long known that professions maintain their autonomy and prestige by convincing the world of two things: (1) we professionals possess valuable skills that the uninitiated do not; and (2) these valuable skills cannot be easily "canned" or reduced to reproducible components easily taught to outsiders.[18] Resistance, moreover, would not just come from the supply side of the economic equation. Chapter 2 showed that, on the demand side, there is a strong desire among mass-public consumers to believe that they live in a predictable world and an equally strong desire among more elite consumers in the media, business, and government to appear to be doing the right thing by ritualistically consulting the usual suspects from widely recognized interest groups. The fainthearted should be forgiven for concluding that we are fated to fail to break this tight symbiotic

---

[18] H. Wilensky, "The Professionalization of Everyone?" *American Journal of Sociology* 70 (1964): 137–58.

embrace between self-confident suppliers of dubious products and their cling-on customers.

But even fierce resistance can be overcome. Low-transaction-cost index funds have benefited—very substantially—from slowly spreading knowledge of how hard-pressed stock-pickers are to best dart-throwing chimps and other mindless algorithms. And prediction markets—in which people put their money where their mouths are—have boomed in popularity.[19] We should not take it for granted that incumbents will forever be successful in creating a Wizard-of-Oz-like mystique around their inner-sanctum knowledge. We live in a world of rapidly advancing information technology and more gradually advancing artificial intelligence. It is arguably only a matter of time before these new technologies encroach on well-established professions, including medicine, law, science, and even that last redoubt of obfuscation, politics.

And if the resistance were overcome, where would we be then? Age of Reason optimists would announce that the long-heralded end-of-ideology thesis has been vindicated—a prediction that, incidentally, has used up its allotment of off-on-timing defenses.[20] Lord Rutherford's era of "gentlemen and women, let us calculate rather than debate" would finally be upon us. My own guess is that the announcement would again be premature. Human nature being what it is, and the political system creating the perversely self-justifying incentives that it does, I would expect, in short order, faux rating systems to arise that shill for representatives of points of view who feel shortchanged by even the most transparent evaluation systems that bend over backward to be fair.[21] The signal-to-noise ratio will never be great in a cacophonously pluralistic society such as ours.

But that does not mean we must reconcile ourselves to the noisy status quo. A coordinated initiative—from those in academia, foundations, and the media who view public intellectuals as purveyors of credence goods, not just solidarity and entertainment goods—could sharpen the signals and dampen the noise. Imperfect though they are, the research tools in this book should be of use to professionals in applied fields such as intelligence analysis, risk assessment, and journalism. Deployed thoughtfully, these tools can help professionals build self-correcting epistemic

---

[19] Of course, there has also been resistance to prediction markets, especially those in which participants might profit from the grief of others, raising the moral specter of taboo trade-offs (see Weber and Tetlock, "Pentagon Futures Trading.")

[20] Daniel Bell, *The Coming of Post-industrial Society: A Venture in Social Forecasting* (New York: Basic Books, 1976).

[21] "True believers" are quick to claim they are victims of bias: L. Ross and D. Griffin, "Subjective Construal, Social Inference, and Human Misunderstanding," in *Advances in Experimental Social Psychology*, Vol. 24, ed. M. Zanna (New York: Academic Press, 1991), 319–59.

communities devoted to monitoring complex events as they unfold in real time, reflecting on the implications of these events for their evolving worldviews, and specifying benchmarks for defining and checking biases.[22] Progress will not be as easy as techno-enthusiasts hope. There are ineradicable pockets of subjectivity in political judgment. But progress is not as hopeless as opponents of social science never tire of insisting.

---

[22] The recommendations of this book are much in the spirit of Sherman Kent, after whom the CIA named its training school for intelligence analysts. We can draw cumulative lessons from experience only if we are aware of gaps between what we expected and what happened, acknowledge the possibility that those gaps signal shortcomings in our understanding, and test alternative interpretations of those gaps in an evenhanded fashion. This means doing what we did here: obtaining explicit subjective probability estimates (not just vague verbiage), eliciting reputational bets that pit rival worldviews against each other, and assessing the consistency of the standards of evidence experts apply to evidence. (S. Kent, *Collected Essays*, U.S. Government: Center for the Study of Intelligence, 1970, http://www.cia.gov/csi/books/shermankent/toc.html).

Methodological Appendix

THIS APPENDIX is divided into six sections, each dedicated to describing the research participants, procedures, and stimulus materials used in one of the six major types of studies presented in the book: (1) the regional forecasting exercises in chapters 2 and 3 (from which we derived the correspondence indicators of good judgment such as probability scores and their components); (2) the reputational bet exercises in chapter 4 (from which we derived the Bayesian belief-updating indicators and measures of belief system defenses); (3) the reactions to historical discoveries exercises in chapter 5 (from which we derived turnabout tests of double standards); (4) the reactions to close-call counterfactual exercises in chapter 5 (from which we derived measures of perceptions of the "mutability" of historical outcomes); (5) the unpacking scenarios of possible futures exercises in chapter 7 (from which we derived coherence measures of good judgment, such as violations of formal principles of probability theory); (6) the unpacking scenarios of possible pasts exercise in chapter 7 (from which we derived inevitability and impossibility curves and measured contradictions between the two sets of perceptions).

I. REGIONAL FORECASTING EXERCISES (CHAPTERS 2 AND 3)

Participants and Individual Difference Measures

Our operational definition of an expert was "a professional who makes his or her livelihood by commenting or offering advice on political and economic trends of significance to the well-being of particular states, regional clusters of states, or the international system as a whole." Expertise could thus take diverse region-specific forms (from southern Africa to the Middle East, etc.) and functional forms (knowledge of local political scenes, of macroeconomic policies and their effects, of interstate relations, of military balances of power and proliferation risks, etc.). We classified the 284 experts (who satisfied the overarching definition and who answered at least half of our forecasting questions) into the following demographic, educational, disciplinary background, current employment, and political affiliation categories (measured in the Professional Background Questionnaire). Participants were mostly male (76 percent), with an average age of 43 (standard deviation of 7.3 years) and an average of 12.2 years of relevant work experience (standard deviation of 4.7).

Most had doctoral degrees (52 percent) and almost all had postgraduate training (96 percent). Our participants came from a potpourri of disciplines, including most branches of area studies (41 percent), international relations (24 percent), economics (12 percent), national security and arms control (11 percent), journalism (9 percent), diplomacy (2 percent), and international law (1 percent). They worked in a range of settings, including academia (41 percent), government (26 percent), think tanks and foundations (17 percent), international institutions (8 percent), and the private sector (including the media) (8 percent). Approximately 61 percent of participants had been interviewed at least once by a major media outlet and 21 percent had been interviewed more than ten times. Approximately 80 percent of participants had served at least once as formal or informal consultants on international political or economic issues to government, the private sector, international agencies or think tanks. The vast majority of the sample (82 percent) participated in forecasting exercises initiated between 1988 and 1995.

We also tried—as often as possible—to measure individual differences in ideological orientation (the thirteen-item Worldview Questionnaire that was factor analyzed in chapter 3) and in cognitive style (the thirteen-item Styles-of-Reasoning Questionnaire that was also factor analyzed in chapter 3). In each case, experts responded to items on nine-point scales ranging from "completely disagree" (1) to "completely agree" (9), with 5 defined as a point of maximum uncertainty.

The items in the Worldview Questionnaire included the following: "I see an irreversible trend toward global economic interdependence"; "Free markets are the best path to prosperity"; "Our society underestimates the adverse environmental side effects of free markets"; "Our society underestimates the adverse effects of markets on social equality"; "I believe balance-of-power politics remains the reigning principle in world politics"; "It is a mistake to dismiss international institutions as subordinate to whims of great powers"; "I am optimistic about long-term growth trajectory of the world economy"; "I am concerned about pushing the limits of sustainable development"; "In dealing with potential adversaries, reassurance is generally a more useful diplomatic tool than deterrence"; "We should weight financial contagion as a greater threat than moral hazard in deciding whether to aid insolvent governments"; "I expect powerful ethnic and religious identifications to transform the boundaries of dozens of existing states in the near future"; "There is a widespread tendency to underestimate fragility of ecosystems"; and "On balance I see myself as more liberal/conservative." Maximum likelihood factor analysis with quartimin rotation yielded the three-factor solution in table 1 in chapter 3. The high-loading items on each factor (above 0.25) defined the belief system scale used in later analyses (average Cronbach's alpha = 0.79).

Of the thirteen items in the Styles-of-Reasoning Questionnaire, we drew eight from Kruglanski's need-for-closure scale: (1) "Having clear rules and order at work is essential for success"; (2) "Even after I have made up my mind about something, I am always eager to consider a different opinion"; (3) "I dislike questions that can be answered in many different ways"; (4) "I usually make important decisions quickly and confidently"; (5) "When considering most conflict situations, I can usually see how both sides could be right"; (6) "It is annoying to listen to someone who cannot seem to make up his or her mind"; (7) "I prefer interacting with people whose opinions are very different from my own"; (8) "When trying to solve a problem I often see so many possible options that it is confusing." The remaining items (9–13) were as follows: (9) In a famous essay, "Isaiah Berlin classified intellectuals as hedgehogs or foxes. The hedgehog knows one big thing and tries to explain as much as possible within that conceptual framework, whereas the fox knows many small things and is content to improvise explanations on a case-by-case basis. I place myself toward the hedgehog or fox end of this scale"; (10) "Scholars are usually at greater risk of exaggerating how complex the world is than they are of underestimating how complex it is"; (11) "We are closer than many think to achieving parsimonious explanations of politics"; (12) "I think politics is more cloudlike than clocklike ("cloudlike" meaning inherently unpredictable; "clocklike" meaning perfectly predictable if we have adequate knowledge)"; (13) "The more common error in decision making is to abandon good ideas too quickly, not to stick with bad ideas too long." Maximum likelihood factor analysis of all thirteen items (with quartimin rotation) yielded the two-factor solution reported in table 2 of chapter 3. Our analyses focused on the first and largest factor—the hedgehog-fox factor—in large part because the second factor (decisiveness) explained so little of the variance in theoretically significant outcomes. The high-loading items on the first factor (0.25 and greater) defined the hedgehog-fox measure used in most of the analyses in the book (Cronbach's alpha = 0.81).

Research Procedures and Materials

All respondents were given a Possible-Futures Questionnaire that introduced the study in this way: "Although political forecasting is obviously an inexact science, educated guesswork is still critical for setting priorities and making contingency plans. Your answers to the forecasting questions posed here will not be traceable either to you personally or to any institution with which you may be affiliated. Our goal is not to proclaim 'winners' and 'losers' in a forecasting contest but rather to study how highly trained professionals reason about complex real-world processes under conditions of uncertainty."

We began systematic collection of forecasts, and reactions to the degrees of confirmation or disconfirmation of those forecasts, in 1987–1988 and continued in periodic spurts through 2003. The forecasting exercises solicited subjective probability judgments of possible futures of approximately sixty nations. These nations had been clustered into nine categories: (1) the Soviet bloc, which initially included the Soviet Union (time series discontinued at end of 1991 and broken into Russia, the Ukraine, and Kazakhstan), Poland, German Democratic Republic (discontinued in 1990 with German reunification), Czechoslovakia (broken into the Czech Republic and Slovakia in 1993), Hungary, Romania, Bulgaria, and non–Warsaw Pact member Yugoslavia (discontinued in 1991 and broken into three of its republics, Slovenia, Croatia, and Serbia); (2) a European Union cluster that included the four largest economies—the United Kingdom, France, Federal Republic of Germany, and Italy; (3) North America (United States and Canada); (4) Central and Latin America, including Mexico, Cuba, Venezuela, Brazil, Argentina, and Chile; (5) the Arab world, including Egypt, Syria, Iraq, Saudi Arabia, Libya, and Sudan, plus Israel, Turkey, and Iran; (6) sub-Saharan Africa, including a "Horn of Africa" subgroup (Somalia, Ethiopia, and, as of 1993, Eritrea), a west Africa subgroup (Nigeria, Ghana, Ivory Coast, Sierra Leone, and Liberia), a central Africa group (Zaire, Angola, Zimbabwe, Uganda, Rwanda, and Burundi), and a southern Africa group (South Africa and Mozambique); (7) China; (8) Northeast Asia (Japan, North and South Korea); (9) Southeast Asia (Vietnam, Thailand, Malaysia, and Indonesia). We also conducted several more specialized exercises that cut across regional expertise (described later). The pool of respondents included at least ten specialists in each region or functional domain examined here, and, in the cases of the Soviet bloc, the Arab world, North America, and the European Union, in excess of twenty.

The typical testing session was divided into three phases. First, experts answered the previously described questions that probed their professional backgrounds, preferred styles of thinking, and ideological and theoretical commitments. Second, they judged the probabilities of short- and longer-term futures for at least two nations within their regional specialty. Third, experts played the role of "dilettantes" and ventured probability judgments of possible futures for at least two nations drawn from regions of the world with which they were less familiar (nations chosen to balance the number of dilettante predictions obtained across regions of the world). Experts working within their specialty were also sometimes asked to make more complex reputational bets that required estimating the likelihood of possible futures conditional, first, on their own perspective on the underlying forces at work being correct and conditional, second, on the most influential rival perspective being correct. These reputational bets allowed us to assess the degree to which experts updated their beliefs like good Bayesians and are the focus of chapter 4 and section II of this appendix.

We assured experts that we understood no human being could possess detailed knowledge of all the topics covered in these exercises and urged experts to assign just-guessing confidence whenever they felt they knew nothing that would justify elevating one set of possibilities over the others. We also gave participants brief facts-on-file summaries of recent developments ("to refresh memories and ensure a minimal common knowledge base"). And it is worth emphasizing that all data were collected with strict guarantees of confidentiality to both individuals and to the organizations with which they were affiliated. These assurances were necessary for both practical reasons (many experts would participate only under such ground rules) and substantive reasons (the objective of our measurement efforts is to tap into what experts really think, not what public positions experts deem it prudent to take).

Forecasting questions had to satisfy five criteria:

1. Pass the clairvoyance test. This test requires defining possible futures clearly enough that, if a genuine clairvoyant were in the room, that person could gaze into her crystal ball and tell you whether the forecast was right or wrong, with no need to return to the forecaster with bothersome requests for ex post respecifications of the sort typically needed in less formal forecasting exercises ("What exactly did you mean by 'a Polish Peron' or 'continuing tension in Kashmir' or 'moderate growth in Japan'?"). We sought easily verifiable public indicators.

2. Pass the exclusivity and exhaustiveness tests. We relied on formal probability theory to assess the accuracy and coherence of the probability judgments that forecasters attached to possible futures. But probabilities are supposed to add to 1.0 if and only if the possibilities do not overlap and if and only if the possibilities exhaust the universe of outcomes. It was necessary therefore to define the boundaries between possible futures with care. Sometimes this was easy. Certain criterion variables had "natural" break points. In the language of measurement theory, they formed either nominal scales that took 0 or 1 values or ordinal scales that permitted rough rank-order comparisons of degree of change. Examples include leadership transitions (e.g., Will "X" still be president or prime minister?) border changes (e.g., Will the state's borders remain the same, expand, or contract?) and entry into or exit from international security

regimes (e.g., NATO, Warsaw Pact, nonproliferation treaty) or trade regimes/monetary union (e.g., GATT, WTO, EU, NAFTA).

Other criterion variables were continuous in character. In the language of measurement theory, they formed ratio scales with equal-spaced intervals between values and nonarbitrary zero points. Examples include GDP growth rates, central government debt as percentage of GDP, state-owned enterprises as percentage of GDP, defense spending as percentage of GDP, stock market closes, and currency exchange rates. The confidence interval was usually defined by plus or minus 0.5 of a standard deviation of the previous five or ten years of values of the variable. Experts were then asked to judge the subjective probability of future values falling below, within, or above the specified band. For example, if GDP growth had been 2.5 percent in the most recently available year, and if the standard deviation of growth values in the last ten years had been 1.5 percent, then the confidence band would have been bounded by 1.75 percent and 3.25 percent.

3. Pass the "don't bother me too often with dumb questions" test. Questions that made sense in some parts of the world made little sense in others. No one expected a coup in the United States or United Kingdom, but many regarded coups as serious possibilities in Saudi Arabia, Nigeria, and so on. Experts guffawed at judging the nuclear proliferation risk posed by Canada or Norway but not at the risks posed by Pakistan or North Korea. Some "ridiculous questions" were thus deleted.

4. Include questions that vary in difficulty and allow us to assess wide individual or group differences in forecasting skill. Range of item difficulty was ensured by varying the temporal range of forecasts (short versus long-term), the regional focus (zone of turbulence versus stability) and the anticipated variance in outcomes (judging from past base rates, border and regime changes are rare, whereas shifts in unemployment or inflation are quite common).

5. Avoidance of value-charged language. This "just the facts, ma'am" rule requires defining possible futures in a reasonably neutral fashion designed to minimize offense among even stridently partisan participants. We could say that central government debt rises above 120 percent of GDP but not that pork-barrel politics is out of control; that cross-border violence is rising but not that the bloodthirsty Israeli or Pakistani aggressors have struck again; that nondemocratic regimes change but not that nations have been liberated or have fallen under even more oppressive yokes. Of course, perfect value neutrality is unattainable, but it is worth trying to approximate it.

Scoring Rules

Although experts sometimes made "0" and "1" predictions (saying that *x* was impossible or inevitable), they mostly expressed degrees of uncertainty about what would happen. And—with the exception of card-carrying Bayesians—they mostly preferred to express that uncertainty via familiar verbal hedges: Gorbachev will "almost certainly" fail or John Major will "probably" lose or there is a "good chance" Pakistan will set off a nuclear test or the likelihood of peaceful transition to majority rule is "vanishingly small."

We had to coax participants to translate these idiosyncratic estimates of uncertainty onto standardized probability scales. From a psychometric perspective, however, the advantages of quantifying uncertainty outweighed the inevitable complaints about "the pseudoscientific artificiality" of affixing probability estimates to unique events. There is just no systematic way to check the accuracy of casual talk about alternative futures, but we can check the accuracy of subjective probability judgments. Quantification gives us a framework for assessing—across many forecasts on many occasions—the correspondence between the subjective likelihoods and objective frequencies of events (e.g., calibration and discrimination measures).

The methods of eliciting subjective probabilities were quite similar for variables with different metric properties. We carved possible futures into logically exhaustive and mutually exclusive sets, usually three of them. Experts then assigned probabilities to each set of possibilities, with the constraint that those judgments had to sum to 1.0. A typical three-possible-futures scale looked like this:

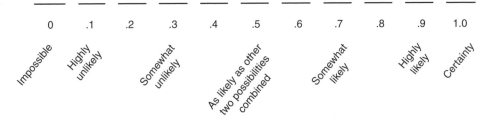

We told experts that, for three-possible-futures forecasts, they should treat 0.33 as the point of maximum uncertainty. We gave them a special "maximum uncertainty" box, which, we stressed, they should use only if they felt that they had *no relevant knowledge* for judging one possible set of futures to be more likely than the other(s) ("just-guessing" values). We also told experts the conditions for assigning the values of zero (only if sure that it is impossible one of the possible futures could occur in the specified period) and of 1.0 (only if sure that it is inevitable one of the possible futures will occur in the specified period). Although at opposing ends of the scale, ratings of zero and 1.0 share a critical psychological property: both represent movement from uncertainty into certainty.

For continuous, ratio-scale variables, experts were given the most recently available value of the variable and presented with a confidence interval around that value. The confidence interval was usually defined by plus or minus 0.5 of a standard deviation of the previous five years of values of the variable (or previous five elections). Experts then judged the subjective probability of future values falling below, within, or above the specified band. For example, if GDP growth had been 2.5 percent in the most recently available year available, and if the standard deviation of growth values in the last five years had been 1.5 percent, then the confidence band would have been bounded by 1.75 percent and 3.25 percent. For experimental purposes, we occasionally broke the set of possible futures into four or even more categories to capture variation in judgments of extreme possibilities (e.g., severe recessions or sustained economic booms) as well as to assess the impact of "unpacking" possible futures into increasingly differentiated subsets.

In principle, the total number of subjective probability forecasts obtained in the regional forecasting exercises should have numbered 95,472: the logical result of 284 forecasters each making short-term and long-term predictions for each of four nations (two inside and two outside their domains of expertise) on seventeen outcome variables (on average), each of which was typically broken down into three possible futures and thus required three separate probability estimates. In reality, as the result of substantial amounts of missing data due to forecasters not answering each question posed, there were 82,361 subjective probability estimates (derived from responses to approximately 27,450 forecasting questions).

Types of Forecasting Questions

Most questions were posed in exercises that were conducted in 1988 and 1992, came in both short-time-horizon and longer-time-horizon versions, and fell in one of the following four broad "content" categories.

CONTINUITY OF DOMESTIC POLITICAL LEADERSHIP

For established democracies, should we expect after either the next election (short-term) or the next two elections (longer-term) the party that currently has the most representatives in the legislative branch(es) of government will retain this status, will lose this status, or will strengthen its position (separate judgments for bicameral systems)? For democracies with presidential elections, should we expect that after the next election or next two elections, the current incumbent/party will lose control, will retain control with reduced popular support, or will retain control with greater popular support? Confidence bands around the status quo option were based on the variance either in seats controlled or in popular vote over the last five elections.

For states with shakier track records of competitive elections, should we expect that, in either the next five or ten years, the individuals and (separate judgment) political parties/movements currently in charge will lose control, will retain control but weather major challenges to their authority (e.g., coup attempts, major rebellions), or will retain control without major challenges? Also, for less stable polities, should we expect the basic character of the political regime to change in the next five or ten years and, if so, will it change in the direction of increased or reduced economic freedom, increased or reduced political freedom, and increased or reduced corruption? Should we expect over the next five or ten years that interethnic and other sectarian violence will increase, decrease, or remain about the same? Finally, should we expect state boundaries—over the next ten or twenty-five years—to remain the same, expand, or contract and—if boundaries do change—will it be the result of peaceful or violent secession by a subnational entity asserting independence or the result of peaceful or violent annexation by another nation-state?

DOMESTIC POLICY AND ECONOMIC PERFORMANCE

With respect to policy, should we expect—over the next two or five years—increases, decreases, or essentially no changes in marginal tax rates, central bank interest rates, central government expenditures as percentage of GDP, annual central government operating deficit as percentage of GDP, and the size of state-owned sectors of the economy as percentage of GDP? Should we expect—again over the next two or five years—shifts in government priorities such as percentage of GDP devoted to education or to health care? With respect to economic performance, should we expect—again over the next two or five years—growth rates in GDP to accelerate, decelerate, or remain about the same? What should our expectations be for inflation and unemployment over the next two or five years? Should we expect—over the next five or ten years—entry into or exit from membership in free-trade agreements or monetary unions?

NATIONAL SECURITY AND DEFENSE POLICY

Should we expect—over the next five or ten years—defense spending as a percentage of central government expenditure to rise, fall, or stay about the same? Should we expect policy changes over the next five to ten years with respect to military conscription, with respect to using military force (or supporting insurgencies) against states, with respect to participation in international peacekeeping operations (contributing personnel), with respect to entering or leaving alliances or perpetuation of status quo, and with respect to nuclear weapons (acquiring such weapons, continuing to try to obtain such weapons, abandoning programs to obtain such weapons or the weapons themselves)?

SPECIAL-PURPOSE EXERCISES

These eight exercises included (1) the weapons of mass destruction proliferation exercise (1988) in which forecasters judged the likelihood of twenty-five states acquiring capacity to produce weapons of mass destruction, nuclear or biological, in the next five, ten, or twenty-five years as well as the possibility of states—or subnational terrorist groups—using such weapons; (2) the Persian Gulf War I exercise (fall 1990) in which forecasters took positions on whether there would be a war (and, if so, how long it would last, how many Allied casualties there would be, whether Saddam Hussein would remain in power, and, if not, whether all or part of Kuwait would remain under Iraqi control); (3) the transitions from Communism exercise (1991–1992) that asked for predictions—over the next three, six, or twelve years—of both economic reform (rate of divesting state-owned enterprises; degree to which fiscal and monetary policy fit templates of "shock therapy") and subsequent economic performance (unemployment, inflation, GDP growth); (4) an exercise on human-caused or -facilitated disasters in the next five, ten, or twenty-five years, including refugee flows, poverty, mass starvation, massacres, and epidemics (HIV prevalence) linked to inadequate public health measures (1992); (5) the EU exercises that focused initially on adoption of the euro (1992–2002, 1998–2008) but that later broadened to address the prospects of former Soviet bloc countries, plus Turkey, in meeting entry requirements); (6) the American presidential election exercises of 1992 and 2000 (Who will win? By how much?); (7) the Internet–New Economy exercise (1999) that focused on the overall performance of the NASDAQ (Is it a bubble? If so, when will it pop?) as well as the revenues, earnings, and share prices of selected "New Economy" firms, including Microsoft, CISCO, Oracle, IBM, HP, Dell, Compaq, Worldcom, Enron, AOL Time Warner, Amazon, and e-Bay; (8) the global-warming exercise that focused on CO_2 emissions per capita (stemming from burning fossil fuels and manufacturing cement) of twenty-five states over the next twenty-five years, and on the prospects of states actually ratifying an international agreement (Kyoto Protocol) to regulate such emissions (1996–1997).

Reality Checks

We relied on the following reference sources to gauge the accuracy of forecasts on the following variables.

CONTINUITY OF DOMESTIC POLITICAL LEADERSHIP

We derived indicators of stability/change in individual leadership, dominance in legislative bodies, and character of regime from the *CIA Factbook* (www.odci.gov/cia/publications/factbook/index.html) as well as supplementary sources such as Facts on File. We derived measures of political liberalization from Freedom House: Freedom in the World (wysiwyg://11http://www.freedomhouse . . . /research /freeworld/2000/index.htm); the annual *Amnesty International Report*, London; the U.S. State Department's Human Rights Reports released by the Bureau of Democracy, Human Rights, and Labor (http://www. state.gov/www/global /human_rights/hrp_reports_mainhp.html); and the United Nations' *World Economic and Social Survey* (1997). We derived indicators of economic liberalization from James Gwartney, Randall Holcombe, and Robert Lawson, "Economic Freedom and the Environment for Economic Growth," *Journal of Institutional and Theoretical Economics*, 155 (4) (December 1999): 1–21. We derived indicators of corruption from Transparency International, *2000 Corruption Perceptions Index*, (http://transparency.de /documents/cpi/2000/cpi2000.html) and from PRS Group, *International Country Risk Guide* (various issues).

GOVERNMENT POLICY AND ECONOMIC PERFORMANCE

We derived data on GDP growth rates (purchasing power parity [PPP]), unemployment, and inflation from the World Bank, *World Development Indicators 2000* (CD-ROM) as well as the *Economist Intelligence Unit*, various issues. We derived indicators of educational and health expenditures and, for a set of twenty wealthy countries, foreign aid, from the United Nations Development Project, *Human Development Report 2000* (http://www.undp.org/hdr2000), as well as from the World Bank. We derived data on marginal tax rates from Price Waterhouse, *Individual Taxes: A Worldwide Summary* (various issues); OECD, *Economic Surveys* (various issues); and L. Bouten and M. Sumlinski, *Trends in Private Investment in Developing Countries: Statistics for 1970–1995* (Washington, DC: World Bank, 1996). We derived miscellaneous data on the degree to which states have developed the institutional and legal infrastructure for market economies from the IMF, *World Competitiveness Report 2000*, as well as from the *International Country Risk Guide* (various issues). We derived key economic policy indicators—central bank interest rates, central government expenditure as a percentage of GDP (PPP), annual central government operating deficit as a percentage of GDP (PPP), and state-owned enterprises as a percentage of GDP (PPP)—from a combination of the World Bank (WDI's CD-ROM, various editions), International Monetary Fund annual summaries, *International Financial Statistics* (various issues) and the *Economist Intelligence Unit*. We derived data on currency fluctuations against the U.S. dollar and stock market closes from the *Economist Intelligence Unit* and data on membership in trade pacts from the *CIA Factbook*. We derived indicators on CO_2 emissions from the World Bank's *World Development Indicators*.

NATIONAL SECURITY AND DEFENSE POLICY

We derived data on nuclear arms control outcomes, unilateral use of military force, participation in multilateral peacekeeping, defense spending (as a percentage of GDP), and entry into/status quo/exit from international alliances and security regimes from the *CIA Factbook*. We derived data on military conscription from the International Institute for Strategic Studies, *The Military Balance* (various issues). We derived data on human-caused disasters—famines, refugee flows, massacres—from United Nations, *Global Humanitarian Emergencies* (New York: UN/ECOSOC, 1997). We relied on the Minorities at Risk project (developed by Ted Gurr)—which monitors the status and conflicts among politically active communal groups in all countries with populations of at least 500,000—for assessments of whether interethnic bloodshed had waxed or waned in "trouble spots."

Coding Free-flowing Thoughts

The analyses of thought protocols drew on two well-validated methods for quantifying properties of thinking styles that, if the cognitive-process account is right, should differentiate better from worse forecasters. The methods assessed: (a) evaluative differentiation—the number, direction, and balance of the thoughts that people generate in support of, or in opposition to, the claim that a particular possible future is likely; and (b) conceptual integration—the degree to which people make self-conscious efforts to resolve the contradictions in their assessments of the likelihood of possible futures.

The thought coding for evaluative differentiation gauged the degree to which the stream of consciousness flows in one dominant direction. Coders counted the reasons—pro, neutral, or con—that forecasters generated for supposing that the possible future that they had judged most likely would materialize. Intercoder agreement ranged from .74 to .86. We then constructed a ratio for each respondent in which the numerator was the number of pro or con thoughts (whichever was greater) and the denominator was the total number of thoughts. Ratio balance indicators of 1.0 imply that thought is flowing in only one evaluative direction. Ratio balance indicators that approach or fall below 0.5 imply that thought is profoundly conflicted. At 0.5, every thought in support of the view that x will occur can be matched with a thought that either runs in the opposite direction or runs in no discernible direction at all. Scores ranged from 0.39 to 1.0, with a mean of 0.74 and a standard deviation of 0.10. This meant that the average expert generated thoughts favoring his or her most likely scenarios by a ratio of roughly 3:1.

The procedure for assessing conceptual integration drew on the widely used integrative complexity coding system.[1] We singled out three indicators of the extent to which experts reflected on the problems of managing tensions between contradictory arguments:

1. Do the forecasters consider each causal connection piecemeal (low integration) or does the forecaster think "systemically" about the connections among causes (high integration)? Systemic thinking acknowledges the possibility of ripple effects that slowly work through networks of mediating connections or of positive or negative feedback loops that permit reciprocal causation in which A causes B and B, in turn, causes A. Do forecasters try to capture the logic of strategic interdependence between key players in the political game? For example, forecasters could do so by analyzing the incentives for each player to pursue specific strategies given what others are doing, in the process drawing conclusions about whether they are observing games with single or multiple equilibrium "solutions" and about whether the equilibria are of the pure-strategy or mixed-strategy type. Forecasters could also do so by considering the possibility that players are constrained by the logic of two-level games in which moves that players make in one game (say, in international negotiations) must count as moves they make in a completely separate game with different competitors (say, in the domestic struggle for electoral advantage).

2. Do forecasters acknowledge that decision makers have to grapple with trade-offs in which they must weigh core values against each other (high integration)? Do forecasters recognize that perspectives on what seems an acceptable trade-off might evolve and, if so, do they identify factors that might affect the course of that evolution?

[1] For details on integrative complexity coding, see P. Suedfeld, P. E. Tetlock, and S. Streufert, "Conceptual/Integrative Complexity," in *Motivation and Personality: Handbook of Thematic Content Analysis*, ed. C. P. Smith (Cambridge: Cambridge University Press, 1992).

3. Do forecasters acknowledge that sensible people, not just fools or scoundrels, could view the same problem in clashing ways (high integration)? Do they explore—in a reasonably nonjudgmental way—the root cultural or ideological causes of the diverging perceptions of conflicting groups?

As with the ratio balance indicator, we computed an index that took into account the total number of thoughts generated (and thus controlled for long-windedness). This procedure counted the integrative cognitions in the texts and divided by the total number of thoughts. Intercoder agreement ranged from .72 to .89. Integrative cognitions were quite rare, so the integrative-cognition ratios ranged from 0.0 to 0.21, with a mean of 0.11 and a standard deviation of 0.05. Only 16 percent of experts qualified as "integrative" by our scoring rules.

Evaluative differentiation is necessary but not sufficient condition for integration, so it should be no surprise that integration was correlated with evaluative differentiation ($r = 0.62$). Given this correlation, it should also be less than astonishing to learn that the integration and ratio balance indicators (RBI) have the same profile of correlates. To simplify later mediational analyses, we (a) reversed the scoring of ratio balance so that now the higher the score, the more evaluatively differentiated (and less lopsided in favor of one position) the forecaster's arguments (this just involved computing the value of $(1 - RBI)$ for each respondent); (b) standardized both the revised ratio balance $(1 - RBI)$ and integration-cognition indicators and added them to produce a composite indicator that will go by the name of integrative complexity.

II. Bayesian Belief-updating Exercises (Chapter 4)

The goal here shifts from assessing "who got what right" to assessing how experts react to the apparent confirmation or disconfirmation of their forecasts.

Respondents

All participants in belief-updating exercises ($n = 154$) were drawn from subgroups that (a) participated in the forecasting exercises described in the regional forecasting exercises; and (b) qualified as "experts" in one of the eleven topics where belief-updating measures were obtained. These topics included the Soviet Union (1988), South Africa (1988), the Persian Gulf War of 1991, Canada (1992), Kazakhstan (1992), the U.S. presidential election of 1992, and the European Monetary Union (1992), as well as a different format in four other domains, including the European Monetary Union (1998), China, Japan, and India.

Research Procedures and Materials

EX ANTE ASSESSMENTS

Respondents were told: "We want to explore in greater depth the views of subject matter experts on the underlying forces—political, economic, cultural, etc.–that are likely to shape the future of [x]." We then posed variants of the following questions:

a. "How confident are you in the correctness of your assessment of the underlying forces shaping events in [x]?" (Respond to 0 to 1.0 likelihood scale, anchored at 1.0 [completely confident that point of view is correct], at 0.5 [50/50 chance], and at 0 [completely confident that point of view is wrong]).

b. "In many domains we study, experts often feel there are other schools of thought that need to be taken into account. Think of the most influential alternative view to the one you currently hold. How likely do you feel it is that this alternative position might be correct?" Experts were asked to make sure that the likelihood assigned to questions (a) and (b) summed to 1.0. Experts who felt there was more than one major alternative view were asked to assign likelihoods to these alternative views being correct and to make conditional probability judgments (described later) for these views as well.

c. "Assuming your assessment of the underlying forces shaping events in [x] is correct and continues to be correct, please try to rank order the following scenarios in order of likelihood of occurrence (from most to least likely). If you feel that you just cannot distinguish the likelihood of two or more scenarios, feel free to specify a tie." After the initial rank ordering, respondents then assigned a subjective probability to each scenario. The scenarios were designed to be exclusive and exhaustive, so experts were asked to ensure that the subjective probabilities they assigned to each scenario summed to 1.0. Respondents were told that if they felt an important "possible future" had been left off the list of scenarios, they should feel free to insert it (few did so, and the requirement of summation of subjective probabilities to unity remained). Respondents were reminded that the subjective probabilities assigned to the option chosen as most likely should always be equal to, or greater than, the point on the likelihood scaled labeled as maximum uncertainty (in the two-scenario case, 0.5; in the three-scenario case, 0.33; and so forth). The instructions also stressed that "it is perfectly acceptable to assign guessing confidence to each scenario if you feel you have absolutely no basis for concluding that one outcome is any more likely than another."

d. "For sake of argument, assume now that your understanding of the underlying forces shaping events is wrong and that the most influential alternative view in your professional community is correct." Experts then repeated the tasks in case (c).

e. "Taking all the judgments you have just made into consideration, what is your best bottom-line probability estimate for each possible future?"

In the Soviet case, possible futures included a strengthening, a reduction, or no change in community party control; for South Africa, movement toward more repressive white minority control, continuation of the status quo, and major movement toward black majority rule; for Kazakhstan, a decline, no change, or an increase in interethnic violence; for Canada, the formal secession of Quebec, continuation of the constitutional status quo, or a new successful effort (commanding the assent of all ten provinces and the federal government) to work out an intermediate "special status" solution of autonomy within confederation; for the European Monetary Union, abandonment of the goal of a common currency, serious delays (in the order of several years, with several major countries "falling out" to varying degrees) or successful progress toward the goal exactly on or close to schedule; for the Persian Gulf crisis, war (brief or protracted), or no war (which could take the form of negotiated compromise or continued confrontation); for the U.S. presidential election of 1992 (George H. W. Bush vs. Bill Clinton vs. Ross Perot) and of 2000 (George W. Bush vs. Al Gore).

An alternative procedure for eliciting reputational bets depersonalized the process so that experts were no longer pitted against their rivals. For example, in addition to asking experts on Western Europe in 1998 to judge the likelihood of countries adopting the euro in the next three to five years, we asked them to judge the truth or falsity of the hypothesis that "there is a long-term process of economic and political integration at work in Europe" and then make two sets of conditional-likelihood judgments: (a) assume the hypothesis is definitely (100%) true and then judge the likelihood of countries adopting the euro in three to five years; (b) assume the opposite and make the same likelihood judgements.

EX POST ASSESSMENTS

After the specified forecasting interval had elapsed, we recontacted the original forecasters (reinterview rate between 61 percent and 90 percent depending on exercise—average of 71 percent). In six regional forecasting exercises, we first assessed experts' ability to recall their original answers (data used in the six hindsight studies reported in chapter 4) and then diplomatically reminded them of their original forecasts and presented them with a Taking Stock Questionnaire that posed nine questions to which experts responded on nine-point scales, anchored at 1 by "strongly disagree" and 9 by "strongly agree," with 5 anchored as "completely unsure." In the other five exercises, we simply reminded experts of their forecasts ("our records indicate . . . ") and went directly to the Taking Stock Questionnaire, which invited experts to look back on their original forecasts and on what had subsequently happened and to rate their agreement or disagreement with the following propositions:

a. A key premise of my original forecast—the assumption that the same underlying forces at work five years ago would continue to be influential—was not satisfied.

b. Another premise of my original forecast—that all other things would remain equal and there would be no major shocks from outside the system—was not satisfied.

c. The more carefully you look at what actually happened, the more you appreciate how close we came to obtaining a very different outcome (but for some minor accidents of history, events could have taken a very different course).

d. The more carefully you look at the current situation, the more you appreciate how easily one of the alternative outcomes might yet still occur (it is still premature to say which predictions will turn out to have been right).

e. Forecasting exercises can yield valuable insights into the validity of competing points of view.

f. Politics is inherently unpredictable.

g. Forecasting exercises are profoundly misleading (they assign too much credit to the lucky winners and too much blame to the unlucky losers).

h. Looking back now, I'd say my assessment of the underlying forces shaping events at the time of the original forecast was sound.

i. Looking back now, I'd say the conceptual or theoretical principles I used to generate the original forecast were sound.

j. Looking back now, I'd say it was a good idea to overestimate some probabilities and to underestimate other probabilities.

Finally, experts were asked "posterior probability questions" prefaced by these instructions: "It is sometimes tempting to argue what happened had to happen and that if only we were wiser, we would have judged what happened as inevitable. And this may indeed be true for some events. But not for all: improbable events do sometimes occur. For example, the number that turns up on any given spin of the roulette wheel was, before the wheel was spun, a highly improbable outcome. We are interested in how, with the benefit of hindsight, you classify the events you once predicted. Do you think the 'subjective probabilities' you originally assigned to possible futures (conditional on your understanding of the underlying forces at work back then) were essentially correct? If so, just insert the same estimates you assigned in your prior assessment into 'Your Current Point of View' boxes. If not, feel free to change the numbers in any way you now consider appropriate as a result of intervening events (subject only to the constraint that the numbers must still sum up to 1.0)."

Scenario I □	Scenario I □
Scenario II □	Scenario II □
Scenario III □	Scenario III □
Other Scenarios (if applicable) □	Other Scenarios (if applicable) □
Confidence	Confidence
Must Sum to _____	Must Sum to _____
1.0	1.0
Your prior assessment	*Your current point of view*

(Numbers on left were filled in, except for hindsight studies.)

Experts were also asked: "Given the political outcomes that did occur, how much confidence do you *now* have in: (a) the correctness of the understanding (you held at the time of the original forecast) of the underlying forces shaping events; (b) the correctness of the major competing point(s) of view you perceived at the time of the original forecast? Recall that a value of 1.0 indicates absolute confidence in a point of view, 50/50 (0.5) indicates no more confidence than you would have about the outcome of the toss of a fair coin, 0 indicates absolute confidence that a point of view is false."

Confidence in your prior point □ of view or theory	Confidence in your prior point □ of view (or theory)
Major Alternative position □	Major Alternative position □
Other Alternatives □ (if applicable)	Other Alternatives □ (if applicable)
Confidence	Confidence
Must Sum to 1.0 _____	Must Sum to 1.0 _____
YOUR ASSESSMENT AT THE TIME OF ORIGINAL FORECAST	YOUR CURRENT ASSESSMENT OF POINTS OF VIEW

(Numbers on left were filled in except for hindsight studies.)

III. Turnabout Tests to Probe for Double Standards (Chapter 5)

The goal here was to assess the magnitude and pervasiveness of "epistemological hypocrisy" in the evaluation of evidence bearing on the plausibility of "lessons of history" that liberals or conservatives deem either politically correct or incorrect.

Participants

These experts were drawn from both the forecasters and belief updaters in sections I and II as well as the experts who made retrospective judgments of close-call counterfactuals in section IV. The turnabout-test exercise reported in chapter 5 focused on the former Soviet Union, with data collection "tacked on" to the questions posed in the forecasting and close-call counterfactual exercise so that initial data collection occurred in 1992 and the number of respondents grew gradually through 2001 (now standing at eighty-nine, of whom approximately half qualify as specialists in either Russian history or the Soviet Union and the other half of whom qualify as specialists in national security policy or international relations with substantial familiarity with the former Soviet Union but not possessing in-depth area knowledge and relevant language skills).

Research Procedures and Materials

Respondents received these instructions: "Since the collapse of the Soviet Union, scholars have gained greater access to once carefully guarded secrets of the Soviet state. We want to explore your reactions to some hypothetical scenarios in which research teams working in the Kremlin archives make discoveries that shed new light on some old controversies."

At this juncture, participants were randomly assigned to the 2 (evidence-tilt) × 2 (methodological precautions) between-subjects conditions of a factorial experiment conducted in 1992–1993. In the *liberal-tilt* condition, participants were asked "to imagine that a research team has uncovered evidence in Kremlin archives that indicates history could easily have gone down very different paths at three junctures: specifically, there is evidence that Stalinism could have been averted in the late 1920s, that the U.S. missed major opportunities to end the cold war in the mid-1950s in the aftermath of Stalin's death, and that Reagan brought the world precariously close to a serious escalation of American-Soviet hostilities in the early 1980s." In the *conservative-tilt* condition, participants were asked to imagine the discovery of the same types of evidence, but the evidence now indicates that "history could not have gone down a different path at three much-debated junctures in Soviet history: there is evidence that the Soviet Union would have evolved in a 'Stalinist' direction even if Stalin had not been present in the late 1920s, that the U.S. did not miss any opportunities to end the cold war in the mid-1950s, and that there was virtually no risk of a serious escalation of American-Soviet hostilities in the early 1980s." In each case, "the evidence takes the form of notes, letters, and transcripts of meetings of senior Central Committee or Politburo officials that reveal a strong inclination (disinclination) to pursue a different line of policy: more tolerance for private enterprise and political dissent in the late 1920s, dramatic Soviet concessions on Germany and troop strength in Eastern Europe in the mid-1950s, and confrontational Soviet responses to the American defense buildup in the early 1980s." In the *high-research-quality* condition, participants are told that the Kremlinological research team was sensitive to the political implications of their findings and took special precautions to check the authenticity of documents, to consider alternative explanations, and to ensure that all interpretations of text were carefully grounded in historical context. The composition of the team also ensured representation of a broad band of perspectives on the former Soviet Union. In the *unspecified-research-quality* condition, participants received no such assurances, only a summary description of the team's goals, work, and findings.

After reading about each discovery, participants agreed or disagreed with the following assertions on nine-point scales (with the midpoint of 5 always labeled "unsure"):

1. There are compelling reasons for accepting the conclusions that the investigators want to draw from the evidence.
2. There are strong grounds for suspecting that the motives of the research team as a whole may be political rather than scholarly.
3. There are strong grounds for doubting the authenticity of documents "discovered" on this topic (fears of forgeries and plants).
4. There are strong grounds for suspecting that when the documents and relevant texts are placed in full historical context, they will not make the point that it is claimed.

Participants were also encouraged to offer free-response commentaries on both the counterfactuals and the evidence.

IV. CLOSE-CALL COUNTERFACTUAL EXERCISES (CHAPTER 5)

The goal here was to test two principal hypotheses. Experts' openness to historical counterfactuals was expected to be a function of (a) the degree to which the counterfactual reinforced or undercut favorite ideological or theoretical generalizations; and (b) the degree to which experts valued explanatory closure ("foxes" versus "hedgehogs"). Studies 1 and 2 focus on the first hypothesis; Studies 3–5 test both hypotheses (as well as the theoretical-beliefs-by-cognitive-style interaction hypothesis).

Study 1: Perceptions of Close Calls in Soviet History

PARTICIPANTS

This study was first conducted in 1992 and asked forty-seven specialists on the former Soviet Union (a sample that consisted of M.A.- and Ph.D.-level professionals working in government and academia) to judge the plausibility of seven counterfactuals that explored contested choice points in Soviet history.

RESEARCH PROCEDURES

We presented respondents with the following instructions: "Making sense of the past often requires making 'counterfactual' assumptions about what would have happened if history had taken a different turn. But these counterfactual claims—'If x had worked out differently, then y would have occurred'—often provoke sharp controversy within the scholarly community as well as in the broader political world. We want to explore your reactions to some controversial counterfactual claims. For example: If World War I had not occurred or taken the form it did, the Bolshevik Revolution never would have succeeded.

"Offer your assessment of how realistic the underlined antecedent condition is. Do we have to rewrite a great deal of history to suppose that the underlined antecedent could have become true, or do we need to alter only one or two minor details or coincidences?

1   2   3   4   5   6   7   8   9

Necessary to make only minor revisions	Completely unsure	Necessary to alter a great deal of history

Assuming, for sake of argument, that the antecedent condition were true, how likely do you believe it is that the hypothesized consequence would have occurred?

1   2   3   4   5   6   7   8   9

Virtually impossible	About a 50/50 choice	Virtual certainty

Assuming, for sake of argument, that the hypothesized consequence occurred, how significant would the long-term impact on history have been? (nine-point scale from 1 [very insignificant] to 5 [moderately significant] to 9 [extremely significant])."

Respondents in Study 1 then made the same three judgments for each six remaining Soviet counterfactuals:

If Lenin had lived ten years longer, the Bolshevik regime would have evolved in a much less repressive direction than it did.

If Stalin had been deposed as head of the Communist Party in the late 1920s, the Soviet Union would have moved to a kinder, gentler form of Communism fifty years earlier than it did.

If Malenkov had prevailed in the post-Stalin succession struggle, the cold war would have thawed in the 1950s.

If Gorbachev had suddenly died at the same time as Chernenko, the Communist Party would have moved in a much more conservative direction than it did.

If Reagan had not adopted so tough a posture toward the Soviet Union in the early 1980s, the Soviets would not have been as accommodating as they were in the late 1980s.

If Gorbachev had timed and planned his reforms more shrewdly, he could have presided over a reformed and democratic federation of the former Soviet republics.

Study 2: Perceptions of Contingency in South African History

PARTICIPANTS

This study was conducted in 1995 and drew on the expertise of twenty-four specialists who had considerable knowledge of South African politics. As in the Soviet case, these respondents judged the plausibility of the antecedent in each counterfactual, the plausibility of each antecedent-consequent linkage, and the plausibility of supposing the effects will be long lasting.

RESEARCH PROCEDURES AND MATERIALS

The counterfactuals included the following:

1. *If it were not for the leadership of F. W. de Klerk,* the South African government would have persisted with white-minority rule.
2. *If it were not for Nelson Mandela's leadership,* the negotiations between the minority white government and the African National Congress never would have been successful.
3. *If the United States had not imposed economic sanctions,* the South African government would have persisted with white-minority rule.
4. *If there had not been overwhelming pressures to reach accommodation—the rapid growth of the black population and the requirements of labor markets—*the South African government would have persisted with white-minority rule.

5. *If Soviet-style Communism had not collapsed*, the National Party would have been much more reluctant to relinquish white-minority control.

Ideology scale. Nine-point scale, anchored at 1 by strongly agree, at 9 by strongly disagree, and at 5 by unsure:

Unregulated capitalism creates unacceptably large inequalities of income.

There is a viable third path between capitalism and Communism.

A good rule of thumb is: the more government interference in the economy, the poorer the people will be.

The most effective way to preserve peace is to maintain a strong defense posture against would-be aggressors.

I sympathize more strongly with liberal than with conservative causes in contemporary politics.

Studies 3, 4, and 5: Rewriting Twentieth-century History

PARTICIPANTS

Participants were drawn from distinct, but overlapping, populations of scholars who specialized in diplomatic and military history, security studies, and international relations. The eighty-seven participants in Studies 3, 4, and 5—which focused on the origins of World War I, the outcomes of World Wars I and II, and the resolution of various cold war conflicts—were randomly sampled from Divisions 18 (International Conflict) and 19 (International Security and Arms Control) of the American Political Science Association (APSA) and from the Society of Diplomatic and Military Historians. In addition to the measures described next, respondents completed a nine-item version of the need-for-closure scale (items 1–9 in section I).

RESEARCH PROCEDURES AND MATERIALS

Covering-law beliefs. The most relevant statements for Study 3 explored beliefs about causal forces often hypothesized to increase the likelihood of war in general and of World War I in particular:

a. International systems with several great powers are no more likely to erupt into war than are those with only two great powers (reverse scored).

b. It is a myth that multiethnic empires are inherently unstable and a threat to world peace (reverse scored).

c. Changes in the international balance of power—induced by differential growth rates in population and economic power—have historically been the greatest threat to world peace.

    d. War is most likely when the state of military technology leads decision makers to believe that the side that strikes first will possess a decisive advantage.

The neorealist-balancing items—especially relevant to the counterfactuals assessed in Study 4—were as follows:

    a. For all the talk about a new world order, world politics is still essentially anarchic—the strong do what they will and the weak accept what they must.

    b. Whenever one state starts to become too powerful, other states find a way of combining forces and preventing it from dominating them.

    c. The security policies of states are often driven by morality, not just by rational calculations of the impact of those policies on the balance of power.

    d. It is naïve to suppose that the failure of would-be conquerors such as Philip II, Napoleon, and Hitler to achieve lasting dominance in Europe was predetermined by balance-of-power politics—it might just have been an accident.

The robustness-of-nuclear-deterrence items—especially relevant to Study 5—were as follows:

    a. For all the talk about the risk of nuclear accidents, the USA and USSR never really came close to nuclear war.

    b. Nuclear weapons played a key role in moderating the behavior of both the American and Soviet governments during the cold war.

    c. It is unrealistic to assume that leaders working under great stress will always act with great restraint in crises that raise the risk of the use of nuclear weapons.

Beliefs about close-call counterfactuals. These measures assessed endorsements of the covering laws on nine-point agree-disagree scales. The close-call counterfactuals for Study 3 cast doubt on the inevitability of the First World War:

    a. If the carriage driver of Archduke Ferdinand had not taken a fateful wrong turn that gave the Serbian assassins a remarkable second chance to carry out their previously botched assassination plot, war would not have broken out in August 1914.

    b. If Bethmann-Hollweg had pressured Austro-Hungary more strongly not to declare war on Serbia, war would have been averted.

    c. If Britain had clearly communicated to Germany its support of France in case of war, Germany would have exercised much more restraint on Austro-Hungary, thereby defusing the crisis.

d. If Germany had accepted Britain's suggestion in late July of a great power conference to deal with the crisis and had pressured Austro-Hungary to do so too, war would been averted.

The close-call scenarios for Study 4 undid the outcomes of either World Wars I or II:

a. If Germany had proceeded with its invasion of France on August 2, 1914, but had respected the Belgian neutrality, Britain would not have entered the war and France would have quickly fallen.
b. If the German High Command had implemented the Schlieffen Plan more aggressively in August 1914, the miracle of the Marne would have been impossible and Paris would have fallen.
c. If Germany had avoided antagonizing the United States by meddling in Mexico and by initiating unrestricted submarine warfare, the United States would not have entered World War I and Germany would have prevailed against the French and British in its spring offensive of 1918.
d. If Hitler had not invaded the Soviet Union and concentrated German resources on defeating the British, Germany would have defeated Britain.
e. If Hitler had more consistently focused on taking Moscow in the summer of 1941, he could have knocked the Soviet Union out of the war.
f. If Hitler had not declared war on the United States on December 11, 1941, the British and the Soviets could never have defeated Nazi Germany.

The close-call counterfactuals for Study 5 explored the feasibility of turning the cold war into thermonuclear war:

a. If Stalin had lived several years longer (surviving his stroke but in an irrational state of mind that encouraged high-risk adventures), World War III could easily have broken out in the mid-1950s.
b. If bad weather had delayed the discovery by U-2 reconnaissance planes of Soviet missiles in Cuba until the missiles were operational, the Soviets would have refused American demands to dismantle and withdraw the weapons.
c. If the Soviets had refused to withdraw their missiles, the U.S. would have launched air strikes against the Soviet bases.
d. If the U.S. had launched such air strikes, the Soviet commanders in Cuba would have launched at least some missiles at the eastern seaboard of the United States.
e. If the Soviets had fired Cuban-based nuclear missiles at American cities, retaliatory nuclear strikes would have been launched at Soviet cities.

f. If Soviet hard-liners had taken charge of the Communist Party in the mid-1980s, the cold war—far from ending peacefully and quickly—coming to an early and peaceful end—would have intensified.

Study 6: Unmaking the West

PARTICIPANTS

The sixty-three participants were either randomly drawn from the membership roster of the World History Association or recruited from two conferences at the Mershon Center of the Ohio State University on the rise of the West. Respondents were contacted by either regular mail or by e-mail, and promised both anonymity and detailed feedback on the purposes of the study. The response rate was 31 percent. In addition to the measures described next, participants completed a nine-item abbreviated version of the need-for-closure scale in section I (items 1–9).

RESEARCH PROCEDURES AND MATERIALS

Covering-law Beliefs. The most relevant beliefs revolved around the theme of the survival-of-the-fittest civilizations:

a. History is, in the long run, an efficient process of winnowing out maladaptive forms of social organization.
b. Western societies and institutions, with their greater emphasis on the rule of law, property rights, free markets, and the practical applications of science, were better adapted to prevail in long-term competition with other civilizations.

Beliefs about Close-call Counterfactuals. The close-call counterfactuals explored the feasibility of unmaking the West via hypothetical interventions that either enfeebled European civilization or empowered rival civilizations:

a. If China had had, at key junctures, emperors more sympathetic to economic and technological development, it could have emerged as the world's first superpower.
b. If the Mongols had continued their advance into central and western Europe and not been distracted by the death of Genghis Khan, later European development would have been impossible.
c. If Islamic armies had made a serious attempt to conquer France and Italy in the eighth century, later European development could have been radically sidetracked.
d. If the Black Death had been even more lethal, killing, say, 70 percent of the population, Europe could not have arisen as the dominant region in the second half of the millennium.

For each counterfactual, experts judged the following on nine-point scales:

a. How plausible was the antecedent condition of the argument? (Do we have to "rewrite" a little or a lot of history?)
b. Assuming the plausibility of the antecedent, how likely was the hypothesized consequence?
c. Assuming the plausibility of the hypothesized consequence, what would the long-term ramifications have been?

V. UNPACKING OF POSSIBLE FUTURES EXPERIMENTS (CHAPTER 7)

The goal here was to explore the impact of encouraging divergent scenario thinking about possible futures on both correspondence indicators of good judgment (e.g., forecasting accuracy) and coherence indicators (e.g., susceptibility to sub-additivity effects).

Participants and Context

These experiments were conducted roughly five weeks after the initial (baseline) subjective probability estimates were obtained in the regional forecasting exercises (section I) for Canada and for Japan (long enough for memories of their original answers to fade). Participants in the Canadian experiment included both experts on Canadian politics ($n = 28$) and dilettantes ($n = 33$). Participants in the Japanese experiment included both experts ($n = 16$) and dilettantes ($n = 19$).

As part of the rationale for recontacting them, we told participants there was growing interest in using "scenario methods for preparing for possible futures" and that we were soliciting experts' reactions to a series of "stories about possible futures" of either Canada or Japan.

Research Procedures and Materials

UNPACKING POSSIBLE FUTURES OF CANADA

The Canadian experiment took the form of a 2 (experts or dilettantes) × 4 (timing of four measures) factorial that required participants to make four sets of judgments: the pre-scenario-exercise assessment of subjective probabilities, a second wave of assessments after doing the status quo scenario exercises, a third wave of assessments after doing the disintegration-of-Canada scenario exercises, and a fourth wave of reflective equilibrium assessments in which experts reconcile possible conflicts among the probabilities they assigned in earlier exercises and ensure those probabilities sum to 1.0.

The stories fell into two broad categories: (a) possible futures that featured either a continuation of the status quo (federal and provincial governments agree to continue disagreeing over constitutional prerogatives) or a strengthening of Canadian unity (in which some agreements are reached); (b) possible futures in which Canada unravels, a secessionist referendum in Quebec succeeds, and controversy centers on terms of the divorce.

The continuation-of-Canadian-confederation scenarios solicited likelihood judgments of four possible futures. In the first, the combination of an economic downturn and skillful handling of federal-provincial relations by the prime minister leads (risk-averse) voters in Quebec to hand defeat to the Parti Québecois (PQ) in the next election. In a second scenario, the same antecedents are at work and the Parti Québecois wins the next election but loses the secessionist referendum because voters are reluctant to take big risks in hard times. In a third scenario, the combination of an economic upturn and skillful handling of federal-provincial relations by the prime minister leads to the defeat of the Parti Québecois in the next election. In a fourth scenario, the same antecedents are at work and the Parti Québecois wins the next election but loses the secessionist referendum because voters are reluctant to gamble with their new prosperity. Experts were also invited to consider all other possible futures consistent with either a continuation or strengthening of Canadian unity. Experts then (a) assigned subjective likelihoods to each of the four possible futures as well as to the fifth residual category; and (b) rated the "ease of imagining" each possible future.

The disintegration scenario presented stories about futures in which Quebec secedes from Canada. These stories again split into four versions. In one, an economic downturn plus a confrontational prime minister who provokes separatist sentiment (with remarks about francophone "linguistic fascism") lead the PQ to victory in both the next election and in the secessionist referendum (the poor economy increases voters' willingness to take risks), and the resulting divorce is surprisingly amicable. In the second, the same antecedents are in place, and the result remains the same (PQ victory in next election and secessionist referendum), but the divorce is acrimonious. In the third and fourth scenarios, all is the same except now there is an economic upturn, Quebec still secedes (the strong economy gives voters confidence that they can "go it alone"), and the divorce is either easy or hard. Again, experts (a) judged the subjective likelihood of the four sets of possible futures as well as that of a residual category containing all other secessionist possibilities; and (b) rated the ease of imagining each story line.

UNPACKING POSSIBLE FUTURES OF JAPAN

The Japanese experiment took the form of a 2 (experts or dilettantes) × 5 (timing of repeated measures) design. The five-level factor included a baseline assessment of the subjective probabilities of three sets of possible futures (status quo and change for either better or worse), assessment of the same possible futures after unpacking each of the three sets, and finally a reflective equilibrium exercise in which participants confronted and tried to resolve logical contradictions created by the unpacking exercises.

In the Japanese scenario study, the perpetuation-of-status-quo set of possibilities included these two subclasses: (a) the ruling Liberal Democratic Party (LDP) maintains its electoral lock on power and resists the economic reforms and restructuring necessary to jumpstart growth but makes sufficient accommodations to reality to prevent serious deterioration and a slide into a deep, prolonged recession; (b) the LDP fractures and briefly loses power to a reformist coalition that begins to implement some politically painful economic reform, loses popularity, falls from power, and the LDP regains power and returns to policies that maintain the status quo. The improvement-on-status-quo set included these two subsets: (a) a reformist faction in the LDP gains power and implements politically painful economic reform; the government becomes unpopular during the transitional period but succeeds in laying down a new legal-financial infrastructure that will be conducive to growth in the future; (b) the LDP disintegrates into factions and a reformist coalition of parties takes power and implements the policies necessary to create a legal-financial infrastructure that will support more robust future growth. The deterioration-relative-to-status-quo set included these two subsets: (a) special interests inside the LDP patronage network succeed not only in blocking reform but also in thwarting essential accommodations to financial reality (e.g., writing off bad bank loans) and, as a result, Japan suffers a protracted slump; (b) the LDP loses power, but the weak coalition and minority successor governments lack the political support and economic wisdom to implement necessary reform and, as a result, Japan enters a protracted slump. As in the Canadian study, we allowed for residual categories into which participants could dump the likelihood of all other possible pathways to the specified superordinate classes of outcomes.

VI. UNPACKING-OF-HISTORICAL-COUNTERFACTUALS EXPERIMENTS (CHAPTER 7)

The goal here was to assess the impact of divergent scenario-based thinking about possible pasts on the hindsight bias (Studies 1 and 2) and on judgments of how quickly historical outcomes became (inevitability curves) or alternative outcomes became impossible (impossibility curves) (Studies 3 and 4).

The Cognitive Style (Hedgehog-Fox) Measure in this Set of Studies

Respondents gave answers on a nine-point agree-disagree scale to the following nine items: (a) "I think that having clear rules and order at work is essential for success"; (b) "Even after I have made up my mind about something, I am always eager to consider a different opinion"; (c) "I dislike questions that can be answered in many different ways"; (d) "I usually make important decisions quickly and confidently"; (e) "When considering most conflict situations, I can usually see how both sides could be right"; (f) "I prefer interacting with people whose opinions are very different from my own"; (g) "When trying to solve a problem I often see so many possible options that it is confusing"; (h) "Scholars are usually at greater risk of exaggerating the complexity of political processes than they are of underestimating the complexity of those processes"; (i) "Isaiah Berlin [1997] classified intellectuals as hedgehogs or foxes. A hedgehog knows one big thing and tries to integrate the diversity of the world into comprehensive and parsimonious vision whereas a fox knows many small things and tries to improvise explanations on a case-by-case basis. I would place myself toward the hedgehog or fox style of thinking about politics."

Participants in Studies 1 and 2

Participants were drawn from the regional forecasting exercises for China and North Korea reported in chapter 7. The studies were conducted in 1997–1998 in the context of the recontact interviews for the belief-updating exercises described in section II. Sample sizes were twenty-one and fourteen, respectively.

Research Procedures

We noted in Chapter 4 that in six of the eleven belief-updating exercises, we asked participants to recall their earlier predictions before we reminded them of what those predictions actually were and before we asked them to respond to the Taking Stock Questionnaire (results described in chapter 4). In two of these six exercises, we informed participants—after they had tried to recall their predictions but before we reminded them of the truth—of the following: "Looking back on what has happened in China/North Korea over the last five years, we would value your expert opinion on how close we came to experiencing alternative outcomes— alternative outcomes that are either significantly better politically or economically than the current situation or significantly worse. What specific scenarios come to mind?" Given the timing and context of the exercise, it was important to create a social atmosphere in which (a) experts felt they would not lose face if they revised their recollections so soon after just expressing them; (b) experts did not, however, feel pressured to change their recollections in a direction that would confirm the experimental hypothesis that counterfactual scenario exercises help to check hindsight bias. Accordingly, we also offered the following additional information: "There is a lot of controversy surrounding the usefulness of scenario exercises of this sort. Some say such exercises give us a keener appreciation of how the world looked before we knew how things would work out. Others say such exercises give us a keener appreciation for why things had to work out as they did. Still others say such exercises rarely cause anyone to change his or her mind. We are doing this research, in part, to find out which of these ideas is right."

Participants then sketched counterfactual alternatives to reality for roughly twenty minutes (responses that we could code for number of distinct scenarios, valence of scenarios [better or worse worlds], and amount of detail within and across scenarios). After this exercise, we then asked participants: "In light of the exercise you just did, do you want to modify any of your earlier estimates of the subjective probabilities that you assigned five years ago?"

Participants in Studies 3 and 4

Respondents were initially sampled from faculty at two midwestern universities (pilot groups), but for the Cuban missile crisis study, they were subsequently randomly selected from the membership lists of Divisions 18 and 19 (International Conflict; International Security and Arms Control) of the APSA and the Society for Historians of American Foreign Relations, and for the Rise of the West study, they were randomly sampled from the membership roster of the World History Association.

Respondents in the missile crisis study completed (a) a nine-item version of the need-for-closure scale (items 1–9 in section I); (b) a measure of faith in the robustness of nuclear deterrence (same as used in Study 5 in section IV). Respondents in the Unmaking the West study completed the same nine-item need-for-closure scale and the survival-of-the-fittest civilizations scale used in Study 6 in section IV.

Research Procedures for the Cuban Missile Crisis Experiment (Study 3)

The 64 subjects were randomly assigned to: (a) a no-unpacking control group ($n = 30$), which responded to the "perceptions-of-inevitability" scale for judging the actual peaceful outcome of the crisis and to the "perceptions-of-impossibility" scale for judging alternative more violent endings of the crisis; (b) an unpacking-of-alternative-violent-outcomes conditions ($n = 34$) in which, before judging anything, participants unpacked the set of alternatives into those in which violence is localized or spreads outside the Caribbean, then unpacked those subsets into those in which violence claims less or more than 100 casualties, and then finally unpacked the subsets with 100 or more casualties into those in which only conventional weaponry is used and those in which one or both superpowers employed nuclear weapons. Respondents then judged the "imaginability" of each of the six sets of scenarios (nine-point scale: easy–difficult) and generated both inevitability curves for peace and impossibility curves for war. Order of elicitation of inevitability and impossibility judgments was always counterbalanced.

BACKGROUND INFORMATION

To assist recall, we provided a chronology of key events, which began on October 16, 8:45 A.M., when Bundy broke the news to JFK that Soviet surface-to-surface missiles were being deployed in Cuba and ended on October 29 when Stevenson and McCloy meet with Kuznetsov in New York to work out details of the settlement that Kennedy and Khrushchev had already reached.

RETROSPECTIVE PERCEPTIONS OF INEVITABILITY AND IMPOSSIBILITY

The order of administration of these questions was always counterbalanced. The instructions for the inevitability curve exercise were as follows: "Let's define the crisis as having ended at the moment on October 29 when Kennedy communicated to the Soviet leadership his agreement with Khrushchev's radio message of October 28. At that juncture, we could say that, barring unforeseen problems of implementing the agreement, some form of peaceful resolution was a certainty—a subjective probability of 1.0. Going backward in time, day by day, from October 29 to October 16, trace on the graph your perceptions of how the likelihood of a peaceful resolution rose or fell during the fourteen critical days of the crisis. If you think the U.S. and USSR never came close to a military clash between October 16 and 29, then express that view by assigning consistently high probabilities to a peaceful resolution across all dates (indeed, as high as certainty, 1.0, if you wish). If you think the superpowers were very close to a military conflict throughout the crisis, then express that view by assigning consistently low probabilities to a peaceful resolution across all dates. Finally, if you think the likelihood of a peaceful resolution waxed and waned from episode to episode within the crisis, then express that view by assigning probabilities that rise or fall in accord with your intuitions about how close the U.S. and USSR came to a military clash at various junctures in the crisis. To start, we have set the subjective probability of peace at 1.0 (certainty) for October 29, marking the end of the crisis."

The instructions for filling in impossibility curves were as follows: "Let's think of the Cuban missile crisis from a different perspective. Rather than focusing on the outcome that did occur (some form of peaceful resolution of the dispute), let's focus on the set of all possible more violent endings of the crisis. So, let's define the crisis as having ended at the moment on October 29 when Kennedy communicated to the Soviet leadership his agreement with Khrushchev's radio message of October 28 (offering to withdraw missiles in return for a public pledge not to invade Cuba and a private commitment to withdraw U.S. missiles from Turkey). At that juncture, we could say that, barring unforeseen problems with implementing the agreement, the likelihood of alternative more violent endings of the crisis had fallen to zero. The alternative outcomes had, in effect, become impossible. Now, going backward in time, day by day, from October 29 to October 16, trace on the graph your perceptions of how the likelihood of all alternative, more violent, endings of the crisis rose or fell during the fourteen critical days of the crisis. If you believe that the USA and USSR never came close to a military clash at any point between October 16 and 29, then feel free to express that view by assigning consistently low probabilities to a violent ending across all dates (indeed, as low as impossibility or zero, if you wish). If you think the superpowers were very close to a military clash throughout the crisis, then feel free to express that view by assigning consistently high probabilities to a violent ending across all dates. Finally, if you think the likelihood of a peaceful resolution waxed and waned from episode to episode within the crisis, then you should feel free to express that view by assigning probabilities that rise or fall in accord with your intuitions. To start, we have set the subjective probability of war at 0.0 (impossible) for October 29, marking the end of the crisis."

Research Procedures for the Rise of the West Experiment (Study 4)

This study included two conditions: (a) a no-unpacking control condition ($n = 27$) in which experts generated inevitability curves for some form of Western geopolitical domination and impossibility curves for the set of all possible alternatives to Western geopolitical domination (order counterbalanced); (b) an intensive unpacking condition ($n = 36$) in which experts were first asked to unpack the set of all possible alternatives to Western geopolitical domination into progressively more detailed subsets, beginning with classes of possible worlds in which either no region of the world achieved global hegemony (either because of a weaker Europe or stiffer resistance from outside Europe, and moving on to classes of possible worlds in which a non-Western civilization itself achieved global hegemony—perhaps China, Islam, or the Mongols, or a less familiar alternative), then to rate the "imaginability" of each subset of scenarios, and then to complete the inevitability and impossibility curves that began at A.D. 1000 and moved by fifty-year increments up to A.D. 1850 (where the subjective probability of Western dominance was fixed at 1.0 and that of possible alternatives at 0.0). Order of inevitability and impossibility judgments was, again, always counterbalanced.

Technical Appendix

Phillip Rescober and Philip E. Tetlock

WE DIVIDE our analysis into two sections: one organized around correspondence indicators of good judgment that focus on the degree to which probability judgments mirror regularities in the external world and the other section organized around logical-coherence indicators that focus on the degree to which probability judgments obey the formal axioms of probability theory.

PART A: CORRESPONDENCE INDICATORS OF GOOD JUDGMENT

Probability Scoring

Our primary correspondence indicator is the probability score (PS). We shall discover that it is useful (1) to decompose this measure of the goodness of fit of subjective probabilities to objective reality into a variety of indicators (variability, calibration, and discrimination); (2) to modify this measure to take into account a variety of objections (we shall examine five types of scoring adjustments designed to address five categories of objections).

The simplest equation is

$$(p_i - x_i)^2$$

where x_i (a dummy variable) equals 1 if outcome i occurs or 0 otherwise, and p_i is the forecaster's prediction (or forecast) for a given outcome i.

Forecasters receive the ideal score, zero, when they always assign predictions of 0 to outcomes that do not occur (in this case, $(p_i - x_i)^2 = (0 - 0)^2 = 0$) and always assign predictions of 1 to outcomes that do occur (in this case, $(p_i - x_i)^2 = (1 - 1)^2 = 0$).

When the forecaster makes many (M) dichotomous predictions, the probability score is

$$PS = \frac{\sum_{i=1}^{M} (p_i - x_i)^2}{M}, \text{ subject to the constraint that } \sum_{i=1}^{M} p_i = 1$$

Example:

We can readily adapt this procedure for forecasting problems with multiple outcomes. Assume a forecaster assigns probabilities of $p_A = 0.1$, $p_B = 0.4$, $p_C = 0.5$ to three mutually exclusive and exhaustive possibilities: the future value of an outcome must be (a) "better than," (b) "the same as," or (c) "worse than" its current value. Suppose (c) occurs. The probability score is

$$PS = \frac{\sum_{i=1}^{M}(p_i - x_i)^2}{M} = \frac{(p_A - x_A)^2 + (p_B - x_B)^2 + (p_C - x_C)^2}{3}$$

$$= \frac{(0.1 - 0)^2 + (0.4 - 0)^2 + (0.5 - 1)^2}{3} = 0.14$$

Probability Score Decomposition

Probability scoring has a certain elegant simplicity. It does not, however, tell us all we need to know to answer key questions about judgmental performance. It is necessary to take additional steps: (a) to decompose the variance in probability scores to obtain more refined estimates of how good a job people are doing at assigning realistic probabilities to possible futures (measures of environmental variability and forecaster calibration and discrimination); (b) to adjust probability scores to address a host of potentially valid objections (introducing difficulty, value, controversy, fuzzy-set, and probability-weighting adjustments).

A forecaster could get a high or low PS as a result of many distinguishable influences. Our analytical starting point is the Murphy decomposition, which breaks probability scores into three components: *variability index (VI)*, *calibration index (CI)*, and *discrimination index (DI)*.[1] The decomposition of the equation in the two-outcome case is

$$PS = \frac{\sum_{i=1}^{N}(p_i - x_i)^2}{N} = b(1-b) + \frac{1}{N}C_T - \frac{1}{N}D_T$$

$$= b(1-b) + \frac{1}{N}\sum_{t=1}^{T}n_t(p_t - b_t)^2 - \frac{1}{N}\sum_{t=1}^{T}n_t(b_t - b)^2$$

$$\underbrace{\hspace{2cm}}_{VI} \underbrace{\hspace{4cm}}_{CI} \underbrace{\hspace{3cm}}_{DI}$$

where *b* is the base rate for a particular outcome (proportion of times an outcome occurs over all events)

[1] A. H. Murphy and R. L. Winkler, "Probability Forecasts: A Survey of National Weather Service Forecasters," *Bulletin of the American Meteorological Society* 55 (1974): 1449–53; Murphy, "Probability Forecasts."

b_t is the base rate for a particular prediction category. For example, if a forecaster predicted that ten events would occur with probability X, and the events occurred six of those ten times, then $b_x = 0.6$.
N is the total number of events
n_t is the number of predictions in the tth category
T is the number of categories of predictions
p_t is the prediction of the tth category

Components of Probability Scores: Variability, Calibration, and Discrimination

Figure A.1 lays out the interpretive challenges raised by each of the three components.

Variability is a measure of environmental (un)predictability. The range of values for the variability index is $0 \leq VI \leq 0.25$.

> CASE 1   *Easiest-to-predict environments:* If the base rate is either 0 or 1, there is no variability ($VI = 0$) and a simple always-predict-the-base-rate strategy is perfectly accurate and receives a perfect probability score, zero.
>
> CASE 2   *Increasingly-difficult-to-predict environments:* As the base rate approaches 0.5, it becomes harder to predict which outcome will occur. Suppose the base rate is 0.8. This situation is easier to predict than 0.5 because, in the former case, one outcome occurs four times more often than the other (.8/.2). An always-predict-the-base-rate strategy yields a better expected probability score in the 0.8 environment (0.16) than in the 0.5 environment (0.25). More generally, the probability score will be inflated by increasingly large VI values as the base rate approaches 0.5 (and VI approaches its maximum value of .25).

Calibration is the weighted average of the mean-square differences between the proportion of predictions correct in each probability category and the probability value of that category. The range of values for the calibration index is $0 \leq CI \leq 1$, with zero corresponding to perfect calibration and representing the best possible score.

Consider five ideal-type cases for the two-outcome model:

> CASE 1   A perfect calibration score of zero is achieved if no events assigned 0.0 occur, 10 percent of events assigned 0.1 occur, and so forth. One could achieve this score by possessing a keen awareness of the limits of one's knowledge (from experience, one has learned that when one feels x degree of confidence, things happen x percent of the time). Or one could achieve this score by adopting a cautious

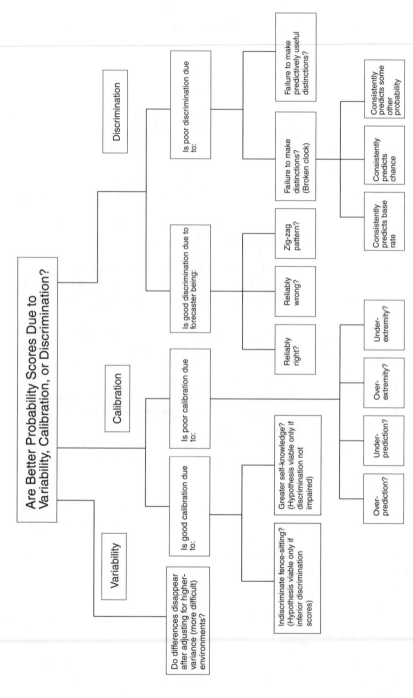

Figure A.1. Possible interpretations of different components of probability scores.

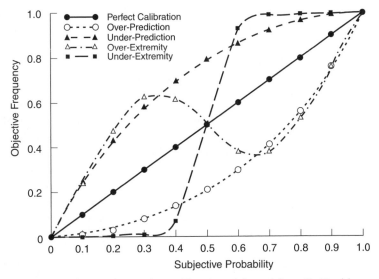

Figure A.2. Four forms of imperfect calibration. Adapted from D. Koehler et al, The calibration of expert judgment. In T. Gilovich et al. (eds), *Heuristics and biases*. Cambridge, 2002.

fence-sitting approach to assigning probabilities that never strays from the base-rate probability of events.

There are even more ways to be poorly calibrated. Cases 2 through 5 present four ways (each captured in figure A.2) of obtaining the same (rather poor) calibration score of 0.48.

CASE 2 Overprediction is across the entire probability scale (subjective likelihood always exceeds objective likelihood).

CASE 3 Underprediction is across the entire probability scale (estimated likelihood always less than objective likelihood).

CASE 4 The overextremity pattern of underprediction for subjective probabilities below 0.5, and overprediction for subjective probabilities greater than 0.5.

CASE 5 The underextremity pattern of overprediction for subjective probabilities below 0.5, and underprediction for subjective probabilities greater than 0.5.

Discrimination indexes the judge's ability to sort the predictions into probability categories (zero, 0.1, etc.) such that the proportions of correct answers across categories are maximally different from each other. Higher scores indicate greater ability to use the probability scale to distinguish occurrences from nonoccurrences than could have been achieved by always predicting the base rate of occurrence for the target event (*b*).

The range of possible values for the discrimination index is $0 \leq DI \leq b(1 - b)$, with $b(1 - b)$ corresponding to perfect discrimination and representing the best possible score. Note that the inequality statement can be rewritten as $0 \leq DI \leq VI$, where VI denotes the variability index.

Consider five ideal-type cases for the two-outcome model:

CASE 1   A perfect discrimination score can be achieved by being phenomenally prescient and assigning zero probability to all events that do not happen and a probability of 1.0 to all events that do happen.

CASE 2   As a squared indicator, the discrimination index is insensitive to the direction of differences between the frequency with which events in a probability category occur and the base-rate frequency of those events. Thus, it is possible to achieve a perfect discrimination score by being phenomenally inaccurate and assigning a probability of 1.0 to nonoccurrences and a probability of zero to occurrences.

CASE 3   A perfect discrimination score can be achieved when the probability of the predicted outcome materializing randomly alternates between 0 and 1 as one moves across the subjective probability scale.

The worst discrimination score, zero, can be achieved when the probability of the predicted outcome materializing within each subjective probability category always equals the overall base rate. This happens when either:

CASE 4   The forecaster fails to make any discriminations and always predicts the same probability—whether it is the base rate, the chance prediction, or some other value—for all possible outcomes. (Thus, $T = 1$ and $b_t = b$).

CASE 5   The forecaster assigns different subjective probabilities, but these distinctions have no predictive value: the base rate within each probability category equals the overall base rate. (Thus, $T > 1$ and $b_t = b$ for all $t = 1, 2, \ldots T$).

Normalized Discrimination Index (NDI)

Discrimination scores can fall between total ignorance (zero) and omniscience (equal to VI). The NDI tells us how well forecasters discriminate occurrences from nonoccurrences relative to the benchmark of omniscience:

$$NDI = \frac{DI}{VI}$$

Calibration versus Discrimination: Distinguishing the Self-aware from Fence-sitters

It is possible to have good calibration but poor discrimination scores if one is a fence-sitter who assigns only a narrow range of probability values (say, 0.4 to 0.6) and the target events occur between 0.4 and 0.6 of the time. And it is possible to have stellar discrimination and terrible calibration scores if one has a flair for making consistently and dramatically wrong predictions. Forecasters with good calibration and discrimination scores give us the best of both worlds: a realistic sense of what they can deliver and the ability to differentiate lower from higher probability events.

Overconfidence versus Regression toward the Mean: Distinguishing Facts from Artifacts

Demonstrating overconfidence requires more than demonstrating that, when experts assign 100 percent probability to x, x occurs less than 100 percent of the time, or that when experts assign zero probability to x, x occasionally occurs. We should expect such effects from regression toward the mean. For example, suppose that "overconfidence" is merely a by-product of measurement error in both subjective probabilities and objective frequencies. The best prediction of the objective frequency ($\hat{y}$) for events at a given level of subjective probability (x_i) would be

$$\hat{y} = \frac{s_y}{s_x} r_{xy} (x_i - \overline{X}) + \overline{Y}$$

where $\overline{X}$ is the average subjective probability
s_x and s_y represent standard deviations of subjective probabilities and objective frequencies
r_{xy} is the correlation of subjective probabilities and objective events
$\overline{Y}$ = average objective frequency

The substantive question is whether forecasters are so overconfident—across probability values—that it becomes implausible to dismiss the phenomenon as a "mere regression artifact." We have a compelling argument against this claim if we can show that the average probability judgment is significantly different from the average objective frequency (or the base rate) for well-specified classes of events. A significant difference is evidence of systematic forecasting error that is logically independent of regression.

$$t = \frac{(\bar{p} - b)}{\sqrt{\dfrac{s_p^2}{N} + \dfrac{s_b^2}{N}}}$$

where $\bar{p}$ is the average prediction
b is the base rate
N is the number of predictions made
s_p^2 is the unbiased sample variance in the predictions made; it is calculated by

$$S_p^2 = \frac{\sum_{event\ j} (p_{ij} - \bar{p})^2}{N_i - 1}$$

s_b^2 is the variance in the base rate; it is calculated by

$$s_b^2 = b(1 - b)$$

Another approach for escaping the regression-toward-the-mean criticism is to demonstrate that the average forecasting error in one group differs from that of another group. To do this, one compares the difference of differences between subjective probability and objective frequency.

$$t = \frac{(\bar{p}_1 - b_1) - ((\bar{p}_2 - b_2)}{\sqrt{\dfrac{s_1^2}{N_1} + \dfrac{s_2^2}{N_2}}}$$

where $\bar{p}_i$ is the average prediction for group i
b_i is the base rate for group i
N_i is the number of predictions that group i had to make
s_i^2 is the unbiased sample variance for group i defined by

$$s_i^2 = \frac{\sum_{event\ j} (p_{ij} - \bar{p}_i)^2}{N_i - 1}$$

A substantive, as opposed to chance-driven, interpretation should gain in credibility to the degree one can show that, measurement error roughly constant, the probability-reality gap varies predictably as a function of independent variables hypothesized to inflate overconfidence (cognitive style, expertise, extremism, short-term versus long-term forecasts, etc.)—in effect, a construct-validational argument.

EXTENSION TO MULTIPLE OUTCOME CASE

In the three-outcome case, we can compute variability, calibration, and discrimination indices by averaging across all possible pairwise discrimination tasks: the ability to differentiate the status quo from change for either the better or the worse, the ability to differentiate change for the worse from either the status quo or change for the better, and the ability to differentiate change for the better from either the status quo or change for the worse.

OPERATIONALIZING THE "MINDLESS" COMPETITION

We could have operationalized the dart-throwing chimp by selecting probability predictions from random number tables. However, the long-term expected value of this strategy (assuming we counterbalance the order in which the three possible futures were assigned probability values) converges on .33. To compute the probability score, the formula was

$$ PS \text{ (chimp)} = \frac{\sum_{i=1}^{M} (c_i - x_i)^2}{M} $$

where c_i is the long-term expected value of just guessing, which is $1/M$
x_i takes on the values of 0 or 1 depending on whether the event in question occurred
M is the number of outcomes for this particular event

Note that this strategy will underperform the base-rate extrapolation algorithms to the degree outcomes were not equiprobable.

We operationalized the base-rate prediction strategy by selecting probability predictions that corresponded to the observed frequency with which outcomes occurred for particular variables and populations of comparison cases. Table 6.1 (Chapter 6) presents the percentages used in the contemporaneous base-rate algorithm: the frequency with which the status quo, change for the better, and change for the worse occurred across all outcome variables in the forecasting periods in which we were assessing the accuracy of human forecasters. To compute the probability score for an event with M outcomes, the formula was

$$ PS(\text{br}) = \frac{\sum_{i=1}^{M} (b_i - x_i)^2}{M} $$

where b_i is the base-rate probability prediction and

x_i takes on the values of 0 or 1 depending on whether the event in question occurred

M is the number of outcomes for this particular event

Base rate estimates depend on how restrictively or expansively, historically or contemporaneously, we define comparison populations. But, as noted in chapter 6, the current results are robust across a wide range of plausible estimates used for computing difficulty-adjusted probabilities scores.

We operationalized the case-specific and time series extrapolation algorithms by basing predictions on the trend lines for specific variables and countries. Cautious case-specific extrapolations assigned probabilities 50 percent greater than guessing (.33) to possible futures that simply extended recent trends. For trichotomous futures, the values would thus be 50 percent (trend continuation), 25 percent, and 25 percent. Aggressive case-specific extrapolations assigned probabilities twice the value of guessing (67 percent, 16.5 percent, 16.5 percent). Hyperaggressive extrapolations placed 100 percent confidence in the proposition that the recent past of country x would also be its near-term future.

OPERATIONALIZING THE SOPHISTICATED COMPETITION

If experts could not beat informal predict-the-past algorithms, one might wonder what motive, aside from Schadenfreude, would prompt us to bring on even more formidable competition from formal statistical algorithms.

It turns out, however, that, although experts do indeed lose by greater margins to formal statistical models (generalized autoregressive distributed lag models), they do not lose by massively greater margins. This is so because the formal models, although they outperform the informal ones, do not do so by massive margins. This result suggests that the true stochastic process governing many of the variables being forecast (call them y_t) is well approximated by autoregressive processes of order one. In this situation, forecasters will do well by adopting simple rules such as "always predict rho $* y_{t-1} + (1 - \text{rho}) * m$," where rho is some constant less than or equal to 1 which indicates the variable's "persistence" and m is the unconditional mean to which the variable reverts over time (e.g., when rho = 1, the variable follows a random walk).

There are other good reasons for determining, at least roughly, the predictability of the outcome variables that confronted forecasters ("roughly" because there is no guarantee that any statistical model incorporates all useful information available ex ante). To obtain crude approximations of predictability, we relied on generalized autoregressive models that lagged each outcome variable by two time periods on itself (first- and second-order autocorrelations) as well as by one time period on the three most highly correlated variables in our dataset (variables that should not have predictive power in pure AR1 processes but do occasionally have predictive power here).

$$y_t = \alpha + \beta_1 y_{t-1} + \beta_2 y_{t-2} + \gamma_1 x_{1,t-1} + \gamma_2 x_{2,t-1} + \gamma_3 x_{3,t-1}$$

The squared multiple correlations in these "optimal" forecasting equations ranged from .21 (long-range predictions of inflation) to .78 (short-term predictions of government spending priorities). These equations define plausible maximum performance ceilings for each outcome variable. Indeed, we can compare human forecasters directly to these equations if we treat the statistically predicted values of the outcome variables as if they were subjective probability forecasts. For instance, one translation rule is to stipulate that, whenever the statistically predicted value falls within one of the three-possible-future ranges of values, and the 95 percent confidence band around the predicted value does not cross the borders between possible futures, assign a value of 1.0—otherwise assign .75. When we implement rules of this sort, across outcome variables, we discover that the discrimination scores for the equations handily surpass those of all groupings of human forecasters (equation ranges between .05 and .10 versus human range between .01 and .04) and the calibration scores rival those of the best human forecasters (average CI for equations is .011). Such results demonstrate there was considerable predictability that experts, regardless of cognitive style, failed to capture (a point underscored by figures 2.5 and 3.2).

These equations also allow us to gauge how the relative size of the group gaps in forecasting performance varied as a function of the relative predictability of outcome variables (we discover, for example, that the fox advantage over hedgehogs was relatively evenly spread out across outcome variables with small to large squared multiple correlations). These equations also remind us that, although each expert made many short-term and long-term predictions across three policy domains, each predictive failure or success should not be viewed as an independent statistical estimate of predictive ability—hence the importance of making conservative assumptions about degrees of freedom in significance testing (treating forecasters rather than forecasts as the principal observational unit).

Adjustments of Probability Scores to Address Conceptual Objections

One can raise at least five categories of objections to probability scoring as a valid measure of forecasting skill:

1. Probability scores are sensitive to irrelevant factors, such as variation in the predictability of political environments (hence, the need for difficulty adjustments).

2. Probability scores are insensitive to relevant factors, such as variation in the political values that forecasters try to achieve (hence the need for value adjustments that reflect the shifting weights experts place on avoiding errors of underprediction and overprediction).
3. The reality checks used to index accuracy are flawed and require controversy adjustments that reflect disagreement over what actually happened.
4. The reality checks used to index accuracy are flawed and require fuzzy-set adjustments that reflect disagreement over what almost happened or might yet happen.
5. Probability scores are based on the assumption that subjective probabilities have simple linear properties, but there is considerable evidence that subjective probabilities have nonlinear properties and that people treat errors in the middle range of the scale as less consequential than errors at the extremes.

Difficulty-adjusted Probability Scores

Probability scores can be inflated by two logically separable sources of variation: the shortcomings of forecasters and the unpredictability of the world. Difficulty adjustments "control" for the second source of variation, thereby giving us a "cleaner" measure of forecasting skill. The rationale is simple. A weather forecaster in Arizona (where it rains 5 percent of the time) has an easier job than one in Oregon (where it rains 50 percent of the time). Winkler's method of difficulty-adjusting probability scores takes into account such variation in predictability, and tells us whether performance differentials between groups persist after leveling the playing field.[2] We slightly modify Winkler's original difficulty-adjusted formula so that

$$S^*(p) = \frac{S(b) - S(p)}{T(b)}$$

where $S^*(p)$ is the skill score that is applied to the expert's forecast, p, $S(p)$ is the expert's probability score based on the quadratic scoring rule, and $S(b)$ is the expert's probability score if she always used the base rate for her forecasts. $T(b)$ is the denominator, and its value depends on whether the forecast is higher or lower than the base rate (taking on the value of $(1 - b)^2$ when a prediction is greater than or equal to the base

[2] R. Winkler, "Evaluating Probabilities: Asymmetric Scoring Rules," *Management Science* 40 (1994): 1395–1405.

rate, and b^2 when the prediction is lower than the base rate). A score of zero implies that the forecaster tells us nothing about future states of the world that we could not glean from crude base-rate summaries of past states of the world. For example, a weather forecaster in Phoenix might have a fantastic probability score (close to zero, say .0025) but will get a skill score of zero if the base predictor (say, always assign a .95 to sunshine) has the same fantastic probability score: $S^* (p) = (.0025 - .0025)/T_B = 0$. (Note that now higher skill scores are better.) A weather forecaster in Portland, however, with the same probability score, .0025, will have an impressive skill score because the base-rate predictor (say, always assign a .5 to "sunshine") has such an anemic probability score (.25) and T_B must take on a relatively small value because the forecaster, in order to achieve his probability score in the high-variance Portland environment, had to make a lot of predictions that both strayed from the base rate and strayed in the correct direction.

Difficulty adjustments take into account that when the base rates are extreme, anyone can look farsighted by predicting that rare outcomes will not occur and common ones will. To give experts the incentive to outperform predictively potent base rates, we need to reduce the penalties for going out on a limb and overpredicting low-base-rate events that fail to materialize, and to increase the penalties for mindlessly relying on the base rate and underpredicting low-base-rate events that do materialize. Difficulty-adjusted scoring does that. Figure A.3 shows that the difficulty-adjusted scoring curves for events and nonevents always intersect at the probability value on the x axis that corresponds to the base rate and at the score value on the y axis that corresponds to zero. In effect, the policy is "If you cannot tell us anything more than we would know from looking at the base rate, you deserve a score of zero." The sharp inflection in the scoring curves at the intersection point in skewed base-rate environments serves two purposes: it punishes experts who miss uncommon outcomes because they always predicted the base rate (hence the sharp downward slope into negative territory for experts who assign probabilities close to zero for rare events that occur as well as for experts who assign probabilities close to 1.0 for common events that fail to occur), and it rewards experts for having the courage to assign greater-than-base-rate probabilities to uncommon events that occur and lower-than-base-rate probabilities to common events that fail to occur (hence these curves rise into positive territory much earlier than the curves of experts who endorsed the base-rate prediction and were correct).

When skill scoring is applied to a dichotomous event, the computational formulas for S_p^* take the following specific forms:

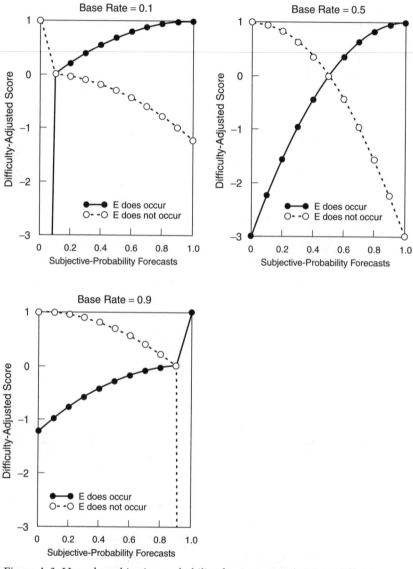

Figure A.3. How the subjective probability forecasts translate into difficulty-adjusted forecasting scores when the target event either does or does not occur and the base rate for the target event is low (0.1), moderate (0.5), or high (0.9). Higher scores represent better performance, and scores fall off steeply when forecasters underpredict rare events that do occur (left panel) and overpredict common events that fail to occur.

$$S_1^*(r) = \frac{(b-1)^2 - (p-1)^2}{(b-1)^2} \qquad \text{if the event is 1 and } p \geq b \text{ (hit)}$$

$$S_1^*(r) = \frac{(b-1)^2 - (p-1)^2}{(b)^2} \qquad \text{if the event is 1 and } p < b \text{ (miss or underprediction)}$$

$$S_0^*(r) = \frac{(b)^2 - (p)^2}{(b-1)^2} \qquad \text{if the event is 0 and } p \geq b \text{ (false alarm or overprediction)}$$

$$S_0^*(r) = \frac{(b)^2 - (p)^2}{(b)^2} \qquad \text{if the event is 0 and } p < b \text{ (correct rejection)}$$

Figure A.3 also shows how subjective probability forecasts translate into difficulty-adjusted forecasting skill across the full range of possible values. The easiest environments are those with extreme base rates in the first and third panels. The specified outcome occurs either 10 percent or 90 percent of the time. The hardest environment is the middle panel. Here, the base rate offers no more guidance than one could glean from chance (in the two-possible-futures case, a base rate of 0.5).

Difficulty-adjustment formulas level the playing field for comparisons of the forecasting performance of experts who work in easier-versus harder-to-predict environments. There are, however, good reasons for caution in interpreting such scores. First, the scoring procedure is open to a general challenge. By aggressively encouraging experts to search for regularities beyond the safe predict-the-base-rate strategy, the formula reduces the scoring penalties imposed on suboptimal prediction strategies (such as probability matching discussed in chapter 2) that look for patterns in randomness. Critics can argue, in effect, that difficulty adjustments encourage the sorts of specious reasoning that led the Yale undergraduates to do a worse job than Norwegian rats in guessing which side of the T-maze would contain the yummy pellets.

Second, the difficulty-adjusted scoring is open to the objection that, in contrast to fields such as radiology, where there is consensus on the right reference populations for estimating the base rates of malignancy of tumors, there is often sharp disagreement among political observers over what, if any, statistical generalizations apply. This is so, in part, because of the heterogeneity of the polities, cultures, and economies of the entities being judged and, in part, because of the dearth of well-established laws for guiding judgment.

We hedged our bets. We reported a range of difficulty adjustments that reflected experts' judgments of which base rates were most relevant to particular nations and periods. One can raise the estimated base rate of an outcome (such as nuclear proliferation between 1988 and 1998) by limiting the reference population to only high-risk states such as Iran, North Korea, and Pakistan, in which case proliferation definitely occurred 33 percent of the time, or one could lower the base rate by expanding the population to encompass lower-risk states such as Libya, Egypt, Brazil, and so on, in which case proliferation occurred less than 10 percent of the time. Chapter 6 assessed the stability of difficulty-adjusted scores by varying values of the base-rate parameter.

Value-adjusted Probability Scores

Value adjustments give forecasters varying benefits of the doubt when they under- or overpredict status quo, change-for-better, and change-for-worse outcomes. Overprediction (or a "false alarm") occurs whenever a forecaster gives a probability greater than zero to a nonoccurrence. Underprediction (a "miss") occurs whenever a forecaster gives a probability less than 1.0 to an occurrence. Overprediction was defined mathematically as

$$\frac{\sum_{j=1}^{N_0}(p_j - 0)^2}{N_0} = \frac{\sum_{j=1}^{N_0}(p_j)^2}{N_0}$$

where p_j is the forecast on the jth occasion of events that did not occur
N_0 is the number of events that did not occur

Similarly, underprediction was defined as

$$\frac{\sum_{j=1}^{N_1}(p_j - 1)^2}{N_1}$$

where p_j is the forecast on the jth occasion of events that occurred
N_1 is the number of events that occurred

We explored two methods of value-adjusting probability scores:

1. The k method that searched for a single value k designed to minimize gaps between subjective probabilities and objective reality; and
2. The "differential-weighting" method that explored the impact of a wide range of adjustments on errors of overprediction (a_0) and underprediction (a_1), within certain mathematical constraints on a_0 and a_1.

The former method gives forecasters the most unconditional benefit of the doubt: whatever mistakes experts are most prone to make, it assumes that those mistakes are purposeful, and introduces a correction factor k that reduces the gaps between specific subjective probabilities and objective frequencies by the average magnitude of the gap. The latter method requires the researcher to specify the direction and degree of the bias to be corrected (drawing, for instance, on experts' expressed error-avoidance priorities), without looking at the mistakes experts actually made.

The k Method

This method of value adjusting takes the following form:

$$PS_j = \frac{\sum_{i=1}^{M} ((p_i - k_i) - x_i)^2}{M}$$

where PS_j is the probability score for the jth occasion when one of M outcomes must occur
p_i is the forecast (probability estimate) of the ith outcome
k_i is the value adjustment for the ith outcome
x_i is either 0 or 1 depending on whether the ith outcome occurred
M is the number of possible outcomes for a given occasion

The restriction is such that

$$\sum_{i=1}^{M} p_i = 1 \text{ and } \sum_{i=1}^{M} k_i = 0$$

DERIVING k_i

Consider an occasion j with M possible outcomes. The unadjusted probability score is

$$PS_j = \frac{\sum_{i=1}^{M} (p_i - x_i)^2}{M}$$

Summing up the PS_j over N occasions, we find that

$$PS = \frac{\sum_{j=1}^{N} PS_j}{N} = \frac{\sum_{j=1}^{N} \left(\frac{\sum_{i=1}^{M} (p_{ij} - x_{ij})^2}{M} \right)}{N} = \frac{\sum_{j=1}^{N} \sum_{i=1}^{M} (p_{ij} - x_{ij})^2}{NM}$$

where p_{ij} is the forecast (probability estimate) of the ith outcome for the jth occasion

x_{ij} is the outcome of the ith outcome for the jth occasion

The value-adjusted probability score would be

$$\text{Val-adj PS} = \frac{\sum_{j=1}^{N}\sum_{i=1}^{M}((p_{ij} - k_i) - x_{ij})^2}{NM}$$

Now we can find the value of k_i that minimizes the probability score:

$$\frac{\partial(Val - adj\ PS)}{\partial k_i} = \frac{\sum_{j=1}^{N} 2((p_{lj} - k_l) - x_{lj})(-1)}{NM} = 0$$

$$\rightarrow \sum_{j=1}^{N}(p_{lj} - k_l - x_{lj}) = 0 \quad \rightarrow \quad \sum_{j=1}^{N}p_{lj} - \sum_{j=1}^{N}x_{lj} = \sum_{j=1}^{N}k_l$$

$$\rightarrow \sum_{j=1}^{N}p_{lj} - \sum_{j=1}^{N}x_{lj} = Nk_l \quad \rightarrow \quad k_l = \frac{\sum_{j=1}^{N}p_{lj}}{N} - \frac{\sum_{j=1}^{N}x_{lj}}{N}$$

$$\rightarrow \quad k_l = \bar{p}_l - b_l \quad \text{where } b_l \text{ is the base rate of outcome } l$$

Thus, the best value adjustment, k_l, for the lth outcome is equal to the average forecast for the lth outcome minus the base rate for the lth outcome. The k parameter adjusts experts' probability estimates by whatever amount they on average differed from the mean observed outcome. Note that applying k in this fashion requires pushing some individual forecasts, $p_i - k_i$, above 1.0 or below 0 and, for this reason, k-adjusted probability scores should be interpreted only at the aggregate level.

Example:

Imagine three possible outcomes: status quo (SQ), change for the better (UP), and change for the worse (DOWN). Suppose a forecaster always predicts 0.8 for SQ, 0.1 for UP, and 0.1 for DOWN. Assume that the base rate for SQ, UP, and DOWN are 0.5, 0.25, and 0.25 respectively.

Note that the value adjustments are

- $k_{SQ} = \bar{p}_{SQ} - b_{SQ} = 0.8 - 0.5 = 0.3$
- $k_{UP} = \bar{p}_{UP} - b_{UP} = 0.1 - 0.25 = -0.15$
- $k_{DOWN} = \bar{p}_{DOWN} - b_{DOWN} = 0.1 - 0.25 = -0.15$

The expected unadjusted probability score is given by

$$\frac{1}{2} PS(SQ) + \frac{1}{4} PS(UP) + \frac{1}{4} PS(DOWN) = 0.253$$

The expected value-adjusted probability score is given by

$$\frac{1}{2}(\text{value-adjusted } PS(SQ)) + \frac{1}{4}(\text{value-adjusted } PS(UP))$$

$$+ \frac{1}{4}(\text{value-adjusted } PS(DOWN)) = 0.208$$

This method of value-adjusting probability scores says to forecasters: "It doesn't matter whether you over- or underpredict. We will take out the difference between your average forecast and the base rate for the outcome." This value adjustment will thus have larger effects to the degree that forecasters repeatedly make errors in the same direction and to the same degree.

There is understandable controversy over how far to take value adjustments. For instance, one possible concession to the "I made the right mistake defense" would be to apply separate adjustments to underprediction and overprediction, thus correcting for the average error in each direction. This concession is, however, too generous. For one thing, it makes broken-clock predictors (that always make the same mistakes) look perfectly calibrated. For another, separate adjustments "assume away the forecasting problem." They rest on the far-fetched assumption that forecasters always knew in advance which error they were going to make. Accordingly, we opt here for single, one-size-fits-all-forecasts adjustments, but we recognize that others may legitimately opt to go further by configuring value adjustments to specific country-variable combinations.

Just as we recognized earlier that probability scores can be decomposed into VI, CI, and DI, the same can be done for the k-value adjusted probability score for N two-outcome events:

$$PS = \frac{\sum_{i=1}^{N}(p_i - x_i - k)^2}{N}$$

$$= b(1-b) + \frac{1}{N}\sum_{t=1}^{T} n_t(p_t - b_t - k)^2 + \frac{1}{N}\sum_{t=1}^{T} n_t(b_t - b)^2,$$

which correspond to VI, CI, and DI respectively. Notice that the only difference between the original and the adjusted decomposition is that k appears in the CI term. This value adjustment improves probability scores entirely by improving calibration scores.

The Differential-weighting Method

Another method of value-adjusting probability scores avoids the logical paradoxes of the k method. This alternate method applies differential weights to errors of overprediction (a_0) and underprediction (a_1):

$$\text{Value-adjusted PS} = \frac{\sum_{i=1}^{N_0} a_0 (p_i - 0)^2 + \sum_{j=1}^{N_1} a_1 (p_j - 1)^2}{N}$$

where N_0 is the number of events that did not occur
N_1 is the number of events that occurred
$N = N_0 + N_1$

When $a_0 = a_1 = 1$, the value-adjusted PS is the unadjusted PS. When a_0 and a_1 take on different values, the value-adjusted PS has the potential to stray far from the unadjusted PS (depending, of course, on the gap between a_0 and a_1, and the size of the gap between errors of under- and overprediction).

We tested many combinations of a_1 and a_0, subject to a "constraint function", $h(a_1, a_0)$. The special case of an unadjusted probability score occurs when $a_1 = a_0 = 1$. Thus, the point (1, 1) must fall in the domain of this function. All other (a_1, a_0) must satisfy the equality $h(a_1, a_0) = h(1, 1)$.

For example, if we set $h(a_1, a_0) = a_1 + a_0$, then $h(1, 1) = 2$. Thus we should test the points (a_1, a_0) such that $a_0 + a_1 = 2$. As Figure A.4 illustrates, other constraint functions we explored include $h(a_1, a_0) = a_1 a_0$ and $h(a_1, a_0) = \exp(a_0) + \exp(a_1)$.

Recall that overprediction was defined as

$$\text{overprediction} = \frac{\sum_{i=1}^{N_0} (p_i - 0)^2}{N_0} = \frac{\sum_{i=1}^{N_0} (p_i)^2}{N_0}$$

and underprediction was defined as

$$\text{underprediction} = \frac{\sum_{i=1}^{N_1} (p_i - 1)^2}{N_1}$$

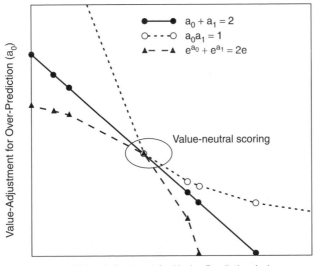

Figure A.4. applies three value-adjustment functions to the data: linear, multiplicative, and natural logarithmic, each subject to constraints on the weights listed in the box. As the functions descend, they place progressively less value on avoiding false alarms (lower values of a_0) and progressively greater importance on avoiding misses (higher values of a_1). The functions intersect at value neutrality.

Figure A.4 shows the results of multiplying the original under- and over-prediction by the new a_1 and a_0. The circled area represents no value adjustment ($a_1 = a_0 = 1$).

The constraints placed on a_0 and a_1 are obviously somewhat arbitrary, but if we arrive at the same conclusion about group differences in forecasting skill after applying a wide range of plausible (a_0, a_1) adjustments, we can be reasonably confident that the observed group differences reflect differences in forecasting skill, not policy priorities.

Probability-weighting Adjustments to Probability Scores

In expected-utility theory, probability estimates enter the utility calculus in a straightforward, linear fashion. In choice theories that specify belief-weighting functions, probability estimates undergo complex transformations into decision weights.[3]

Drawing on this latter tradition, we developed a method of adjusting probability scores that takes into account the nonlinear nature of

---

[3] A. Tversky and D. Kahneman, "Advances in Prospect Theory: Cumulative Representation of Uncertainty," *Journal of Risk and Uncertainty* 5 (1992): 297–323; A. Tversky and C. R. Fox, "Weighing Risk and Uncertainty," *Psychological Review* 102 (1995): 269–83.

subjective probabilities. For instance, prospect theory posits that the shape of the probability-weighting function is determined by the psychophysics of diminishing sensitivity: marginal impact diminishes with distance from reference points. For monetary outcomes, the status quo serves as the sole reference point that distinguishes losses from gains. The resulting value function is concave for gains and convex for losses. For probability assessments, there are two reference points: impossibility (zero) and certainty (1.0). Diminishing sensitivity here implies an S-shaped weighting function that is concave near zero and convex near 1.0. This means that the weight of a probability estimate decreases with its distance from the natural boundaries of zero (impossibility) and 1.0 (certainty). Among other things, the probability-weighting function helps to explain the Allais paradox in which increasing the probability of winning a prize from .99 to 1.0 has more impact on choice than increasing the probability of winning from .10 to .11.

We apply the formula directly to the forecast p as follows:

$$w(p, \gamma) = \frac{p^{\gamma}}{(p^{\gamma} + (1-p)^{\gamma})^{\frac{LN3}{LN2}}}$$

where $0 < \gamma \le 1$. We then enter this adjusted subjective probability forecast into the probability-scoring function which is now defined as

$$(w(p, \gamma) - x)^2$$

When $\gamma = 1$, the adjusted prediction equals the original prediction $(w(p, \gamma) = p)$ and so the adjusted probability score equals the original probability score. As γ approaches zero, we treat all forecasts made with some doubt (subjective probabilities in the broadly defined "maybe zone" from .1 to .9) as increasingly equivalent. In other words, the differences among weighted subjective probabilities in the .1 to .9 range shrinks when the gamma weights approach zero. The question, of course, is how extreme should gamma be?

The most extreme psychological argument asserts: (a) people can reliably discriminate only three levels of subjective probability—impossibility (0), certainty (1), and a clump of intermediate "maybe" values (in which any expression of uncertainty is equivalent to any other); (b) the natural default assignment for the weighted probability is the state of maximum uncertainty in a trichotomous prediction task (.33), hence the rationale for the exponent $LN3/LN2$. More moderate psychological arguments would allow for the possibility that people can reliably discriminate several levels of subjective probability along the belief continuum from zero to 1.0. From this standpoint, the right value of gamma might well be one

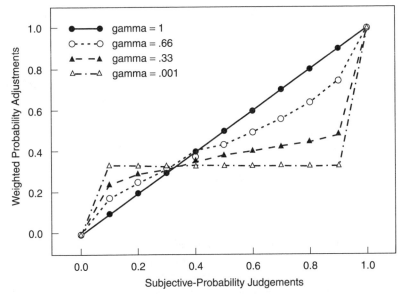

Figure A.5. shows the impact of gamma adjustments of varying extremity on probability scores. Extreme gamma adjustments flatten the midsection of the S-shaped curve by treating all probability judgments in the broadly defined "maybe zone" (from .1 to .9) as increasingly equivalent to each other. The more extreme the gamma adjustment, the less sensitive probability scores become to accuracy in the middle range of the probability scale and the more sensitive they become to accuracy at the end points where outcomes are declared either impossible or inevitable.

that yields a functional form similar to that posited in cumulative prospect theory (say γ between .5 and .7).

The net effect of these probability-weighting adjustments is threefold: (a) to reward experts who get it "really right" and assign undiluted-by-probabilistic-caveats predictions of zero to things that do not happen and predictions of 1.0 to things that do happen; (b) to punish experts who get it really wrong and assign predictions of zero to things that happen and predictions of 1.0 to things that do not happen; (c) to count movement in the wrong direction at the extremes as a particularly serious mistake (moving from 1.0 to .8 when the outcome happens makes one look more inaccurate than moving from .8 to .6).

Controversy-adjusted Probability Scores

Regardless of whether we rely on traditional scores or on adjusted or weighted scoring systems, the computations rest on assumptions about states of the world: either x happened (reality takes on the value of 1.0) or x did not happen (reality takes on the value of 0.0). Notwithstanding our efforts to elicit forecasts that passed the clairvoyance test, controversies sometimes arose as to what happened. Uncertainty shrouded:

   a. Casualty estimates in poorly reported conflicts. How many deaths were traceable to sectarian violence within Nigeria or Liberia or the Congo between 1992 and 1997?
   b. Who was in charge during power transitions or struggles? Was Deng Xiaoping—even in retirement in the early 1990s—still the de facto head of state in China? Was Khatami or Khamenei the real head of state in Iran in the late 1990s?
   c. The classification of powers as nuclear or not (e.g., North Korea in 1998?)
   d. The truthfulness of official government statistics on spending, debt, and macroeconomic performance. Did the Italian government "cook the books" on government finances to squeeze past the Maastricht criteria for currency convergence? How much faith can we put in the official economic growth or government debt or defense spending figures issued by the People's Republic of China?
   e. The treatment of cross-border conflicts (should we count Russian support for separatists in the Abkhazian region of Georgia and Russian military pursuit of Chechen guerrillas into Georgia?).

When plausible challenges surfaced (roughly 15 percent of the time), we recomputed probability scores to ensure that the conclusions drawn about expert performance do not hinge on arbitrary judgment calls. These controversy adjustments provided lower- and upper-bound estimates of accuracy, with lower-bound estimates indicating how poorly a group would perform if we worked with classifications of reality that worked to the maximum disadvantage of the group's forecasts and upper bounds indicating how well the group would perform if the classifications consistently worked to the group's advantage. It is also worth noting that we explored an alternative method of controversy adjustment which operates in the same fashion as fuzzy-set adjustments in the next section and which requires modifying our coding of nonoccurrences as zero and occurrences as 1.0 so that (a) nonoccurrences shift up in value and occurrences shift down; (b) the size of the shift is in proportion to the frequency and credibility of the controversy challenges.

Fuzzy-set Adjustments

The final modification of probability scores has a more radical, even postmodern, character: "fuzzy-set" adjustments that challenge the "binary objectivism" of probability scoring. Advocates of fuzzy-set measurement models argue that it is profoundly misleading to squeeze ambiguous and continuous outcomes into sharply defined, dichotomous categories. They urge us to treat such outcomes as they are: both "perspectival" (formally acknowledge ambiguity by allowing the coding of reality to vary with the vantage point of the observer) and a matter of degree (formally acknowledge the continuous character of such outcomes by allowing the coding of reality to take on values between zero and 1.0 and scoring predictions as true or false to varying degrees).[4]

Rising to this measurement challenge is, however, daunting: we need to figure out defensible ways of quantifying the degree to which things almost happened (or, in the case of controversy adjustments, uncertainty over what actually happened). We do not claim to have final answers. But we do offer our provisional solution, which was to take seriously what forecasters told us after the fact about how far off they felt their own predictions were. As noted in chapter 4, forecasters often invoked a wide range of arguments that asserted that, although the unexpected happened, they were not as wrong as they might appear because (a) their most likely outcome almost happened (close-call defense); (b) that outcome might yet happen (off-on-timing defense); (c) that outcome would have happened but for external shocks that no one could reasonably be expected to have foreseen (exogenous-shock defense).

We initially applied fuzzy-set adjustments simply in proportion to the degree to which forecasters relied on each of these belief system defenses. Let us begin by considering a forecaster who assigns a probability of .9 to a nonoccurrence. The unadjusted probability score is

$$(p - x)^2 = (.9 - 0)^2 = .81$$

The forecaster might also advance one or more of the belief system defenses. Fuzzy sets proceed to give some benefit of the doubt to the forecaster. Rather than assigning $x = 0$, we might estimate the proportion of times groups of forecasters (say, hedgehogs versus foxes) offer belief system defenses and then adjust the classification of reality accordingly (say, if forecasters offer defenses 30 percent of the time when they assigned 0.9 to things that did not happen, the adjustment might shift the reality classification from zero to .30). The probability score would then be given by

$$(p - x)^2 = (.9 - .3)^2 = .36$$

Conversely, consider a forecaster who assigns a probability of zero to an event that does occur. The probability score is

$$(p - x)^2 = (0 - 1)^2 = 1$$

---

[4] C. Ragin, *Fuzzy-set Social Science* (Chicago: University of Chicago Press, 2000).

If forecasters argue 30 percent of the time that x "nearly did not occur or will soon disappear," we let $x = .7$ and the probability score becomes

$$(p - x)^2 = (0 - .7)^2 = .49$$

Thus far, we have implicitly agreed with forecasters whenever they offer a defense, but we can also attach credibility weights to defenses that range from zero (completely reject the defense) to 1.0 (completely accept the defense).

In adjusting the probability score, we can now reduce the gaps between subjective probabilities and objective reality in proportion to both the credibility weighting attached to defenses and the frequency with which defenses were offered. The general formula is

$$PS = \frac{\displaystyle\sum_{\substack{category\ k,\\event\ occurs}} \begin{pmatrix} number\ of \\ predictions\ in \\ kth\ category, \\ defense\ not \\ considered \end{pmatrix} PS_k(E,\ no\ adj.) + \begin{pmatrix} number\ of \\ predictions\ in \\ kth\ category, \\ defense \\ considered \end{pmatrix} PS_k(E,\ adj.)}{}$$

$$+ \frac{\displaystyle\sum_{\substack{category\ k,\\event\ does\ not\\occurs}} \begin{pmatrix} number\ of \\ predictions\ in \\ kth\ category, \\ defense\ not \\ considered \end{pmatrix} PS_k(no\ E,\ no\ adj.) + \begin{pmatrix} number\ of \\ predictions\ in \\ kth\ category, \\ defense \\ considered \end{pmatrix} PS_k(no\ E,\ adj.)}{N}$$

where "adj." is short for "adjustment" and E short for Event.

Consider another stylized example. Suppose that a forecaster only assigns the probability value of 0.3 to each of 100 predictions; suppose further that the event occurs on 40 occasions. Of the 60 remaining nonoccurrences, the forecaster offers a belief system defense 20 times (one-third of the time). If we gave zero credibility to the belief system defenses, we would compute the first part of the numerator in the traditional manner:

$$\sum_{i=1}^{60} (p_i - x_i)^2 = \sum_{i=1}^{60} (0.3 - 0)^2 = 60(.09) = 5.4$$

If we gave 75 percent credibility weight to the defenses (accept 75 percent of what experts say as true), these 60 scores would be calculated as

$$\sum_{i=1}^{45} (p_i - x_i)^2 + \sum_{i=46}^{60} (p_i - (adjusted\ x_i))^2$$

$$= \sum_{i=1}^{45} (p_i - x_i)^2 + \sum_{i=46}^{60} \left(p_i - \left(\begin{array}{c} credibility\ weight \\ of\ given\ defenses \end{array} \right) \left(\begin{array}{c} proportion\ of\ times \\ defense\ offered \end{array} \right) \right)^2$$

$$= \sum_{i=1}^{45} (.3 - 0)^2 + \sum_{i=46}^{60} \left(.3 - (.75)(.333) \right)^2 = 45(.09) + 15(.0025) = 4.0875$$

Conversely, notice that the event occurred 40 times, meaning that the forecaster incorrectly assigned a low probability ($p < 1$) to 40 events that occurred. Of these 40 nonoccurrences the forecaster offers a defense 10 times. Once again, in adjusting the probability score with the fuzzy-set concepts, we may assign credibility weights ranging from zero to 1.0. If we gave zero credibility weight to these belief system defenses, we would compute the second part of the numerator as

$$\sum_{i=1}^{40} (p_i - x_i)^2 = \sum_{i=1}^{40} (0.3 - 1)^2 = 40(.49) = 19.6$$

If we gave 50 percent credibility weight to the defenses (accept 50 percent of what experts say as true), these 40 scores would be calculated as

$$= \sum_{i=1}^{35} (p_i - x_i)^2 + \sum_{i=36}^{40} \left(p_i - \left(\begin{array}{c} credibility\ weight \\ of\ given\ defenses \end{array} \right) \left(\begin{array}{c} proportion \\ of\ times \\ defense\ offered \end{array} \right) \right)^2$$

$$\sum_{i=1}^{35} (.3 - 1)^2 + \sum_{i=36}^{40} \left(.3 - (.5)(.75) \right)^2 = 35(.49) + 5(.0056) = 17.178$$

The previous example illustrates the procedure for calculating the fuzzy-set-adjusted score when $p_t = .3$. In general, for each of the $p_t = \{0, .1, .2, \ldots, 1\}$ subjective probability categories, we can separate the predictions by those in which the event either occurred or did not occur. Within these subcategories, experts may or may not offer a defense. We then have the option of how large a credibility weight to assign these defenses.

For a more general statement of the fuzzy-set adjustment procedure, let A_k^1 be the percentage of defenses considered in the kth probability category when the event occurs, and let A_k^0 be the percentage of defenses considered in the kth probability category when the event does not occur. Let n_k^1 be the number of predictions in the kth probability category when the event occurred, and let n_k^0 be the number of predictions in the kth probability category when the event did not occur.

The probability score would then be calculated by

$$
PS = \frac{\displaystyle\sum_{\substack{category\ k, \\ event\ occurs}} \begin{pmatrix} number\ of \\ predictions\ in \\ kth\ category, \\ defense\ not \\ considered \end{pmatrix} PS_k(E,\ no\ adj.) + \begin{pmatrix} number\ of \\ predictions\ in \\ kth\ category, \\ defense \\ considered \end{pmatrix} PS_k(E,\ adj.)}{N}
$$

$$
+ \frac{\displaystyle\sum_{\substack{category\ k, \\ event\ does \\ not\ occurs}} \begin{pmatrix} number\ of \\ predictions\ in \\ kth\ category, \\ defense\ not \\ considered \end{pmatrix} PS_k(no\ E,\ no\ adj.) + \begin{pmatrix} number\ of \\ predictions\ in \\ kth\ category, \\ defense \\ considered \end{pmatrix} PS_i(no\ E,\ adj.}{N}
$$

$$
= \frac{\displaystyle\sum_{\substack{category\ k, \\ event\ occurs}} \left(n_k^1(1-A_k^1)\right)PS_k(E,\ no\ adj.) + \left(n_k^1 A_k^1\right)PS_k(E,\ adj.) + \displaystyle\sum_{\substack{category\ k, \\ event\ does \\ not\ occur}} \left(n_k^0(1-A_k^0)\right)PS_k(no\ E,\ no\ adj.) + \left(n_k^0 A_k^0\right)PS_k(no\ E,\ adj.)}{N}
$$

Thus far, fuzzy-set adjustments have been applied in direct proportion to how often they were offered. It is noteworthy, however, that forecasters rarely used close-call arguments to imply that they themselves might have been lucky when they got it right (thus implying they were almost wrong). To address this objection, we apply a self-serving correction factor that reduces credibility weights as a function of the following fraction: "percentage of occasions when experts say something else almost happened when they got it right (assign .8, .9, or 1.0 to events that occur and 0.0, .1, or .2 to events that do not occur)" divided by "percentage of occasions when experts say something else almost happened when they got it wrong (assign 0.0, .1, or .2 to events that occur and .8, .9, or 1.0 to events that do not occur)." The smaller the fraction, the lower the credibility weights we give belief system defenses.

$$\sum_{\substack{i \in \text{ events where} \\ \text{no defense given}}} (p_i - x_i)^2 + \sum_{\substack{i \in \text{ events where} \\ \text{defense given}}} \left(p_i - (\text{adjusted } x_i)\right)^2$$

$$= \sum_{\substack{i \in \text{ events where} \\ \text{no defense given}}} (p_i - x_i)^2 + \sum_{\substack{i \in \text{ events where} \\ \text{defense given}}} \left(p_i - \left(\begin{array}{c} \text{self} - \text{serving} \\ \text{correction factor} \end{array} \right) \times \left(\begin{array}{c} \text{credibility} \\ \text{weight of} \\ \text{given defenses} \end{array} \right) \left(\begin{array}{c} \text{proportion} \\ \text{of times} \\ \text{defense offered} \end{array} \right) \right)^2$$

Summing Up Adjustments of Probability Scores

Estimates of forecasting skill rest on assumptions about both the external world (base rates of events and classifications of reality) and the forecasters themselves (their values and how they use probability estimates). That is why we strove to test the robustness of conclusions about the superior forecasting skill of foxes across a wide range of probability scoring adjustments. Recurring questions have been: When do hedgehogs "catch up?" And why?

It was not easy to produce catch-up effects in the current dataset. It is possible, however, to use Monte Carlo simulation methods that treat the current dataset as a special case of the vast range of variation in underlying forecasting-environment and forecaster-response-style parameters, including the base-rate distributions of events (e.g., status quo vs. change for either the better or the worse), the response distributions of forecasters' judgments across probability scales, and the value priorities that forecasters place on avoiding false alarms or misses.

PART B: LOGICAL-COHERENCE AND PROCESS INDICATORS OF GOOD JUDGMENT

We shift here to tests of good judgment that focus not on the empirical accuracy of judgments but rather on the logical defensibility of those judgments. Among other things, good judges should respect each of the following formal principles of probability theory:

a. The additive rule that defines the probability of either of two mutually exclusive events occurring: $p(A \cup B) = p(A) + p(B)$. If we also stipulate exhaustiveness: $p(A \cup B) = p(A) + p(B) = 1$. Subsections I and II of part B, which deal with the power of belief unpacking to inflate subjective probabilities and to warp inevitability and impossibility curves, describe violations of this rule.

b. The multiplicative rule that defines the joint probability of two independent events: $p(A \cap B) = p(A)p(B)$. More generally, if we allow for the possibility the events are not independent: $p(A \cap B) = p(A/B)p(B) = p(B/A)p(A)$. Subsection III, which deals with the power of scenarios to inflate subjective probabilities, describes violations of this rule.

c. Bayes's theorem builds on these identities to define the probability of an outcome (D) conditional on alternative exclusive and exhaustive hypotheses $(H$ and $\sim H)$ being true: $p(D) = p(D/H)p(H) + p(D/\sim H)p(\sim H)$. Subsection IV, which deals with egocentricity gaps between the likelihoods people actually attach to outcomes and those they would if they used the full formula, describes violations of this rule.

d. Bayes's theorem further builds on these identities to define the probability of a hypothesis (H) conditional on an outcome (D) as:

$$p(H/D) = \frac{p(D/H)p(H)}{p(D)} = \frac{p(D/H)p(H)}{p(D/H)p(H) + p(D/\sim H)(\sim H)}$$

In odds form, Bayes's theorem tells us how much confidence people should retain in the relative validity of two hypotheses once they learn outcome D occurred. Their confidence should be a function of the prior odds they placed on each hypothesis being true (the ratio $p(H)/p(\sim H)$) and a function of the conditional likelihoods they placed on the outcome assuming the truth of each hypothesis (the likelihood ratio or "reputational bet"

$$\frac{p(D \mid H)}{p(D \mid \sim H)}):$$

$$\underbrace{\frac{p(H/D)}{p(\sim H/D)}}_{\substack{\text{Posterior} \\ \text{Odds}}} = \underbrace{\frac{p(H)}{p(\sim H)}}_{\substack{\text{Prior} \\ \text{Odds}}} \underbrace{\frac{p(D/H)}{p(D/\sim H)}}_{\substack{\text{Likelihood} \\ \text{Ratio}}}$$

Subsection V, which deals with failures of belief updating (failures to honor reputational bets), describes violations of this rule.

I. Violations of the Additive Rule: Belief-unpacking Effects (Chapter 7)

Amos Tversky's support theory predicts when people will quite routinely violate the additivity rule by making "sub-additive" judgments.[5] Support theory posits that the judged likelihood of a hypothesis A is a monotonic function of the strength of the arguments, $s(A)$, that people can muster for the hypothesis. The judged probability that hypothesis A rather than B holds, $P(A, B)$, assuming only one can be true, is

$$P(A, B) = \frac{s(A)}{s(A) + s(B)}$$

The theory also posits that unpacking the description of an event A (e.g., victory in a baseball game) into its disjoint components, $A_1 \cup A_2$ (e.g., victory by one run or victory by more than one run), generally increases its support and that the sum of the support linked to component hypotheses must be at least as large as the support for their explicit disjunction, so that

$$s(A) \le s(A_1) + s(A_2)$$

assuming that (A_1, A_2) is a partition of A. The psychological rationale is that unpacking reminds us of possibilities, and of evidence for possibilities, that we otherwise would have overlooked. The judged likelihood of the "whole set" can thus often be less than the sum of its parts. Unpacking can magnify the sorts of anomalies portrayed in figure A.6.

II. Further Violations of Additivity: Analytical Framework for Impossibility and Inevitability Curves

Figures 7.8 and 7.9 showed the impact on probability judgments of encouraging observers to unpack counterfactual possibilities into progressively more specific (easily imagined) sub-possibilities. The area between the two impossibility curves represented the power of unpacking to inflate likelihood judgments across time.

In figures 7.8 and 7.9, the data for the impossibility curves with and without unpacking consisted of points (x_i, y_i) where the x_i's were dates and the y_i's were subjective probabilities. The impossibility curve with no unpacking shows that probability judgments of those counterfactual alternatives to reality can be best approximated as a lower-order polynomial function of time:

[5] A. Tversky and D. J. Koehler, "Support Theory: A Nonextensional Representation of Subjective Probability," *Psychological Review* 101 (1994): 547–67.

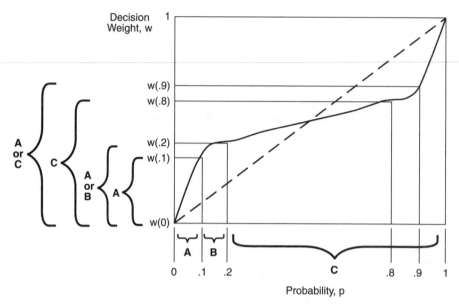

Figure A.6. The probabilities of three exclusive and exhaustive possibilities on its x-axis: A(.1), B(.1), and C(.8). It illustrates how sub-additive judgments result from probability-weighting functions that incorporate the principle of diminishing sensitivity in which the decision weight assigned to events falls off sharply with departures from the natural reference-point boundaries of zero and 1.0. For instance, A's probability of .1 translates into the decision weight w(.1); B also has a probability of .1, which would receive the decision weight w(.1) if judged by itself but of only w(.2)–w(.1) when judged as an addition to A. Thus when we compute the decision weight for the likelihood of either A or B (probability of .2), the resulting w(.2) is far smaller than w(.1)+w(.1). In a similar vein, C has a probability of .8, which translates into the decision weight w(.8) when we judge it by itself. But when we compute the decision weight for the likelihood of either C or A, or C or B (probability of .9), the value w(.9) is far smaller than w(.8)+w(.1).

$$f_{\substack{no \\ unpacking}} = -1.6294x^3 + 5.7373x^2 - 7.0071x + 3.6173$$

The impossibility curves with unpacking of counterfactual alternatives to reality can be best approximated as a higher-order polynomial function of time:

$$f_{\substack{with \\ unpacking}} = 6.803x^6 - 5.6630x^5 + 1.9403x^4 - 3.5043x^3$$
$$+ 3.5196x^2 - 1.8645x + 4.0805$$

Having approximated the two separate functions, we can now calculate the area of the region by integrating both functions:

$$\text{area} = \int_{x_0}^{x_n} P(x)dx$$

To obtain the area of the shaded region, we simply compute the difference of the two areas.

III. Violations of the Multiplicative Rule: Scenario Effects (Chapter 7)

Whenever we construct scenarios with contingent linkages between events (A probably leads to B, which probably leads to C), we should be alert to the possibility that people are not adequately taking into account the rapidity with which likelihood of the "whole" diminishes.

Figure A.7 illustrates the number of logical constraints that people would need to satisfy if they were to judge the Canadian-futures scenarios in a logically consistent manner. Of course, as chapter 7 showed, people often flouted these constraints by assigning far more probability to the lower-level branches than they should have. For example, the probability of the lowest and leftmost node, $A_1B_1C_1$, should equal $P(A_1)P(B_1)P(C_1)$ if A, B, and C are independent. Even if each event had a probability of .7, the joint likelihood of all three is $.7^3 = .343$. Probabilities fall less steeply insofar as A, B, and C are correlated, but usually still more rapidly than do forecasters' probability estimates of multiple-outcome possibilities. The net result is thus also violations of the additivity rule: in particular, big sub-additivity effects in which, for example:

$$P(A_1) < P(A_1|B_1)P(B_1) + P(A_1|B_2)P(B_2)$$
$$P(B_1|A_1)P(A_1) < P(C_1|B_1,A_1)P(B_1|A_1)P(A_1)$$
$$+ P(C_2|B_1,A_1)P(B_1|A_1)P(A_1)$$
$$1 < \sum_{i=1}^{2}\sum_{j=1}^{2}\sum_{k=1}^{2} P(C_k|B_j,A_i)P(B_j|A_i)P(A_i)$$

IV. Violations of the Definitions of the Probability of an Event (Chapter 4)

The violations of the definition of the probability of an event in the previous equation arose because observers often estimated the $p(A)$ to be essentially the same as $p(A/B)$, where A refers to experts' most likely futures and B refers to their favorite working hypotheses about the underlying drivers of events. The result was an egocentricity gap in which observers

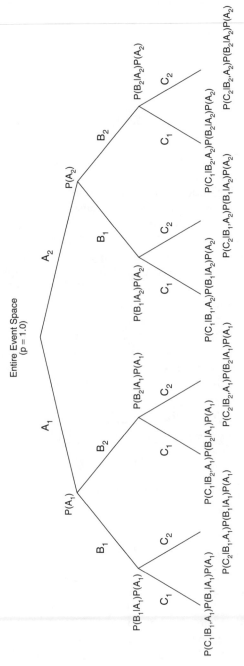

Figure A.7. The complexity of the probabilistic reasoning in which people must engage, and the logical constraints they must respect, to arrive at logically consistent probability estimates for both the bottom-line prediction in the Canadian futures exercise in chapter 7 (will Canada hold together $[A_1]$ or fall apart $[A_2]$?) and the various subsidiary possibilities (economic upturn $[B_1]$ or downturn $[B_2]$) as well as the outcome of the next Quebec election (separatists win $[C_1]$ or lose $[C_2]$). For example, $P(C_1 \mid B_2, A_1) P(B_2 \mid A_1) P(A_1) + P(C_2 \mid B_2, A_1) P(B_2 \mid A_1) P(A_1)$ must equal $P(B_2 \mid A_1) P(A_1)$ and, in turn, $P(B_2 \mid A_1) P(A_1) + P(B_1 \mid A_1) P(A_1)$ must equal $P(A_1)$, and of course $P(A_1) + P(A_2)$ must equal 1.0.

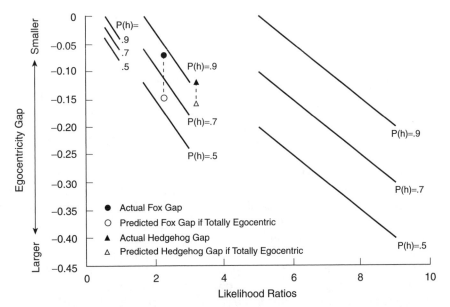

Figure A.8. How the egocentricity gap, produced by estimating p(D) solely from p(D/H), has the theoretical potential to grow as a function of the extremity of the likelihood ratio (all possible combinations of numerator values of .5, .7, and .9 and denominator values of .1, .3, and .5, yielding ratios from 1:1 to 9:1) and the cautiousness of the prior-odds ratio (values for p(H) ranging from .5 to .7 to .9, yielding odds ratios from 1:1 to 9:1). There is the greatest potential for large gaps when experts offer extreme likelihood-ratio judgments and cautious prior-odds ratio judgments. The maximum potential sizes of the egocentricity gap for hedgehogs and foxes are roughly equal; the actual sizes of the egocentricity gaps reveal foxes to be less susceptible to the effect than hedgehogs.

wound up assigning significantly more likelihood to their "most likely futures" (p(A)) than they would have if they had taken other relevant factors into account (taking seriously the possibility that their favorite hypothesis, p(B), might be false).

The sloping diagonal lines in Figure A.8 highlight two factors that moderate the magnitude of the gap: the extremity of two ratios, the prior-odds ratio (experts' subjective probability estimates of their preferred hypothesis about the underlying drivers of events proving correct, divided by their estimates of the most influential alternative hypothesis proving correct) and the likelihood ratio (experts' subjective probabilities that their most likely future will occur if their preferred hypothesis proves correct, divided by their subjective probability of that future occurring if the rival hypothesis proves correct).

Figure A.8 also shows: (a) there is greater potential for large egocentricity gaps when the likelihood ratio, $p(D/H)/p(D/\sim H)$, rises above 1 (reflecting increasingly confident reputational bets). This mathematical necessity should lead us to expect wider gaps among the more intellectually aggressive hedgehogs than among the more cautious foxes (likelihood ratios for foxes' most likely futures hovered around 2.3:1, whereas hedgehogs' ratios hovered around 3.2:1); (b) the potential size of egocentricity gaps shrinks as the prior odds ratio, $p(H)/p(\sim H)$, rises from .5 to 1.0, reflecting increasing confidence in the correctness of one's worldview. This mathematical necessity should lead us to expect narrower gaps among the self-assured hedgehogs than among the more tentative foxes (prior-odds ratio for foxes hovered around 2.2:1, whereas those for hedgehogs hovered around 3.1:1); (c) the offsetting effects in (a) and (b), coupled to the actual differences in likelihood ratios and prior-odds ratios offered by foxes and hedgehogs, imply that if foxes and hedgehogs were equally likely to rely on the $p(D/H)$ as a heuristic for estimating the value of $p(D)$, the actual egocentricity gap would be slightly greater for foxes than for hedgehogs. Figure A.8 shows that: (a) the predicted values of the egocentricity gaps for hedgehogs and foxes are roughly equal (–.16 versus –.149); (b) the actual values of the gap are substantially larger for hedgehogs (–.12) than for foxes (–.07). This result is captured by the steeper rise in the fox circles than in the hedgehog triangles and is consistent with the hypothesis that foxes are less likely to rely on the "consider only my own perspective" heuristic in affixing likelihoods to those futures they judge most likely to occur.

If we replaced experts' actual predictions in all the regional forecasting exercises in section I with those they would have made if they had shown zero egocentricity gaps in the preliminaries to the belief-updating exercises in section II, there would have been considerable shrinkage in the subjective probability–objective reality gaps, with less overestimation of the likelihood of "most likely futures." Foxes' probability-reality gaps would shrink by approximately 18 percent and hedgehogs' gaps would shrink by approximately 32 percent. The fox-hedgehog performance differential would obviously also shrink, but it would remain statistically significant.

V. Violations of Belief-updating Rule

We relied on reputational bets (likelihood ratios) elicited at time 1 to assess how strong a Bayesian obligation experts would feel to change their minds at time 2 when they learn whether their most likely future did or did not materialize.

The Bayesian belief-updating formula in chapter 4 tells us how much one should change one's mind about the validity of competing hypotheses when one confronts evidence that one once thought had probative value for distinguishing those hypotheses. Figure A.9 illustrates how much a card-carrying Bayesian should increase or decrease confidence in a hypothesis when the incoming evidence is either moderately or strongly diagnostic (likelihood ratio equaling 0.6/0.4 in the first case and 0.8/0.2 in the second and .95/.05 in the third). The curves rise much more slowly in response to weaker evidence (likelihood ratio closer to 1.0), and there is more room for rapid upward movement for hypotheses that start from a low baseline prior (say, .1) than from a high one (say, .9 where ceiling effects limit potential change).

Extreme probability assignments, such as assigning 1.0 or total confidence to one's prior hypothesis and zero or no confidence to rival perspectives, create problems within this framework. Key terms, such as the prior-odds ratio, become undefined when forecasters declare unshakeable confidence. When such problems arose, we used replacement value of .95/.05.

There is a straightforward procedure for computing the discrepancy between how much experts update their beliefs and how much Bayes's theorem says they should. The Bayesian prescription for belief change can be obtained in three steps. First, calculate the ex ante likelihood ratio, which is done by dividing the expert's original assessment of the conditional likelihood of each scenario, assuming the correctness of that expert's understanding of underlying forces, by the expert's original assessment of the conditional likelihood of the same scenario, but now assuming the correctness of the most influential alternative view of the underlying forces. Second, calculate the prior-odds ratio, which is done by dividing the subjective probability that experts placed in their understanding of the underlying forces by the subjective probability that experts placed in the most influential rival view of those underlying forces. And third, multiply the prior-odds ratio by the diagnosticity ratio for each respondent's forecasts to yield the posterior-odds ratio, which tells us the relative likelihood of the two hypotheses in light of what we now know has happened.

Just as fuzzy-set adjustments can "correct" probability scores by giving forecasters credit for being almost right, the same can be done for belief-updating equations. In the latter case, though, the correction operates on the likelihood ratio. We might, for example, allow losers of a reputational bet to lower the likelihood ratio (bring it closer to unity so that the outcome of the bet has weaker implications for the correctness of any point of view) in proportion to the frequency with which forecasters offered belief system defenses, in proportion to the credibility weights one assigns the defenses, and in proportion to how self-servingly forecasters offered the defenses. Imagine forecasters have just lost a reputational bet: an outcome

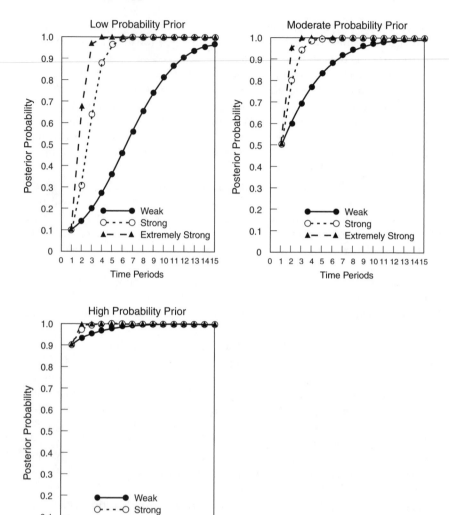

Figure A.9. The impact of repeatedly presenting weak, strong, and extremely strong evidence (likelihood ratios from 1.5:1 to 4:1 to 19:1) on updating of beliefs in a prior hypothesis initially assigned low, moderate, or high probability (from 0.1 to 0.5 to 0.9). Convergence in beliefs eventually occurs across the fifteen trials, but it occurs more rapidly when belief in prior hypothesis is strong and the evidence is probative.

has just occurred that they earlier rated as three times more likely if their rivals' point of view was correct than if their own point of view was correct. This 3:1 ratio could be reduced in proportion to the frequency with which experts claimed other things almost happened or might still happen. Thus a 3:1 ratio could be cut in half if forecasters offered such defenses 50 percent of the time and we grant 100 percent credibility to those claims. But this halving of the original likelihood ratio can be quickly reversed if we adjust the fuzzy-set correction in proportion to experts' tendency to offer more "excuses" when they are on the losing versus winning side of reputational bets. If experts "request" fuzzy-set adjustments nine times more often when they get it wrong, experts would get the benefit of only one-ninth of the original 50 percent reduction in the likelihood ratio (a 5.5 percent reduction).

Of all the adjustments to probability scoring and Bayesian belief-updating indicators, fuzzy-set adjustments are, for obvious reasons, the most controversial.

Concluding Thoughts

In the spirit of the old aphorism that you never know you have had enough until you have had more than enough, we have pushed the objectification of good judgment to its approximate point of diminishing returns, and then perhaps beyond. We recognize, of course, that not everyone will make the same epistemic judgment calls: some readers will conclude that we did not go far enough (and made too many concessions to defensive forecasters and their post-modern apologists) and others will conclude that we went far too far (and created a prime exhibit of pretentious "scientism"). There is no point in disguising the fallibility of our analytical apparatus or in denying the obvious: this effort falls far short if our benchmark is methodological perfection. But this effort fares better if we adopt a more realistic standard: Have we offered a starter framework for drawing cumulative lessons about the determinants of the accuracy of expert judgment in complex real-world situations? This project is intended to begin a conversation, not end it.

Index

Abelson, Robert, 39n. 36, 182–83n. 16
academic hyperspecialization, 233
academic journals, 233–34
accountability, 185–86, 218n. 2
accuracy criteria, 249–50; for domestic political leadership, 249; for government policy and economic performance, 249–50; for national security, 250
Acheson, Dean, 143
actor-dispensability debates, 106–7
additive rule, 301; violations of, 303–5. *See also* sub-additivity; support theory; "unpacking" scenarios
African National Congress (ANC), 109–10
AIDS, 225
Allen, P. G., 42n. 42
Allison, G., xiii n. 4
Almond, G., 134n. 11
Al Qaeda, 6
ambiguity, 38; aversion to ambiguity as factor driving fox-hedgehog performance differentials, 81–82
American Political Science Association, 25
analogical reasoning (from history), 38, 92–100
Anderson, C., 191n. 3
Angell, Norman, 102
antideterminists, 153
Argentina, 114, 115
Arkes, H., 65n. 50, 123n. 2
Armstrong, J. S., 65n. 50, 86n. 16, 1 18n. 46
Arthur, B., 27n. 8
Articles of Confederation, 89
"Asian Tigers," 116

Bartels, L., 25n. 1
base rates, 42n. 43, 49, 220; prediction strategies (using contemporaneous or recent past cross-sectional base rates, defined either restrictively or expansively), 51–52, 281–82. *See also* difficulty-adjusted probability scores
Bayesian belief-updating exercises, 252; ex ante assessments, 253–54; ex post assessments, 254–56; respondents, 252–53. *See also* reputational bets
Bayesians, 17, 18, 122, 123, 126n. 5, 129, 180
belief system defenses, 81, 129, 187, 224; challenging the conditions of hypothesis testing defense, 129–31; close-call counterfactual defense ("I was almost right"), 132–34, 140, 140n. 20, 141, 182; exogenous-shock defense, 131–32; "I made the right mistake" defense, 83, 135; just-off-on-timing defense, 134, 141; the low-productivity outcome just happened to happen defense, 135–36; playing-a-different-game defense, 186–87; politics is hopelessly cloudlike defense, 134–35; protecting, 156; quantitative analysis of, 136–37; really not incorrigibly closed-minded defense, 180–81; wrong questions defense, 184–85, 184–85n. 18
belief systems, minimalist versus maximalist models of constraint, 182–83, 183n. 16
belief-updating rule, violations of, 308–9, 311
Bell, D., 237n. 20
Berlin, Isaiah, 2, 2n. 3, 67, 72–73, 86–87, 88, 162, 241. *See also* hedgehog/fox dimension
Beyth-Marom, R., 123n. 2, 126n. 5
Bhagwati, J., 115n. 42
BJP Party, analogy to Nazi Party, 94, 94n. 22
Blake, William, 216
Blight, J., 5n. 7
Bloom, H., 23n. 44. *See also* meta-cognition (and the art of self-overhearing)
boomsters-doomsters, 71–72
Botha, P. W., 109
Braudel, Fernand, 144
Brazil, 114
Brehmer, B., 37n. 29
British Labor Party, 94